PRESIDENTIAL COMMUNICATION

PRESIDENTIAL COMMUNICATION

Description and Analysis

Robert E. Denton, Jr.,
and
Dan F. Hahn

New York
Westport, Connecticut
London

Library of Congress Cataloging-in-Publication Data

Denton, Robert E., Jr.
    Presidential communication.

    Includes index.
    1. Presidents—United States. 2. Communication in
politics—United States. I. Hahn, Dan F. II. Title.
JK518.D45 1986   353.03'5   86-9294
    ISBN 0-275-92175-1 (alk. paper)
    ISBN 0-275-92176-X (pbk. : alk. paper)

Library of Congress Catalog Card Number: 86-9294
ISBN: 0-275-92175-1
ISBN: 0-275-92176-X (pbk.)

First published in 1986

Praeger Publishers, 521 Fifth Avenue, New York, NY 10175
A division of Greenwood Press, Inc.

Printed in the United States of America

∞

The paper used in this book complies with the Permanent
Paper Standard issued by the National Information Standards
Organization (Z39.48-1984).

10 9 8 7 6 5 4 3 2 1

We dedicate this book to:

Donald and Norma Heater, friends, family, loved ones;

and

The memory of Dan Hahn's mother, Irene Mercy Hahn, who taught that all endeavors, even criticism, ought to be tempered with the power of gentleness.

PREFACE

Historically, much has been written about U.S. presidents. Very little, however, has been written about the U.S. presidency. And even less has been written about the presidency from a purely communication or rhetorical perspective. Most works on the presidency are either historical or contemporary focusing on specific time periods or individual presidents. In addition, they tend to take one of nine basic critical approaches: constitutional–legalistic, institutional, pluralistic, elitist, behavioral, decision-making, systems, policy process, and symbolic–perceptual. Each approach, over time, has proclaimed supremacy in describing the "essence" of the office, the nature of its power, and its salvation as an institution. Yet, each approach necessitates focusing on different aspects of the presidency thus influencing the findings, results, and outcomes of the investigations. Some of the approaches are explanatory while others are descriptive or prescriptive. It is useful to consider each in terms of its theoretical yields as well as shortcomings.[1]

Constitutional–legalistic discussions of the presidency rest on the legal foundations of the institution.[2] Careful analyses of the Constitution, congressional statutes, and Supreme Court decisions provide the primary bases for investigation. The major issue of concern for such scholars is presidential power and authority as revealed in our rather legalistic governmental structure. This approach is perhaps the most "narrow" of all the approaches. Therein lies its greatest limitation. As Myron Hale observes, "a legal analysis is not a political analysis."[3] This approach simply ignores the dynamics of the office. It treats the institution as strictly "empirically" defined, ignoring the emotional, symbolic significance of the office. Questions of presidential power are observable and consequently clearly "right or wrong," "good or bad." This study argues that the emotional, mythical, and symbolic dimensions of the office are more important than even the constitutional definition of the office. The presidency "lives" and "grows" in accordance with societal needs and expectations, regardless of statutes.

The institutional approach primarily views the office from a structural orientation.[4] The continual growth, expansion, and development of the office comprise the key concerns of this perspective. The question of how the institution has grown to meet the needs of the citizenry has led to organizational and management concerns. The epitome of this approach lies in the attempt to find the "best" and most "efficient" political structure. Organizational theory comprises the major emphasis of this orientation today. Again, however, this approach ignores many "political" dimensions of the office. There is a big difference between "efficiency" and "effectiveness." Efficiency does not automatically guarantee psychological or emotional satisfaction. The presidency is more than a management office. To identify a problem, isolate the variables, and construct a solution is not the same as generating support, persuading a public of a law's necessity, and getting the legislation passed through Congress. Leadership, as a quality, differs from simple management. Because the office is "public," structure alone is of little concern when attempting to gauge the significance of the office to the public.

The pluralism or interest group approach to the presidency focuses on the behavior of various groups in society that share common interests or issues.[5] The unit of analysis is the cross section of human activity.[6] This approach views political activity as representation of demands in society founded in social and economic concerns. Various groups of shared interest compete for power, influence, and access to government reins of control. Political actions are evaluated in terms of their effects on specified groups. Thus, political outputs or decisions are really the results of "group behavior." At least this perspective recognizes more dynamics of the office. It recognizes the role of societal factors in influencing the office. The occupant of the office must reflect or at least acknowledge the concerns of various groups in society. Yet, as the literature defines the area, it tends to ignore the influence of elites in controlling the very demands and issues of the "interest groups."

The question arises as to the significance of issues proclaimed. Are the problems announced truly reflective of the opinions of a large number of citizens? Group consensus can certainly be fabricated and manipulated. If the various appeals are abstract enough, we all belong to many groups. The important question is the intensity of affiliation. One can argue that sheep, as a group, seek comfort and safety in numbers, but the shepherd is the one who dictates the parameters of movement and limits of food. Societal laws can be potent independent variables in patterning human behavior. With the powerful but passive role of mass media, it has become rather easy to proclaim wide support. Public versus private interest is largely a matter of myth. Are presidents to be viewed simply as "interest group leaders" with their sole task to function as bargainers of special interests? The office encompasses *all* Americans. Once elected, the president is indeed president of all the people for a set period of four years no matter the margin of electoral victory. In most inaugural addresses, a new president proclaims to speak for "all Americans whether democrat or republican; rich or poor; black or white."

The elitist approach emphatically states that a recognizable "ruling class" exists.[7] This "ruling class" is comprised of a self-conscious elite who controls society. The approach emphasizes clear human differentiation within organized groups. Within each human activity are those individuals who exercise domination over others. Elites comprise the major hierarchies and organizations of society. Consequently, the important decisions in our society are made by a "power elite." Elitists' power may be based upon wealth, education, or social status. Nevertheless, this approach lessens the impact of individual input and freedom. It argues that our government is maintained by a "circulation of elites." Presidents may come and go but the real decision-makers or power brokers simply rotate around in government and comprise a relatively small number of individuals. At least this approach, almost to an extreme, recognizes the role of a select few individuals "contriving," "manipulating," and "leading" the masses. It almost assumes, in a rather strict sense, a unity of agreement among elites in terms of "what to do" and "how to do it." We know, of course, from experience that this is certainly not the case. (One need only investigate the continuous disagreement of "elite" economists about the regulation of our economy to prove the point.) Specifically, in terms of the presidency, no distinction is made between governing and nongoverning elites. We are too well aware of the fact that the "best" does not always win. Leaders are selected for a variety of reasons. There is, in our system above all others, a distinction too often forgotten between campaigning and governing; between leadership and management. In addition, with the continual increase of the role of media in presidential politics a "nobody" can become a "somebody" and be elevated to the presidency despite background or experience (for example, Jimmy Carter). In this age, a "celebrity" is not the same as an "elite" in the traditional usage of the term.

Currently, the popular behavioral approach to the presidency focuses on the individual occupant of the office.[8] The goal of such scholars is to identify the "ideal" or "best" models of personality types to be presidents. Thus, models and categories of personality types are developed. From these models, criteria are established for evaluating and judging potential presidents. The task of the public, therefore, is simply to find the "ideal" type to become president. This approach is founded on the belief that personality variables influence an individual's behavior, approach to the job, and decision-making capabilities. Although the literature in this area is most fascinating and entertaining, it simply suffers from reductionism by ignoring too many variables of influence. The perspective is dangerously interpretive and subjective; it fails to recognize the capabilities of an individual, at various times, to "move across" personality types. In addition, it may be argued, at certain times our nation felt a need for and responded to varied personality types. After World War II our nation felt it needed the stability of an Eisenhower. After the barrage of social legislation of Lyndon Johnson we felt a need for the restraint of Richard Nixon. Perhaps most importantly, the approach diminishes the role of institutional influence. Buchanan argues most effectively that there are common exposures, influences, or experiences all occupants of the presidency must confront.[9] This study will certainly argue that the institution has a "life of its own." An individual must adapt to or adopt the public's historical expectations of the office and presidential behavior. Finally, does the president confront a pre-established "reality" or is a president always compelled to create an acceptable "reality" for the public?

The decision-making approach to the office is also rather narrow.[10] Concrete proposals, actions, or decisions are a product of a decision-making process. Thus, to judge the value, correctness, or quality of a decision, the scholar must focus on the decision-making process. This demands analyzing the organizational context, the accuracy of information, the motivations of participants, and the consequences of the decisions. Within this approach, crisis decision-making has received the most attention (that is, Truman's decision to drop the atomic bomb, Kennedy's Bay of Pigs and Cuban missile crisis, Johnson's Vietnam entanglement, Nixon's Watergate difficulties, Ford's *Mayaguez* mission, Carter's failed rescue attempt of U.S. hostages in Iran, Reagan's sending of troops to Grenada, etc.). This approach attempts to explain, analyze, describe, and evaluate crucial decisions made by presidents. Such analysis isolates and magnifies the importance of many variables in the decision-making process. The difficulty, of course, is that this approach lacks real objective criteria. Description is fine but in the realm of evaluation questions arise. There really is no way to make the decisions with "full," "all," or "complete" information. In reality, this is a rather narrow, fragmented approach. It clearly fails to provide a broad perspective of what the presidency entails as an office.

The systems and policy process approaches to the presidency, in many ways, are the most encompassing of all the approaches.[11] The systems approach views political behavior as a system of behavior subject to many influences from the environment. "The political system is defined as that set of interactions relevant to the process of authoritatively allocating values for a society."[12] The political system is usually depicted as a means for resolving differences that are processed as "outputs." The "outputs," therefore, are results of the policy process. Microscopically, policy process scholars identify models of bargaining, conflict, and negotiation.

Interestingly, both approaches espouse to be empirical, constructively adaptive, and analytic in nature.[13] In terms of the presidency, the office is viewed as only one element of our governmental system. However, as Hale observes, "very few scholars have used a vigorous and demanding systems approach when studying the institutionalized Presidency."[14] Nevertheless, this approach does recognize more variety of variables that affect the nature of the presidency than most other approaches. Yet, the approach fails to assess critically the very nature of "inputs." System "inputs" are not simply a synthesis of societal beliefs, attitudes or values. Rather they are subject to manipulation and control. In fact, it is often hard to distinguish between system "feedback" and system "inputs." Although providing a "holistic" alternative to studying the presidency, the systems approach lacks a clear framework for treating the office as a subsystem.

The symbolic–perceptual approach to the presidency views the impact and significance of the office from the psyche of the occupant and/or from the perspective of the public.[15] The approach is a derivative of the behavioral and systems approaches. The office has power, significance, and impact based largely upon its historical and mythical development. It is the "ceremonial" and "head of state" roles that especially provide the presidency with public expectations, deference, and esteem. The trappings of the office are necessary but dangerous. Although somewhat narrow, the approach is gaining in validity as it attempts to explain the "nonrational" and "public" dimensions of the office.

Does such an abundant number of critical approaches accurately describe the essential nature and essence of the modern presidency? We believe they do not. The above approaches all provide rather deterministic and mechanistic explanations of the U.S. presidency. Increasingly, it is becoming clear that structures are only a small part of the presidency. Structures, in fact, are arranged by individuals with unique perceptions, beliefs, and attitudes which play a significant role in the ultimate uses of those structures. In addition, they exist in a cultural context consisting of specific norms and expectations.

The presidency avoids simple descriptions and explanations. The institution is a paradox.[16] The office always seems too strong or too weak. A president appears to have too much power for the realization of "self rule" while lacking enough power to solve this nation's most critical problems. The U.S. public wants a common man in the White House but expects uncommon leadership. The public demands that a president be above "politics" while forgetting that to be elected an individual must be, above all, a politician. When acting decisively, the president is labeled "dictatorial" and "unconstitutional." But when failing to act decisively, he is called "passive" and "weak." Why has such a paradoxical institution survived for more than 200 years and served the U.S. public well in the process?

Part of the answer lies in the fact that the institution is largely undefined. The Constitution is alarmingly vague on the responsibilities, dimensions, and roles of the office. Although the presidency is indeed a very real office with an elected official, space, desks, and staff, it remains elusive and undefined. "The Presidency is the work of the Presidents."[17] Expectations are created through presidents' rhetoric, use of symbols, rituals, and sense of history. "Americans are taught at home, in the schools, and in pervasive political rhetoric that America is the land of equal opportunity; that there is equality before the law; that government accurately reflects the voice of the people, but does not shape it; that political and economic values are allocated fairly."[18] Within such an environment, as Clinton Rossiter notes, the president becomes ". . . the one-man distillation of the American people" reflecting their perceived dignity and majesty.[19] Consequently, elaborate criteria are envisioned for the man who desires the "sacred" office.

"Candidates must try to conform to the public stereotypes of goodness, a standard which is typically far more demanding of politicians than of ordinary mortals."[20] By being "one of us," the president should naturally reflect the qualities comprising the "average American citizen" perpetuated in the myth of the "American character." "A candidate is helped by being thought of as trustworthy, reliable, mature, kind but firm, a devoted family man and in every way normal and presentable."[21] But these attributes alone are apparently not enough. Americans require a sense of direction and strength. As James Barber recognizes, ". . . children want to believe the President is a good man, that people turn to the President for a sense that things will be all right; that in the midst of trouble is a core of serenity, and that our ordinary ease will be sustained."[22] Herein lies the beginning of the paradox.

We argue that communication — its quantity and quality — defines the nature and essential characteristics of the U.S. presidency. The nature of the office goes beyond the constitutional–legalistic questions, the institutional organizational charts, the pressures of economic elites or interest groups, the specialized "inputs" and "outputs" of policy, and the "real" personality of individual presidents. Communication is at the heart of winning elections and governing the people. Communication is how candidates present themselves to voters; share hopes, desires, and goals for the future; persuade Congress and the governmental bureaucracy to take action; sustain effective leadership; and give life and meaning to the ceremonial import of the office. Communication is the "oil" that keeps the governmental machinery going. It is the mode and means for democratic government. It defines the institution and gives the office a pragmatic dimension.

RHETORIC AND POLITICS

If, as Aristotle proclaimed, politics is the "master science," then the art of rhetoric is its primary disciple.[23] For Karl Wallace, rhetoric is "the knowledge and application of the principles and methods of discourse, informative and persuasive, private and public, in situations that affect the information, attitudes and personal welfare of listener and speaker, reader and writer."[24] Thus, the art of rhetoric serves the master art of politics. If the political society is democratic, then the rhetoric must mirror the values, principles, and processes of democracy. "The character of the instrumental art," according to Wallace, "derives from the master art."[25]

Rhetoric is method, not subject. It is concerned with open issues and questions about which people dispute and falls in the realm of the contingent. "Rhetoric, therefore, is distinguished from the other instrumental studies in its preoccupation with informed opinion rather than with scientific demonstration."[26] It *does* rather than *is*. Consequently, theorist Donald Bryant argues that the function of rhetoric is "adjusting ideas to people and people to ideas."[27] Human ideas, issues, and interests are always in conflict and in need of definition, compromise, and negotiation. As an instrumental discipline, rhetoric is a literary study, a philosophical study (modes of argument, motives, and discovery), and a social study (behavior of people in society).[28]

THE RHETORICAL PRESIDENCY

It is, perhaps, rather obvious that rhetoric is vital to the functioning of a democratic society. We go beyond that assumption and posit that rhetoric, or specifically the nature of the communication activities that comprise the office, best defines the institution of the U.S. presidency. By examining the "rhetoric" of the office, we can best understand the relationship of the office with the public historically or in contemporary times; discover how individuals in the office govern the nation; and how individuals adapt, adopt, reject, or redefine the presidential role in society. Such examinations are both descriptive and prescriptive. To discover the office is to discover ourselves, our nation, and our history. They address issues of public and private motives, public and private concerns, and public and private actions.

The presidency has become the focal point of our political system. This was not always the case. Early presidents seldom gave public addresses. Written statements served as notice of issue positions. Campaigns were conducted by the parties. Only a handful of people were knowledgeable and aware of public issues. Even fewer actually voted or participated in the electoral process. Today, presidential rhetoric and communication activities are sources of tremendous power; power to define, justify, legitimize, persuade, and inspire. Everything a president does or says has implications and communicates "something." A president surrounds himself with communication specialists. Every act, word, or phrase becomes calculated and measured for a response. Every occasion proclaims a need for utterance.

James Ceaser, with several other colleagues, argues that three factors have attributed to the rise of the "rhetorical presidency."[29] The first factor is the modern doctrine of presidential leadership. The public expects a president to set goals and provide solutions to national problems. To be a "leader of men" is a cherished concept and a political expectation and, hence, a necessity for our presidents. The second factor giving rise to the rhetorical presidency is the development of the mass media. The mass media have increased the size of the audience, provided immediate access to the public, and changed the mode of communicating with the public from primarily the written word to the spoken word delivered in dramatic form. The final factor contributing to the supremacy of the rhetorical presidency is modern electoral campaigns. Contemporary presidential campaigns require national travel, public performances, image creation, issue definition, and the articulation of problem solutions. A "common man" can become known and win an election. Competition for communication opportunities is great.

The purpose of our study is to investigate the institutional presidency from the traditional perspectives of communication scholarship. Specifically, we investigate the presidency from interpersonal, intrapersonal, small group, and mass communication orientations. In addition, the presidency as essentially a rhetorical and persuasive institution is argued in separate chapters. This book is one of only a few that systematically considers the presidency from a purely communication perspective. It is the *only* text that focuses on communication variables in relation to the presidency.

Many studies on the presidency are too narrow, episodic, and totally ignore the impact of the institution of the presidency. They often focus on a single president, event, and utilize rather conservative definitions of rhetoric and communication. It is our belief that the theories and concepts of contemporary communication scholarship are applicable to all communicative contexts and situations.

Chapter 1 investigates further the nature of the rhetorical presidency. Chapter 2 discusses presidential persuasion considering both verbal and nonverbal dimensions. Chapter 3 considers the various interpersonal contexts of presidential communication and Chapter 4 views the intrapersonal dimensions of presidential communication. In Chapter 5, the various contexts where small group communication occurs are considered and in Chapter 6, the important role of mass communication activities is investigated. Finally, in Chapter 7 we reflect upon the relationship of rhetoric to democracy and the future of the "rhetorical presidency."

At the conclusion of each chapter we present an "explication" section applying the theories and notions discussed in the chapter to specific officeholders. These "mini-studies" provide examples and further application of the theories discussed in the various chapters. Unless indicated otherwise, we are the authors of these readings. We hope they serve to illustrate theories to specific events or situations as well as to demonstrate the value of communication analyses of presidential behavior.

NOTES

1. Chapter 2 of Hale's forthcoming book on the presidency provides the only synthesis of the various orientations to the office. This chapter plus Michael Weinstein, *Philosophy, Theory, and Method in Contemporary Political Thought* (Glenview: Scott, Foresman, 1971) served as the major source of descriptions provided in this discussion.

2. Nearly all major works on the presidency must, of course, acknowledge the constitutional, historical creation of the office. For an example of a study that totally bases its significance on this approach see Edward Corwin, *The President: Office and Powers* (New York: New York University Press, 1967).

3. Hale, p. 25.

4. For example, see Aaron Wildavsky, ed., *The Presidency* (Boston: Little, Brown, 1969).

5. See David Truman, *The Governmental Process* (New York: Alfred A. Knopf, 1951); David Easton, *The Political System* (New York: Alfred A. Knopf, 1953); Arthur Bentley, *The Process of Government* (Cambridge: The Belknap Press, 1967); William Connolly, *The Bias of Pluralism* (New York: Atherton Press, 1969).

6. For a good discussion on pluralism see Weinstein, *Philosophy, Theory, and Method*, pp. 104–26.

7. See Gaetano Mosca, *The Ruling Class* (New York: McGraw-Hill, 1939); C. Wright Mills, *The Power Elite* (New York: Oxford University Press, 1956); Harold Lasswell, *Politics: Who Gets What, When, How* (Cleveland: World, 1958); Renzo Sereno, *The Rulers* (New York: Frederick Praeger, 1962); Peter Bachrach, *The Theory of Democratic Elitism* (Boston: Little, Brown, 1967).

8. See Harold Lasswell, *Psychopathology and Politics* (Chicago: University of Chicago Press, 1930); Edwin Hargrove, *Presidential Leadership; Personality and Political Style* (New York: Macmillan, 1966); James Barber, *The Presidential Character* (Englewood Cliffs: Prentice-Hall, 1972).

9. Bruce Buchanan, *The Presidential Experience* (Englewood Cliffs: Prentice-Hall, 1978).

10. See Harold Lasswell, *The Decision Process* (College Park: University of Maryland, 1956); Richard Snyder, ed., *Foreign Policy Decision-Making* (New York: Free Press, 1962); David Braybrooke and Charles Linbloom, *A Strategy of Decision* (New York: Free Press, 1963); Graham Allison, *Essence of Decision: Explaining the Cuban Missile Crisis* (Boston: Little, Brown, 1971).

11. See Gabriel Almond and Sidney Verba, *The Civic Culture* (Princeton: Princeton University Press, 1963); David Easton, *A Systems Analysis of Political Life* (New York: John Wiley & Sons, 1965); H. Wiseman, *Political Systems* (New York: Frederick Praeger, 1967); Morton Kaplan, *Macropolitics* (Chicago: Aldine, 1969).

12. Weinstein, *Philosophy, Theory, and Method*, p. 197.

13. Ibid., p. 205.

14. Hale, p. 42.

15. See Robert E. Denton, Jr., *The Symbolic Dimensions of the American Presidency* (Prospect Heights: Waveland Press, 1980); Roderick Hart, *The Political Pulpit* (West Lafayette: Purdue University Press, 1977); and Michael Novak, *Choosing Our Kings* (New York: Macmillan, 1974).

16. For a good treatment of the paradoxical nature of the presidency see Thomas Cronin, *The State of the Presidency* (Boston: Little, Brown, 1975), pp. 1–22.

17. Grant McConnell, *The Modern Presidency* (New York: St. Martin's Press, 1976), p. 9.

18. Murray Edelman, *Politics as Symbolic Action* (Chicago: Markham, 1971), p. 55.

19. Clinton Rossiter, *The American Presidency* (New York: Mentor Books, 1962), p. 16.

20. Nelson W. Polsby and Aaron B. Wildavsky, *Presidential Elections* (New York: Charles Scribner & Sons, 1971), p. 190.

21. Ibid.

22. James D. Barber, "Man, Mood, and the Presidency," in *The Presidency Reappraised,* ed. Tugwell and Cronin (New York: Praeger, 1974), p. 206.

23. Aristotle, *Nicomachean Ethics,* Book I, 2.

24. Karl Wallace, "Rhetoric and Politics," *The Southern Speech Journal* 20 (Spring 1955):195.

25. Ibid., p. 199.

26. Donald Bryant, "Rhetoric: Its Functions and Its Scope," in *Contemporary Rhetoric,* ed. Douglas Ehninger (Glenview: Scott, Foresman, 1972), p. 20.

27. Ibid., p. 26.

28. Ibid., p. 37.

29. James Ceaser et al., "The Rise of the Rhetorical Presidency," in *Essays in Presidential Rhetoric,* ed. Theodore Windt (Dubuque: Kendall/Hunt, 1983), p. 7.

ACKNOWLEDGMENTS

We would like to acknowledge our indebtedness to the legion of scholars whose works on the presidency have informed ours and who are cited and quoted throughout this endeavor. And we would especially like to acknowledge two organizations most responsible for publishing useful manuscripts on presidential persuasion, The Speech Communication Association, publisher of *The Quarterly Journal of Speech* and The Center for the Study of the Presidency, publisher of *Presidential Studies Quarterly*.

Colleagues are invaluable. They are friends, supporters, and motivators. Robert Denton would like to personally thank his colleagues at Northern Illinois University, specifically Arthur Doederlein, Richard Johannesen, Charles Larson, Jon Powell, and Lois Self; and wife and son, who share in every endeavor. Dan Hahn would like to personally thank his colleagues at Queens College and, of course, his wife.

CONTENTS

Part II: COMMUNICATION DIMENSIONS OF THE PRESIDENCY

Part I

THE RHETORICAL PRESIDENCY

Chapter 1

THE RHETORICAL PRESIDENCY

Public sentiment is everything. With public sentiment nothing can fail, without it nothing can succeed.

Abraham Lincoln

Presidents are special beings. When they talk, we listen. We want to know where they are, what they are doing, and how they are doing it. Why are they so special? They are not special physically — we have had fat ones, thin ones, tall ones, short ones, some ugly, some handsome. They are not special intellectually — they have ranged through the many gradations from smart to dumb. They are not special emotionally — some have been strengthened by the pressure, others have cracked under the strain. What makes each and every one special, however, is that they lead us, define us, protect us, and embody us. And they do so, implicitly and explicitly, through communication.

If you doubt the significance and importance of presidential public communication, consider the following two examples. The presidential debates of 1960 demonstrated how important public speech can be in influencing the very nature of our society. The debates were heard and watched by over 101 million Americans.[1] The election was decided by a mere 118,550 votes — votes that may well have been determined by the public debate performances of the candidates. Scholars have concluded that those viewing the debates shifted their opinion toward Kennedy and most of his last minute support came from the "undecided" voter. In fact, Kennedy's support gained about 4 percent with each debate.[2]

By 1979 Carter's public popularity was at an all time low. He decided to retreat with his advisors to Camp David to review his presidency.

3

Upon reflection, Carter believed that his presidential leadership had missed its mark. He had acted, as he told David Broder, as "the head of the government" rather than as the "leader of the people."[3] He also believed that the nation was experiencing a crisis of spirit or "malaise." The answer — a campaign to wake up the American people. The *Washington Post* announced the campaign with the headline that read "Carter Seeking Oratory to Move an Entire Nation."[4]

President Reagan, "the great communicator," has clearly demonstrated that how a president communicates with the public is an important element in governing the nation. The rhetoric of presidents is important on several dimensions. Linguistically, their words shape ideas and stimulate action. Intellectually, their words provide rationales for action and justifications for decisions. Psychologically, their words can inspire, comfort, and motivate the nation. Socially, their words connect us as a social entity, providing the feeling of a human relationship with our leader. Ethically, their words can do good or evil, encourage justice or injustice, selfishness or selflessness. Aesthetically, their words have encompassed our grief (Lincoln's Gettysburg Address), given us hope (Franklin Roosevelt's first inaugural address), and challenged us to address the task at hand (Kennedy's inaugural address).

In this chapter we consider the importance of the "rhetorical presidency." More specifically, we explore the dependency of modern presidents upon public communication activities and provide a basis for citizen analysis of presidential rhetoric.

POLITICS AND COMMUNICATION

Humans are, according to Aristotle's *Politics*, "political beings" and "he who is without a polis, by reason of his own nature and not of some accident, is either a poor sort of being [a beast] or a being higher than man [a god]."[5] And because nature makes nothing in vain, Aristotle continues, humans "alone of the animals are furnished with the faculty of language."[6] Thus, it was recognized over 2,000 years ago that politics and communication go hand in hand because they are essential parts of human nature. Public communication allows us to deal with our social environment. "There are few tools," according to Roderick Hart and his colleagues, "other than public talk with which to maintain the delicate balance between community and jungle."[7]

Indeed, through public speaking by our national, state, and local officials, our values and goals are defined, refined, and articulated. Their words can inspire, move, and articulate but also deceive, destroy, and exploit. Public communication, or rhetoric, serves many purposes. Karlyn Campbell recognizes several general rhetorical purposes that represent an orderly progression in terms of complexity and political utility.[8] First, rhetoric serves to create a "virtual experience." Through rhetoric we experience a range of emotions leading to corresponding behavior. In the process, rhetoric functions to alter perceptions and assist in formulating beliefs. Verbal descriptions by our leaders often serve as rationales, justifications, or motivations for collective action. Finally, much public rhetoric by officials is aimed at maintaining support, action, or the status quo.

According to Doris Graber, "politics is largely a word game. Politicians rise to power because they can talk persuasively to voters and political elites. Once in power, their daily activities are largely verbal."[9] Dan Nimmo concurs and argues that the purpose of political talk is to "preserve other talk." In fact, politics and communication are inseparable. "Politics, like communication, is a process, and like communication, politics involves talk. This is not talk in the narrow sense of the spoken word but talk in the more inclusive sense, meaning all the ways people exchange symbols — written and spoken words, pictures, movements, gestures, mannerisms, and dress."[10] From this perspective we may view politics as an activity of communication between persons.

Political Language

Political consciousness is dependent upon language, for language can determine the way in which people relate to their environment.[11] At the very least, language should be viewed as the medium for the generation and perpetuation of politically significant symbols. Political consciousness, therefore, results from a largely symbolic interpretation of sociopolitical experience. To control, manipulate, or structure the "interpretation" is a primary goal of politics in general. The language of government, in many ways, is the dissemination of illusion and ambiguity.[12] A successful politician will use rather specific linguistic devices that reinforce popular beliefs, attitudes, and values. Politically manipulated language can, therefore, promote and reinforce the existing political regime or order.

From this brief discussion, it is clear that what makes language political is not the particular vocabulary or linguistic form but the *substance* of the information the language conveys, the *setting* in which the interaction occurs, and the explicit or implicit *functions* the language performs. As Doris Graber observes, "When political actors, in and out of government communicate about political matters, for political purposes, they are using political languages."[13]

Functions of Political Language

Graber identifies five major functions of political language: information dissemination, agenda-setting, interpretation and linkage, projection for the future and the past, and action stimulation.[14] It is useful to discuss briefly each of these functions.

There are many ways information is shared with the public in political messages. The most obvious, of course, is the sharing of explicit information about the state of the polity. Such dissemination of information is vital to the public's understanding and support of the political system. This is especially true in democratic nations where the public expects open access to the instruments and decision-making of government officials. But the public, being sensitized to uses of language, can obtain "information" by what *is not* stated, *how* something is stated, or *when* something is stated. Often times, especially in messages between nations, the public must "read between the lines" of official statements to ascertain proper meanings and significance of statements. Such inferences are useful in gauging security, flexibility, and sincerity. Sometimes the connotations of the words used communicate more truth than the actual statements. Are our relations with the Soviet Union "open," "guarded," or "friendly?" There are times, especially in tragedy, that the very act of speaking by an official can communicate support, sympathy, or strength. Thus, the act of speaking rather than the words spoken sometimes conveys the meaning of the rhetorical event.

The very topics chosen by politicians to discuss channel the public's attention and focus issues to be discussed. The agenda-setting function of political language primarily occurs in two ways. First, before "something" can become an issue, some prominent politician must articulate a problem and hence bring the issue to public attention. The issue can be rather obvious (poverty), in need of highlighting (status of American education), or created (the "Great Society"). A major way political language establishes the national agenda is by controlling the information disseminated to the general public. Within this realm there is always a great deal of competition. There are a limited number of issues that can effectively maintain public interest and attention. While certain "self-serving" topics are favored by one person, party, faction, or group, the same topics may be perceived as meaningless or even harmful to other factions, persons, or groups. While President Nixon wanted to limit discussion and public attention regarding the Watergate break-ins and tapes, rival groups wanted public debates and revelations to continue.

The very act of calling the public's attention to a certain issue defines, interprets, and manipulates the public's perception of that issue. Causal explanations are often freely given. Such explanations may be suspect. Control over the definitions of a situation is essential in creating and preserving political realities. Participants in election primaries, for example, all proclaim victory regardless of the number of votes received. The top vote-getter becomes the "front runner." The second place winner becomes "the underdog" candidate in an "up-hill battle." The third place candidate becomes a "credible" candidate and alternative for those "frustrated" or "dissatisfied" with the "same old party favorites." Political language defines and interprets reality as well as provides a rationale for future collective action.

A great deal of political rhetoric and language deals with predicting the future and reflecting upon the past. Candidates present idealized futures under their leadership and predictions of success if their policies are followed. Some predictions and projections are formalized as party platforms or major addresses as inaugurals or state of the union addresses. Nearly all such statements involve promises — promises of a brighter future if followed or Armageddon if rejected. Past memories and associations are evoked to stimulate a sense of security, better times, and romantic longings. An important function of political language, therefore, is to link us to past glories and reveal the future in order to reduce uncertainty in a world of ever increasing complexity and doubt.

Finally, and perhaps most importantly, political language must function to mobilize society and stimulate social action. Language serves as the stimulus, means, or rationale for social action. Words can evoke, persuade, implore, command, label, praise, and condemn. Political language is similar to other uses of language. But it also articulates, shapes, and stimulates public discussion and behavior about the allocation of public resources, authority, and sanctions.

THE RHETORICAL NATURE OF THE PRESIDENCY

George Edwards argues, in a recent work, that "the greatest source of influence for the president is public approval."[15] Today, as never before, presidents want not only to please the public and avoid irritating them, but also want to formulate and lead public opinion. In fact, research has shown that the higher the president's approval rating by the public the more Congress supports presidential policy decisions.[16]

The study of presidential rhetoric is the investigation of how presidents gain, maintain, or lose public support. For Theodore Windt, it is "a study of power, of the fundamental power in a democracy: public opinion and public support."[17] At the very least, the words of a president establish the public record of the administration, reflect the values and goals of the public, and in essence, the vocabulary becomes the favored policy (that is, New Frontier, Great Society, Star Wars, etc.). It is not surprising, therefore, that James Ceaser and his colleagues argue that "the rhetorical presidency is based on words, not power."[18] As Hart observes, the "American citizenry nevertheless require the federal archivists to scurry around behind modern chief executives and record their remarks for posterity, sparing no expense or tree for the sake of president's speeches perhaps because they have become convinced in a media-saturated age that a president is earning his keep only when he stands in public and talks."[19]

The speeches of presidents, indeed, differ from those of ordinary citizens or even celebrities in terms of frequency and how they must communicate.[20] In addition, presidents seldom face their entire audience and must always keep in mind the impact of their remarks on various constituencies. Presidents must be able to speak on a wide range of topics with great detail, knowing that their words are recorded and "live forever."

Despite the notion of the "grand oratory" of the nineteenth century, our early presidents seldom relied upon public address to win public support. George Washington usually gave only one speech a year — the one mandated in the Constitution to address Congress. Prior to 1912, the political parties conducted the presidential campaigns. Woodrow Wilson was the first presidential candidate to engage in active public campaigning.[21] In fact, an argument can be made that the framers of the Constitution did not favor "mass oratory" because it could counter "rational" and "enlightened self-interest" concerns of the citizenry.[22] The government was designed to minimize reliance upon the passions of the people and establish institutions that would be stable, efficient, and effective.

Between 1945 and 1975, public speeches by presidents increased 500 percent. President Gerald Ford, not a particularly effective speaker, delivered 682 public speeches in 1976 and President Jimmy Carter, also not a particularly effective speaker, averaged one speech a day during his entire term of office.[23] The reasons for the rise of the "rhetorical presidency" have already been identified in the preface of this book. But the importance and impact of modern electoral campaign politics plus the role of the mass media cannot be overemphasized. In addition, Gary Woodward argues that today's presidency is a collection of traditions and rhetorical expectations that each new president inherits. The legacies of past presidencies cannot be ignored. Presidents and their public relations staffs "are sensitive to the rhetorical precedents they have inherited. By the time a leader reaches the oval office he has usually spent the better part of an adult lifetime soaking up its unwritten rules and potent traditions. Most presidents come to power as well-versed students of the institutional presidency."[24]

James Barber recognizes the importance and impact of presidential rhetoric upon their administration. In his classic, *The Presidential Character*, Barber searches for patterns in behavior of past presidents and, based upon these patterns, classifies presidents into "character types."[25] He believes there are three major influences upon a person that will shape the presidential performance: style, world view, and character. For our purposes the variable "style" is especially relevant. He defines it as "the president's habitual way of performing his three political roles: rhetoric, personal relations, and homework."[26] This means communication — public, small group, and face-to-face — to write, think, record, and articulate thoughts.

Although it is clear that presidential speechmaking has increased drastically, the question remains, how does it differ significantly from the speechmaking of other public figures? Hart, in his impressive work entitled *Verbal Style and the Presidency*, provides insight into the question.[27] In comparison to corporate leaders, religious leaders, political candidates, and social activists, presidents mention themselves and their actions with great frequency. In addition, presidential speechmaking tends to be more optimistic, practical, "real," and less complex than addresses by other leaders. "Humanity, practicality, and caution are the special sound of presidential discourse."[28]

To talk of the "rhetorical presidency" is to recognize more than the increase of and impact of presidential discourse. It is to identify a way of viewing and analyzing the office.[29] The institution of the American presidency is greater than any individual. The office greatly influences the officeholder, who must confront already established expectations of presidential performance and behavior. The set of expected presidential roles results from the interaction of the office with the public. The role sets are created, sustained, and permeated through interaction comprised of campaigns, socialization, history, and myth. There is a clear, rather systematic process of transformation from candidate to president where the candidate must confront the "political self" and the public definition of the presidential role. Thus, as a result of interacting with the public, historical expectations, and individual views of the office, the person "becomes" president. The office of the presidency, then, dictates the nature and relationship of the president with the public. Rhetoric, broadly defined, is the means of confirming or denying the public's expectations of acceptable role behavior.

The presidency is simply a rhetorical institution. For the public, the office is comprised of a "string of public conversations" rather than a "series of private decisions." Presidents, although they have names, are corporate models of historical images and personae created in the public's collective consciousness. Their messages are persuasive in nature and are carefully constructed for a purpose. Thus, how a policy is defined, articulated, and sold may be more important than the policy itself. For presidential rhetoric constitutes social action, provides a context for collective action, and contributes to the oral history and definition of the nation.

Recognition of the rhetorical presidency is also recognition of potential abuses and concerns. Presidential rhetoric may emphasize style over substance with the belief that "words presented in stylistic finesse can solve real, difficult, even paradoxical problems."[30] There is the danger that symbols and slogans may replace policy discussions. Presidential rhetoric, although increasing, is becoming more one-way communication than two-way interaction. Thus, increased quantity of addresses in no way insures quality of interaction. Finally, too much time spent speaking, Hart observes, leaves too little time for presidential thinking in private to insure "good" policies and decisions. Speechmaking is both an art and a science, a tool for both good and evil uses.

COMMUNICATION ANALYSES OF THE PRESIDENCY

This book is about analyzing the presidency from a communication perspective. This approach implies several assumptions. First, the presidency is primarily and essentially a rhetorical institution. The presidency is defined by public communication and functions through communication in a variety of ways and contexts. But more importantly, the statement implies a need for systematic investigations of the presidency utilizing principles of communication theory, research, and criticism. It is this latter element that most distinguishes our approach from others.

Our analyses are guided by two major dimensions of communication study. The first dimension considers the five elements common to all communication transactions: speaker, listener, message, medium, and situation. Each of these elements contains variables of consideration and special influence relevant to the institutional presidency. The second dimension of traditional communication scholarship revolves around the content areas of interpersonal, intrapersonal, small group, mass, and public communication. Each of these areas provides insight into the variety, uses, and importance of communication phenomena to the presidency. It is our belief that if the theories and concepts of communication scholarship are valid, they are applicable to all communicative contexts and situations. Thus, we are applying the theoretical concepts of the two dimensions of communication scholarship to the single office of the presidency.

Why such an approach? A communication perspective can help us critically to sort out and evaluate the messages and information we receive from the White House. Failure of people to react critically leads to the witch hunts of Salem, to the programs of Nazi Germany, and to the deceptions of Watergate. But those who accept, reject, or ignore messages without filtering them are equally dangerous. What we do or fail to do, believe or reject based upon what we hear and are told by our leaders can indeed affect our lives, the lives of our loved ones, and even the continuation of all life. In addition, it may well shape America and impact upon the quality of life in this country. To be aware of the communication aspects of presidential behavior will help us all to *participate* and become partners in the political process.

NOTES

1.   Frank Stanton, "A CBS View," in *The Great Debates,* ed. Sidney Kraus (Bloomington, IN: Indiana University Press, 1962), p. 66.

2. Saul Ben-Zeev and Irving White, "Effects and Implications," in *The Great Debates*, ed. Sidney Kraus (Bloomington, IN: Indiana University Press, 1962), p. 334.

3. As quoted in James Ceaser et al., "The Rise of the Rhetorical Presidency," in *Essays in Presidential Rhetoric*, ed. Theodore Windt (Dubuque, IA: Kendall/Hunt, 1983), p. 3.

4. "Carter Seeking Oratory to Move an Entire Nation," *Washington Post*, July 14, 1979, pp. 15–16.

5. Aristotle, *The Politics of Aristotle*, trans. Ernest Barker (New York: Oxford University Press, 1970), p. 5.

6. Ibid., p. 6.

7. Roderick Hart, Gustav Friedrich, and William Brooks, *Public Communication* (New York: Harper & Row, 1975), p. 12.

8. Karlyn Kohrs Campbell, *The Rhetorical Act* (Belmont, CA: Wadsworth, 1982), pp. 8–14.

9. Doris Graber, "Political Language," in *Handbook of Political Communication*, ed. Dan Nimmo and Keith Sanders (Beverly Hills, CA: Sage Publications, 1981), p. 195.

10. Dan Nimmo, *Political Communication and Public Opinion in America* (Santa Monica, CA: Goodyear Publishing, 1978), p. 7.

11. The strongest statement of this notion is provided by Benjamin Lee Whorf. For him, "If a man thinks in one language, he thinks one way; in another language, another way." The structure of language "is itself the shaper of ideas, the program and guide for the individual's mental activity, for his analysis of impressions, for his synthesis of his mental stock in trade." See John Carroll, ed., *Language, Thought, and Reality: Selected Writings of Benjamin Whorf* (New York: John Wiley & Sons, 1956).

12. Murray Edelman, *Politics as Symbolic Action* (Chicago: Markham Publishing, 1971), p. 83.

13. Graber, "Political Language," p. 196.

14. Ibid., pp. 195–224.

15. George C. Edwards, *The Public Presidency* (New York: St. Martin's Press, 1983), p. 1.

16. George C. Edwards, *Presidential Influence in Congress* (San Francisco, CA: W. H. Freeman, 1980), pp. 86–100.

17. Theodore Windt, *Presidential Rhetoric (1961–1980)* (Dubuque, IA: Kendall/Hunt, 1980), p. 2.

18. Ceaser et al., "The Rise of the Rhetorical Presidency," p. 17.

19. Roderick Hart, *Verbal Style and the Presidency* (Orlando, FL: Academic Press, 1984), p. 2.

20. Ibid., p. 8.

21. Ceaser et al., "The Rise of the Rhetorical Presidency," p. 14.

22. Ibid., p. 8.

23. Hart, *Verbal Style and the Presidency*, p. 2.

24. Gary Woodward, "The Presidency: Focusing on the Role of Rhetorical Antecedents" (Paper presented at the Annual Convention of the Eastern Communication Association, Providence, Rhode Island, May 2, 1985), 1–2.

25. See James David Barber, *The Presidential Character,* 2nd ed. (Englewood Cliffs, NJ: Prentice-Hall, 1977).

26. Ibid., p. 7.

27. See Hart, *Verbal Style and the Presidency,* especially pp. 32–42.

28. Ibid., p. 41.

29. See Robert E. Denton, Jr., *The Symbolic Dimensions of the American Presidency* (Prospect Heights, IL: Waveland Press, 1982); Hart, *Verbal Style and the Presidency,* especially pp. 5–7; Theodore Windt, *Essays in Presidential Rhetoric*; and Robert E. Denton, Jr. and Gary Woodward, *Political Communication in America* (New York: Praeger, 1985).

30. Hart, *Verbal Style and the Presidency,* p. 231.

READINGS

INTRODUCTION

Chapter 1 argued that the presidency is primarily and essentially a rhetorical institution. The first essay focuses on the public discourse of President Gerald Ford and the *Mayaguez* incident. The essay challenges Ford's public description of the event in three ways: the nature and cargo of the vessel, the true extent of diplomatic endeavors, and the claims of authority for taking military action. The result is a case of "corrupt rhetoric" equal to the lies of the Nixon administration. Analysis of the event reveals that the American people responded positively to the military action by Ford because he was able to structure public perceptions of the event.

The second essay shows how President Richard Nixon utilized three key presidential myths in his rhetoric to identify problems, propose solutions, and enhance his image of leadership. These myths encouraged citizen patience, trust, and sacrifice. The authors conclude that when Nixon utilized the myths, his policies were generally supported. When he did not do so, his policies were largely rebuffed.

The final essay applies Kenneth Burke's "pentad" to Abraham Lincoln's second inaugural address. Such an application suggests why the speech was unpersuasive and Lincoln "out of step" with his auditors. Northerners and Southerners were mere "agencies" fulfilling God's will.

Each essay shows how presidents "lead" us, "define" us, "protect" us, and "embody" us through public communication.

CORRUPT RHETORIC: PRESIDENT FORD AND THE *MAYAGUEZ* AFFAIR*

The public communication of President Ford and his administration concerning the *Mayaguez* incident, I will argue, represents an example of corrupted discourse — one that is particularly significant because the quiet acceptance of it ushered us once again into the "Imperial Presidency" which the Nixon impeachment was supposed to have ended.

The broad outlines of the *Mayaguez* affair are familiar: the Cambodians captured the small American vessel; the U.S. government demanded an immediate release; the Cambodian government did not respond; the United States attacked; the vessel was recaptured; the Cambodians released the crew. In this retelling, and in the administration's original tale, the operation sounds simple and straightforward. And that is part of the problem: the discourse was corrupted by a false description of the situation.

The Cambodians captured a small U.S. vessel named the *Mayaguez*. Why? The American press, thus the people, never asked that question; and the U.S. government never answered it. The ostensible reason for the capture was that the boat lay eight miles off the coast of a Cambodian island, well within the twelve miles Cambodia claimed as territorial waters. Let us suppose for a moment that that *was* the reason for the capture. Is it an unreasonable reason? Does the United States recognize the twelve-mile territorial limit? Ostensibly, no. The United States recognizes a three-mile limit for some purposes (including, presumably, the purpose that the *Mayaguez* was pursuing) and a twelve-mile limit for other purposes. The nine miles of waters between what the United States recognized in this situation and what the Cambodians recognized could reasonably be described as "contested" waters. How did our government describe them? In the original release describing the capture, the location was depicted as "on the high seas."[1] That is a phrase normally taken to mean "those seas not under the jurisdiction of any government." But ... jurisdiction as decided by whom? That we do not know. All we know is that, for the purpose of this operation, the U.S. government chose to define eight miles out as "high seas." When the miles are off the U.S. coast rather than the Cambodian, the government utilizes a different

*Originally published by Dan F. Hahn, "Corrupt Rhetoric: President Ford and the *Mayaguez* Affair," *Communication Quarterly* 28 (Spring 1980):38–43. Reprinted with permission.

standard: "The U.S. Coast Guard regularly seizes vessels that have strayed inside the twelve-mile limit."[2]

Did not the U.S. government consider the twelve-mile Cambodian limit valid? Indeed, President Ford acted against the interpretation of his legal counsel, who ". . . cautioned him that . . . the ship's capture was not 'piracy.' Under international law, they said, Cambodia had a legal right to seize the ship after it steamed within the twelve-mile limit which Cambodia claims as its territorial waters."[3] That made Ford's description of the location ("high seas") and the act ("piracy") not just "dissembling," but lying. President Ford chose to describe a legal Cambodian action as illegal, and then, on the basis of his own false description, to engage in military action in retribution for that legal action.

Note, also, that his description made it a clear case of good guys versus bad guys. Any citizen who accepted his description had little choice but to accept his action. The situation seemed simple; the resultant action seemed legitimate. The corrupt discourse of President Ford established a climate in which the actions of President Ford had to be applauded.

It should be remembered that the foregoing hinges on the assumption that the Cambodian action was motivated by the infringement of their territorial waters. Could they have had other, perhaps more plausible, motivations? Certainly, in a time when the shenanigans of the C.I.A. were being aired, it was possible to suspect that the boat was not the simple "American merchant ship"[4] described by Ford. Indeed, the *Mayaguez* does seem to have dealt in rather strange merchandise. The trip immediately preceding this one was from Saigon to Hong Kong, and the cargo was, according to White House press secretary Ron Nessen, "some administrative material" from our Saigon embassy.[5] For this trip the boat was under contract to the U.S. Army, carrying meat, liquor, Coca Cola, and the like to U.S. troops stationed in Thailand.[6] Assuming that the Cambodians had good enough intelligence information to know that the *Mayaguez* had been recently and/or currently was in the employ of the U.S. government, could that information have been specific enough for them to have known that the cargo was meat rather than mortars, cokes rather than C.I.A. spies? And could they have known for sure that the supplies were for U.S. troops in Thailand rather than rebels in Cambodia? Indeed, do *we* know that for sure even today?

In short, the U.S. assumption that this was an innocent civilian boat may not have been the assumption upon which the Cambodians were operating when they captured it. Thus, the description of the boat as merely "an American merchant ship"[7] glossed over the important detail that the merchandise of this merchant ship was military cargo and that, without specific knowledge of the nature or destination of the cargo, the Cambodians could have perceived the *Mayaguez* as a dangerous military threat. Again, President Ford chose to overlook these factors in his description of the ship, a description that made a complicated situation look like a simple case of piracy, logically answerable by simple application of military power.

A second major way in which the Ford administration corrupted the discourse surrounding this affair was by not allowing "solution-by-discourse" (that is, diplomacy) a chance to work — and by talking as though it had.

It is difficult to piece together the sequence of events in order to determine if diplomacy was given a fair chance. The best information available to the public provides the following sequence:

May 12, 5:03 A.M. The U.S. government learned of the capture of the *Mayaguez*.[8]

May 12, 2:00 P.M. The U.S. government announced the seizure and began diplomatic efforts.[9]

May 13, 6:20 A.M. U.S. aircraft fired warning shots across the bow of the *Mayaguez*.[10]

May 13, evening (exact time not divulged). U.S. forces destroyed three Cambodian patrol boats and immobilized four more.[11]

May 14, 1:00 A.M. First U.S. air attacks.[12] (Note: this may be redundant of the May 13, 6:20 A.M. entry; not enough is known about either event to be sure.)

May 14, morning (exact time not divulged). The National Security Council decided to utilize military action to recapture the *Mayaguez* and its crew.[13] (Note: the action previously reported was not to recapture but merely to prevent movement of boat and crew to the mainland.)[14]

May 14, 5:55 P.M. "Consultation" with Congress begun.[15]

May 14, 8:15 P.M. Cambodian offer to return the *Mayaguez* received.[16]

May 14, 8:20 P.M. "Consultation" with Congress concluded.[17]

May 14, 9:00 P.M. *Mayaguez* recaptured by U.S. forces.[18]

May 14, 9:15 P.M. Ford demanded release of the crew.[19]

May 14, 10:53 P.M. U.S.S. *Wilson* announced crew was approaching.[20]

May 14, 10:57 P.M. U.S. planes bombed Cambodian airport.[21]

May 14, 11:14 P.M. Ford told crew was safe.[22]

May 14, 11:30 P.M. Crew rescued.[23]

May 14, 11:50 P.M. U.S. planes bombed Cambodian oil refinery.[24]

May 15, 12:27 A.M. Ford announced the successful completion of the mission.[25]

The time schedule is somewhat confusing, and most entries relate to military, rather than diplomatic, ventures. This is not to say that there was no diplomacy, but that the times for these were never indicated. We know, for instance, that the Chinese representative in Washington was asked to deliver a message to the Cambodians and refused formally, although the president believed the message was sent despite the refusal.[26] We do not know when the Chinese representative was approached. We do know that, subsequent to the Chinese refusal, the U.S. ministry in Peking delivered a message to the Cambodian embassy in Peking.[27] We do not know when that took place. More important, we do not know if the Cambodian embassy was able to get the message to the decision-makers in Cambodia. Finally, we know that the United States appealed to the U.N. for help some time after the United States attacked the Cambodian boats, but we do not know whether it was after the May 13 warning attack or after the main attack began the evening of May 14.

We do, however, know a few things which impinge upon our assessment of the diplomatic endeavors. We know that from the time Washington heard of the capture of the *Mayaguez* until it started military operations to recapture it, approximately 60 hours elapsed. That is the most extensive time schedule for diplomacy that can be deduced. The most contracted schedule, that between the reported beginning of our diplomatic efforts and the firing of our first bullet, was 16 hours. Thus, the amount of time devoted to diplomacy was somewhere in the 16–60 hour range.

That leaves a number of imponderables: Were 16 hours enough? Were 60 hours enough? Were sufficient diplomatic channels explored? Were the diplomatic channels that were utilized able to contact the appropriate authorities in Cambodia? Was the first message from Cambodia (May 14, 8:15 P.M.) a response to the diplomatic efforts begun up to 60 hours before or to the military attempt at recapture begun approximately two hours before? Why, when the first communication from Cambodia — a conciliatory one — was received, were the U.S. forces not ordered to cease fire in place (in effect, taking a defensive rather than offensive posture)? The answers to these questions, absent the missing information, require each of us to make value judgments. For me, the answer to the key question whether enough time was devoted to diplomacy before military intervention was employed must be negative.

Too few diplomatic attempts are reported, and those few seem too nonpersistent, for me to see them as anything but perfunctory at best, hypocritical at worst (hypocritical in the sense that they seem only to have been undertaken to provide a legalistic screen through which the desired military action could be sifted).[28]

Be that as it may, it is clear that the administration's rhetoric surrounding the capture and recapture of the *Mayaguez* corrupted the discourse by implying that all appropriate diplomatic efforts had been taken when, at best, that is a doubtful proposition. In the official announcements concerning the *Mayaguez* only three references — two direct and one indirect — to diplomatic efforts were located. In the original announcement of the capture, the official press release says, "He has instructed the State Department to demand the immediate release of the ship."[29] In announcing the decision to utilize force to recapture the boat and its crew, the statement of the press secretary began, "In further pursuit of our efforts to obtain the release . . . ,"[30] implying that diplomatic efforts had been "pursued." Finally, in the letter to Congress explaining and justifying his efforts, President Ford contended, "Appropriate demands for the return of the *Mayaguez* and its crew were made, both publicly and privately, without success."[31]

The sequence in these three official announcements is simple and clear: we *will make* a diplomatic demand; we *have been* pursuing nonmilitary means; we *did make* the "appropriate demands" but "without success." The simplicity, of course, is deceptive. The government did not deem it necessary to tell us what diplomatic channels were available to it, which of those it chose to utilize and why, or whether any of the messages reached their target within the Cambodian government. Rather, it chose to imply that all appropriate channels had been utilized and that the Cambodians had refused to negotiate. Perhaps that is the case. However, it is not reflected in the public communication surrounding the event. On the basis of that information, I must conclude that the government willingly lied to us about the "failed" diplomacy in order to attain our support for the military operation. For those unwilling to travel that far with me, I submit that at the least the discourse was corrupted by the withholding of information concerning the diplomatic attempts, thus forcing us to evaluate the efficacy of the diplomacy with inadequate information.

The third major corruption of the public discourse was through false claims of authority for taking the military action. These false claims were put forward by President Ford and his legal counsel, Roderick Hills. President Ford contended, "This operation was ordered and conducted pursuant to the President's constitutional Executive Power and his authority as Commander-in-Chief of the United States Armed Forces."[32] His counsel added that Ford "acted under his constitutional war powers to protect the lives and property of Americans."[33]

Let us examine the first claim of authority, the president's "constitutional executive power." Such powers are enumerated in Article II of the U.S. Constitution. Nowhere in that enumeration is found the power to engage in military operations outside a declaration of war. In fact, the only military reference among the enumerated executive powers says, "The President shall be commander in chief of the army and navy of the United States." But this was Ford's second "authorization." Unless authorization number one was identical to authorization number two, President Ford claimed to be acting under "constitutional executive power" which simply does not exist. If there is additional executive power permitting military action, beyond the commander-in-chief position, it is not *constitutional*. Thus, Ford corrupted the discourse by claiming to have acted under powers delegated by the Constitution, when such powers do not appear in the Constitution.

Ford's second rationale was that he was acting under his authority as commander-in-chief. What authority does the commander-in-chief have? What is a commander-in-chief? Clearly, it is a military title, the highest military title. Logically, it means that the president is the number one general. But no general, even number one, has the right to engage in an act of war without a declaration of war (the power to declare war is specified in the Constitution as belonging to Congress — Art. 1, Sec. 8, par. 11). For the president to take that power unto himself, in the name of his military position as commander-in-chief, is as clear a violation of the Constitution as is imaginable.

Yet, it may be argued, presidents have been utilizing such powers for some time. Precisely; and for that reason the Congress passed the War Powers Act of 1973. "The act requires a president, before sending troops into action, to 'consult' with Congress."[34] Thus, it appears that Congress — the war-declaring body — has determined that some military action can be undertaken without a declaration of war but that such actions must be decided upon in consultations between the president and the Congress.

Did such consultations take place? That depends, does it not, upon what is meant by "consultation?" If your son, Gerry, has one of his friends call to tell you that Gerry is going to the movies tonight, is that a consultation? I think not. Rather, I imagine "consultation" to mean that the two of you get together and come to a mutual understanding about whether he is going to the movies. The understanding, the decision, grows out of a dialogic process we call consultation.

What was the nature of the "consultation" in the *Mayaguez* decision? We find that the decision to take military action was made on the morning of May 14, while the first "consultation" did not take place until 5:55 that afternoon. Obviously, the consultation could not have been of the "let's decide what to do" type (and since that is the only type of consultation that exists, it must be that this later "consultation" was not a consultation at all).

Other anomalies appear. The "consultations" were not among principals. President Ford did not talk to the congressmen; he had them called by members of the White House staff.[35] Nor was it a "consultation" with the 535 people who constitute Congress; only 18 members of Congress were contacted.[36] The president had some of his friends tell some of Congress, "We are going to war tonight." To call that a consultation that fulfills the requirements of the War Powers Act takes us past credulity — perhaps to an "incredibility gap."

So much for the president's "constitutional executive power" and his authority as "commander-in-chief." What about his "constitutional war powers to protect the lives and property of Americans," the argument of his legal counsel? We must first note that there is no such thing as *constitutional* war powers of the president, above and beyond the commander-in-chief appellation. And, even if there were, they surely would not be "operational" absent a declaration of war. Congress has, during our many wars, conferred special war powers upon the president, but at the conclusion of each war those powers have reverted automatically to the Congress. It is nonsensical at best, dictatorial at worst, for the president to assume these special war powers in peacetime.

But certainly, it may be argued, even if we forget the constitutional argument and the war powers argument and the commander-in-chief argument, the president has the power to which his counsel alluded, the power to protect the life and property of Americans; did not President Johnson utilize such powers to land troops in the Dominican Republic? The answers are: yes, President Johnson utilized such powers; and no, they do not exist legally. The controlling law in this circumstance is still the congressional act of July 27, 1868, which says that when a foreign country deprives a U.S. citizen of his liberty the president is directed "to use such means, *not amounting to acts of war,* to obtain the release, and promptly to report to Congress."[37]

I conclude that President Ford acted unconstitutionally and illegally in sending troops to recapture the *Mayaguez.* (It should be noted that this judgment concerning legality is, of necessity, based purely on the evidence here presented. To date, no interpretations have appeared in any law journals, domestic or international; no claims have been filed with the World Court; no mention of *Mayaguez* has appeared in any Admiralty case.) Additionally, I conclude that President Ford's false claims for authority to take the actions corrupted the public discourse surrounding the event.

President Ford, by his illegal acts, tore asunder the Constitution and emasculated the War Powers Act of 1973. For the society to condone his actions would be, in the words of constitutional historian Raoul Berger, "to undermine the foundations of our democratic society."[38] And for those of us concerned with public rhetoric to condone the false descriptions, misleading simplifications, and lies of President Ford and his lieutenants would be to allow the loosening of the cement of public civility. Our role, I suggest, is not just to be concerned about isolated cases of corrupt rhetoric, for such cases can have widespread insidious results. As Edwin Black has argued, we must be alert to discourse that disposes "an audience to expect certain ways of arguing and certain kinds of justifications in later discourses that they encounter."[39] The Ford stance on the *Mayaguez* can be presumed to have done precisely that: by reinstituting the "president knows best" syndrome of the Imperial Presidency, Mr. Ford reinstituted a form of argumentation that the Nixon impeachment hearings had sought to eliminate.

Assuming that the foregoing provides a reasonable evaluation of the rhetoric surrounding the *Mayaguez* event, a nagging question remains: why did the American people so overwhelmingly approve Ford's handling of the situation? Are we so imperialistic, nationalistic, chauvinistic, and messianic that we will support any foreign military adventure the president desires? No doubt some people think so, but the evidence here is insufficient to demonstrate such an evaluation. In addition, such a sweeping indictment of the U.S. population is not necessary to explain their positive reactions in this case.

A case can be made for understanding their positive response to the *Mayaguez* actions in terms of the historic situation. We had just "lost" Vietnam and were feeling somewhat abused, tired of being pushed around by every second-rate power in the world. Our historic senses remembered, with some shame, an earlier capture of a U.S. ship, the *Pueblo*, by North Korea. *Mayaguez* gave us an opportunity to flex our muscles, to "reassert our manhood."

While this historic explanation may establish that the administration and people were predisposed toward face-saving actions somewhere in the world, it does not establish why the specific action in question was perceived to be so exemplary. Yet an explanation of that perception is implied in the foregoing analysis: the American people responded positively because the Ford administration was able to structure their perceptions. "In the field of foreign affairs, the public is not able to scrutinize an empirical reality. . . . Especially in such cases where . . . [the public does] not have firsthand access to an objective situation, their perceptions are based upon pictures or images constructed through their linguistic interaction with others."[40]

The American people are not conversant with international law, and thus had no reason to doubt the "high seas" and "piracy" descriptions given by President Ford. In similar manner, not knowing much about the possibilities of international diplomacy, the American people had no trouble believing that all possible diplomatic avenues had been explored.

As Richard Cherwitz has demonstrated, "the primary character of a crisis is defined by the President's discourse."[41] The president's definition, then, provides the "terministic screen" through which the population views the event, while at the same time providing him with a "terministic compulsion" to follow the implications of the terminology to their logical conclusions. In this case, Ford's terminology logically required military action. And a population whose perceptions were determined by that terminology had no trouble in accepting and applauding the resulting action.

All of this does not, of course, prove that the action was wrong. But it does demonstrate that corrupt discourse poisons the possibility of evaluating action, and — to the degree the action was taken because of terministic compulsion — it demonstrates that action, right or wrong, can be taken for the wrong reasons if the terminology is incorrect. Corrupt rhetoric corrupts decision-making.

NOTES

1.   "The White House: Statement by the Press Secretary," May 12, 1975, p. 1.

2.   Ron Chernow, "Of the United States, Cambodia and the Mayaguez Affair," *The New York Times,* May 22, 1975, p. 38.

3.   Jack Anderson, "Veterans' Benefits," *New York Post,* May 28, 1975, p. 41.

4.   "The White House: Statement," p. 1.

5.   "West German Magazine Asserts Mayaguez Carried C.I.A. Data," *The New York Times,* May 23, 1975, p. 3.

6.   Ibid.

7.   "The White House: Statement," p. 1.

8. Anthony Lewis, "The Morning After," *The New York Times*, May 12, 1975, p. 29.

9. Ibid.

10. Gerald R. Ford, "Text of a Letter to the Speaker and the President Pro Tem," May 15, 1975, p. 1.

11. Ibid.

12. Lewis, "The Morning After," p. 29.

13. I. F. Stone, "Conned in Cambodia," *The New York Review*, June 12, 1975, p. 16.

14. Ford, "Text of a Letter," p. 1.

15. Stone, "Conned in Cambodia," p. 16.

16. Lewis, "The Morning After," p. 29.

17. Stone, "Conned in Cambodia," p. 16.

18. Ford, "Text of a Letter," p. 2.

19. Lewis, "The Morning After," p. 29.

20. Ibid.

21. Ibid.

22. Ibid.

23. Ford, "Text of a Letter," p. 2.

24. Lewis, "The Morning After," p. 29.

25. Ford, "Text of a Letter," p. 1.

26. Jack Anderson, "Dissension Over Mayaguez," *New York Post*, May 21, 1975, p. 45.

27. Ibid.

28. "Waldheim Raps U.S.," *New York Post*, May 20, 1975, p. 5.

29. "The White House: Statement," p. 1.

30. "The White House: Statement by the Press Secretary," May 14, 1975, p. 1.

31. Ford, "Text of a Letter," p. 1.

32. Ibid., p. 2.

33. Raoul Berger, "The Mayaguez Incident and the Constitution," *The New York Times*, May 23, 1975, p. 37.

34. Stone, "Conned in Cambodia," p. 16.

35. Ibid.

36. Ibid.

37. Berger, "The Mayaguez Incident," p. 37.

38. Ibid.

39. Edwin Black, *Rhetorical Criticism: A Study in Method* (Madison: University of Wisconsin Press, 1978), p. 35.

40. Richard A. Cherwitz, "The Contributory Effect of Rhetorical Discourse: A Study of Language-in-Use" (Paper presented at the 1979 Speech Communication Association convention), 5–6.

41. Ibid., p. 6.

RICHARD NIXON AND PRESIDENTIAL MYTHOLOGY: AN INSTITUTIONAL PERSPECTIVE*

Malinowski contends that myths in general define ". . . the rights and privileges of groups and persons to particular positions of social power. . . ."[1] Myths deal with power relationships and thus reveal the social fabric of a society. *Political* myths relate specifically to authority and legitimize the use of power by validating the establishment. The major effect of political myth, then, is ". . . to validate the existing order, to show that it is right for the rulers to rule and for the governed to be governed."[2] Since myths are concerned with power and ultimate power in this country resides in the presidency, it is reasonable that American myths envelop that office. As Clinton Rossiter suggests, "The final greatness of the Presidency lies in the truth that it is not just an office of incredible power but a breeding ground of indestructible myth."[3]

Richard Nixon imbued the office of the presidency with his own special brand of myth, influenced by his personal political style, world-view, and character. Identified as an active-negative president,[4] Nixon repeated in his actions the following political themes which impinged upon and influenced the particular shape of his own presidential mythology: personal involvement in a failing course of action, the emergent enemy, the fight against "giving in," the lone struggle, the answer is effort, and the appeal to faith.[5] From these themes, three specific presidential myths emerged: (1) all problems are caused by outgroups (the emergent enemy); (2) our leaders are benevolent heroes who will lead us out of danger (personal involvement, the lone struggle, effort); and (3) the function of the citizen is to sacrifice and work hard to do the bidding of the leaders (appeal to faith, effort).[6] We refer to these as "specific Presidential myths" because each of them supports the status quo and thus strengthens the power of the incumbent president. Because the president is the major "identifier" of problems, the major "proposer" of solutions, and the one person representative of all the people, the three myths support and enhance his position.[7] Richard Nixon utilized all three presidential myths in his rhetoric, each one to identify problems and propose solutions; the second, the myth of the benevolent hero, he also used to enhance himself.

*Originally published by Dan F. Hahn and Ruth M. Gonchar, "Richard Nixon and Presidential Mythology," *Journal of Applied Communication Research* 1 (Winter-Spring 1973):25–48. Reprinted with permission.

THE ORIGIN OF PROBLEMS

All problems are caused by outgroups, whether the ubiquitous "they" or some specified group. Our problems are never caused by us. Some omnipresent "others" caused poverty, so we can mount a war against them. Our police never make mistakes — they just respond to a ghostly sniper who eludes the vision of all but the police. Do we have racial problems? Outside agitators! Inflation? Greedy union leaders!

The idea that outsiders create our problems is a comfortable myth, of course, because it means we do not have to engage in soul-searching or do much evaluating of our own actions except in terms of whether the actions were sufficient to destroy the evil influences of those terrible others. The conspiracy theory of politics embraced by both Right and Left is, therefore, merely the logical extension of the myth accepted by the Center. Theoretically, then, that means that either end of the political spectrum is capable of capturing much of the vast middle at any given time.

Did Nixon believe in and act on the basis of this myth? The evidence seems to be affirmative. Certainly his early career as an anti-Communist was based on the "outside agitator" myth. Discovering his presidential stand on the myth was somewhat more difficult until we noticed that "outsiders," for Nixon, meant his traditional enemies: the press, Congress, the "liberal community," and some members of his own administration. In short, all dissatisfaction with the Nixon leadership was perceived by Nixon as being caused by outsiders — and the Nixon response was to isolate those dissatisfied persons from access to him, the result of which, of course, was an exacerbation of the natural isolation of a president so eloquently described by George Reedy,[8] or to mount an attack upon them.

Hostility between Nixon and newsmen dates back to 1948, and Nixon saw the press as "outsiders." Two forms of news isolation were observable. First, the press, at least the critical, White House press corps, was isolated deliberately from the president. Unable to obtain complete information of administrative policies and procedures, not only because of isolation but because of an infrequent number of press conferences, the "critical press" had to resort to leaks and speculations to fill the columns of its dailies. The resulting lack of verification led them to make mistakes, and those inaccuracies, in turn, left them open to administration charges of intentional misleading of the public. Second, Nixon deliberately isolated himself from direct commentary about his administration in both print and electronic media, citing for his defense the exaggerations and over-dramatizations of news media presentation.[9] Nixon's attack strategy against the industry was mounted primarily by Vice-President Spiro Agnew.

Nixon's distrust and isolation from Congress also was traditional. As vice-president, Nixon had observed Eisenhower's difficulties in dealing with a "hostile" Democratic Congress. Assuming that "his" Democratic Congress would behave similarly, Nixon made few attempts to establish communication channels. His weekly breakfasts with top congressional leaders became briefings rather than consultations. Having instituted nightly summer cruises on the Potomac for Congressional big-wigs, Nixon rarely attended. When Congress disapproved of presidential policy (the Haynsworth and Carswell nominations provide a good example), Nixon lashed out at the "outgroup," calling them hypocrites and racists.

Nowhere was Nixon's isolation from the "liberal community" more apparent than in his reactions to campus dissent. Clearly, students were outsiders. Years of distrust and isolation desensitized Nixon to student voices so that when he did try to communicate he misunderstood their interests. While students, the night before an anti-war rally, anguished over the killings at Kent State, Nixon reminisced about his college days. While they bemoaned the escalation into Cambodia, Nixon discussed the upcoming football season. That Nixon appointed Bud Wilkenson, a former football coach, as his special consultant for youth affairs is testimony to this desensitization. So was the speech in which he called them "bums" and the announcement that he would watch a football game during the November 15, 1969 Moratorium March.

Finally, Nixon also discovered "outsiders" in his own administration, isolated himself from them, and finally got rid of them. Walter Hickel and James Farmer are two examples of this syndrome. Nixon even isolated himself from the reports of his own commissions (for instance, his Commission on Obscenity and Pornography) when they conflicted with his own viewpoint.

But it was in reference to the Vietnam conflict that Nixon most clearly relied upon the myth that outsiders caused the problem. The number of "outsiders" arrayed against him was truly colossal. First, of course, were the North Vietnamese and the Viet Cong. These two, known as "the enemy," supposedly caused all the problems. He said they were characterized by ". . . intransigence at the conference table, belligerence in Hanoi, massive military aggression in Laos and Cambodia and stepped-up acts in South Vietnam. . . ."[10] The myth is unscathed: the American military does not cause any problems — it just selflessly responds to aggressors.

The other "outsiders," Nixon's traditional enemies, also were at fault. The press was unfair in its coverage, Congress tried to block his program, the liberal community gave aid and comfort to "the enemy" and even the usually supportive Far Right, with its insistence upon a military victory, caused problems. Nixon described himself as standing in a cross fire between the "superhawks" and the "superdoves."[11] Rarely has Aristotle's Golden Mean been subscribed to with more vehemence.

In sum, Nixon supported the myth that all problems are caused by outsiders, but he supported it in a novel way — by labeling anyone who opposed him an enemy (or "outsider"). He utilized this redefinition process both for those who denied the validity of his goals and those who thwarted the success of his proposals for reaching those goals.

If problems are caused by outsiders, the American tendency is to turn to a benevolent hero to save us. So we turn now to Nixon's relation to the "hero" myth.

THE BENEVOLENT HERO

The second specific presidential myth can be summarized thusly: our leaders are benevolent heroes who will lead us out of danger. The myth of the benevolent hero president is one grounded in the very heart of modern political mythology. Its development, particularly over the past 50 years, can be seen most clearly in the political science texts written on the presidency. Influenced by the expanded power given the office by Franklin Delano Roosevelt, political scholars mythologized the presidency. Examine, for a moment, descriptions of the office appearing in representative textbooks: "The President is the most strategic policy maker in the government. His policy role is paramount in military and foreign affairs." "He reigns, but he also rules; he symbolizes the people, but he also runs their government." "He is . . . a kind of magnificent lion who can roam widely and do great deeds. . . ."[12] These are the descriptions to which the past two generations have been exposed in their classrooms and upon which these generations approach the political scene. These are, to a great extent, the bases for the myth. Perhaps the culmination of the "benevolent hero" myth occurred some years ago in a television cartoon series entitled "Super President."

Two dimensions of the "benevolent hero" president are apparent — the omnipotent dimension and the moralistic-benevolent dimension.[13] The omnipotent dimension itself develops along two interacting lines. First, only the president is or can be the genuine architect of U.S. public policy, and only he, by attacking problems frontally and aggressively, can be the engine of change to move this nation forward. It should be noted here that actions the president initiates need not be successful; they just must be taken. Second, the president is the strategic catalyst in the U.S. political system and the central figure in the international system. This second line expresses the importance of the president's centrality to the cosmos. As such, it provides the justification for line one of the omnipotent dimension, for if the myth envisions the world revolving around the president, it follows that only he can shape its destiny and engineer its progress.

The moralistic-benevolent dimension divides and develops similarly along two lines. First, the president must be the nation's personal and moral leader; by symbolizing the past and future greatness of America and radiating inspirational confidence, a president can pull the nation together while directing us toward the fulfillment of the American dream. Second, if only the right man is placed in the White House, all will be well, and, somehow, whoever is in the White House is the right man. This final dimension line, self-reflexive in nature, binds the others together; it provides a self-fulfilling prophesy for the myth.

The myth of the textbook president, the omnipotent hero, was personified in the rhetoric of President Richard Nixon. Not only did it provide him with justification for his actions ("I've taken this action because that's what the myth of the presidency calls for") but it also furnished him with subjects and content for whole addresses.

The first line of the omnipotent dimension can be analyzed in terms of the president as (a) the genuine architect of U.S. policy, a man who (b) attacks problems frontally and aggressively, and who (c) interprets this power expansively. Nixon gave support to the "genuine architect" aspect of the myth by citing constantly in his speeches his various presidential roles. From his interview with Howard K. Smith: ". . . and as Commander in Chief I have met that responsibility. I have met it and I believe this is correct."[14] Another example: "I think the time has come for me as President, and as Commander in Chief of our Armed Forces, to lay all of the pertinent facts before you and let you judge for yourself as to the success or failure of our policy."[15] Again: "Tonight, I again warn the North Vietnamese that if they continue to escalate the fighting when the United States is withdrawing its forces I shall meet my responsibility as Commander in Chief of our Armed Forces to take the action I consider necessary to defend the security of our American men."[16] Finally: ". . . I announced, as you will recall . . . that I, as President and as Commander in Chief, would exercise the authority which I had in such cases to review the case — that I would not pass the buck to a commission; I would not pass it to the Secretary of the Army."[17] Nixon used this "identification of roles" strategy to speak on behalf of those who served him in his "role": "I have visited Vietnam many times, and speaking now from that experience as Commander in Chief of our armed forces, I feel it is my duty to speak up for the two and a half million fine young Americans who have served in Vietnam."[18]

As a "genuine architect," the president must develop policy. Nixon's creating of the Nixon Doctrine satisfied that mythic need; his constant rhetorical references to his creation reinforced his myth-role accomplishment. Here is one of his many references to the Nixon Doctrine: ". . . however, everything we see there [Vietnam] is a new philosophy of United States policy. It is the most complete and accurate description of the Nixon Doctrine. This doctrine is designed for the specific purpose of maintaining a U.S. policy role in the world rather than a withdrawal from the world and international responsibilities."[19] Inherent in his discussion of the Nixon Doctrine was the reinforcement of an American (as differentiated from democratic) political myth — the myth of messianic diplomacy. The most powerful nation in the world, so the myth goes, has the responsibility as Messiah to save the rest of humanity from the enemies of their survival. The Nixon Doctrine substantiated the American myth. Finally, as "genuine architect," the president must know when to initiate action. This Nixon did with aplomb: "To protect our men who are in Vietnam and to guarantee the continued success of our withdrawal and Vietnamization programs, I have concluded that the time has come for action."[20]

Not only must the president be the genuine architect of U.S. public policy, he also must approach that policy-making process with vigor, attacking problems frontally and aggressively. Nixon's approach to this myth characteristic was to speak before national audiences only when he was describing the reasons for and the results of action he had taken. In those speeches his formula for attacking problems frontally and aggressively was: "I act, and you reap the benefits of my actions."[21] Perhaps a mini-analysis of excerpts from Nixon's April 7, 1971 speech to the nation on Vietnam can demonstrate the action formula. He began: "Over the past several weeks you have heard a number of reports on TV, radio, and in your newspapers on the situation in Southeast Asia. I think the time has come for me . . . to lay all of the pertinent facts before you and let you judge for yourselves as to the success or failure of our policy." (Note that "our" is being used here royally, that is, as a monarch would use the term.) So "you" will judge what "I" am doing and have

done. "I have decided to increase the rate of American troop withdrawals
. . ." and to explain why, "I would like to review briefly what I found
when I came into office. . . ." He goes on to tell us that no
comprehensive plan for ending American involvement in the war had
been devised, so "I implemented a plan to train and equip the South
Vietnamese . . . and you can see how our plan has succeeded. . . .
Every decision I have made in the past, and every decision I make in the
future will have the purpose of achieving that goal. . . ." I make
decisions, so Nixon says, "that contribute to the achievements of our
goals. . . ." What is the "you" role in the speech? "You will recall . . .
As you know . . . as you can see . . . most of you will recall . . . as
you can see . . . you look at the record. . . ."[22]

Finally, a president must give an expansive interpretation to his
official powers. Nixon first indicated that he recognized the extent of his
presidential powers in this rhetorical development: ". . . I will continue
to use the power of my office to persuade business and labor to act
responsibly in making further progress against inflation."[23] He repeated
this assertion later in the same speech: "That is why I shall do all that a
man in my office can do to preserve the economic freedom that built this
nation."[24] But "doing all that a man in my office can do" was not enough
for Nixon. It did not fulfill completely the mythic requirement of
"expansive interpretation." And so, Nixon identified situations as crises
and thereby justified the further expansion of his presidential powers: "I
have asked the Congress to extend for one year the Economic
Stabilization Act, which gives the President the power he needs to stop
inflation."[25] Identified as a crisis, inflation could be stopped only by
broader presidential power. Similarly, the need for a "vigorous activist
role in the world" caused Nixon to move ". . . drastically at home and
abroad to deal with the basic problems at home and abroad."[26] The
upshot of expansive interpretation of power was Nixon left free to take
risks in crisis situations. Indeed, for Nixon, the fulfillment of the
omnipotent dimension myth was his appearance as a leader who was not
afraid to take risks to achieve his goal. As he said: "When Americans are
risking their lives in war, it is the responsibility of their leaders to take
some risks for peace."[27]

The second line of the omnipotent dimension, that the president is the
strategic catalyst in the American political system and the central figure in
the international system, was manifested in Nixon's rhetoric by his
attempt to picture his presidential role as "the defender and upholder of
democracy." And so, in response to a question regarding his approval of
F.B.I. wiretapping, Nixon said: "Let's remember that the President of the

United States has the responsibility for the security of this country and the responsibility to protect the innocent from those who might engage in crime or which would be dangerous to the people of this country."[28] This view of the president as defender of democracy was not new for Richard Nixon. It was apparent after his 1960 presidential defeat that Nixon held to this myth view. Commenting on the reason he did not demand a recount of the 1960 election returns, Nixon said:

> I could think of no worse example for nations abroad, who for the first time were trying to put free electoral procedures into effect, than that of the United States wrangling over the results of our presidential election, and even suggesting that the Presidency itself could be stolen by thievery at the ballot box. It is difficult enough to get defeated candidates in some of the newly independent countries to abide by the verdict of the electorate. If we could not continue to set a good example in this respect in the United States, I could see that there would be open-season for shooting at the validity of free elections throughout the world.[29]

Nixon characterized the "strategic catalyst" myth throughout his speeches. His concern with history is one manifestation of that myth.[30] James Reston noted that Nixon ". . . put aside his old partisan and ideological arguments. He is now beginning to see himself in historical terms. . . ."[31] From Nixon's own rhetoric comes proof of that transcendence: "I realize that in this war there are honest and deep differences in this country about whether we should have ever become involved. There are differences as to how the war should have been conducted. But the decision announced tonight transcends those differences."[32] Nixon, as "strategic catalyst," transcended the ordinary, everyday bickering. Moreover, Nixon prescribed policies as "strategic catalyst" for not only the United States, but the world, fashioning his policies for the good of humanity across the globe: "We must strike a balance between doing too much and preventing self-reliance, and suddenly doing too little and undermining self-confidence. We intend to give our friends the time and the means to adjust, materially and psychologically, to a new form of American participation in the world."[33] He invoked the Taft-Hartley injunction to end a West Coast dock strike because it was his "natural and necessary duty."[34]

It was when Nixon was challenged by opposition that the "strategic catalyst" myth became most evident. To justify his decisions regarding Vietnam, Nixon called upon this second myth: "I don't question the motives of those who oppose me. But I know this world. I have traveled about and talked to many leaders, and I know we have a chance to play a role in this world."[35] Another example: when Wilbur Mills, chairman of the House Ways and Means Committee, challenged the president and worked out a textile import bargain with the Japanese, Nixon overrode the bargain, indicating, as he did, that Mills' ". . . maneuvers have challenged the President's authority to conduct foreign affairs. . . ."[36] By calling upon the "strategic catalyst myth," Nixon justified his action. Likewise, in the Calley case Nixon took this position:

> The widespread public interest was a factor in the sense that when people all over the Nation, their Congressmen and their Senators, are stirred up about a particular issue, a President — the President — has a responsibility to do what he can within the law to try to quiet those fears, to try to bring some perspective into the whole matter.[37]

The second dimension of the U.S. presidency myth we call the moralistic-benevolent dimension. Like the omnipotent dimension, it has two components. First, that the president must be the nation's personal and moral leader; by symbolizing the past and future greatness of America and radiating inspirational confidence, a president can pull the nation together while directing us toward the American dream. Second, that if only the right man is placed in the White House all will be well, and, somehow, whoever is in the White House *is* the right man.

The first component of the moralistic-benevolent dimension calls for the president to symbolize the morality and faith upon which this U.S. democracy is based. Here is an example of myth used to substantiate myth. The kind of "morality" demonstrated by a president is no less mythic than the general myth of the president as moral leader. In Nixon's case, he testified to nothing short of the Boy Scout code. In response, for example, to a question regarding Governor Rockefeller's actions at Attica, Nixon characterized the governor's responses (and his own through transference) as moral: "I believe people in public positions, heads of government or Prime Ministers, or maybe even Presidents [note the transference from Rockefeller to himself] cannot give in to demands for ransom, as was the demand made in this instance."[38] From not giving in to unjust demands, morality generalized for Richard Nixon to never backing down from a difficult situation. Still responding to the question of Attica, and his support of Governor Rockefeller, Nixon continued: "When a man [Rockefeller] is in a hard place and makes a hard decision and steps up to it, I back him up and I don't try to second-guess him. The next day, when some of the other returns come in, I still back him."[39] This, of course, was long before the Watergate revelations forced him into uncharacteristic withdrawals of support and second-guessing.

Nixon's verbalizations regarding moral actions did not always correspond with his political actions. During his Kansas State speech, Nixon abhorred the use of violence on campus and in the nation. Yet he excepted the use of violence in Vietnam. "He did so on grounds that the proper objective is not only to end the war but do it in a way that contributes to a just and lasting peace. . . . He is citing a particular goal as justifying violence — and on a dreadful scale — in a lecture purporting to rule out violence as an acceptable instrument, and accurately depicting how the 'acceptance of violence' corrodes a society."[40] Further, Nixon's labeling of violence as despicable did not prevent him from welcoming the so-called "hard hat" leaders to Washington just after they had beaten up peace demonstrators on the streets of New York, nor did it stop him from publicly congratulating a sky marshall for shooting a would-be hijacker who turned out to be a mentally unbalanced man in possession of a blank pistol.

Morality and faith are synonymous to Richard Nixon, and so to demonstrate his personal and moral leadership to the nation, Nixon utilized "faith" to symbolize moral leadership. A note should be included here: apparently faith and religion were not synonymous for Nixon. He manifested a "Cecil B. DeMille" approach to religion.[41] The religious ceremonies he confected for his entry into the White House included a second viewing of the three-hour film, *The Shoes of the Fisherman*.[42] This religiosity impelled him to bring the church to the president rather than the president to the church. Sunday services in the Nixon years were held in the White House, not in a Washington church. We projected a time when Nixon would televise his White House services on Sunday mornings for the nation to witness, and, yea, it was done.

With this view of religion/faith as a backdrop, Nixon's use of "faith" as an affirmation of his moral leadership becomes clear. A typical Nixon speech dealing with faith ran something like this: The war, the dissension, the purposelessness of the nation are merely symptoms of a greater crisis — the crisis of the spirit. Therefore, "To a crisis of the spirit, we need an answer of the spirit." Where is that answer? Not in God, as Billy Graham might suggest: ". . . and to find that answer we need only look within ourselves." "Here is Nixon rejecting the doctrine of original sin, a doctrine to which he generally adheres, and accepting the naive hope that the 'silent majority' can alter fundamentally the conditions of existence."[43] What are the attributes Nixon ascribed to the American spirit? "They are the specific historical attributes of the Christian deity: a healing power, compassion for the helpless, forgiveness to the sinner, and to all mankind, the freedom to choose their own ultimate destiny. The God of Christian theology is alive and well in the patriotism of Richard Nixon."[44] So for Nixon, faith and patriotism, morality and faith were combined into a monolith of benevolence. "Lacking a God, he [Nixon] has made patriotism his religion, the American dream his deity."[45] The equation, religion-patriotism-morality, could be seen frequently in Nixon's rhetoric:

> The older a nation and a people become, the more they become conscious of history and also of what is possible. Now I will explain to you what I mean. I rate myself as a deeply committed pacifist, perhaps because of my Quaker heritage from my mother. But I must deal with how peace can be achieved and how it must be preserved.[46]

Later in the same interview: "I can assure you that my words are those of a devoted pacifist. My very hardest job is to give out posthumous Medals of Honor."[47] Again, Quaker pacifism and American patriotism conjoin.

Faith in the nation, faith that the nation can heal itself, was a keystone of Nixonian oratory:

> I want all of you to know that as I stand here today ... I have great faith. I have faith in it [the nation] not because we are the strongest nation in the world, which we are, and not because we are the richest nation in the world, which we are; but because there is still, in the heartland of this country, and the heartland of America is in every State of America, there is still a strong religious faith, a morality, a spiritual quality which makes the American people not just a rich people, or a strong people, but makes the American people a people with that faith which enables them to meet the challenge of greatness.[48]

In short, Nixon had faith in the nation because the nation had faith. This circular relationship appeared frequently in Nixon's rhetoric and was nearly always equated with patriotism and the greatness of America. Nixon assured the nation that we ". . . can be confident that certain American values are not going to change."[49] Those American values he intended to preserve were the same ones which he extolled — the American dream, Horatio Alger values that forced this benevolent leader into stating: "I do say, however, that I think it is very important for those of us in positions of leadership not to tell a large number of people in America, whoever they are, that because of the accident of their birth they don't have a chance to go to the top."[50]

A benevolent leader also must radiate confidence, and this Richard Nixon did constantly. Let's not talk about the things that are wrong with the country, Nixon said, let's talk about the things that are right with it. After all, this is the job a president has; his critics will illuminate the problems often enough. His mythic assignment is to publicize the goodness of the nation. In a way, the president must act as the country's number one P.R. man.

Nixon gave "talks on confidence,"[51] detailing ". . . a few of the things I believe you have a right to be confident about."[52] What did this nation have a right to be confident about? In sum, that the Nixon foreign and domestic policies were succeeding, but more so that the greatness of this nation will not deteriorate: "Let us never lose the quality of greatness that has made today better than yesterday. Let us always hold fast to the quality of confidence that will help us make tomorrow better than today."[53] How can this confidence be activated? Nixon concluded, "We will succeed only if we cherish our right to be confident in our ability to shape the future."[54] Again, he returned to the nation's ability to heal itself and determine its future. Nixon exuded confidence in his programs by heralding the nation's future greatness. From his address of Phase 2 of his Economic Program: "We often hear people say these are troubled times. I say these are great and exciting times. We are at the threshold of a great new era, an age of movement in challenge and change. We have an unparalleled opportunity to create a better world for ourselves, for our children."[55] On his Vietnam policies: "But while I will never raise false expectations, my deepest hope, as I speak to you tonight, is that we shall be able to look back on this day, at this critical turning point when U.S. initiative moved us off dead center and forward to the time when this war would be brought to an end and when we shall be able to devote the unlimited energies and dedication of the American people to the exciting challenges of peace."[56]

Political observers often identified Nixon's reliance on the "future greatness" myth. James Reston, for example, noted it in his comments on the 1971 state of the union message: Nixon ". . . stood on a box and talked more about the State of Tomorrow than about the State of the Union today. His speech was in some ways like an insurance salesman's dream of the 'golden years' in which there would be no more war, inflation, unemployment, indolence, or unpaid hospital bills."[57] In fact, Nixon even went so far as to predict the end of these critical problems: "This war is ending. In fact, I seriously doubt if we will ever have another war. This is probably the very last one."[58]

The final aspect of the moralistic-benevolent dimension, that if only the right man is placed in the White House all will be well, and, somehow, whoever is in the White House is the right man, is the most difficult to isolate when examining Richard Nixon's rhetoric. But implicitly within his speeches is the indication that "he is the President." How lucky it is for the nation, then, to be told reassuringly: "That is why I shall do all that a man in my office can do to preserve the economic freedom that built this nation."[59] At times Nixon addressed himself to the future, indicating that any presidential successors would have no trouble living with his policies, because they would be the "right men in the White House" too: ". . . I want the American people to be able to be led by me, or by my successor, along a course that allows us to do what is needed to help keep the peace in this world."[60]

How did Nixon explain this myth of the right man at the right moment? The historical power and perspective of the office fashions the man to the job: "Obviously it was a political temptation when I started office to state simply that we would get out right away without any responsibility for what came next. But I knew too much about history, about Asia, about the basic feeling in the United States. . . ."[61] A similar statement clarifies even further Nixon's belief in the myth: "This would have been the easy thing to do, withdraw from Vietnam. It might have been the popular move. But if I had done so, I would have betrayed my solemn responsibility as President of the United States."[62]

Finally, the "right man" demonstrates he is "right man" by utilizing the powers of the office. If the powers of the office are being utilized correctly, the man holding the office must be the right man. So Nixon capitalized on this myth with statements such as: "With all the moral authority of the office which I hold, I say that America could have no greater and prouder role than to help end this war. . . ."[63] Again, in response to the uproar surrounding the Calley court-martial: "And I think a pretty good indication that the action I took was effective in that respect is that since that action we've seen the fears with regard to the Calley case subside — because they know that he is going to get a fair review and a final review from the President of the United States."[64] Nixon was the president, the right man; all would be well.

THE CITIZEN'S FUNCTION

If we are threatened by outside forces from which we can be saved by a benevolent hero, the third myth is obvious: the function of the citizen is to sacrifice and work hard to do the bidding of the leader. After all, a leader can only lead if there are followers to follow. The folklore supporting this myth is voluminous — "Too many cooks spoil the broth," "Too many chiefs, not enough Indians," etc.

Leaders reinforce the myth of the sacrificing followers with their rhetoric. Churchill offered Great Britain "blood, sweat, toil, and tears," and Kennedy reminded Americans to "ask not what the country can do for you, but what you can do for the country." Indeed, Robert Cathcart has held that one of Nixon's weaknesses was that he did not inspire followers. Analyzing Nixon's inaugural address, Cathcart lamented, "The speech shows his reluctance to ask for sacrifice or new government programs to meet our mounting crisis. His appeal is to those who want to occupy that comfortable moral middle ground between ease and sacrifice."[65]

An analysis of Nixon's rhetoric concerning Vietnam would seem to validate Cathcart's observation. The average citizen is asked to do little beyond feeling proud of our fighting men and responding to some unspecified responsibility: "This is the most difficult war in America's history, fought against a ruthless enemy. I am proud of our men who have carried the terrible burden of this war with dignity and courage, despite the division and opposition to the war in the United States. History will record that never have America's fighting men fought more bravely for more unselfish goals than our men in Vietnam. It is our responsibility to see that they have not fought in vain."[66] The only suggestion of any role for the average citizen to play in fulfilling that responsibility was that of supporting Nixon: "Nothing could have a greater effect in convincing the enemy that he should negotiate in good faith than to see the American people united behind a generous and reasonable peace offer."[67]

Indeed, it is not surprising that both Johnson and Nixon were unpopular or that we were critical of their Vietnam policies. They made it too easy; they minimized our sacrifices and maximized their responsibilities. In short, they overemphasized their roles as heroes and underemphasized the citizen role as sacrificing followers.

If the leader does not tell us how we can help, we feel unfulfilled, useless and we experience anomie. Our myth structure collapses and the leader becomes one of the "others," one of the outsiders. "Our" leader at that point must be defeated by a "man on a white horse," a new leader who will utilize our following and chase out the shadowy figure who is arrogantly posing as our leader and justifying his leadership by reference to a largely non-existent followership called "the silent majority." In short, Nixon's mythical following destroyed the American myth about the role of followers and created a vague, uneasy feeling of helplessness. This, in turn, weakened his ability to be perceived as a heroic leader and led us to wonder who the enemy really was.

So Nixon's failure to get support for his Vietnam policy can be attributed, in part, to the fact that instead of asking us to sacrifice for a specific policy, he led us to what Cathcart called "that comfortable moral middle ground between ease and sacrifice."

Nixon took an approach more in keeping with the myth in his economic policies. In explaining Phase 2 he specifically asked for sacrifices from everyone: ". . . working men and business men, farmers and consumers, members of Congress, of our state and local government. That means all of us."[68] The result? The people supported his plan — 66 percent favored his wage and price controls.[69]

When Nixon supported the myth by asking for sacrifice he found support. When he did not ask for sacrifice he had his policies rebuffed.

NOTES

1.   Max Gluckman, *Politics, Law and Ritual in Tribal Society* (New York: Mentor, 1965), p. 54.

2.   John Beattie, *Other Cultures* (New York, 1964), p. 161.

3.   James David Barber, *The Presidential Character* (Englewood Cliffs: Prentice-Hall, 1972), p. vii.

4.   Barber, *Presidential Character*, pp. 347–442.

5.   Ibid., pp. 56–57.

6.   These points and much of the rationale of this section are generalized from Murray Edelman, "Myths, Metaphors, and Political Conformity," *Psychiatry* 30 (1967): 217–228.

7.   For an excellent discussion of the transformation of the presidency from a law-enforcing to a problem-solving institution, see Joseph E. Kallenbach, *The American Chief Executive* (New York: Harper & Row, 1966), pp. 320–344.

8.   George Reedy, *The Twilight of the Presidency* (New York: World, 1969).

9.   *New York Post*, April 21, 1970, p. 4.

10.   Richard Nixon, "Radio and Television Address on the Situation in Southeast Asia," *The New York Times*, April 30, 1970, p. 5.

11.   Richard Nixon, "Interview with C. L. Sulzberger," *The New York Times*, March 10, 1971, p. 14.

12.   Thomas E. Cronin, "The Textbook Presidency and Political Science," *Congressional Record* 116 (1970).

13.   Ibid.

14.   Richard Nixon, "Interview with Howard K. Smith," *The New York Times*, March 23, 1971, p. 15.

15. Richard Nixon, "Address by the President," *The New York Times*, April 8, 1971, p. 6.

16. Richard Nixon, "Radio and Television Address by the President on the Situation in Southeast Asia," *The New York Times*, April 30, 1970, p. 4.

17. Richard Nixon, "Interview with Six Newsmen," *The New York Times*, April 17, 1971, p. 14.

18. Richard Nixon, "Address by the President," *The New York Times*, April 8, 1971, p. 6.

19. Nixon, Sulzberger interview.

20. Nixon, April 30, 1970 address.

21. For more detail see Ruth Gonchar and Dan Hahn, "The Rhetorical Predictability of Richard Nixon," *Today's Speech* 19 (1971):3–13.

22. Nixon, April 8, 1971 address.

23. Richard Nixon, "Talk on Confidence," *The New York Times*, April 27, 1971, p. 32.

24. Ibid.

25. Richard Nixon, "Text of Nixon's Address on Phase 2 Plans," *The New York Times*, October 8, 1971, p. 27.

26. Richard Nixon, "Transcript of the President's News Conference on Foreign and Domestic Affairs," *The New York Times*, September 17, 1971, p. 14.

27. Richard Nixon, "The Terms of Peace," *Setting the Course, The First Year: Major Policy Statements by President Richard Nixon*, ed. Richard Wilson (New York: Funk and Wagnalls, 1970), p. 12.

28. Nixon, "Interview with Six Newsmen."

29. Richard Nixon, *Six Crises* (New York: Pyramid, 1962), pp. 446–447.

30. Gonchar and Hahn, "Rhetorical Predictability," p. 6.

31. James Reston, "The State of Tomorrow," *The New York Times*, January 24, 1971, p. 13E.

32. Nixon, April 30, 1970 address.

33. Richard Nixon, Radio Talk to the Nation, quoted in Robert E. Semple, "The Many Shades of Meaning in His Doctrine," *The New York Times*, February 28, 1971, p. E1.

34. Max Frankel, "Nixon's Activism: A New Personality for '72," *The New York Times*, September 27, 1971, p. 12.

35. Nixon, Sulzberger interview.

36. Robert E. Semple, "The President's Image," *The New York Times*, March 22, 1971, p. 24.

37. Nixon, "Interview with Six Newsmen."

38. Nixon, September 17, 1971 news conference.

39. Ibid.

40. Tom Wicker, "In the Nation: Violence, Corrosion and Mr. Nixon," *The New York Times*, September 20, 1970, p. 17.

41. Garry Wills, *Nixon Agonistes; The Crisis of the Self-Made Man* (Boston: Houghton Mifflin, 1970), p. 182.

42. Ibid.

43. Charles P. Henderson, Jr., "Richard Nixon, Theologian," *The Nation*, September 21, 1970, p. 233.

44. Ibid., p. 235.

45. Ibid., p. 236.

46. Nixon, Sulzberger interview.

47. Ibid.

48. Richard Nixon, "Remarks of the President at Billy Graham Day," *The New York Times,* October 15, 1971, p. 23.

49. Nixon, confidence talk.

50. Nixon, September 17, 1971 address.

51. Excerpts from a typical "confidence" talks included in *The New York Times,* April 27, 1971, p. 32.

52. Ibid.

53. Ibid.

54. Ibid.

55. Nixon, Phase 2 address.

56. Nixon, Terms of Peace address.

57. Reston, "State of Tomorrow," p. 13 E.

58. Nixon, Sulzberger interview.

59. Nixon, Confidence excerpts.

60. Nixon, Sulzberger interview.

61. Ibid.

62. Nixon, Terms of Peace address.

63. Ibid.

64. Nixon, "Interview with Six Newsmen."

65. Robert Cathcart, "The Nixon Inaugural Address," in J. L. Ericson and R. F. Forston, *Public Speaking as Dialogue: Readings and Essays* (Dubuque: Kendall-Hunt, 1970), p. 130.

66. Nixon, Terms of Peace address.

67. Ibid.

68. Nixon, Phase 2 address.

69. Wallace Turner, "California Poll Assesses Agnew," *The New York Times,* November 28, 1971, p. 55.

A BURKEAN ANALYSIS OF LINCOLN'S SECOND INAUGURAL ADDRESS*

Lincoln's second inaugural address ". . . discloses a cluster of opinions which was certainly alien to the auditors of 1865 in its detachment from chauvinism, its historical perspective, and its pervasive sense of tragedy. Add to the list the tone of compassion in the speech and its rejection of retributive justice, and a universe begins to take shape."[1]

How did Lincoln arrive at such a non-typical stance? Did his detachment come from a tendency of his personality? Was his compassion the result of increasing revulsion to the bloody carnage over which he reigned as commander-in-chief? The answers to these questions we may never know, but to the degree we approach them, we will probably do so through rhetorical analysis. Most presidents act primarily via the rhetorical mode, so if the motivations for their actions are embedded within those actions it will be rhetorical analysis which will tease them out.

Of all contemporary rhetorical theorists, the name Kenneth Burke is most intimately associated with a concern for motive. For Burke, language use is an act and an act is motivated. An analysis of a speaker's language, then, should "get at" the individual's impressions of reality, as "Much that we take as observations about 'reality' may be but the spinning out of possibilities implicit in our particular choice of terms."[2] But those choices, we should remember, are made within particular circumstances. Burke's stress upon language, then, functions to restore to the text ". . . its value as activity and its meaning as a gesture and a response to a determinate situation."[3]

We propose, therefore, to re-analyze Lincoln's second inaugural, using as our "terministic screen" Burke's Pentad, his device for analyzing language as "symbolic action." Our goal is to determine why Lincoln, in this speech, was so "out of step" with his auditors.

At first glance, applying the Pentad results in an analysis which views Lincoln as the AGENT at the SCENE of his second inauguration. Through his speech (AGENCY) he equates (ACT) the plight of North and South in the midst of fighting the war. His PURPOSE was to pave the way for the eventual reunification of the North and South and an amicable reconstruction of the South.

---

*Originally published by Dan F. Hahn and Anne Morlando, "A Burkean Analysis of Lincoln's Second Inaugural Address," *Presidential Studies Quarterly,* 9 (Fall 1979):376–379, by permission of the Center for the Study of the Presidency.

Although these *are* aspects of the speech, the analysis appears too superficial. On closer inspection, we find a more appropriate analysis is triggered by the last sentence of the fourth paragraph, in which Lincoln has been equating the North and South: "The prayers of both could not be answered — that of neither has been answered fully." The question which naturally occurs at this point is, whose purpose *could* be completely fulfilled in this situation? That question is not asked outright, but is induced by that last portion of the sentence, which provides a smooth transition to the actual intent of Lincoln's speech. The transitional paragraph begins, "The Almighty has His own purposes" — and we have our answer: God is the AGENT. The Pentad can be drawn from that one entire paragraph to which Lincoln has been leading us throughout the address. The North and South are the AGENCIES in "this terrible war" (ACT) which God (AGENT) has provided for the PURPOSE of abolishing slavery and punishing "those by whom the offense came." The SCENE is the United States in the throes of the Civil War.

Lincoln's chosen language directs attention to the points which would persuade his audience to a particular perception of the "reality" of the events at hand. This "reality" was that, although four years ago we thought two sets of agents with opposing purposes were following their respective courses of action, we now realize that they were actually mere agencies for a greater Power who possessed His own purpose. Although "both parties deprecated war," and each faction would fight the war for its own purpose, the war was actually fought for the Almighty's purpose. Being mortals, it is difficult to discern the Almighty's reason; nevertheless, Lincoln attempts to offer an interpretation.

> If we shall suppose that American slavery is one of those offenses which, in the providence of God, must needs come, but which having continued through His appointed time, He now wills to remove, and that He gives to both North and South this terrible war, as the woe due to those by whom the offense came, shall we discern any departure from those divine attributes which the believers in a living God always ascribe to Him?

What can we do but the will of God? This war is out of our hands — we did not want it, although we would fight it for our own cause, but it comes as God's will. We hope that it ends quickly, especially since the cause of it has been abolished.

> Yet, if God wills that it continue until all the wealth piled up by the bondsman's two hundred and fifty years of unrequited toil shall be sunk and until every drop of blood drawn with the lash shall be paid by another drawn

with the sword, as was said three thousand years ago, so still it must be said, "The judgments of the Lord are true and righteous altogether."

The rhetoric is geared to the perception of God as AGENT. In his opening statement and at other points in the beginning of the speech, Lincoln refers to a time four years ago on the occasion of his first inauguration. Reference is being made to a time when he was the AGENT (or thought he was); a time when ". . . a statement, somewhat in detail, of a course to be pursued, seemed fitting and proper." There is an anticipation in his opening paragraph that this is no longer the case. At this early point we assume that another statement laying out the "course to be pursued" would not be "fitting and proper" because the last one still has not been completed. But no, the reason is different — it would not be appropriate because the speaker no longer perceives himself as the AGENT.

The extensive use of the passive voice verb form indicates the type of role the president sees for himself. Also indicative of his role is the absence of references to himself as the doer of an action. If, as Burke says, "There is an implied sense of negativity in the ability to use words at all,"[4] then the concept of language as action implies that language can also indicate inaction. And inaction is exactly the course Lincoln announces in the second inaugural, the only course appropriate for an AGENCY, especially since the role of AGENT has been claimed by another to whom it rightfully belongs.

We find it significant that in a piece of only six paragraphs, four are devoted to stating the conditions of the situation. This is an important aspect of the speech since it demonstrates the care taken to set the stage and to prepare the audience for the introduction of another AGENT. These conditions are presented in a logical order which leads us smoothly into the transition, which is the crux of the oration. This occasion is compared to that of four years ago and, since all the issues have been publicly discussed and the audience is aware of them, there is no reason to discuss them again. Indicative of Lincoln's relinquishment of power as AGENT is his proclamation: "With high hope for the future, no prediction in regard to it is ventured." Neither a prediction nor a course of action nor a morale booster is offered. This does not have the ring of an inaugural speech of a man who is retaining the reins of authority and the obligation for an entire nation in the midst of a civil war. This is no inflammatory speech to spur the citizenry on to win the war. A purposeful choice of inaction has been made.

Although he deems it unnecessary to speak of the issues, Lincoln does indeed call attention to them. He does so without naming or directly accusing the South. He mentions that slavery was exclusively a characteristic of the South and that it "was, somehow, the cause of war." "Somehow" is a deliberately cautious term. The intention here is to diminish the role of the South in causing the war. No accusing finger is pointed since both sides attempted to win their ends through peaceful means, but each was willing to wage war if those proved unsuccessful.

Lincoln painstakingly equates the plight of the North and the South in an effort to dispel feelings of hostility:

> Neither party expected for the war the magnitude or the duration which it has already attained. Neither anticipated that the cause of the conflict might cease with, or even before, the conflict itself should cease. Each looked for an easier triumph, and a result less fundamental and astounding. Both read the same Bible, and pray to the same God; and each invokes His aid against the other. It may seem strange that any men should dare to ask a just God's assistance in wringing their bread from the sweat of other men's faces; but let us judge not, that we be not judged. The prayers of both could not be answered — that of neither has been answered fully.

This is the reason for attributing the war to God. (As a handiwork of His design, no side need bear the blame.) Anyone who believes in Him and ". . . those divine attributes which the believers in a living God always ascribe to Him" will accept the war as His will. Therefore, we, as His AGENCIES, will fight this war as long as He sees fit, as retribution for "the offense." As AGENCIES:

> With malice toward none; with charity for all; with firmness in the right, as God gives us to see the right, let us strive on to finish the work we are in; to bind up the nation's wounds; to care for him who shall have borne the battle, and for his widow, and his orphan — to do all which may achieve and cherish a just and lasting peace among ourselves, and with all nations.

Although Lincoln indicated that he dared not predict the outcome of the war, there is a strong intimation here that a Union victory is inevitable. With this in mind, the words "With malice toward none" express the essence of the entire address. Feelings of animosity are natural between opposing AGENTS, but AGENCIES cannot be held responsible. Through a skillful rhetorical maneuvering, he has directed attention and energies away from a conflict of Northern AGENTS against Southern AGENTS and has positioned God at the focal point. The war, strange as it may seem, was God's will and both sides must bear it even without understanding how a just God could let it drag on. But once peace arrives, as it eventually must, we all know how God wants us to treat each other: not with malice, but with charity. As AGENCIES, in war *and* peace, we can do no better than fulfill the desires and purposes of the AGENT, the Prime Mover, and thus deserve a "just and lasting peace."

And now we know, do we not, why the second inaugural, although today considered a rhetorical masterpiece, was unpersuasive in 1865: his auditors were unwilling to accept the "reality" that pictured them as AGENCIES rather than AGENTS, unable to adjust away from the hatred and malice of wartime toward the love and charity of a Christian peacetime. Lincoln, with his call for compassion, was not just ahead of his time; unfortunately, he was ahead of all times.

NOTES

1.   Edwin Black, *Rhetorical Criticism: A Study in Method* (Madison: University of Wisconsin Press, 1978), p. 172.
2.   Kenneth Burke, *Language as Symbolic Action* (Berkeley: University of California Press, 1966), p. 46.
3.   Frederic R. Jameson, "The Symbolic Inference; or, Kenneth Burke and Ideological Analysis," *Critical Inquiry* 4 (1978):509.
4.   Burke, *Language, p. 12*.

Chapter 2

PRESIDENTIAL PERSUASION

> The principal power that the president has is to bring people in and try to persuade them to do what they ought to do without persuasion. That's what I spend most of my time doing.
>
> Harry S. Truman

In Chapter 1, we began our consideration of politics and communication by noting Aristotle's observation of humans as "political beings" and the importance of the "faculty of language" in establishing and maintaining social life. Our concern with presidential persuasion follows rather naturally our discussion of the rhetorical presidency. Aristotle defines rhetoric as "the faculty of observing in any given case the available means of persuasion."[1] For him, "the modes of persuasion are only true constituents of the art [of rhetoric]: everything else is merely accessory."[2]

Contemporary scholars view persuasion as an essential part, if not the very essence, of all communication activities. On the surface, the process of persuasion appears rather simple. In selecting an automobile, we may desire one that is primarily inexpensive, or elegant, or fuel efficient, or fast, or stylish, or suggests social status. A car salesman will demonstrate how their vehicle meets our criteria, present "new" evidence suggesting alteration of our criteria, or may attempt to simply change our criteria directly. The process becomes more subtle and complex, however, when one notices the range of appeals for products in advertising. The ad for the Volkswagen Rabbit differs greatly in *People* magazine versus *National Geographic*. In one, the ad focuses upon lifestyle and social setting while the other on efficiency and engineering. Each ad, for the same product, makes specific and very different assumptions about the readers of the magazines.

This trivial example reveals the complexity of the process of persuasion. Each element of a communication transaction contributes to the persuasive process: a speaker's motives, wants, and desires; a listener's motives, wants, and desires; a message's appeals, evidence, and structure; the medium's delivery attributes and limitations; and environmental variables.

In this chapter we will investigate the nature of presidential persuasion. We think persuasion is an essential part of all presidential behavior. We will focus on the verbal and nonverbal persuasive dimensions of the office as well as identify some of the more overt ways presidents influence public opinion.

PERSUASION DEFINED

Although Aristotle defined rhetoric as being primarily concerned with persuasion, the definition is rather narrow. A more contemporary definition by Douglas Ehninger characterizes rhetoric as the "rationale of symbolic inducement; as that discipline which studies all of the ways in which men may influence each other's thinking and behavior through the strategic use of symbols."[3] This definition broadens the scope of rhetoric and defines the act of persuasion. Persuasion is the process of how people influence each other. It consists of both the elements (verbal and nonverbal symbols) and the process (alignment, realignment, or identification of beliefs, attitudes, or values) of negotiating everyday life. As a process, persuasion is neither good nor bad. It is a tool of human beings.

PERSUASION TODAY

Today, persuasion surrounds our life. Every American is exposed to over 1,600 advertising messages daily.[4] In our jobs, decisions are most often products of advocacy presentations rather than analyses of information. Much of the persuasion we encounter daily, however, is not direct but subtle and operates at the subconscious level. In the mid 1950s, Vance Packard became concerned "about the large-scale efforts being made, often with impressive success, to channel our unthinking habits, our purchasing decisions, and our thought processes by the use of insights gleaned from psychiatry and the social sciences. . . . The result is that many of us are being influenced and manipulated, far more than we realize, in the patterns of our everyday lives."[5] What bothered Packard is that persuasion today tries "to invade the privacy of our minds. It is this right to privacy in our minds — privacy to be either rational or irrational — that I believe we must strive to protect."[6]

Politics today is much more a science than an art. And without doubt, the kingmakers of contemporary politics are the new breed of political and media consultants.[7] Today's professional politicians are "politicians" only insofar as they earn their living working for political candidates and campaigns and are "professionals" in the sense that they possess unique skills and knowledge relevant to human motivation and mass communication technology.

The political professional is needed today because of what Blumenthal calls "the permanent campaign." The "permanent campaign," a direct result of the new technology in the age of information, has become "the steady-state of reality of American politics. In this new politics, issues, polls, and media are not neatly separate categories. They are unified by the strategic imperative . . . the elements of the permanent campaign are tangential to politics: they are the political process itself."[8]

POLITICS AND PERSUASION

The process of persuasion is not only an essential element of politics but lies at the heart of democratic government. The more open a society, the more important the process of persuasion. Open societies encourage citizens to take part in public debate and discussion. Liberty makes choices possible and choices encourage competition and advocacy. The greater the diversity of opinions and choices within a nation, the greater the need for vigorous public debate and issue discussion. Persuasion, then, is the tool of a free people.

The presidency, which serves as the focal point of our government for all citizens, is indeed an office of persuasion. As Donna Cross observes, "once the selling of the president has been completed, selling *by* the president can begin."[9] A chief executive leading the masses by various means of persuasion is, of course, nothing new. Louis XIV declared that "the people are happy when attending a spectacle: this is the means by which we hold their mind and their heart."[10] Even Napoleon set up a press bureau that he called the Bureau of Public Opinion. Its function was to "manufacture political trends to order."[11] Today, presidential addresses are primarily sales pitches designed to persuade more than inform, endorse more than enlighten.

As citizens, we should be aware of the various strategies and methods of presidential persuasion. Persuasion is a powerful instrument for the advancement of both personal and social causes. To understand the process of persuasion is to protect ourselves and society from selfish and evil elements. Cross effectively argues, "people should be educated, beginning as schoolchildren, to recognize propaganda. There is a distinction between argument and sophistry, between persuasion and demagoguery, between information and dogma. A rational democracy requires that people be able to recognize that distinction."[12]

PRESIDENTIAL PERSUASION

Political Language, Symbols, and Persuasion

As argued in Chapter 1, political consciousness is clearly dependent upon language, for language can determine the way in which people relate to their environment.[13] At the very least, language should be viewed as the medium for the generation and perpetuation of politically significant symbols. Political consciousness, therefore, results from a largely symbolic interpretation of sociopolitical experience. To control, manipulate, or structure the "interpretation" is a primary goal of politics in general. The language of government, in many ways, is the dissemination of illusion and ambiguity.[14] A successful politician or leader will use rather specific linguistic devices that reinforce popular beliefs, attitudes, and values. To complete the circle, "politically manipulated language can function as agents promoting the stability — whatever its attributes — of a political order."[15]

From this perspective, we argue that most official presidential language is an expression of dominant societal symbols and predefinitions. When evoked, rather specific expected behavior occurs. In addition, the use of highly evocative and ritualistic language may indeed structure a political reality which also influences behavior. The paramount questions become whether or not ritualistic language has any positive effect on the decision-making process and to what extent citizens are "manipulated" by highly abstract, ambiguous rational symbols. For example, the term "national security" was evoked frequently by the Carter and Reagan administrations. During the Carter administration, the American people were instructed to consume less oil, not to sell grain to the Soviet Union, and to support nuclear power endeavors, all in the interest of national security. During the Reagan administration, Americans were encouraged to support large defense expenditures, the MX missile system, and the development of a "star wars" defense system, also in the interest of national security. Obviously the term has become a rather potent linguistic device. However, perhaps what is more important is the "reality" that is created each time the term is evoked: does it make a difference upon behavior if it is evoked by the president, a senator, or newsperson; what values do the symbol (or term) have resulting from conditioning and socialization? Major considerations, therefore, become how situations are developed, how terms become significant symbols, and how the presidency as a part of the "process" becomes an influential symbolic artifact affecting societal behavior.

Michael Novak argues that a president's symbolic power consists of five components: identification, interests, action, moral fulfillment, and authority.[16] These components focus on the extent an individual, looking at the president says "we"; the degree a president suggests knowledge and concern for the public's interests; the degree a president's actions stimulate actions in the general public; the degree that a president conveys a sense of admiration and inspiration; and the extent to which a president appears to know what he is doing as well as the ability to direct the nation. Each of these aspects is conveyed through interaction, molded in language, and is more pervasive than any legal power granted in the Constitution.

How do political symbols work? It is their abstract, "semantic hollowness" that makes symbols so powerful. Although political symbols function as objects of common identification, they simultaneously allow for individual idiosyncratic meanings to be attached. Two individuals may disfavor abortion but do so based on religious (that is, "Thou shalt not kill") or constitutional grounds (that is, the right to life, liberty, and the pursuit of happiness). The same two individuals may disagree about abortion for rape victims but clearly support a general appeal by a president disavowing the practice of abortion. Political symbols are powerful not because of the broad commonalities of shared meaning but because of the intense sentiments created and attached to them resulting in the perception that the symbols are vital to the system.[17] Cobb and Elder even argue that the stability of the U.S. polity is a direct result of an abstract, shallow symbolic consensus. "This type of consensus rests upon symbols that are commonly viewed as important and are the objects of relatively homogeneous affective attachments but which lack any commonality of substantive meaning across individuals and groups."[18]

Political symbols, then, are the direct link between individuals and the social order. As elements of a political culture, political symbols function as a stimulus for behavior. The use of appropriate symbols results in the people's acceptance of certain policies that may or may not provide tangible rewards, their support for various causes, and their obedience to governmental authority. Political symbols become, according to Dan Nimmo, means to material and social ends and not ends in themselves.[19]

There is, however, a long process from symbol creation, definition, acceptance, and subsequent behavior. For implicit in the argument is the notion that successful leadership and control is dependent upon the successful manipulation of political symbols. There is a constant competition and struggle for national symbols. At one level, a president attempts to manipulate symbols in order to mobilize support, deactivate opposition, and insulate himself from criticism. On a broader level, national symbols are perpetuated in order to preserve the prevailing culture, beliefs, and values. Thus, the ongoing manipulation of political symbols takes place in the context of an existing set of symbols grounded in the political culture. For the cynic, the key to political power and authority is simply a matter of "pushing the right buttons" or manipulating the right symbols. Yet, even in a democracy where logic, rationality, and open discussion are greatly valued, such a notion of manipulation should not be quickly dismissed.

In attempting to explain social action, Robert Pranger argues that three variables present themselves: experience (symbols), perception (meaning), and a system linking experience and perception.[20] The "linking system," of course, is politics. Political activities attempt to define "experience" thus resulting in a desired "perception." The reverse is also possible.

We must caution, however, that few scholars agree that hard-sell media campaigns and the evoking of patriotic clichés alone alter the attitudes and behavior of large numbers of people.[21] But many studies are short term and merely focus on clearly persuasive messages while ignoring the more subtle effects of educational or informational messages upon attitudes. Our point is that persuasion is a complex process and people interpret messages in such a way that is compatible with long-term commitments, with the beliefs that are created by events and current perceptions of reality. Public views on issues are mobilized rather than fixed. Issues themselves are largely created, identified, and permeated throughout society. Neither issues nor specific positions on issues exist in a vacuum. Advocates of a "systems or process" orientation to government are mistaken to conceive of "outputs" as public policy "goals." Rather, governmental "outputs" are results of the *creation* of political followings and mass support.

Obviously, mobilization of public support is much easier when revolved around a potent political symbol. A president can justify nearly any action or policy or mobilize public support for a specific policy by defining the issue in terms of national security. Not only is the concept potent, but the expectations of presidential performance dictates that the president will take care of constituents in any emergency; has the best access to needed sources of information in order to make policy decisions; and will always act in the best interests of the nation. "Government affects behavior," as Murray Edelman so masterfully notes, "chiefly by shaping the cognitions of large numbers of people in ambiguous situations. It helps create their beliefs about what is proper; their perceptions of what is fact; and their expectations of what is to come."[22] The principal task becomes, therefore, not to grant public demands but to change or control the demands and expectations of the public. To accomplish this is to control the cognitions and perceptions of the people. And this is best achieved by the manipulation of broad, abstract, national symbols. In political terms, a symbol can be understood as a way of organizing a repertory of cognitions into meanings.[23]

The mass media play a significant role in providing immediate access of information to the citizenry of the nation — as well as providing powerful techniques of creating and permeating desired "images" for public consumption. A president can, nearly at any time, command the attention of the media and speak directly to the American people. In addition, a president constantly attempts to create a favorable image in the minds of the public utilizing the media. The use of media by presidents will be discussed in much greater detail in Chapter 6.

Nevertheless, the dynamics of political images can only be appreciated by understanding the interaction of two key societal processes.[24] The first process is that of political images being created and distributed among the individuals of a society. The second dynamic of political life is the distribution of specialized skills and knowledge among the people of the society. Political images include not only role expectations but also symbolic or personalized images of institutions themselves.

Nearly every American has a rather clear or concrete image of the presidential role. The image is perpetuated from generation to generation and is modified over time by agencies of formal instruction and, more importantly, face-to-face communication.[25] The long-term process and dynamics of the presidential image developed are described by Kenneth Boulding as

> a role image which originated in the minds of the founding fathers and in the course of the long political and constitutional discussions which preceded the founding of this republic. It is an image which is partly enshrined in the transcript of the constitution. It is an image, however, which has been changing slowly in the course of history and which is derived in part from the recorded experience of the occupants of the role. The role is the center of a complex network of communications both in and out, part of which each occupant of the role inherits and part of which he creates for himself.[26]

Many images and perceptions comprise any situation. These images and perceptions do not exist in a vacuum. Rather, they are created and evolve from the interaction among people, government, and political leaders. Culture is not transmitted like a telegraph message. Culture is taught in human endeavors which are largely created, staged, and performed by people in the community who have been trained and who are, in turn, training others in cultural presentation. Society results from the blending together of the vast separate lines of action of the members of a group. Such a process Herbert Blumer calls "joint action." The basis for joint action is "the establishment through interpretive interaction of common definitions of the situation. Even though much of joint action is in the form of repetitive, patterned responses to common situations, each instance of it has to be recreated, reconstituted, and reenacted."[27] A presidential contest is really a contest of competing definitions of situation. The winner is one who successfully articulates the "definition of situation" held by the majority or one who successfully creates a potent "definition of situation" that has been adopted by a majority of the voters.

Situations, the context for politics, are not neutral. They are created, manipulated, and permeated throughout society. Consequently, the "definition of situations" is a commodity that politicians compete to control and own. Public cognitions and impressions are influenced by the investment and utilization of "significant symbols" that are emotional, intense, and cultural in nature. Society, therefore, is a dynamic, interacting entity consisting of many levels acting simultaneously.

The presidency is itself a "significant symbol" also comprised of many levels and elements. The institution influences and affects the beliefs, attitudes, and even values of the public already established through socialization. As an institution, legitimacy is guaranteed and thus deference to presidential authority is largely a matter of impression management. Presidential elections are also largely a contest for symbolic legitimation.

Leadership and Persuasion

Leadership is a term that is often used in connection with the presidency. In a recent work, Theodore Sorensen renewed the argument for a strong and powerful presidency. Sorensen believes that "Congress can legislate, appropriate, investigate, deliberate, terminate and educate — all essential functions. But it is not organized to initiate, negotiate or act with the kind of swift and informal discretion that our changing world so often requires. Leadership can come only from the presidency."[28] It is, however, much easier to call for strong leadership than to define the concept.

Nimmo argues that political leadership "actually refers to a particular relationship that exists between a leader and his followers in specific settings."[29] The focus of much modern leadership theory is upon the willingness of followers to follow. There are no specific lists of traits that constitute leadership although certain traits are helpful in any specific situation. It is more useful, according to Murray Edelman, to look for leadership dynamics "in mass responses, not in static characteristics of individuals."[30]

In terms of the presidency, one should recognize the importance of what Orrin Klapp calls "symbolic leadership."[31] The real appeal of public officials is what they symbolize rather than what they have done. Klapp argues that certain persons have enormous effect, not because of achievement or vocation but because they stand for certain things; they play dramatic roles highly satisfying to their audiences; they are used psychologically and stir up followings. Symbolic leadership is an emergent phenomenon resulting from the interaction of the public and the politician. As political drama begins, according to Klapp, roles are identified, interpreted, and projected upon the politician and no distinction is made between what a thing "is" and what the audience sees that it is. The key, therefore, in becoming a symbolic leader is to take advantage of the dramatic elements in any setting. Settings become drama when "things happen to audiences because of parts played by actors; the function of the actor is to transport an audience vicariously out of everyday roles into a new kind of 'reality' that has laws and patterns different from the routines of the ordinary social structure."[32]

The sources of images or preconceptions people have of the qualities of leadership are vast. There are, however, three major influences upon such leadership construction. First, history rather carefully characterizes past national leaders. Washington was a man of integrity ("the cherry tree"), determination ("Valley Forge"), and was democratic (refusal to be "king"). Lincoln was a man of patience ("preserve the union"), forgiveness ("with malice toward none"), and a lover of freedom ("Emancipation Proclamation"). Second, television greatly contributes to the creation of leadership ideals. The open forums give the impression of being able to assess candidate qualities. Finally, leadership qualities are portrayed in dramatic programs and literature. Often voters openly compare the qualities of politicians to those of professional entertainers. Even Walter Cronkite, former evening news anchor for CBS, was mentioned as a credible vice-presidential running mate for the 1980 Anderson independent presidential bid.

Presidential Power

We would be remiss if we did not recognize the classic argument of Richard Neustadt that the power of the presidency lies in the power to persuade and "the essence of a President's persuasive task with Congressmen and everybody else, *is to induce them to believe that what he wants of them is what their own appraisal of their own responsibilities requires them to do in their interest, not his.*"[33] Presidential power, for Neustadt, consists of three elements: professional reputation (that is, the skill and the will to use various bargaining assets), public prestige (that is, popularity), and formal constitutional powers. Two of the three elements demand consistent and continual persuasive communication activities.

The point is rather obvious. Formal constitutional powers alone are no guarantee of influence nor provide the basis for effective leadership. Presidents simply must engage in persuasion across all levels of audiences and activities.

Strategies of Persuasion

As noted in Chapter 1, George Edwards argues that the greatest source of presidential influence today is public approval.[34] Without it, no policy or legislation is likely to pass Congress. A president must not only follow public opinion but most often attempt to lead and generate public support for a wide range of policy positions. Some attempts are direct while others are much more subtle. Presidential persuasion, as a complex process, involves a multitude of factors and approaches: verbal and nonverbal, skill and instinct, art and science. Although it is virtually impossible to identify all strategies and tactics of presidential persuasion, it is useful to explore some major ways presidents attempt to influence public opinion.[35]

Direct Appeal to the Public

Roderick Hart correctly observes that today every presidential message is the product of a "persuasive factory." Each president has "a gaggle of wordsmiths to help him stoke the fires of invention, and with political advisors to help him assess each drafted word for its presumed impact . . . a president's speech is a sociopsychological composite: of circumstance, of supporters and detractors, of diverse motivations."[36] Such help, however, is no guarantee of success. The quality of public performance has become an essential element to success. Carter's lack of skill in public speaking is noticeable in contrast to Reagan. Even Walter Mondale, the day after his presidential defeat by Reagan, stated that his lack of effectiveness in communicating through the mass media hurt his candidacy.

But good public speaking performances alone are not enough to capture and motivate public sentiment. It involves, as Hart describes, a "complex of factors constituting modern communications."[37] In the case of Ronald Reagan, labeled the "Great Communicator," the factors include: skilled public relations staff and media experts, sophisticated polling techniques, carefully staged media events, blue suits and undyed hair, a carefully orchestrated casual air of informality and personableness, an elegant, image-conscious wife, and the "God-given ability to dominate by force of personality almost any social gathering in which he finds himself."[38] It is a preference, as most scholars reluctantly agree, for style rather than content that seems most effective in imparting public opinion.

Historically, except in cases of foreign affairs, direct appeals to the nation usually do not succeed. Wilson's failure to gain approval of the League of Nations, Ford's failure to sell the anti-inflation "WIN" campaign, and Carter's futile attempt to encourage energy conservation and the expansion of nuclear power are obvious examples. Even Reagan's attempts to solicit public support for increased defense spending, building the MX missile, and major tax reform were largely met with a "wait and see" attitude.[39] The fact is that the general public does not maintain a sustained interest in politics and the details of policy formation. But the presidential threat to Congress of "taking the issue to the American people" is an enduring tactic and myth of American political democracy.

Media Events

Much will be said about media and mass communication in Chapter 6. Suffice it to say here that carefully staged and controlled media events greatly help a president to project the desired image, obtain free publicity, and establish a national agenda for issue discussion and debate. No president is more aware of the need and value of projecting the right image or using the media than Ronald Reagan. Michael Deaver's sole job in the Reagan administration was to orchestrate the president's image and stage television events. In fact, upon Reagan's election in 1980, he created the Office of Planning and Evaluation to monitor the president's performance in the first 100 days in office. Reagan also retained Mark Goode, a media consultant and former television producer, whose office was next to the White House.

Many media events are rather obvious. Lyndon Johnson was the first president to request live network coverage to sign legislation. Similarly, President Nixon requested coverage of vetoing key legislation in order to focus on aspects of an issue that required explanation and justification. Although Reagan stayed one inning at the opening day of the 1984 baseball season in Baltimore, he was seen the next day in the media throwing a ball and eating a hot dog in the dugout. And presidential phone calls are, today, rather commonplace — to astronauts, to winning sports teams, or to "ordinary" citizens with unique needs or situations.

Presidential trips, of course, provide great drama and show the president as a world leader. Carter received great publicity with his "town meetings" and staying in the homes of "ordinary folks." And how ironic, in 1980, when President Reagan, who spent most of his political career opposing the Chinese Communists, not only visited mainland China but offered U.S. economic and technological assistance. The trip was Reagan's first major television spectacle. Michael Deaver spent nine days in China scouting locations for the president to visit.[40] The Republican National Committee sent a special film crew to record footage for use in the 1984 presidential campaign. Even Reagan's itinerary was influenced by the potential of media coverage. A trip down the Yangtze River was canceled because there was no way to get the tapes to the networks for showing.[41]

Presidential elections, finally, provide countless attempts at creating and controlling media events. Conventions are totally created for media coverage and impact. Even the selection of the theme song "Rocky" by Mondale was no accident. Media and image considerations overshadow issue concerns in staging presidential debates. In the debates of 1976, the issues of lighting, staging, position of cameras, use of reaction shots, camera movement, and the height of the podiums became major points of discussion and negotiation between the candidates.[42] For the 1980 and 1984 presidential debates, Reagan developed a Debate Task Force that negotiated the formats, prepared briefing materials, conducted research, developed debate strategies, and provided professional consultation on performance variables.

Politics as a "spectator sport" has both empowered the media as well as made it the object of control for all presidents. It is the primary channel of access and instrument of image control.

Symbols

For Nimmo, governmental groups and individuals are political symbols to "assure people that problems are solved even if current policies actually achieve relatively little" and to "arouse and mobilize support for action."[43] The use of euphemism, puffery, and metaphor are vital in creating a sense of assurance. During the Ford administration, the word "detente" was avoided because it had become associated with a controversial policy. Carter consistently referred to the Iranian students as "terrorists" in their takeover of the U.S. embassy and Reagan called the Soviet pilot who shot down a Korean airliner a "murderer." Such uses may define situations and communicate informational and evaluative aspects of events. Puffery attempts to exaggerate or to overstate matters of subjective experience. Especially in election years, every issue is of the "gravest importance to the future of our country." Metaphor, as a language device, is useful for explaining the unfamiliar by associating it with something more immediate, clear, or known. A "war on poverty" or a "war on crime" reveals a degree of seriousness, priority, and intensity. Simply labeling a problem a crisis often mobilizes support. Appeals to the national good and self-sacrifice induce cooperation and support which may restrain free choice. Each of these uses of symbols influences individual and group behavior.

Political symbols work because of their abstract semantic hollowness. Although political symbols function as objects of common identification, they simultaneously allow for idiosyncratic meanings to be attached. Political symbols are powerful not because of the broad commonalities of shared meaning but because of the intense sentiments created and attached to them resulting in the perception that the symbols are vital to the system. As elements of the political culture, political symbols serve as stimuli for political action. They serve as a link between mass political behavior and individual political behavior. Political symbols, then, are vital to both the functioning of the individual and society.

Presidents influence public opinion utilizing verbal political symbols in two primary ways. First, they can reduce complex policies or issues to a single term or slogan such as Franklin Roosevelt's "New Deal" or Lyndon Johnson's "Great Society." Second, redefining or changing the name of something is effective in altering public perceptions or images. The basic principle is simply to replace emotively charged names, labels, or words with more neutral ones. In late 1982, Reagan directed the Defense Department to replace the term "MX missile" with "Peacekeeper" to be used in all conversations and correspondence.[44] During the Vietnam War, Nixon used such explanatory terms as: pacification center (that is, concentration camp), surgical strike (precision bombing), strategic withdrawal (retreat), and selective ordinance (napalm). Carter described the failed rescue mission of the Iranian hostages as an "incomplete success." Such uses of language can mask true meanings, heighten emotions, or reduce emotional impact.

Presidents can also maximize influence and impact by reinforcing verbal symbols with the nonverbal trappings of the office. The presidency is a national political symbol. The occupant of the office is given a great deal of deference. The presidency is both our administrative and ceremonial office. Michael Novak characterizes the president as America's "priest, prophet, and king."[45] Any individual who holds the office is perceived as rational, intelligent, and often charismatic. The pageantry, history, and majesty of the office is transferred to its occupant. Use of the presidential seal and podium, "Hail to the Chief," and various other official backdrops communicate the strength and grandeur of the office. They serve to remind the audience that they are listening to the president of the United States and not just an average citizen. It is not surprising, therefore, that in April 1984, President Reagan changed the location of the televised press conferences to the open doorway in the East Room of the White House revealing a long, elegant corridor. The cameras record a majestic setting and a stately exit that dramatizes the importance of the office. Ronald Reagan, more than any contemporary president, clearly understands the importance of the historic, patriotic, symbolic aspects of the presidency. Early in his presidency Reagan deliberately set out to restore the grandeur of the office lost by Carter with drastically increased state parties, dinners, and receptions. Robert Dallek asserts that "while Reaganites may be seen in part as practitioners of traditional politics ... they should also be viewed as caught up in symbolic politics: their public goals satisfy psychological needs as much as material ends."[46]

Public Relations and Publicity Activities

Every president has a full-time staff whose sole job is to help manage image and information. As an advocate for the president, they ensure that the administration gets its side of the story or issue to the American people as well as ensure that the proper image of presidential behavior is conveyed. While the impact and importance of such activities upon presidential influence are obvious, the size of the staff dedicated to these activities may be surprising. According to the *1985 White House Phone Directory*, Reagan has: 3 people in the Office of Communication; 10 people in the Office of Speechwriting and Research; 2 people in the Office of Media Relations and Planning; 3 people in the Office of Public Affairs; 2 people in the Office of Communication Planning; 12 people in the Office of Public Liaison; 14 people in the Office of the Press Secretary; and 5 people in the Office of News Summary and Audio Service. In addition, there are numerous other individuals within the Office of Deputy Chief of Staff that clearly have public relations and related duties (that is, communication director, press advance director, press secretaries, etc.). Thus, there are well over 50 communication specialists whose jobs are to plan, coordinate, and orchestrate presidential public appearances and information.

Control of Information

As the adage goes, information is power. To control the dissemination of information is a powerful technique of influencing public opinion. Some of the ways of controlling information are simple and expected. Others, however, are devious and unethical. Perhaps the most common method of controlling information is simply to withhold it. For years the Johnson and Nixon administrations withheld the true costs and military situation in Vietnam. Today, because of our lenient information classification system, much of our involvement and activities in foreign countries are classified. By suppressing evidence, administrations can provide explanations or justifications of policies or programs more to their liking. In the 1970s, America's high rate of inflation was attributed to the high rate of OPEC oil yet both Japan and Germany had much lower rates than the United States but equally dependent on foreign oil.

At the daily press briefings, only good news is given to reporters. If "housing starts" are up or the "cost of living" is down they will be prominent in the daily White House press releases. If they are not favorable, however, reporters must rely upon other sources to obtain the current information. Administrations can also try to de-emphasize bad news by focusing on some other matter. The day unemployment climbed to 10 percent in 1982, Reagan called a press conference to announce the suspension of Poland's status as a "most favored nation."

An interesting technique of controlling information is to simply *not* collect certain data that tends to support the status quo and to alter the method or criteria of collecting certain information. The Reagan administration, for example, started including people in the military in calculating the monthly rate of employment.

The timing of the release of information can increase impact. On the eve of the New Hampshire primary in 1980, Carter had the U.S. Olympic Hockey Team that defeated the Soviets visit the White House. Much "free" and favorable press resulted. On the mornings of the Wisconsin and Kansas primaries, Carter made a public announcement of a "positive step" toward the release of the U.S. hostages held in Iran.[47]

Perhaps the easiest way to control information is to control media access. During the 1972 presidential election campaign, Nixon only left the White House for formal gala events thus reducing having to answer and address difficult questions concerning Watergate and Vietnam.

Finally, the most extreme form of controlling information is presidential lying. Despite Carter's promise of never lying to the public he was "caught" in a "white lie" in telling Bill Moyers that he never reviewed requests to use the White House tennis courts. More seriously, however, were Eisenhower's claim of no role in the 1954 coup in Guatemala, Kennedy's claim of no role in the Bay of Pigs invasion, and Nixon's claim of no role in Watergate.[48]

While not exhaustive, these categories do represent broad ways presidents can influence public opinion that is essential for legislative policy and issue support.

CONCLUSION

If, as we argued in Chapter 1, the presidency is primarily a rhetorical institution it is equally a persuasive one as well. Our argument here is simply that every individual occupant of the office must engage in persuasion: as an advocate for specific policies, as motivator for legislative action and support, and as chief arbitrator and negotiator of societal wishes and desires. Not only is the individual occupant a persuader by definition, however, but the office itself possesses a great reservoir of influence and social significance that makes it a powerful and persuasive office. It is the one man distillation of the American people: their hopes, desires, and majesty. Thus, *everything* a president says or does is potentially persuasive and will carry meaning or significance to some people or groups of people whether it is a state dinner or a state of the union address, a phone call to astronauts orbiting earth or a town meeting, a photo session with world leaders or a short weekly radio broadcast. The variety of activities and significance may vary greatly but each are persuasive in nature nonetheless. And a "successful" president will so design them.

NOTES

1. Aristotle, *Rhetoric*, trans. Rhys Roberts (New York: The Modern Library, 1954), p. 24.
2. Ibid., p. 19.
3. Douglas Ehninger, *Contemporary Rhetoric* (Glenview, IL: Scott, Foresman, 1972), p. 3.
4. John O'Toole, *The Trouble With Advertising* (New York: Chelsea House, 1981), p. 5.
5. Vance Packard, *The Hidden Persuaders* (New York: Pocket Books, 1957), p. 1.
6. Ibid., p. 229.
7. For a review and discussion of the political consulting industry see Robert E. Denton, Jr. and Gary Woodward, *Political Communication in America* (New York: Praeger, 1985), pp. 50–70.
8. Sidney Blumenthal, *The Permanent Campaign* (New York: A Touchstone Book, 1982), p. 311.
9. Donna Cross, *Media-Speak* (New York: Mentor Books, 1983), p. 188.
10. As quoted in ibid., p. 188.
11. As reported in Packard, *The Hidden Persuaders*, p. 155.
12. Cross, *Media-Speak*, p. 214.
13. The strongest statement of this notion is provided by Benjamin Lee Whorf. For him, "If a man thinks in one language, he thinks one way; in another language,

another way." The structure of language "is itself the shaper of ideas, the program and guide for the individual's mental activity, for his analysis of impressions, for his synthesis of his mental stock in trade." See John Carroll, ed., *Language, Thought and Reality: Selected Writings of Benjamin Whorf* (New York: John Wiley & Sons, 1956).

14. Murray Edelman, *Politics as Symbolic Action* (Chicago: Markham, 1971), p. 83.

15. Claus Mueller, *The Politics of Communication* (New York: Oxford University Press, 1973), p. 19.

16. Michael Novak, *Choosing Our King* (New York: Macmillan, 1974), pp. 29–31.

17. Rodger Cobb and Charles Elder, "Individual Orientations in the Study of Political Symbolism," *Social Science Quarterly*, vol. 53, no. 1 (June 1972):80.

18. Ibid., p. 87.

19. Dan Nimmo, *Political Communication and Public Opinion in America* (Santa Monica, CA: Goodyear Publishing Company, 1978), p. 90.

20. Robert J. Pranger, *Action, Symbolism, and Action* (Nashville, TN: Vanderbilt University Press, 1968), p. 67.

21. For example, see R. Sigel, "Political Socialization: Its Role in the Political Process," *Annals of the American Academy of Political Science* 361 (September 1965); R. E. Dawson and K. Prewitt, *Political Socialization* (Boston: Little, Brown, 1969); D. Sears, "Political Behavior," in *The Handbook of Social Psychology*, ed. Lindzey and Aronson, vol. 5 (Mass.: Addison-Wesley, 1969), pp. 315–388; J. Dennis, *Socialization to Politics: A Reader* (New York: Wiley, 1973); and S. Kraus, 'Mass Communication and Political Socialization: A Reassessment of Two Decades of Research," *Quarterly Journal of Speech* 59 (December 1973):390–400.

22. Edelman, *Politics as Symbolic Action*, p. 7.

23. Ibid., p. 34.

24. Ibid., pp. 97–114.

25. Ibid., p. 104.

26. Ibid., pp. 103–104.

27. Peter Hall, "A Symbolic Interactionist Analysis of Politics," *Sociological Inquiry* 42 (1972):41.

28. Theodore Sorensen, *A Different Kind of Presidency* (New York: Harper & Row, 1984), p. 10.

29. Dan Nimmo, *The Political Persuaders* (Englewood Cliffs, NJ: Prentice-Hall, 1970), p. 8.

30. Edelman, *Politics as Symbolic Action*, p. 73.

31. See Orrin Klapp, *Symbolic Leaders* (Chicago: Aldine, 1964).

32. Ibid., p. 32.

33. Richard Neustadt, *Presidential Power* (New York: John Wiley & Sons, 1980), p. 35.

34. See George Edwards's *The Public Presidency* (New York: St. Martin's Press, 1983).

35. There are a tremendous number of works that identify various attempts at presidential persuasion. For several books that provide broad classifications and examples see Robert E. Denton, Jr., *Symbolic Dimensions of the American*

Presidency (Prospect Heights, IL: Waveland Press, 1982); Denton and Woodward, *Political Communication in America*; Edwards, *The Public Presidency*; Roderick Hart, *Verbal Style and the Presidency* (Orlando, FL: Academic Press, 1984); Kathleen Jamieson, *Packaging the Presidency* (New York: Oxford University Press, 1984); Dan Nimmo and James Combs, *Mediated Political Realities* (New York: Longman, 1983); Judith Trent and Robert Friedenberg, *Political Campaign Communication* (New York: Praeger, 1983); and Larry Sabato, *The Rise of Political Consultants* (New York: Basic Books, 1981). For this section, Edwards's broad categories are used to provide the structure for discussion.

36. Hart, *Verbal Style,* p. 7.

37. Ibid., p. 212

38. Ibid.

39. The eventual public support for large defense expenditures during Ronald Reagan's first term was due to the Soviet Union's activities in Poland, Afghanistan, and South America as well as worldwide terrorism activities in Iran, Germany, Beirut, and Granada. The large defense expenditures were questioned by many segments of the public in 1984 and 1985.

40. "It's Show Time for President in China," *U.S. News and World Report,* May 7, 1984, p. 23.

41. As reported in ibid.

42. See Robert R. Tiemens, "Television's Portrayal of the 1976 Presidential Debates: An Analysis of Visual Content," *Communication Monographs,* vol. 45, no. 4 (November 1978):362–370.

43. Dan Nimmo, *Political Communication and Public Opinion in America* (Calif.: Goodyear Publishing, 1978), pp. 83-86.

44. Howard Kahane, *Logic and Contemporary Rhetoric,* 4th ed. (Belmont, CA: Wadsworth, 1984), p. 139.

45. See Novak, *Choosing Our King,* pp. 3–57.

46. Robert Dallek, *Ronald Reagan: The Politics of Symbolism* (Cambridge, MA: Harvard University Press, 1984), p. viii.

47. As reported in Richard Watson and Norman Thomas, *The Presidential Contest* (New York: John Wiley & Sons, 1980), p. 34.

48. Edwards, *The Public Presidency,* p. 63.

READINGS

INTRODUCTION

Chapter 2 argued that the process of persuasion is not only an essential element of politics but lies at the heart of democratic government. And the fundamental power of the presidency lies not in policy pronouncements or enactment of legislation, but in the ability to mobilize public support. In addition, the office itself possesses a great reservoir of influence and social significance independent of the specific occupant.

The first essay explores the persuasiveness of Ronald Reagan. The authors suggest that Reagan's choice of metaphors in his public discourse contribute to his success as "The Great Communicator."

The second essay investigates the rhetorical strategies of Richard Nixon during the 1972 presidential campaign which included: minimizing commitments while maximizing control, minimizing information about self while maximizing information about the opponent, and minimizing program commitments while maximizing promises through allusions and busyness. The goal of the strategies was to maintain power and the major rhetorical lesson of Watergate may be that crises will not be perceived as crises if handled by non-crisis rhetoric.

The final essay considers persuasive form in presidential rhetoric by considering the power of definition, identification, action, emotional involvement, logical and rational argument, strength, honesty, grandeur, and ideology. The essay challenges the notion that form is wedded to content and suggests that critics cannot consider content without also considering form.

REAGAN'S PERSUASIVENESS:
AN EXPLORATORY INTERPRETATION

There have been a plethora of explanations for Reagan's rhetorical success. Ernest Bormann attributes it to Reagan's "Restoration" fantasy theme;[1] Blankenship, Fine, and Davis point to Reagan's ability to encompass and embody the "American Dream";[2] Steven Weisman argues that the president's ability to take advantage of media propensities is decisive;[3] Hedrick Smith claims Reagan's anti-political stance is what does the trick;[4] while Richard Reeves sees Reagan's success at defining "Americanism" as setting him apart.[5] James Fallows perceives Reagan as a genial variety-show host who deflects all criticism with "dramatic narrative based on unverifiable material about his personal life,"[6] and Robert Kaiser attributes the appeal to Reagan's gift of simplification.[7] Steven Weisman points to Reagan's self-confidence and optimism,[8] while John Corry stresses Reagan's certainty.[9]

We could go on, but you get the idea: every academic and journalistic critic has set forth a reason for Reagan's success. And yet, no one of them has, for us, captured the essence of Reagan's appeal. Each interpretation is, in its own way, right. Yet none of them strike us as truly explanatory; that is, other politicians have utilized the restoration theme, other politicians have embodied the American Dream, other politicians have taken advantage of the media, etc. None of those explanations, then, truly explains why this specific man, giving these specific speeches, to specific Americans at a specific point in our history is so persuasive.

Therefore, we propose a theory which may be worthy of further consideration. We present it as a stimulus to thinking rather than as a definitive answer.

We know that no speaker can be persuasive with an audience unless he somehow aligns self with audience predispositions. It is on the basis of this knowledge that Reagan partisans claim that the American society has taken a turn to the Right and that Reagan merely is echoing audience beliefs. While there is some little evidence for this conclusion, there is much that militates against it. For instance, even while Reagan was rolling up an impressive victory over Mondale in 1984, poll data suggested that "on many issues, ranging from arms control to abortion, the public [was] closer to the Democrat's stand than to Mr. Reagan's."[10] Thus, there seems not to have been an ideological conversion in the nation, and we should seek the bases of Reagan's persuasiveness elsewhere.

Nonetheless, Reagan's rhetorical effectiveness must somehow be tied to audience predispositions. As Kenneth Burke has pointed out, "Only those voices from without are effective which can speak in the language of a voice within."[11] And if we are convinced that the answer in this case is not to be found in the substance of Reagan's stands, we have little choice but to turn our search to stylistic elements. To again quote Burke, "we might well keep it in mind that a speaker persuades an audience by the use of stylistic identifications. . . ."[12]

Without denying that style is multi-faceted and that more than one component of Reagan's style may contribute to his persuasiveness, we propose to suggest the possibility that Reagan's choice of metaphors may explain, or at least help explain, the achievement of his status as "The Great Communicator."

In short, we posit that Reagan is popular and persuasive, in part, because his metaphoric language taps into fads and feelings and beliefs of the average person on the subconscious level. The two major metaphors in Reagan's rhetoric, path metaphors and disease/health metaphors, both seem to echo affirmatively with contemporary audiences.

Let us first examine Reagan's path metaphors. Here are some representative constructions:

- "I will not stand by and watch this great country destroy itself under mediocre leadership that drifts from one crisis to the next."[13]
- "The question is, are we simply going to go down the same path we've gone down before. . . ."[14]
- "The important thing now is to hold to a firm, steady course. Tonight I want to talk with you about the next steps that we must take on that course. . . ."[15]
- "The best view of Big Government is in a rear-view mirror as we leave it behind."[16]
- "The nation's fiscal policy is now firmly embarked on a new, sound, and sustainable course."[17]
- "We live now at a turning point."[18]
- "All of us have been swamped by a sea of economic statistics. . . ."[19]
- "We're not going to go down the dead-end street. . . ."[20]

- "My greatest satisfaction is . . . that a country that was skidding dangerously in the wrong direction . . . has been set on the right course."[21]
- "The great nation is moving forward again and we're not turning back. . . ."[22]

These metaphors are not strikingly novel. Indeed, that is part of their power. Precisely because they are everyday, ordinary metaphors they do not arouse our suspicions. Because they are the metaphors *we* use, they sound reasonable to us. Additionally, path metaphors suggest choosing between alternative roads — an activity familiar to the U.S. audience, and one they expect politicians to engage in.

On a slightly deeper level, path metaphors suggest movement and action, and thus fit the U.S. penchant for being on the move, striving, mobile. After all, in our language "action" normally is assumed to be positive while inaction is assumed to be negative, so that locutions like "stern action," "resolute action," and "immediate action" ring positively with us while "inaction" and "indecision" are presumed to be weak, negative, and wishy-washy.

Thus the first of Reagan's two major metaphors does "speak the language of the audience," but it is, in our opinion, Reagan's second metaphor, disease/health, which taps most deeply into the U.S. psyche.

Let us look at a representative sample of these metaphors from Reagan's speeches:

- "Our federal government is overgrown and overweight. Indeed, it is time for our government to go on a diet."[23]
- "This Administration's objective will be a healthy, vigorous, growing economy. . . ."[24]
- "The 1981 budget . . . hemorrhaged badly. . . ."[25]
- "We're not proposing . . . an artificial stimulant to the economy. . . ."[26]
- "Unless you get at the root causes of the problem . . . you may be able to temporarily relieve the symptoms, but you'll never cure the disease. You may even make it worse."[27]
- "The pounding economic hangover America's suffering didn't come about overnight and there's no single, instant cure."[28]
- "Crime today is an American epidemic. . . ."[29]
- "Our nation has labored to purge itself of the inflationary disease that . . . had progressively undermined the economy's ability to generate

growth. . . . Those inflationary fevers have largely subsided. . . ."[30]

- "Not providing our friends the weapons they need . . . is a prescription for disaster."[31]

We suggest that these medical metaphors reverberate positively in a citizenry that is "into" health — jogging and other forms of exercise (the names Jane Fonda and Richard Simmons, for instance, come to mind), beds that raise and lower to ease back pain, diets (from Beverly Hills to Scarsdale, from Pritikin to Berger to Hass), herbs, vitamins, chiropractors, iridologists, psychologists, and health foods. (It is interesting to note, by the way, that health foods often have been equated with ideology, from C. W. Post's touting of cereal breakfast as part of an anti-sex campaign, to the Rightist juice bars in Southern California in the 1950s and their campaign against flouridated water in the early sixties, the Leftist back to nature movement in the mid-to-late sixties, etc.).

At a deeper level, Reagan's metaphoric language is also positive in a selfish, narcissistic, yuppie-dominated society where everybody is looking out for self — almost literally concerned for the health of number 1. This confluence of health and economics is found in the widespread use of medical metaphors in economic discussions — "a healthy economy," "a growing economy," "inflationary fever," etc.

At an even deeper level the disease/remedy metaphors echo with truth for the citizen who mistakenly perceives a link between health and morality, who looks down upon the disabled as somehow poisoned, who thinks homosexuals are both "sick" and immoral, believing that A.I.D.S. was visited upon homosexuals by a God angry at their immorality. Indeed, the tendency of Americans to label as "sick" those things they perceive as wrong and immoral exemplifies this tendency.

So it may well be that part (maybe even much) of Reagan's success can be attributed to his metaphors, stylistic artifacts to which a receptive audience responds favorably even though they do not necessarily endorse the programs that make up the substance of the president's oratory.

ASSESSMENT

Thus far we have addressed only the practical question, might Reagan's metaphors be persuasive with his audience? But a rhetorical critic's job extends beyond the sphere of practicality. If the metaphors are persuasive we want to know why they are, and we may even want/need to delve into that most problematic of all spheres, the ethical.

Turning first to the path metaphors, it may be noted that they can be subdivided into land imagery and sea imagery. The sea metaphors are the traditional ones — the captain of the ship of state steering us out of the stormy seas, launching new projects, etc. They do not, in our opinion, create any problems.

The path and road metaphors, however, strike us as somewhat dangerous in a pluralistic society. This is largely because a path or a road traditionally (and as Reagan uses them) provides only two choices — forward or backward. Further, only one of the two is acceptable. So Reagan can say, "We have no choice but to continue down the road toward a balanced budget. . . ."[32] and "what we're doing is the only course that can stimulate the economy. . . ."[33] and "The path I have outlined is fair, balanced and realistic. . . . It is the only path that will lead to a strong sustained recovery."[34]

We submit that the thought that your way is the *only* way is the seed that can grow into fanaticism. As such, it is inappropriate in a pluralistic society. And metaphors that insinuate such a viewpoint are likewise inappropriate.

The notion of all following a path together sounds unobtrusive, almost reminiscent of *The Wizard of Oz*. But instead of Dorothy skipping down the yellow brick road, it is all of us, and there are no signposts to tell us if we are following the road to Oz or to the Wicked Witch of the West.

Finally, let us assess the medical imagery. It is not any stretch of the imagination to suppose that one who utilizes medical images accrues some of the patina of a doctor's reputation. And, as we all know, the doctor image is one of scientific impartiality. Therefore, we would speculate that use of medical imagery would impart an aura of impartiality to the user. Perhaps that is why Reagan is so much more popular than Reaganomics, and why he is believed even when again and again caught in misstatements, distortions, and lies.

Additionally, we know that the doctor does not *cause* the disease. Thus, a speaker who chooses metaphorically to identify self as a doctor may thereby escape blame for the problem. In the political arena such a stance carries the added benefit that opponents can be identified as the cause, the carriers of the disease. Here is how Reagan identified our national disease as the result of Carter's poisoning influence: "We must overcome something the present administration has cooked up: a new and altogether indigestible economic stew, one part inflation, one part high unemployment, one part runaway taxes, one part deficit spending, and seasoned by an energy crisis. It's an economic stew that has turned the national stomach."[35]

Another advantage of using medical metaphors is that doctors seldom are held accountable when the prescribed medicine fails to effect a cure. Sometimes the patient is even blamed for rejecting the cure. And in the political arena, a doctor-president is especially blameless because he can always claim that the Congress voted the wrong cure or an insufficient dosage.

Whenever Congress tries to pass a tax bill to cover some of the massive deficits created by Reaganomics, Doc Reagan attacks them as "quick fixes" and explains that, historically, "Each time they were applied, they gave a little temporary relief to the patient, but left him weaker than he was before."[36]

Finally, we all know that surgery always causes pain. Thus, there is a temptation to believe that any present pain is indicative of future health. President Reagan encourages that belief by pointing out that unemployment had to go up to cure inflation, but that now we must not attend directly to unemployment with an infusion of money because "artificial stimulants . . . are what brought on the inflationary disorders that we have now paid such a heavy price to cure."[37] In short, the suffering of the unemployed proves that the economic cure is working.

But perhaps all that are really working are Reagan's medical metaphors. For he does seem to be perceived as impartial, blameless both as to the cause of our national problems and to his inability to cure them, and he does seem to have been successful in defusing the outcry about unemployment by his treatment of it as a natural, albeit painful, result of his economic surgery.

While we probably will never know if we were wise to follow the path Doc Reagan took us down, it should be clear by now that a major component in our willingness to follow him was that he spoke our language, thereby gaining our acquiescence for the journey even though we were suspicious of some of his chosen vehicles.

NOTES

1. Ernest G. Bormann, "A Fantasy Theme Analysis of the Television Coverage of the Hostage Release and the Reagan Inaugural," *Quarterly Journal of Speech* 68 (May 1982):133–145.

2.   Jane Blankenship, Marlene G. Fine, and Leslie K. Davis, "The 1980 Republican Primary Debates: The Transformation of Actor to Scene," *Quarterly Journal of Speech* 69 (Feb. 1983):25–36.

3.   Steven R. Weisman, "The President and the Press; The Art of Controlled Access," *The New York Times Magazine,* October 14, 1984, pp. 34 *passim.*

4.   Hedrick Smith, "The Politics of Blame," *The New York Times Magazine,* October 7, 1984, pp. 36–48.

5.   Richard Reeves, "The Republicans," *The New York Times Magazine,* September 9, 1984, pp. 56–59 *passim.*

6.   James Fallows, "The Reagan Variety Show," *The New York Review of Books,* April 12, 1984, pp. 8–12.

7.   Robert G. Kaiser, "Your Host of Hosts," *The New York Review of Books,* June 28, 1984, pp. 38–41.

8.   Steven R. Weisman, "Can the Magic Prevail?" *The New York Times Magazine,* April 29, 1984, pp. 38–56.

9.   John Corry, "Critic's Notebook: Candidates, How Democrats and the President Size Up on TV," *The New York Times,* February 1, 1984, p. C25.

10.   David E. Rosenbaum, "Poll Shows Many Choose Reagan Even if They Disagree With Him," *The New York Times,* September 19, 1984, p. A1.

11.   Kenneth Burke, *A Rhetoric of Motives* (New York: Prentice-Hall, 1950), p. 39.

12.   Ibid., p. 46.

13.   Ronald Reagan, "Acceptance Speech," *The New York Times,* July 18, 1980.

14.   Ronald Reagan, "America's New Beginning: Program for Economic Recovery," *Los Angeles Times,* February 19, 1981, p. 10.

15.   Ronald Reagan, "Transcript of President's Address on Proposed Spending Cuts," *The New York Times,* September 25, 1981, p. A28.

16.   Ronald Reagan, "Excerpts from Address by Reagan on Role of Private Groups," *The New York Times,* January 15, 1982, p. A14.

17.   Ronald Reagan, "Text of the President's Budget Message to Congress," *The New York Times,* February 7, 1982, p. 25.

18.   Ronald Reagan, "Transcript of Reagan's Address to Parliament on Promoting Democracy," *The New York Times,* June 9, 1982, p. A16.

19.   Ronald Reagan, "Transcript of Reagan's Speech to Nation on G.O.P. Policy and the Economy," *The New York Times,* October 14, 1982, p. B14.

20.   Ronald Reagan, "Transcript of President's News Conference on Foreign and Domestic Matters," *The New York Times,* November 12, 1982, p. B6.

21.   Ronald Reagan, "Transcript of President's News Conference on Foreign and Domestic Matters," *The New York Times,* January 21, 1983, p. A14.

22.   Ronald Reagan, "Excerpts from Reagan's Speech to Hispanic American Group," *The New York Times,* August 13, 1983, p. 15.

23.   Ronald Reagan, "Acceptance Speech," *The New York Times,* July 18, 1980.

24.   Ronald Reagan, "Let Us Begin an Era of National Renewal," *The New York Times,* January 21, 1981.

25.   Ronald Reagan, "Transcript of President's Address on Proposed Spending Cuts," *The New York Times,* September 25, 1981, p. A28.

26.   Ronald Reagan, "Transcript of the President's Televised Speech on Tax Policy," *The New York Times,* August 17, 1982, p. D16.

27.   Ronald Reagan, "Transcript of Reagan's Speech to Nation on G.O.P. Policy and the Economy," *The New York Times,* October 14, 1982, p. B14.

28.   Ibid.

29.   Ronald Reagan, "Text of President's Speech on Drive Against Crime," *The New York Times,* October 15, 1982, p. A20.

30.   Ronald Reagan, "Text of the Budget Message Sent to Congress by the President," *The New York Times,* February 1, 1983, p. A18.

31.   Ronald Reagan, "Text of President Reagan's Speech on Threat to Latin America," *The New York Times,* May 21, 1983, p. 4.

32.   Ronald Reagan, "Transcript of President's Address on Proposed Spending Cuts," *The New York Times,* September 25, 1981, p. A28.

33.   Ronald Reagan, "Transcript of President's News Conference on Foreign and Domestic Matters," *The New York Times,* November 12, 1982, p. B6.

34.   Ronald Reagan, "Transcript of President's State of Union Message to the Nation," *The New York Times,* January 26, 1983, p. A14.

35.   Ronald Reagan, "Acceptance Speech," *The New York Times,* July 18, 1980.

36.   Ronald Reagan, "Transcript of Reagan's Speech to Nation on G.O.P. Policy and the Economy," *The New York Times,* October 14, 1982, p. B14.

37.   Ronald Reagan, "Text of the Budget Message Sent to Congress by the President," *The New York Times,* February 1, 1983, p. A18.

THE WATERGATE STRATEGIES OF RICHARD NIXON DURING THE 1972 CAMPAIGN*

That complex of activities known as "Watergate," from the break-in (June 1972) to Nixon's resignation (August 1974), was extraordinary in American politics. A reasonable hypothesis, then, would be that the break-in was kept from affecting the outcome of the 1972 election by extraordinary rhetorical strategies. Indeed, that was our hypothesis as we began this study. But the data do not support that hypothesis; they refute it completely.

We are now prepared to argue that no new rhetorical strategies were developed to cope with Watergate. Further, because it could be and was encompassed in the normal Nixon rhetorical approach, "Watergate" was perceived by the electorate as an event less than extraordinary. A new rhetorical approach, we now believe, would have signaled the people that

---

*Originally published by Dan F. Hahn and Ruth M. Gonchar, "The Watergate Strategies of Richard Nixon During the 1972 Campaign," *The Communicator,* 10 (Spring 1980):64-75. Reprinted with permission.

something unusual was brewing, while the normal had the effect of soothing them into quiescence. Jeb Magruder was undoubtedly including the Watergate cover-up when he said that the Nixon administration strategy ". . . really did not change to any great extent from the beginning of '71 when we started contemplating the campaign. . . ."[1]

Briefly, the overall strategy can best be described as a minimax system: minimize your commitments while maximizing your control. The first portion of the strategy, the minimizing of commitments, required the Nixon administration to keep its options open; that, in turn, required several second-order minimax strategies: (1) minimize the information about yourself while maximizing that about your opponent; and, (2) minimize your program commitments while maximizing your promises, preferably by allusions and busyness rather than by specific oral promise.

Minimizing information about self was a Nixon strategy that reappeared throughout his career; its first appearance dates back to the Voorhis campaign of 1948 and was the game-plan Murray Chotiner designed for Nixon.[2] The strategy was manifested in Nixon's 1968 "Secret Plan for Ending the War in Vietnam" and remained and intensified when Nixon entered the White House. The Nixon administration's penchant for secrecy is well known and well documented, but some specifically rhetorical examples will exemplify the strategy. During the planning for the 1972 campaign, the November Group (Nixon's media advisors) discovered that Nixon was perceived as lacking warmth. Rather than attack the problem with contradictory information, the group decided to proceed indirectly, implying that Nixon was not cold — just shy. Peter H. Dailey, a member of the November Group, explained: "Interwoven into the documentaries and into some of the commercials were little touches of lightness to try to show this shyness. In one, for example, there was a thing with Tricia Nixon talking about the fact on the night before her wedding, the President wrote her a note and slipped it under the door. It was a very warm, personal note from father to daughter, but he just couldn't tell her his thoughts personally and he felt that he could express them better in a note. Our testing showed that by using things like this we were beginning to create an understanding of the President as a shy man rather than a cold man."[3] The strategy of minimizing information about self in this instance was accomplished by the tactic of substituting other, less revealing, information.

In the case of Watergate, the tactic used to accomplish minimization was denial — denial of the facts, and of the importance of the facts. This tactic was utilized consistently from the onset of the Watergate revelations right through the November elections:

- June 18, John Mitchell: The burglars were not "operating either on our behalf or with our consent."[4]
- June 19, Ron Zeigler: "A third-rate burglary attempt."[5]
- June 20, Ron Zeigler: Charles Colson has "assured me that he has in no way been involved in this matter."[6]
- June 22, Richard Nixon: "Mr. Zeigler and also Mr. Mitchell, speaking for the campaign committee, have responded to questions on this in great detail. They have stated my position and have also stated the facts accurately . . . and, as Mr. Zeigler has stated, the White House has had no involvement whatsoever in this particular incident."[7]
- August, Attorney General Kleindienst: ". . . a simple burglary."[8]
- August 8, Maurice Stans: No money intended for CREEP financed the break-in.[9]
- August 29, Richard Nixon: ". . . this very bizarre incident."[10]
- September 29, CREEP spokesperson: There is "no truth" to the story that there existed a secret CREEP fund controlled by John Mitchell.[11]
- October 25, Ron Zeigler: Haldeman never had access to any secret CREEP fund — besides, such a fund never existed.[12]
- October 26, Clark MacGregor: Yes, there was a private fund to be used to gather information on "possible organized disruption of GOP rallies in New Hampshire" but H. R. Haldeman did not have access to it and it was not a secret fund.[13]

For six months the strategy did not deviate: deny the facts, deny the significance of the facts. It is interesting to note that President Nixon's first response to Watergate (June 22) implied that the matter was not important enough for the president's time, directly (by suggesting that Zeigler and Mitchell had already exhausted the topic) and indirectly (by devoting only 117 words to answering the question in a press conference in which the average answer ran 282 words). Also interesting in this regard is the fact that it was the very next day that Nixon had the meeting with Haldeman that is now called the "smoking gun" conversation, where it was decided to call Patrick Gray, Director of the F.B.I., off the case. The easiest way to reveal as little as possible about yourself was to curtail information-gathering in the first place. Even the reason Nixon suggested Gray be given for the curtailment lacked information: ". . . don't lie — to the extent to say there is no involvement, but just say this is a comedy of errors, without getting into it, the President believes that it is going to open the whole Bay of Pigs thing up again."[14]

Eventually the strategy of revealing as little as possible about himself was Nixon's undoing. Better, perhaps, if he had admitted all at the beginning. In admitting just enough to make the secrecy and denials palatable, he finally ran out of admissible materials, and exploded: "What the hell does one disclose that isn't going to blow something?"[15] But that was in 1973. In 1972 his strategy of denying information worked effectively and almost effortlessly.

The other side of the minimax strategy is to maximize information, preferably negative, about the opposition. This strategy explained the 1972 focus on anti-McGovern ads as well as the obsession with investigating the events at Chappaquiddick. An interesting rhetorical example of maximizing information about the opposition was Nixon's acceptance speech at the 1972 Republican Convention. In that address, Nixon was expected to trace the accomplishments of his first administration and chart the course of his second; that is the pattern of most incumbent speeches.

Nixon did not follow the pattern. Rather, after some perfunctory opening remarks, he said: "And in asking for your support, I shall not dwell on the record of our administration, that has been praised, perhaps too generously, by others at this convention."[16] With that transition, he swung into a scathing attack of McGovern and the Democratic party platform. "It was as if Mr. Nixon (had) not been President at all but (was) still the office-seeker and partisan sharpshooter, ever on the attack."[17] Whatever else that speech did, it gave a minimum of information about Nixon's program and a maximum of negative information about McGovern's.

This strategy, which in part may have set the tone for Watergate itself, was continued after the break-in arrests. On the undercover side, it was continued by the Segretti unit. Above board, it was continued by attacking the Democrats and their attempts to "exploit" Watergate. Thus, when the Democrats filed a lawsuit against CREEP for the break-in, John Mitchell labeled the suit a piece of "demagoguery."[18] Then, when the lawsuit was broadened in September to include some White House employees, the Republicans accused the Democrats of using the federal courts as "an instrument for creating political headlines."[19] And Clark MacGregor, on behalf of CREEP, filed a countersuit ". . . seeking $2.5 million in damages from O'Brien. It accused O'Brien of having used the court 'as a forum in which to publicize accusations against innocent persons which would be libelous if published elsewhere' and of 'using his civil action to improperly conduct a private inquisition while a grand jury investigation is in progress.'"[20]

What was being revealed about the enemy in all of this was their motivation. The formula was: we are innocent and helpful to the courts; they are trying to capitalize on the situation and obstruct the courts. Spiro Agnew got so taken with the "look at them, not us" approach that in September he ". . . told reporters in Minneapolis that the apprehension of the five men in the headquarters of the Democratic National Committee was a 'set-up' designed to embarrass the Republicans and damage their Presidential campaign."[21] That probably took him beyond the latitude of acceptance of most Americans, even then, but it was a perfect example of the "revealing the opposition" approach in operation.

If the minimizing of information about self maintains power by keeping options open, the maximizing of negative information about your opponent accomplishes the same thing by channeling aggression. The Nixon administration channeled aggression by naming (that is, defining enemies to hate) and by manipulating issues.

The naming of enemies is familiar to most rhetorical critics.[22] In Nixon's case, the enemies were legion: the press, liberals, students and the academic community in general, peaceniks, the Vietcong, some Congressmen (and Congress generally), and even some members of Nixon's own administration. The "enemies list" which surfaced during the Watergate inquiry was unpredictably lean, considering the number of people and groups identified and treated as enemies by the administration.

But the important point to be made is not that the administration had, and recognized, its enemies. Rather, what is significant is how the enemies were used, for they provided foci against which the aggression felt by ordinary citizens could be channeled. The naming of enemies tactic explained the contempt heaped upon students, the anger hurled at the academic community upon the release of the report of the President's Commission on Pornography and Obscenity, the savage bombing raids in and near the largest cities of Vietnam. Most of all, it explained the attacks by Vice-President Agnew against the press. The enemies identified, the aggression was given a reasonable target, and the administration was spared criticism.

Naming the enemy in the Watergate contest has already been seen in the White House naming of Democrats as demagogues and in identifying the lawsuit as an attempt to utilize the courts for political purposes. The classic *ad hominem* argument developed: debunk the attacker so you need not deal with his argument.

But the Democrats were not the major enemy in this situation, so the *ad hominem* approach also was used against the central enemies, the *New York Times* and the *Washington Post*. In response to stories linking

Segretti to Chapin and Hunt to Mardian, Zeigler called the charges "hearsay, innuendo, and guilt by association," and Clark MacGregor "attacked the *Post* for using 'unsubstantiated charges' to 'maliciously' link the White House to Watergate."[23] The day before MacGregor finally admitted the existence of a "special fund," Zeigler responded to a *Post* story alleging its existence by typing the story as ". . . a 'political effort,' 'character assassination,' and 'the shoddiest type of journalism.'"[24] Commenting on all these charges against the media, Robert Semple wrote: "At the moment, the White House spokesman's principal tactic seems to be to create the impression, and have the public believe, that the charges of espionage are no more than stories printed in newspapers — and not very reliable newspapers at that. 'Do you know why we're not uptight about the press and the espionage business?' one White House aide — not Mr. Ziegler — asked rhetorically the other day. 'Because we believe that the public believes that the Eastern press really is what Agnew said it was — elitist, anti-Nixon, and ultimately pro-McGovern.'"[25]

The traditional behavior of blaming bad news on the messengers not only applied to the naming of enemies strategy, but the fact that it had begun before the break-in made the assertions against the press more believable in regard to Watergate. No new strategy was called for precisely because the old one had been so successful.

The second way the aggression of the citizenry was channeled was by a manipulation of the issues. From "benign neglect" to busing, Nixon played upon the racial fears of middle-class whites. No attempt was made to allay those fears, no steps toward racial harmony were taken. With both inflation and unemployment increasing, Nixon seized upon the issue of the economy, not necessarily to nurture it to health, but, rather, to milk it for the votes he saw as "reachable." He ". . . set his own priorities, which favored defense, manufacturing, and business quite heavily, and restricted funds for fields like ecology, teaching, social services, and public employment generally. . . . Those youths and adults in the parts of the economy favored by economic expansion became defenders of Nixon's policies and of the system. McGovern sympathizers were almost always hard pressed economically or wanted to work in fields which fared poorly or were locked out under Nixon's jobmaking and spending priorities."[26]

Those who could not find jobs, because of Nixon's priorities, went on welfare, and then Nixon channeled aggression at them for undermining the work ethic. Said, he, "The person whose values are most directly threatened is the American worker, and it is up to the

American worker to understand the nature of the challenge and to move strongly to turn it back."[27] But what could a worker do to "move strongly" and "turn back" those who threatened his way of life? He could channel his aggression against them — and fulfill his patriotic duty by voting for Nixon in 1972.

Nixon also manipulated the Watergate controversy. The issue of the Watergate affair should have been: Was Nixon (or the White House) involved in the break-in and ensuing cover-up? But if that issue had remained paramount, voter aggression would have been directed against the Oval Office. The Nixon administration was able to divert aggression to other issues and overcome the appearance of culpability by implying, "I didn't do it but here's why it looks like I did." While there were many "here's whys" used by the Nixon administration, the most popular seemed to be "they are out to get me," in which the attempt was made to divert attention from the question at hand to the motives of the questioners — from "Is Nixon involved in Watergate?" to "Is the *Washington Post* attempting to elect McGovern?" Thus, a straw man tactic accomplished its purpose by diverting aggression to another source by manipulating the issues.

Another "issue" which was manipulated concerned the significance of the event — naming an event a "third-rate burglary" and "a very bizarre incident," implying that spying was a common tactic, asserting that Watergate was analogous to the antics of Democratic trickster Dick Tuck. Probably the strangest application of this tactic came from Spiro Agnew, who held that the outcry was clearly partisan because "I didn't see any of these cries of moral indignation against the person accused of stealing the Pentagon Papers."[28]

But the most consistent issue manipulation that occurred was the question of fairness. In Nixon's first public statement on Watergate (June 22), he said, "I will not comment on those matters, particularly since possible criminal charges are involved."[29] This approach continued throughout the campaign. When asked on October 5 why the administration did not just make a "clean breast" of what had happened, Nixon said: "I would say finally with regard to commenting on any of those who have been indicted, with regard to saying anything about the judicial process, I am going to follow the good advice, which I appreciate, of the members of the press corps, my constant, and I trust will always continue to be, very responsible critics. I stepped into one on that when you recall I made inadvertently a comment in Denver about an individual who had been indicted in California, the Manson case. I was vigorously criticized for making comment about the case, so, of course, I know you would want me to follow the same single standard by not commenting on this case."[30]

A related minimax tactic was found in the promise-performance dichotomy. In 1972, Nixon seemed to be running against the incumbent, or at least against the government in Washington. That is, rather than pointing to his performance and calling for more of the same, he was asking for a change from the "old ways" as though he were divorced from them. Peter H. Dailey of the November Group explained how this tactic evolved: ". . . the more we looked at the research, the more we found that the President really had the beginnings of a unique position, and that was that while people were dissatisfied with the direction of the country, their feelings seemed directed more at intangibles of government, and bureaucracy, than at the President. So, very early, we felt that the most important single thing we could do was to have the President take a position on the side of change. He had to be somebody who was identified as being for change. . . ."[31]

Yet, nowhere did the November Group identify or advertise a desire on Nixon's part for any specific change or proposals for accomplishing the changes desired by the electorate. The change format was strategy. According to the Republican Ripon Society: "To the Nixon White House the sole purpose of public statements was to influence, not to inform. When a statement is issued as part of a game plan, the truth of that statement becomes only strategically relevant — relevant, that is, if the assertion might be contested or the statement might sound implausible. The assertion that a statement is either 'operative' or 'inoperative' betrays a strategic mentality that regards statements as instruments."[32]

Thus did the Nixon administration promise, albeit obliquely, what it did not intend to deliver. It is not surprising, therefore, that the performance did not live up to the promises. Nixon could run on the same platform — and stock speech — in 1972 as he had in 1968 because none of the problems of 1968 had been solved. Some movement, visible busyness, had occurred. But, "promising administration programs, such as the Family Assistance Plan, the Philadelphia Plan, the New American Revolution, and many others were brought forth for their symbolic significance and then quietly shelved when their public relations value declined."[33] Programs created enemies and closed options, while promises created friends and, as long as they were not enacted, left options open. "The administration, then, sought to increase its power position by concentrating on image-building. The problem was that whenever the time came to *use* some of the power for a policy commitment, the argument usually prevailed that to do so would sacrifice support that might be used later."[34] Since there were few domestic programs to which the administration was committed, it seemed reasonable not to squander any of its potential power.

Again, the minimax formula was employed — minimize commitments by avoiding programs, maximize promises by allusions to change, by busyness, by proposals for strategically expendable programs. The options remained open; the power and control were intact.

In the Watergate affair, the "promises" strategy surfaced immediately after the break-in and continued throughout the 1972 campaign:

- June 19: The F.B.I. announced a full-scale investigation.[35]
- June 22, Richard Nixon: "As far as the matter now is concerned, it is under the investigation, as it should be, by the District of Columbia police and by the F.B.I."[36]
- August 30, Richard Nixon: "With regard to who is investigating it now, I think it would be well to notice that the F.B.I. is conducting a full field investigation. The Department of Justice, of course, is in charge of the prosecution and presenting the matter to the grand jury. The Senate Banking and Currency Committee is conducting an investigation. The Government Accounting Office, an independent agency, is conducting an investigation of those aspects which involve the campaign spending law. . . . In addition to that, within our own staff, under my direction, counsel to the President, Mr. Dean, has conducted a complete investigation of all leads which might involve any present members of the White House staff or anybody in the Government."[37]
- September 15, Richard Kleindienst: "In announcing the indictment (he) said the investigation was 'one of the most intensive, objective, and thorough . . . in many years, reaching out to cities all across the United States as well as into foreign countries.'"[38]
- October 6, Richard Nixon: "The F.B.I. has assigned 133 agents to this investigation. It followed out 1,800 leads. It conducted 1,500 interviews. Incidentally, I conducted the investigation of the Hiss Case. . . .The F.B.I. did a magnificent job, but that investigation, involving the security of this country, was basically a Sunday school exercise compared to the amount of effort that was put into this."[39]

The strategy of making promises, then, was effected primarily by pointing with pride to the number and extent of the investigations. The other portion of the "promises" strategy was to keep so busy with other things that Watergate would recede into the background. True, most presidents are almost always busy, so it cannot be proven that keeping busy was a consciously chosen strategy. However, there is one interesting clue to the "busyness" strategy in Nixon's news conferences: in his June 22 conference, when the opening question concerned Watergate, he used verbs of movement throughout the conference 48 times ("We're moving on that problem," "we will go forward," "an on-going program," "going ahead," "the biggest step," etc.). Yet, in his next conference, five weeks later, when Watergate was not a subject of questioning, verbs of movement were not used even once. While there may be another explanation for the correlation, it seems to indicate a strategy of obfuscation through promising.

The final tactic in the promise-performance dichotomy, not performing, also was followed. The investigations, it now seems, were generally bogus. But at the time they looked and sounded real, truly exonerating the Nixon White House. The tactic worked. Nixon's re-election was assured.

The issue, then, was manipulated to become a question of "fairness" — Were the Democrats being fair in their use of the courts? Was the press being fair in making absurd charges and asking Nixon to comment inappropriately on court cases? Was Nixon being fair by letting the court do its work, by following the democratic idea of "innocent until proven guilty?" Somehow, in all that, the central question, "Was Nixon involved?" got lost. The aggression was deflected from the White House to the Democrats and the elite newspapers.

CONCLUSION

That, then, was the strategy which allowed the 1972 Nixon campaign to cope with the Watergate affair. The goal was to maintain power. The minimax strategies were (1) to keep the options open by concealing as much about the self as possible while revealing as much negative information about the opposition as possible, and by promising a lot (as obliquely as possible) while delivering as little as possible, and (2) to channel aggressions by naming the enemies and manipulating the issues.

Watergate did not harm Nixon in the 1972 campaign. Because he was able to follow his normal rhetorical strategies in coping with the emerging scandal, the event seemed more normal than it really was. The major rhetorical lesson of Watergate may be that crises will not be perceived as crises if handled by non-crisis rhetoric. Whether, in the long run, Nixon chose the correct strategy in 1972 is not ours to say, although the events following the landslide election victory lead us to suggest that the 1972 campaign was not unlike the incident described by Robert Southey in his poem, "The Battle of Blenheim":

> "But what good came of it at last?"
> Quote Little Peterkin.
> "Why that I cannot tell," said he;
> "But 'twas a famous victory."

NOTES

1. Ernest R. May and Janet Fraser, eds., *Campaign '72: The Managers Speak* (Cambridge: Harvard University Press, 1973), p. 193.

2. Garry Wills, *Nixon Agonistes: The Crisis of the Self-Made Man* (Boston: Houghton Mifflin, 1970), p. 86.

3. May and Fraser, *Campaign '72*, p. 198.

4. Edward W. Knappman, ed., *Watergate and the White House: June, 1972–July, 1973*, vol. 1 (New York: Facts on File, 1973), p. 11.

5. Anthony Ripley, "Simple Watergate 'Caper' Sends Ripples Over U.S.," *The New York Times*, June 23, 1972, p. 14.

6. Ibid., p. 11.

7. Richard M. Nixon, "Transcript of the President's News Conference Emphasizing Domestic Matters," *The New York Times*, June 23, 1972, p. 14.

8. Ripley, "Simple Watergate 'Caper,'" p. 14.

9. Knappman, *Watergate and White House*, p. 12.

10. Richard M. Nixon, "Transcript of News Conference by the President on Political and Other Matters," *The New York Times*, August 30, 1972, p. 20.

11. Knappman, *Watergate and White House*, p. 14.

12. Ibid., p. 16.

13. Ibid.

14. "Conversation between the President and H. R. Haldeman, June 23, 1972," in "Statement of Information Appendix 3," *Hearings before the Committee on the Judiciary, House of Representatives* (Washington: Government Printing Office, May, 1974), p. 39.

15. Richard M. Nixon as quoted in Arthur Miller, "The Limited Hang-Out," *Harper's*, September 1974, p. 18.

16. Richard M. Nixon, "Transcript of Nixon's Acceptance Address," *The New York Times*, August 24, 1972, p. 47.

17. "Call to Fear," *The New York Times*, August 25, 1972, p. 32.

18. Knappman, *Watergate and White House*, p. 11.

19. Ibid., p. 12.

20. Ibid.

21. Spiro T. Agnew as quoted in James T. Wooten, "Agnew Confirms His Faith in Nixon about Watergate," *The New York Times*, April 26, 1973, p. 34.

22. Ruth M. Gonchar and Dan F. Hahn, "Richard Nixon and Presidential Mythology," *Journal of Applied Communication Research* 1 (1972):27.

23. Knappman, *Watergate and White House*, p. 15.

24. Ibid., p. 16.

25. Robert B. Semple, Jr., "G.O.P. and 'Spy' Plot," *The New York Times,* October 31, 1972, p. 45.

26. Samuel Lubell, *The Future While It Happened* (New York: W. W. Norton, 1973), p. 36.

27. Richard M. Nixon as quoted in Robert B. Semple, Jr., "President Scores 'Welfare Ethic,'" *The New York Times,* September 4, 1972, p. 1.

28. Tom Wicker, "Ellsberg and Apathy," *The New York Times,* October 31, 1972, p. 45.

29. Nixon, "Transcript . . . Domestic Matters," p. 14.

30. Richard M. Nixon, "Transcript of the President's News Conference on Domestic and Foreign Matters," *The New York Times,* October 6, 1972, p. 28.

31. May and Fraser, *Campaign '72*, p. 197.

32. Ripon Society and Clifford W. Brown, Jr., *Jaws of Victory: The Game-Plan Politics of 1972. The Crisis of the Republican Party and the Future of the Constitution* (Boston: Little, Brown, 1973), p. 6.

33. Ibid., p. 5.

34. Ibid., p. 6.

35. Knappman, *Watergate and White House*, p. 11.

36. Nixon, "Transcript . . . Domestic Matters," p. 14.

37. Nixon, "Transcript . . . Political and Other Matters," p. 20.

38. Knappman, *Watergate and White House*, p. 13.

39. Nixon, "Transcript . . . Domestic and Foreign Matters," p. 28.

PERSUASIVE FORM IN PRESIDENTIAL RHETORIC

In the novel, *Still Life with Woodpecker,* author Tom Robbins depicts one female character as being so naive that she "thought fellatio was an obscure Italian opera and was annoyed that she couldn't find the score."[1] In the study of rhetorical form we all are naive, and perhaps annoyed that the "score" has never been printed. This is not a matter of a conspiracy of silence; scholars just now are beginning to study this subject. And most of what has been written, including what follows here, can best be described as conjecture, or, at the most, informed conjecture. Nonetheless, conjectures, the bases of hypotheses, are the necessary first steps to knowledge. Thus, we dare to present this essay, not in the hope of providing the right answers, but more with the prayer that we will ask the right questions, explore the relevant phenomena, and provide intelligent conjectures upon which the next scholar can build.

Language, like every other human artifact, comes in many forms. Just as there are many ways to say "I love you," there are multiple means of expressing, "I'm the best person for the office." These "means" include, but are not limited to, the elements of rhetorical form to be considered in this essay.

Unfortunately, the consideration of rhetorical form must lead us into much speculation, for, while we know a good deal about forms in terms of grammatical correctness, we know next to nothing in terms of what forms communicate, that is, how they work upon auditors or how they provide insight into speakers. Nor is this ignorance surprising:

> It must always be remembered that it is not the normal communication situation for hearer or reader to examine messages closely. If communication is to succeed in its purpose, the desired modification of conduct which the sentence or sentences as a whole are intended to produce must be understood quickly and the response given quickly, if social interaction is to continue normally. Under such circumstances, then, it must be supposed that it is inevitable that the form and content of most utterances will not be subjected to close examination, and that it is not merely the result of communicational laziness that this should be so.[2]

Yet as students of political language we must attempt to understand how discourses work, how rhetors attempt to persuade us.

It is not enough to be "up" on all the current political issues so that we will know when the speaker is lying. Politics, by its very nature, seldom deals in truths; it deals with actions today which will produce reactions tomorrow. It deals with hypotheses, speculations, arguments about which actions among those possible for today will produce which reactions, desirable and undesirable, possible for tomorrow. Thus politics, inherently, is involved with rhetoric about the unknowable. How, then, do people come to believe so fervently that they do know? How do they become so positive that the strip-mining bill will hurt the economy or that failure to build a certain weapon system will doom us to another war? And how do they go about convincing us to agree with them?

Obviously, decision-making and persuasion depend on many elements. But one such element that often is overlooked is rhetorical form. Political discourse

> seeks from its auditors commitments that are implicit in its formal characteristics: in the way it argues, [in addition to] the substance of its argument; in its ways of coming to judgment that it implicitly recommends,

[in addition to] the judgment that it actually advocates; in the way it uses language, [in addition to] the proposition expressed by that language. The form of the discourse — ... the way it uses evidence, the forms of reasoning it employs — solicits from the auditor commitments to certain ways of thinking, of viewing the world, of making decisions, that are not necessarily implied in the substance of the discourse.[3]

When the Far Right, in the 1964 campaign, said of Barry Goldwater, "In your heart you know he's right," and the Far Left countered with, "In your guts you know he's nuts," both were doing more than stating positions. They were recommending ways of knowing. You know with your heart. You know with your gut. These forms of knowing were being recommended; by implication, knowing with your brain was being denigrated.

We understand, somewhat implicitly, that form accomplishes these things. We do not know how or why it does so. Our purpose here, then, is to engage in some speculation about the hows and whys of form.

POWER OF DEFINITION

In the same common-sense mode in which most of us think a person's clothing tells us something about him or her, it is reasonable to assume that his or her language "gives something away." But, given the imponderables in the relation between a person's language and his or her epistemology, what is it that is being "given away" and how do/should we react to those language clues? Richard Weaver contended that a sure "index" to a person's political position could be found "in his characteristic way of thinking, inevitably expressed in the type of argument he prefers."[4] And while Weaver the political conservative probably would have applauded President Reagan's conservatism, it is possible that Weaver the rhetorical theorist would have abhorred Reagan's "characteristic way of thinking," for Reagan's

mind does not proceed according to logical or empirical principles. It works in an essentially imagistic way. Its most characteristic device is the figure of speech known as synecdoche: the use of a part to stand for a whole. Again and again Mr. Reagan uses this device, in the form of anecdotes. And again and again the parts he uses to stand for the whole — from the celebrated Chicago "welfare queen" who did not exist to the ... slander of the disabled Virginia welder whom the President accused of taking welfare while working — are shown to be false. Even if they were true, that would be small comfort, for complex social realities still would have been reduced to simple, and by no means typical, examples. But the President's anecdotes are not true. Which means that he represents social reality to himself with false images, and then, guided by a light that is darkness, acts into that reality. All is illusory — except the real pain caused by these false metaphors.[5]

While it is not important for us to determine whether Richard Weaver would have applauded or abhorred Reagan's rhetorical form, we should at least realize that his evaluation would have been determined by the perspective (political conservative or rhetorical critic) from which the evaluation was being made.

And the question of perspective, in turn, can be controlled somewhat by the form into which the rhetor casts the remarks. Ronald Carpenter, for instance, has noted that presidential discourse is more often designed to reflect citizen attitudes than to change them:

In these instances, audience decisions are not about the past, or in the Aristotelian paradigm, *re*structurings of previously formed convictions; nor are they decisions about the future and whether or not to engage in new, different behaviors. Rather, discourse which basically reflects or rearticulates prevailing attitudes is, in essence, epideictic or demonstrative. The audience renders a decision for the present, and the focus of approval or disapproval is how well the President articulates values with which listeners *already* agree.[6]

Even when a president does seem to be talking about policy-making, presenting information for the consideration of the citizenry, such as in a crisis, the form of the address need not be perceived as an example of deliberate oratory in the Aristotelian sense. It may be that the president in question just needed a pretext to appear "presidential." Gary Woodward contends that what is critical is to note whether such events "come to the forefront of our attention because of the seriousness attached to them by presidents who obliged themselves to shape suitable responses," and Woodward concludes, "A crisis is sometimes most profitably studied as an act of presidential *labeling*."[7]

Thus, the ability to define the issues should be considered one of the foremost powers of rhetorical form. Yet it also is one of the simplest, for much of the power derives merely from the nouns employed. So, the nouns of a president should tell you which portions of the world he finds relevant. They will, in a sense, show you the arenas of his consciousness, and thus the areas in which you can expect concern and activity. From 1976 to 1980 the country focused on energy because President

Carter focused on it. Since 1980, the "energy crisis" has disappeared —
not so much because objective conditions have changed but because
"energy" is not a field of interest to Ronald Reagan.

Nouns function, then, to direct attention. And looking in one
direction sometimes precludes looking in another; thus, President
Reagan's emphasis on individualism implicitly denies our
interrelatedness, making easier his task of dismantling the welfare
programs of Johnson's "Great Society."

IDENTIFICATION

The concept of identification is central to presidential rhetoric, for an
important job of a president is to persuade the audience that he identifies
with their interests and thus it is in their interests to identify with him.
Kenneth Burke, the rhetorical theorist who has made identification the
basic thrust of his analytic framework, contends that identification
concerns ". . . one's ways of sharing vicariously in the role of leader or
spokesman . . . allegiance and change of allegiance . . . one's way of
seeing one's reflection in the social mirror . . . positive and negative
responses to authority."[8]

To examine a president's modes of identification, one can isolate such
words as "and," "too," "also," etc. Such connectives establish
relationships, thus tell you what the president thinks goes with what. But
they may also suggest dominance and fear of being dominated. That is,
one who utilizes an abnormally high number of connectives may do so
out of fear of being interrupted.

Pronoun use also can tell us a good deal about identifications. For
instance, Nixon's use of pronouns identified him as a benevolent
dictator. The pronoun "I" tended to be followed by action verbs, while
"we" and "us" tended to be used in the receiving position. The Nixonian
formula, then, was "I, President Nixon, have acted . . . and we, the
citizens, reap the benefits of the action."

Pronoun frequency also is revealing. Consider, for example, the
implications of the fact that Nixon used "I" 10 times as often in foreign
policy as in domestic policy speeches, or that in the White House tapes he
utilized "I" 16 times as often as is found in normal conversation.

Jimmy Carter's references to the populace also are instructive. He ran
for the presidency as a repository of *our* goodness. In line with this
theme, in his inaugural address he used "we" 43 times and "our" 36
times, while employing the personal pronoun "I" only 6 times. Of the 35

paragraphs of the speech, 25 began with "we," "our," or "let us." Yet, by 1980 the president had taken a new orientation. The change was from Carter the commoner, the man of the people, who by relying on us would accomplish things with us, to Carter the president, who was above us, who relied on himself and his Georgia mafia and did things for us.

Every president, of course, comes to be seen as an "insider," but that was an especial problem for Carter because he had run on the rhetoric of an outsider in 1976. To offset the changed circumstances, the 1980 campaign plan was to utilize an "insider-outsider" approach, to run as

> the same man, with the same instincts and concern for ordinary citizens as the Jimmy Carter of 1976 — but with four years of practical experience, the outsider who now knows how Washington works, but is still prepared to take on the oil companies, the special interest groups.[9]

However, Carter was unable to shake off his new orientation and return to his 1976 emphasis. For instance, in the three 1976 debates with Ford he had employed the phrase "the people" over 70 times,[10] on the average of 23 times per debate, but in the 1980 debate with Reagan he "referred to 'the people' only 9 times . . . while invoking references to the presidency 27 times."[11] Furthermore, when he did mention "the people" in 1980, it was clear that his perception of their role had changed:

> Rather than providing the source of wisdom and knowledge for his presidency, the people [had become] subjects, to be commanded by the president. For example, in discussing energy, Carter said, "We have demanded that the American people sacrifice and they've done very well."[12]

ACTION

It is axiomatic that we elect presidents to act for us. Obviously, then, a central component in the rhetoric of officeholders is to demonstrate that they have been taking the right actions. As Gary Woodward has commented, ". . . few presidents can resist the urge to use the imagery of movement, even if only to transpose calculated *in*action as significant *action*. . . ."[13]

President Reagan's favorite metaphor, for instance, is a metaphor that implies action — the path metaphor. It is difficult to find a Reagan speech in which he does not talk about "choosing the right road," taking the "first step" and "staying the course."

In addition to the metaphors, a president's verbs and adverbs contain messages of action. The kind of verbs employed explain the president's behavior patterns and even give insight into his attitudes toward leadership. Active presidents use active verbs; passive ones employ more passive verbs. The weak, passive verbs employed by Jimmy Carter in his inaugural, "to help shape" and "a step forward," should have forewarned us of his approach to the presidency. Meanwhile, it should be noted that there is no verb form for "incursion," thus no actors. An "incursion" apparently just happens.

It should also be noted that some judgments of political import are built into our language. For instance, action normally is assumed to be good. Thus, locutions like "stern action," "resolute action," "immediate action," etc., are presumed positive. Inaction is assumed to be bad. One wonders, therefore, if our language doesn't push us toward action for action's sake. We find it suggestive that in earlier ages, when the mind was more highly valued, they wrote "confessions," whereas in our time, when actions are more highly valued, we write "autobiographies."

The adverbs of a president suggest salience and intensity, and will tend to show you not only what is to be done, but how he plans to do it. Thus, those who expected Jimmy Carter to be an active president in the F.D.R. mold obviously overlooked his heavy campaign reliance upon adverbs like "gradually," "modestly," "accurately," and "slowly."

EMOTIONAL INVOLVEMENT

Not only do presidents desire to indicate what actions they favor, they also want to communicate how deeply they are committed to their actions. One way they do so is through the adjectives they choose to utilize. In the adjectives are lodged opinions of the world, judgments about what is worth saving, developing, etc. And if you examine the adjective clusters you should be able to discover the categories utilized to make judgments — moral, practical, aesthetic, etc. Military attitudes toward death, for instance, are found in the fact that in the language of war there are only two kinds of death — "prompt" death and "dilatory" death. Compare the attitude expressed toward life in those adjective choices with George McGovern's 1972 tendency toward an excessive use of modifiers. He would not say, "American blood," nor "young American blood," but "precious young American blood."

However, because the citizens are not unified in their commitments, presidents sometimes want to speak in such a way that those who favor an action will perceive them as being supportive while those who are opposed to the action can hope that action will not necessarily follow the words. A common method of accomplishing this purpose is to speak on one side of an issue but to act on the other, thus giving the rhetoric to one group and the policy to the other.

Closely related is the penchant of presidents for protecting themselves by couching their promises in the subjunctive mood. For example, the *New York Times* attacked President Carter for hedging when he promised, "I would never give up full control of the Panama Canal as long as it had any contribution to make to our national security." The *Times* complained that the "conditional note . . . opens a wide realm of judgmental freedom."[14]

We will never know, of course, whether Carter really was hedging on the Panama Canal, saying what his audience wanted to hear, or if his "conditional note" was the careful language of a realistic politician who understood that the political world is a probabilistic world, best dealt with through hypotheses, contingencies, and possibilities, that is, with the subjunctive. As George Will has noted, "Most of what a President says is politically, if not grammatically, in the subjunctive mood because he can do little alone. A President's principal power is the highly contingent power to persuade Congress. And Congress hears a discordant clamor of other voices."[15] From this perspective, the subjunctive only brings the rhetoric into realistic alignment with the political world.

Another form useful in avoiding overcommitment, employed in politics as well as in the rest of life, is what I call *affirmation by denial*. It is the same form Ralph Waldo Emerson had in mind when he said, "The louder he talked of his honor, the faster we counted our spoons." J. Hillis Miller gives this example: "If I say, 'I shall not compare thee to a summer's day, a rose, a running brook,' I have in spite of myself made those comparisons, and the day, rose, and brook have a positive existence in my speech."[16] When a politician says, "I wouldn't think of doing . . . X," we only know one thing for sure — that he did think of doing it, that is, it did cross his mind. When Henry Kissinger, after the *Mayaguez* affair, said, 'We are not going around looking for opportunities to prove our manhood," one critic responded, "It was a curious comment for the question had never been asked, and it made it clear that at a level very close to his consciousness, Secretary Kissinger knew that this was precisely what America's reaction had been all about."[17] Of course, you understand, we wouldn't think of saying that the good secretary had lied.

A favorite Nixonian variant of "affirmation by denial" was the "I would never have said that myself" form, in which Nixon reported the attacks the Silent Majority had made against his critics: "When I say I inherited this war, I want to point out that I am actually quoting what others say. I'm not going to cast blame for the war in Vietnam on either of my predecessors." Nixon disassociated himself from the statement by indicating that he personally did not hold with this view, but the jury was not instructed to disregard the testimony. The variant allowed Nixon to vindicate his action without having to specify blame. We just knew that the blame lay elsewhere.

LOGICAL/RATIONAL

We expect our president to be logical and rational (as we understand logicality and rationality). And the expectations of the audience are a part of the milieu in which form operates. Consider, for example, the area of foreign policy. Do we want our presidents to be logical and rational, or childish and petulant? Assuming we agree on the audience preference here, does it give us any insight into the popularity of Lyndon Johnson and Richard Nixon versus the anti-war protesters of the late 1960s and early 1970s? Look, for a moment, at Nixon's second inaugural in 1973. He demonstrated his own "logical" approach through what I call the *law of semantic equality*. That is, the grammatical structure and word choices that he employed seemed to say, "look how calm and logical I am being." For instance, and this is just one of many possible examples from that speech, Nixon said, "Just as America's role is indispensable in preserving the world's peace, so is each nation's role indispensable in preserving its own peace." The parallel structure of the sentence argued rationality; the parallel word choices argued rationality. But the argument was highly irrational. The given, the indispensability of America in preserving peace, was based upon the "fact" that other nations were too weak to preserve peace. Therefore, the conclusion that other nations must preserve their own peace flew in the face of the weakness posited about them in the premise. Or, stated the other way, if the other nations were capable of preserving their own peace, America would not have had an "indispensable" role in preserving peace. Regardless, the point remains that the structure and word choices suggested a rationality that the content belied. The form (or structure) was persuasive in much the same way that many men find 36–24–36 persuasive, that is, regardless of the unrevealed and unexamined content. Richard Nixon, through the form of the discourse, demonstrated his rationality, even though the content was irrational, even nonsensical.

Compare, now, one of the major rhetorical forms employed by the protesters, the slogans of demonstrators: "Hey, hey, L.B.J., How many kids did you kill today?" or "One, two, three, four, we don't want your fucking war." The form of the slogans suggested childishness: the simple rhymes of nursery-land, the cadences of high school cheerleaders, the directness of the naive child. The form was childish, but "misleadingly childish."[18] For there is nothing less childish, more the province of grown-ups, than killing and war. But more, "Hey, hey, L.B.J., How many kids did you kill today?" said something serious about who should be blamed for the war and who was taking the brunt of it. (The assertions of responsibility and victimage may have been right or wrong; regardless, they were serious assertions.) Likewise, the phrase "fucking war" was a serious phrase. It was not merely an obscenity designed to shock; more importantly, it implicitly argued that war is obscene — a serious argument.

No matter. The forms of the protagonists carried the day. The form of President Nixon was rational, misleadingly so. And the American people chose the form their expectations led them to prefer, despite the fact that the public opinion polls suggested that close to a majority preferred the anti-war content of the protesters.

President Reagan sometimes accomplishes his proof of rationality in a somewhat unique way. Having come to politics from the world of Hollywood, a tinsel-town which thrives on illusion, he was attacked as living in a "fantasy world." Jimmy Carter sneered, "It is a make-believe world of good guys and bad guys, where some politicians shoot first and ask questions later."[19] But Ronald Reagan has been able to turn his liability into an asset. Where most presidents rely upon their knowledge of the real world to prove that their own programs are realistic, Reagan can reverse the usual form. As an expert on the world of illusion, he occasionally "proves" his own rationality by branding his opponent's positions as illusionary.

STRENGTH

Another goal of presidents is to seem strong. One can do so, of course, by taking extreme or tough positions. But the other possibility is to talk tough about your moderate stance. In another place, Hahn argued that the 1980 election pitted two semi-tough rhetoricians — Ronald

Reagan, who had polar positions but talked moderately, versus Jimmy Carter, who took moderate positions but employed polar language.[20] The two approaches of 1980 are common in politics, described earlier in this essay as giving the rhetoric to one side and the policy to the other, a way to fulfill the something-for-everyone impulse that runs through American politics. Kenneth Burke has identified the form as "secular prayer" and suggested that it is a perfectly reasonable form for a president to employ when the public wants a more drastic measure than he wants to endorse:

> In this case, you would try to put through a more moderate measure — but you would make up the difference stylistically by thundering about its startling scope. One could hardly call this hypocrisy; it is the normally prayerful use of language, to sharpen up the pointless and blunt the too sharply pointed. Hence, when Roosevelt, some years ago, came forth with a mighty blast about the death sentence he was delivering to the holding companies, I took this as evidence on its face that the holding companies were to fare quite favorably. Otherwise, why the blast?[21]

Ronald Reagan became president, at least in part, because he was perceived as having a kind of toughness President Carter lacked. Yet that perception of toughness was almost exclusively from the content of his rhetoric rather than the form. Indeed, we would argue that an examination of rhetorical form would yield the conclusion that President Reagan is not a tough president. Reagan repeats such phrases as "let me say" and "let me repeat," which ask for permission to speak, instead of the more aggressive "I say" and "I repeat." Additionally, his vocabulary is not as vivid or exciting as one might expect from an aggressive person. Instead, he uses words like "well" and "now" and "I might add," creating a sort of archetypically California laid-back, almost sedated, language. Even in describing events that are in no way colorless, such as nuclear war, Reagan employs colorless words. In fact, his lexicon is never so bland and dull as when he is depicting the weapons of nuclear war.

Which is the real Ronald Reagan, the president with the "strong" policies or the one with the "weak" rhetorical form? We do not yet know for sure, but the relative softness of his actions against the Soviet Union following the "massacre" of the Korean airliner and the withdrawal of the Marines from Beirut suggest that the rhetorical form may be the more accurate gauge of the man.

HONESTY

At least since Watergate, it has become mandatory that presidents demonstrate their honesty. Fortunately for them, there are rhetorical forms available for that purpose. But unfortunately for them, overuse of the major form has undermined its power.

In our capitalistic society we are all familiar with the Latin, *caveat emptor*, the notion that the buyer should beware. Yet, we have all had the experience of having a salesperson tell us, almost conspiratorially, that it is a good thing you came in today because tomorrow the item you are interested in will be $10 more. The form of the dialogue says, "I'm on your side. I'll level with you and sell it to you today, even though my commission would be better if you delayed your purchase 24 hours." Maybe we believe him. Maybe we buy the item. And just maybe . . . we end up in the same store the next day shopping for another item. How do we now act toward our salesperson? Yesterday, his form told us, "Today I'm looking out for you; tomorrow I'll be lining my own pocket." If we are smart, we will take him at his word. (Of course, if we were *that* smart we probably would not have believed him yesterday, but that's another story.) The present point is that his manner of telling us yesterday of his trustworthiness makes him suspect today.

Politics has its own version of the personal *caveat emptor*. It is the senator asking, "Can I speak frankly?" the president averring, "I'll be honest with you." This form may enjoy temporary success, but it implicitly conveys to us that these times are exceptions to the nonfrank, dishonest norm. And, misused often enough, they can turn into liabilities, just as Nixon's phrase, "Let me make one thing perfectly clear," came to signal us to watch for the obfuscation, the muddying phrase, the escape clause in what he was about to say.

And practically any piece of meta-communication (that is, communication about the communication) underlines in about the same way. When a professor says, "Listen carefully, this point is important," he underlines that point, but also, implicitly, says, "the rest of my presentation is not important, you do not need to listen to it."

GRANDEUR

One goal of all presidents is to depict themselves as wonderful, perhaps grander than they are. Their language helps them do so. Take, for instance, the line from John Kennedy's inaugural that so caught the imagination of America, "Ask not what your country can do for you, but what you can do for your country." Think about the meaning here. What can most of us do? Pay taxes. Die in a war. Work, and thereby avoid welfare. Be law-abiding. Etc. Pretty gruesome or pedestrian behaviors he asked of us. So why the positive response? One part of the answer, we would contend, relates to the form.

> Word orders like "Ask not what . . ." are not used in ordinary conversation or even ordinary speech-making. We associate the unusual deployment of verb, adverb, and accusative pronoun with biblical language and with eloquent oratory of the past, and we respond to the poetry of those associations.[22]

That is, the form recalls other deployments of the same form and we react to the speaker as though he or she were of the other genre — a poet, or maybe a minor prophet — rather than a politician. The form deflects our thought from the content of the line to the image of the speaker, simultaneously transforming the speaker from a grubby politician to a poet or prophet.

Another president, Jimmy Carter, was more obvious in deflecting our evaluation of him from the political arena to the religious sphere. James Reston referred to Carter's inaugural as a "revival meeting,"[23] Hedrick Smith said it was "less rallying cry than sermon,"[24] and Anthony Hillbruner entitled his analysis of it, "Born Again: Carter's Inaugural Sermon."[25] Certainly these commentators noted the most obvious subject in the speech.

In defining the world as two distinct parts, physical and spiritual, and then emphasizing the latter, President Carter set a religious mood in his inaugural address. In the very first sentence, when Carter thanked President Ford for "all he has done to heal our land," he implied that one of the presidential responsibilities is that of "healing," a job that can be seen either in medical terms, or, metaphorically, as a divine responsibility.

Carter specifically referred to his faith by talking of the *two* Bibles before him and by quoting the prophet Micah. And, throughout, the speech was sprinkled with religious language. He declared that the inauguration attested to the "spiritual" strength of the nation, that there was "a new spirit among us all," that "ours was the first society openly to define itself in terms of . . . spirituality," etc. He used the word "spirit" 7 times and other clearly religious words — "pray," "moral," "religious," etc. — an additional 27 times.

In addition to his Christian faith, Carter asserted his faith in the nation and in the American people. He seemed to ask the citizens to have that same faith in him. In this manner he became a missionary with his own church of political believers. He had made a commitment to America; in return, he sought a commitment from the people. Again, the religious overtones drowned out the political ones.

At the end of the speech the president listed six goals. Although they were stated in the past tense, the aphoristic form made them resemble the Ten Commandments. One statement followed another without explication, each with its own ideology, each pertaining to moral and spiritual issues. Any could be converted from aphorism to commandment by replacing "that we had" with "thou shalt." "That we had strengthened the American family," then, would become, "Thou shalt strengthen the American family."

Clearly, Carter was deflecting our attention from the political to the religious world. Yet he may have overdone it. We Americans do not like to be preached to; the descriptive phrase for somebody who does so is the negatively toned "preachy." While we expect a little religion to be interspersed in our political addresses, when the religious references become overbearing we get nervous about unbending fanaticism.

IDEOLOGICALLY CORRECT

The forms into which presidents choose, or are internally forced, to place their arguments, then, obviously are important, but are they purely idiosyncratic? That is, are the forms determined solely by reference to unknown, highly personal characteristics or are forms determined in part by political ideology? Do liberals and conservatives tend to gravitate to certain predictable forms? The evidence is not all in yet; in fact, it has hardly begun to be collected.

For instance, some of the most common-sense notions about metaphors and ideology have not even been tested yet: Do conservatives utilize more rural metaphors than liberals? Do conservatives utilize more Biblical metaphors than liberals? Since sports metaphors are basically competitive, are they more useful in supporting *laissez faire* positions than welfare state formulations? Do liberals rely on metaphors of becoming (what humans can become) while conservatives rely on metaphors of being (what humans are) or of heritage (what humans were)? Do conservatives utilize more familial metaphors than liberals? Do the land and property metaphors in our national tradition predispose us to conservatism? etc.

While very little research along these lines has been reported, minor preliminary work on sloganeering would seem to indicate that there may be political differences in rhetorical form. Compare, for instance, these four slogans of the Right, "If guns are outlawed, only outlaws will have guns," "Support your local police," "America — love it or leave it," and "Honor America," with four from the Left, "Free the Soledad Brothers," "Right on," "Up the revolution," and "Power to the people." Beyond the obvious ideological content, are there differences?

> It is notable, first, that all the slogans of the right form complete sentences, atomic syntactic units whose metaphoric force arises from the involutions of the syntax itself. The slogans of the left, on the other hand, tend to be sentence-fragments, elements rather than units of meaning, depending upon the ambiguity of their unstated context for their power. Listening to the right, in other words, one feels the force of prepared and authoritative pronouncements; listening to the left, one has the impression of having entered into an ongoing and not always verbalized conversation.[26]

Perhaps there are other differences, perhaps the ones identified here are superfluous and could not be duplicated with other, more randomly drawn, samples of Right and Left discourse. But it appears a promising avenue. If there are correlations between preferred language forms and ideological positions, and if we want to understand the language of politics, this kind of minute examination will have to continue.

CONCLUSION

One of the bizarre effects of language is that the speaker comes to believe his or her own language. Undoubtedly, Ronald Reagan probably believes he has placed a "safety net" under the poor and that he has slammed shut a "window of vulnerability." Thus, language that is ostensibly descriptive can shade into self-fulfilling prophecies. For instance, President Carter's use of language as self-fulfilling prophecies seems to have been related to his whole desire for and promise of trust. In the Carter lexicon, we are what we think we are; our feelings capture reality; our programs are as we describe them. We must trust ourselves, our feelings, our solutions. Then, as we see how well everything works, we will be able to trust each other and, eventually, even trust our government. Somehow, the key to this whole political approach was revealed and reflected in his language. It was, in a sense, the politics of biofeedback wherein trust and confidence flowed from actions, but successful actions flowed from trust and confidence. So the most logical, because the easiest, point at which to begin to repair the damage to public confidence was the rhetorical. Hence the "trust me" campaign of 1976, the symbolism of his first year, the 1978 presentation of the liberation of the Panama Canal as an act of atonement, the malaise speech of 1979, and perhaps even his overall preference for the straightforward and banal rather than the eloquent.

Unfortunately for Carter, the result was merely that he was seen as lacking eloquence, and his "plain" style was heard as one that reduced

> great phrases into banalities. Lincoln's "we must think anew and act anew. We must disenthrall ourselves" degenerated into Carter's "we must change our attitudes as well as our policies." And the Founding Fathers' ringing pledge of "our lives, our fortunes and our sacred honor" became, in Mr. Carter's pallid paraphrase, "their property, position, and life itself."[27]

So Carter was defeated in 1980 and Ronald Reagan read his overwhelming victory as a mandate for his announced programs. Yet we would argue that the Carter-Reagan-(Anderson) race was determined largely on the basis of images constructed from their differing rhetorical forms.

While it is a banality to say that form and content are wedded, we hope we have been able to demonstrate that the old truism is not necessarily true. But beyond the question of the truth of the form-content equation, a greater problem is that rhetorical critics have tended to mouth the truism then go on to examine the content without considering the form. Thus we know little of the hows and whys of form, and it is free to work its magic unbeknownst to us. Like Tom Robbins's unfortunate lady, we miss out on the action because we do not know the score.

NOTES

1. Tom Robbins, *Still Life with Woodpecker* (New York: Bantam, 1980), p. 11.

2. Archibald A. Hill, "Analogies, Icons and Images in Relation to Semantic Content of Discourses," *Style* 2 (1968):209.

3. Christopher I. Johnstone, "Thoreau and Civil Disobedience: A Rhetorical Paradox," *Quarterly Journal of Speech* 60 (1974):313–314.

4. Richard M. Weaver, *The Ethics of Rhetoric* (Chicago: Regnery, 1953), p. 112.

5. Jack Beatty, "The President's Mind," *The New Republic*, April 7, 1982, p. 12.

6.   Ronald H. Carpenter, "The Symbolic Substance of Style in Presidential Discourse," *Style* 16 (1982):39.

7.   Gary C. Woodward, "Toward a Model of Recurring Form in Presidential Rhetoric: An Overview" (Paper presented at Central States Speech Association convention, April 8, 1983), 13.

8.   Kenneth Burke, *The Philosophy of Literary Form; Studies in Symbolic Action*, 3rd ed. (Berkeley: University of California Press, 1973), p. 227.

9.   Terence Smith, "Jimmy Carter, Now the Insider, Dusts Off the Outsider Appeal," *The New York Times*, April 29, 1979, p. E4.

10.   Steven R. Brydon, "Outsider vs. Insider: The Two Faces of Jimmy Carter" (Paper presented at Western Speech Communication Association convention, February, 1981), 3.

11.   Ibid., p. 8.

12.   Ibid., p. 16.

13.   Woodward, "Toward a Model," p. 7.

14.   "Mr. Carter's World . . . Under Scrutiny," *The New York Times*, June 25, 1976, p. A26.

15.   George F. Will, "Jimmy Draws His Sword," *New York Post*, April 27, 1977, p. 35.

16.   J. Hillis Miller, "The Still Heart: Poetic Form in Wordsworth," *New Literary History* 2 (1971):305.

17.   Lucy Komisar, "You Won't Have Uncle Sam to Kick Around Any More," *The New York Times*, June 30, 1975, p. 29.

18.   Frank D. McConnell, "Toward a Lexicon of Slogans," *Midwest Quarterly* 13 (1971):80.

19.   Jimmy Carter, "Text of President Carter's Convention Address," *Chicago Tribune*, August 15, 1980, p. 2.

20.   Dan F. Hahn, "The Semi-Tough Language of the 1980 Presidential Campaign," *The Pennsylvania Speech Communication Annual* 38 (1982):41–45.

21.   Kenneth Burke, *A Grammar of Motives* (New York: Prentice-Hall, 1945), p. 393.

22.   Murray Edelman, "Myths, Metaphors, and Political Conformity," *Psychiatry* 30 (1967):226.

23.   James Reston, "Revival Meeting," *The New York Times*, January 21, 1977, p. A23.

24.   Hedrick Smith, "A Call to the American Spirit," *The New York Times*, January 21, 1977, p. A1.

25.   Anthony Hillbruner, "Born Again: Carter's Inaugural Sermon" (Paper presented at Speech Communication Association convention, December, 1977).

26.   McConnell, "Toward a Lexicon," p. 82.

27.   William Safire, "The New Foundation," *The New York Times*, January 25, 1979, p. E21.

Part II

COMMUNICATION DIMENSIONS OF THE PRESIDENCY

Chapter 3

INTERPERSONAL DIMENSIONS OF THE AMERICAN PRESIDENCY

White House staff members are chosen, not according to any geographical, political, or other pattern, but for their ability to serve the President's needs and to talk the President's language.

Theodore Sorensen

Although the president is a single individual, the presidency, as an institution, is comprised of many people. To be close to the president is to be in a position of power, recognition, and social status. From these people we seek to know the "true nature" of the occupant — his likes and dislikes, his daily routine, and his darkest secrets. And, those individuals closest to the president are also objects of curiosity. Why are they chosen? What do they do? How much influence do they possess?

In this chapter we are going to explore the interpersonal relationships of presidents and their staff. More specifically, we will investigate the key principles of interpersonal communication, the dynamics of a presidential staff, and the interpersonal communication styles and techniques of American presidents since Harry Truman. Such an investigation emphasizes the impact and importance of staff members upon an administration. And more importantly, while our presidents may be good public communicators, their communication skills behind closed doors between individuals are often lacking. Such skills will tell us more about the "true nature" of the occupant.

INTERPERSONAL COMMUNICATION DEFINED

One way of classifying or understanding communication is according to the number of people involved in the transaction. This approach provides four general orientations: intrapersonal, interpersonal, group, and mass communication. Intrapersonal communication focuses on communication behavior significant to the individual and is the focus of Chapter 4. Interpersonal communication focuses on face-to-face interaction between two or more people. Small group communication, discussed in Chapter 5, usually focuses on the interaction of three to twelve individuals. And mass communication, the focus of Chapter 6, involves large groups communicating through the mass media.

The study of interpersonal communication is the study of relationships among persons. The basic element is the face-to-face interaction between two people. There are two primary functions of interpersonal communication activities.[1] The social function results from the pure pleasure and satisfaction of interaction. Its purpose is to build and maintain relationships. The decision-making function of interpersonal communication serves to exchange information, process information, and influence the attitudes and behaviors of others. It is the latter function that concerns us most in relation to presidential interpersonal communication.

There are several distinct characteristics of interpersonal communication.[2]

1. It is dynamic. Participants are both sending and receiving signals continually and simultaneously.
2. It is interactive. It follows that in interpersonal communication there is mutual influence and interdependence between the participants. Each person is constantly aware of the other and assumes the roles of both sender and receiver which involves constant adaptation and adjustment.
3. It is proactive. Interpersonal communication involves the total person. An individual's beliefs, attitudes, values, social background, and previous transactions all influence the nature of the interaction.
4. It is contextual. It follows from the previous characteristic that environmental and situational factors also influence interaction.
5. It is irreversible. Each utterance becomes part of the social history between individuals and helps define future utterances and behavior.

Interpersonal communication, because it is between only two individuals, would appear to be the most simple form of communication activity. This is not true. Interpersonal communication is complex for several reasons. As already mentioned, interpersonal communication involves the whole person. Each participant brings social and psychological "baggage" to the interaction. The content of the interaction is most often personal, intimate, and revealing. Meanings are relational, derived from past experience. To successfully "transfer" meanings to another requires shared experience, mutual understanding, and general agreement on the words that represent the spectrum of experience. Through the interaction participants are trying to maintain self-image, social role consistency, and situational definitions. The forms of dyadic communication range from the most social (intimate) to the most formal (interview) to the most stressful (interrogation). And there are greater risks in interpersonal communication — risks of rejection, withdrawal, exposure, and weakness.

Dan Rothwell and James Costigan recognize three distinct levels of interpersonal communication.[3] The instrumental level of interpersonal communication is directive in nature. On this level, much business is conducted. The superior or boss conveys information, establishes goals, and assigns tasks. This level characterizes, obviously, the majority of presidential interpersonal communication. The manipulative level attempts to seduce favors, action, or consensus with other individuals. This level is, perhaps, the most intriguing. In the last chapter, we argued that persuasion is the essential activity of the presidency. As noted in Chapter 2, presidents differ greatly in their skills of persuasion. The most successful president on this level of interpersonal communication was Lyndon Johnson. He was masterful at getting legislation through Congress and aides to remain loyal. Jimmy Carter, as we will discuss later, spent little time on this level of interpersonal communication to the detriment of his administration. Finally, on the expressive level, individuals share their thoughts, ideas, and feelings through more creative and artistic forms of communication. It is generally recognized that John Kennedy, as an author, journalist, and patron of the arts greatly appreciated the expressive function of literature and drama. He often utilized these forms both in public and private forums.

Interpersonal communication is the tool for achieving three basic interpersonal needs: inclusion, control, and affection.[4] Humans, as social animals, need to be with others. Even so, according to William Schutz, humans differ in the degree and intensity of involvement with others.[5] At one extreme, introverts withdraw and often even fear social interaction. Often the basis for such behavior is the fear of rejection and denial. The social risks prevent interaction. The other extreme, the extrovert, is overly social and continually seeks others. But this type of individual is also problematic. Such individuals are usually overcompensating for feelings of insecurity, low self-esteem, and desperately seeking validation. Of course, the true social individual is one who not only has successful relations with others but also can be either a high or low participator without fear or anxiety.

Several scholars suggest that most of our contemporary presidents have been social extroverts. Psychologically they have been characterized as overachievers, "mommy's boy," possessing low self-esteem.[6] Others argue that our political process itself tends to encourage extroverts to run for the office.[7] These observations are indeed interesting when considering that nearly every president characterizes the job as lonely and isolating. As we will discuss later, most of our contemporary presidents restricted their access to a very few individuals and Lyndon Johnson could not stand to be alone.

Whether or not presidents have a greater need for control than other citizens, the fact remains that the job does require a strong personality. In terms of control, the general public values strong leadership and will reject a submissive president, but few presidents could be truly classified as democratic. With an electoral mandate, they perceive their job as one of providing direction and giving orders, not following and taking orders from others. Hence, our presidents are more autocratic, domineering, power seeking, who expect a rather clear hierarchy of power and control.

Even so, however, Bobby Patton and Kim Giffin recognize several manipulative relationship styles.[8] The *nurturing* style closely resembles that of a mother and son. Underlying the relationship is a strong versus weak dichotomy. This style characterizes the presidency of Richard Nixon. In the face of adversity, Nixon would exhibit strength, determination, and fortitude. He was, until the end, protective and loyal to his staff. Nixon took care of his own.

The *supporting* style shares characteristics of a father and daughter relationship. There tends to be greater mutual trust between the participants. The Reagan presidency characterizes this style. Reagan empowers his staff with the day to day details of administration. He is not only loyal to his staff but also trusts them. There is an ideological and social bond between Reagan and his closest staff members. Many have been with him for years.

The *challenging* style exhibits the extremes of "bitch" and nice guy, love and hate, calm and anger. Nearly every book on Lyndon Johnson describes the "Johnson treatment" noting his extremes of emotion, attitudes, and feelings. All of his staff were subjected to bouts of anger and love, friendliness and rejection.

The *educating* style resembles the master and servant relationship. Even with affection, there is a clear superior-subordinate relationship, with the master possessing all the knowledge, answers, and solutions to problems and daily life. Jimmy Carter possessed a strong belief in his knowledge of America's problems and the best solutions to those problems. Even the title of his book, *Why Not the Best*, suggests a single and "right" solution to America's problems. Carter believed that to identify a problem and articulate a solution was all that was needed for Congress to pass appropriate legislation and to generate public support. He soon discovered that self-evident wisdom and rationality were not enough.

The *confronting* style is characterized by fierce competition and questioning. Franklin Roosevelt drilled his staff, seeking information, perspectives, and alternatives to various issues or dilemmas. He actually encouraged confrontation and competition among his staff.

Finally, within the manipulating relationship style is the mild *accommodating* style where true feelings may be suppressed and harmony is valued above all else. As will be discussed in greater detail, Gerald Ford did not like conflict. He found it difficult to fire staff members and would not do so directly.

The strong need for control plus the hierarchical nature of the presidency does influence the nature and flow of communication.[9] Communication between equals flows much more readily than downward to subordinates or upward from subordinates to superiors. Also, the quantity of messages sent downward are greater in a hierarchical structure. Those lower in the hierarchy will certainly be more cautious about messages sent upward and will avoid being the one sharing "bad" news. Interestingly, those of high status assume that they are clearly understood while those of lower status tend to distort messages received from above in such a way as to fit their purposes. Finally, the simple fact is that people at the extremes of a hierarchy do not talk to each other.

The human need for affection also differs greatly among people. The degree of affection we have for people depends on several factors: accessibility, commitment, and reciprocity of the relationship. Other than anger or outrage, presidents seldom demonstrate emotion in public. But it appears that even in private, presidents seldom demonstrate genuine affection for close staff members.

There are three general types of dialogue in interpersonal communication.[10] Technical dialogue serves primarily for the transmission and reception of information. Pseudo dialogue is self-centered, attempting to satisfy our own needs for interaction. Others become more of a "sounding board" than a partner in conversation. In genuine dialogue, however, we engage in personal sharing with others who are viewed as equal in status and importance.

Finally, conflict is another area of concern for scholars of interpersonal communication. The basic concept is that poor communication results in conflict. There are many kinds, types, and degrees of interpersonal conflict. For our purposes, it is interesting to note how individuals approach conflict.[11] Lyndon Johnson did not avoid interpersonal conflict. In fact, some even suggest he enjoyed arguments. From Johnson's perspective, he had to "win" at all costs. To lose would be a sign of failure and personal weakness. One was either with him or against him. Gerald Ford, however, was more of a friendly helper in conflict, seeking harmony among his staff. He was genuinely sensitive to the feelings of others and would even alter or undervalue his own goals in order to avoid major conflict. Jimmy Carter exhibited a compromise style in dealing with staff conflict. He sought the middle ground, allowing each side to gain something in the outcome. It appears that John Kennedy's style of conflict resolution closely resembled that of Jimmy Carter. Kennedy viewed conflict as natural and useful. He encouraged discussions in the spirit of trust and openness. Ultimately, he sought to integrate the goals of all parties to the satisfaction of those participants. Ronald Reagan, even more so than Gerald Ford, appears to simply detest conflict among his staff. He has no use for conflict and will flee a conflict scene rather than endure. Such situations, if they arise, are handled by staff.

Most presidential interpersonal conflict is over message content, that is, definitions, policy goals, or interpretations of fact. Seldom are such conflicts over values. And frequently, because of the powerful position of the White House staff, conflicts are of an ego nature. At the heart of such conflicts are questions of an individual's perceived status and self worth. Each of these concepts will be illustrated in much greater detail as we focus on the interpersonal communication styles of specific contemporary presidents.

PRESIDENTIAL STAFF AND INTERPERSONAL COMMUNICATION

John Kennedy wrote, in the middle of his presidency, "a president must choose among men, among measures, among methods. His choice helps determine the issues of his presidency, their priority in the national life, and the mode and success of their execution."[12] Theodore Sorensen, however, believes that the nature of the presidential staff tells us a great deal about the president. "A president must be judged in part on whom he is willing to take into his house, there to invoke his name and use his telephone — and affect our lives."[13] Franklin Roosevelt chose people mainly from government and journalism, Truman chose veteran public servants, Eisenhower from business, and Kennedy from governmental agencies and universities.[14] Essentially, the ultimate success or failure of staff members depends upon the success or failure of the president.

The Executive Office of the president was established in 1939. Franklin Roosevelt's Committee on Administrative Management declared that "the president needs help." The Executive Office was created to:[15]

1. ensure that the chief executive is adequately and currently informed;
2. assist him in foreseeing problems and planning future programs;
3. ensure that matters for his decision reach his desk promptly, in condition to be settled intelligently and without delay, and to protect him against hasty and ill considered judgments;
4. exclude every matter that can be settled elsewhere in the system;
5. protect his time;
6. secure means of ensuring compliance by subordinates with established policy and executive direction.

In essence, the staff serves as the president's "eyes, ears, and mouth." In addition, they function as liaisons between the executive branch and Congress, the public, and media. In reality, however, Emmet Hughes claims that key members of a president's staff lack political experience and are there to serve the *personal* needs of the chief executive. "The staff," according to Hughes, "is less concerned with presidential conscience than with presidential comfort."[16] This primary purpose of performing personal services to the president, George Reedy argues, is "a president's most persistent problem in staying in touch with reality."[17] He claims that "the first strong observations to attract the favor of the president become subconsciously the thoughts of everyone in the room."[18] Reedy further notes that a president can be rude, insulting, and even sadistic to close advisors and friends and their only response is most likely to be, "How fortunate that he has people around him who understand the tremendous burdens he is carrying."[19] The presidential staff, then, provides a protective screen around the White House isolating the president from reality. In short, the goal is to please — not to challenge the president. Thus, the original intent of the executive staff has developed into what Hughes describes as the "paradox of the White House Staff." "Where it should be utterly invaluable, it may be nearly insidious. When it should make a president frown, it may prefer to make him laugh. And while its essential role is to keep a president awake and alert, the easier course, always, is to let him drowse."[20]

Interestingly, Michael Medved suggests that presidents and their assistants *should not* be personally close friends. He offers the following ground rules:[21]

1. A president should select a staff whose goals and experience involve more than one individual.
2. Staff members should avoid publicity.
3. Emotional dependence by a president upon his staff should be avoided.

The public usually perceives presidents as men with many friends and who enjoy frequent interpersonal contacts. In reality, this assumption too appears to be falacious. John Kennedy is quoted as saying, "In politics there are no friends, only allies."[22] The truth is that contemporary presidents differ greatly in their desire for and skills in interpersonal relations. For Barbara Kellerman, this dimension is critical to presidential leadership. She argues that a truly successful president must have "an affinity for other persons, some reasonable investment in others, and ... at least a modest ability to perform effectively in interpersonal situations."[23] Thus, an introvert is dysfunctional to our political system.

By focusing on individual president's styles of interpersonal communication we may gain an insight into their personalities and their perceptions of their roles as president.

Harry Truman

Power, according to Harry Truman, is one of three things that can ruin a man. Money and women are the others. "If a man can accept a situation in a place of power with the thought that it's only temporary, he comes out all right. But when he thinks he is the *cause* of the power, that can be his ruination."[24]

The vast majority of Truman's staff were close friends. He referred to his staff as his "crew" and they felt secure in saying what they thought. Sometimes, at the morning staff meetings, arguments would occur and

Truman himself would get angry. But Truman treated his staff as a family. He appreciated the "friendships" and took pride in the fact that of his staff "not one of them went out and wrote a book on me."[25] While in his office, Truman refused to use the "buzzers" on his desk to summon people. Rather, he would go out to the aide's office and request to see someone. In addition, he most often greeted the person at the door of his office. It was this lack of egotism that generated loyalty among his staff. Truman valued humility in others and thus tried to act accordingly. If a staff member would abuse the special access to the president, according to Margaret Truman, the president would serve as an "ego deflator."[26]

Interestingly, at home, Truman seldom raised his voice and preferred to play a peacemaker's role. Although Truman never avoided a political conflict or decision, at home he "made a point of avoiding arguments."[27]

Dwight Eisenhower

In contrast to Truman, Eisenhower's interpersonal communication was primarily instrumental in nature. In terms of his staff, the flow was generally unidirectional with Eisenhower providing "fervent sermons" on general policies and direction.[28] As is well known, his staff was strictly structured. Areas of responsibility were clearly defined and work or tasks were delegated. Personally, Eisenhower detested "aggressive politics" and would avoid direct personal critiques. He had few close, intimate friends. Sherman Adams was perhaps the most powerful presidential aide in history. He had daily and total access to the president as well as the president's trust. Yet, unlike other presidents and key staff members, Adams and Eisenhower never developed a genuine intimacy.[29] It was simply not his style. It was not so much viewed as a sign of weakness but a fact of military command. Although a broad generalization, the quality and quantity of interpersonal communication for Eisenhower appears to be limited.

John Kennedy

John Kennedy wanted to counter the administrative style of the Eisenhower administration. He felt that Eisenhower was actually a slave to the rather strict White House procedures established.[30] Kennedy abandoned the idea of a collective, institutionalized presidency. The corporate model of decision-making was replaced by a more informal, individual process. Weekly staff meetings and cabinet meetings were abolished. Organizational charts and chains of command were ignored. He was simply not interested in committee recommendations. Kennedy preferred informal "give and takes" and direct contacts. Even the cabinet was largely convened as a symbol. As members, they were to be informed, not consulted.[31] Kennedy's self-reliance and confidence "freed him from dependence on orderly administrative arrangements."[32] Such a drastic change in administrative style was not surprising. In his first state of the union address he called for "dissent and daring" in the permanent government.[33]

In terms of his staff, Kennedy wanted a small and personal staff. Although areas of responsibility were recognized they were not exclusive. Kennedy served as his own chief of staff. He implemented the concept of a "wheel and series of spokes."[34] His primary advisors were equal in pay, stature, and access to his office. And, in addition, his principal staff members shared Kennedy's worldviews and policy objectives.

From all indications, it appears that Kennedy genuinely enjoyed rather private and informal interaction. Newspeople and ambassadors who had come to his office for "business" soon found themselves being intensely interviewed. Even "his conversations with visitors sometimes turned to a kind of nineteenth-century court gossip about public figures and private lives, astonishing strangers from all fields with his curiosity about the personalities and politics of their professions, his knowledge of high and low goings-on, and his willingness to spend time in lighthearted conversations."[35]

Kennedy was a good listener. Seldom, even in important cabinet meetings, would he expound his own beliefs. Rather, he would listen to all sides, all ideas, and ask questions. He did not want his position to stifle input. He was, according to Secret Service Chief Baughman, more egalitarian than Truman.[36]

Kennedy also tried to maintain an open and informal office environment. No appointments were necessary to see him. Daily, an hour before lunch and the last hour of the afternoon, Kennedy's office door was "open for business." Staff members would pop in and were welcomed.[37]

Although Kennedy had a good relationship with his staff, according to Theodore Sorensen, the president did not often express open gratitude but showed his appreciation by being intensely loyal. He would not hesitate to defend staff members in public if they were criticized or their actions questioned.

Perhaps the best assessment of Kennedy's interpersonal communication style is provided by close, personal aide Sorensen: "He was informal without being chummy, hard-driving but easy mannered, interested in us as people without being patronizing. While neither he nor we ever forgot that he bore the responsibilities of leadership, he treated us more as colleagues or associates than employees. He made clear that we were there to give advice as well as to take orders."[38] Thus, Kennedy encouraged interaction, recognized the value of others, and exhibited characteristics that would encourage interpersonal relations.

Lyndon Johnson

Lyndon Johnson truly enjoyed interpersonal communication. According to Jack Valenti, there was no dichotomy between working or social friends.[39] Johnson always preferred to keep separate the public and private sides of his personality. But by early 1964, the press was beginning to portray him as a "whiskey drinking, Texas primitive, who told dirty jokes and mistreated his Secret Service bodyguards."[40]

Upon the death of Kennedy, Johnson felt it was important for him to maintain members of the Kennedy staff. To do so, Kearns reports that Johnson used all his interpersonal charm, wit, and influence.[41] Before talking to each member, he would plan his approach. He would evoke Kennedy's name and use a mixture of rational and emotional argument as had been his forte in his years on Capitol Hill.

But what becomes the key characteristic of Johnson's relationship with his staff was his rather frequent verbal tirades. They were often very intense and in the presence of others. Kearns suggests that Johnson "needed to make his staff look ridiculous: that he was strengthened by his exposure of inadequacies in others."[42] Such fits of temper were not limited to his staff. Evans and Novak report that when A. Z. Bhutto, Pakistan's foreign minister, in a meeting with Johnson was critical of U.S. policy, Johnson "dressed him down as he had reporters who had written stories displeasing him."[43] Yet, Johnson could demonstrate gratitude by presenting staff members with lavish gifts. But soon another outpouring of abuse would follow. "To Johnson," according to George Reedy, "loyalty was a one-way street: all take on his part and all give on the part of everyone else."[44]

Staff members, however, largely tolerated the "hot/cold" treatment. For some, Johnson served as a strict father figure. For others, the genius of the social legislation made the sacrifice worth the effort. And for others there was genuine admiration. Bill Moyers even wanted to name his third son "Lyndon Johnson Moyers."[45]

To ensure staff loyalty, Johnson took three actions. First, he avoided fixed staff assignments giving overlapping jurisdictions. Second, he reduced the staff's access to the media. All information, interviews, etc. were to come from the Oval Office or so directed. Finally, he would keep staff members off guard by giving limitless praise one minute and total destruction the next.[46]

The keys to Johnson's interpersonal power were his reliance upon psychological techniques and preparation. For him, there were no casual meetings. According to Reedy, Johnson "was an intensely serious man with intensely serious purposes. He was absolutely convinced that achievement was possible only through careful negotiation in quiet backrooms where public passions could not intrude."[47] Before visitors would arrive his staff would provide a great deal of background information. Then the meetings would be carefully staged: a casual walk around the Rose Garden, a private drink in the president's study, and the sharing of a personalized message or appeal. Legislators especially were made to feel a part of the decision-making process.

But the very factors that made his efforts successful also kept him from having genuine, satisfying interpersonal relations. Johnson had to be always in control and clearly "boss." He alone would set topics or issues for discussion and even would review guest lists. Martin Luther King, Jr. is quoted as saying that when you went to talk with Kennedy, he made you do all the talking, when you talked to Johnson, he did all the talking.[48] His desires took top priority and all were expected to drop everything in order to meet his demands.[49] Ronnie Dugger relates an incident when "from the oval office he went into the bathroom adjacent, leaving the door open behind him. Around the corner from me loud expulsive sounds mixed in with his continuous talking. One of his young men squatted down just outside the open door and made notes. Another was hovering around him somewhere inside the bathroom."[50]

Finally, for Johnson, all communication was a means to an end. As Reedy observes, "he was totally devoid of small talk. Worse, he had no concept of the social usefulness of small talk."[51] Reedy relates that on one occasion an interviewer, to break the ice, asked Johnson about life in the White House. Johnson responded by shouting "What kind of a chicken-shit question is that to ask the leader of the free world?"[52]

Thus, Johnson did not endear himself to others. His need for control, dominance, and the humiliating frequent tirades prevented "quality" interpersonal relations. Dugger best characterizes Johnson as "rude, intelligent, shrewd, charming, compassionate, vindictive, maudlin, selfish, passionate, volcanic and cold, vicious, and generous."[53]

Richard Nixon

Nixon, too, was not successful at interpersonal communication, but for different reasons. Like Johnson, Nixon's White House was one of control. Nixon believed that all events and activities must be managed.[54] But Nixon did not like face-to-face interaction. He was uncomfortable with talking to relative strangers.[55] Nixon, throughout his career, avoided personal invasion of privacy or exposure. He sought privacy and solitude. Nixon, in fact, had *nine* private offices among the White House, Camp David, Key Biscayne, and San Clemente.[56] It is ironic that for a president so jealous of his own privacy, Nixon installed the most elaborate taping system ever, thus invading the privacy of everyone entering his offices.

Nixon was equally unsuccessful, according to Ehrlichman, in managing his cabinet.[57] Members were constantly arguing among themselves and Nixon's treatment of them did not help appeals for unity. By the spring of 1970, even Vice-President Agnew told the president that he should consult with cabinet members more. In terms of access, Nixon would invite cabinet members to the White House but secretaries could never invite themselves. He considered the cabinet to be extensions of the president's staff, to provide public relations and give advice — only when asked.

Nixon found it difficult to express emotion in front of others — even family. He projected a "cold" and "tough" exterior. According to Eli Chesen, Nixon had an exaggerated sense of self-importance.[58] His job demanded that he alone make the tough choices and decisions. If there were to be a savior, he was it. Accordingly, Nixon would not tolerate being corrected or proven wrong.

Psychologically, Nixon truly had low self-esteem. To relate to others was risky. Faults and self-doubt were easily seen. Thus, Nixon's paranoid tendencies are fairly well documented.[59] Fellow politicians could not be trusted. As a loner, even his wife was kept somewhat at a distance.

Because he was an introvert, according to the argument of Kellerman, the Nixon presidency was doomed for problems.[60] Nevertheless, Nixon lacked interpersonal communication skills, primarily by choice.

Gerald Ford

The Gerald Ford White House was indeed different from the Nixon White House. It is not surprising that Ford greatly admired Truman. In many respects, they were similar in style.

As with most new presidents, Ford wanted his staff to function as the "spokes of the wheel." He would be his own chief of staff. But, as Ford reveals in his memoirs, it is impossible to have a true open-door policy.[61] In terms of staff, Ford declares that "most presidents need and use their 'friends' as key members of the White House Staff because it reduces risk, ensures loyalty, and there is familiarity."[62]

As a leader, Ford can best be characterized as an "accommodator" and "compromiser." His many years in Congress taught him the value of working with people. Consequently, Ford did not like conflict or hurting people.[63] At one point, Barber Conable, a colleague in the House of Representatives, wrote "you should control the staff rather than letting the staff control you."[64] Richard Reeves perceives this aspect as one of weakness; working with people is not leadership.[65]

But perhaps no president showed as much respect for staff members as Ford. He never stood on ceremony with staff members and would encourage open dialogue on all subjects. In addition, he would end each meeting with a "thank you" or by saying "good-bye."[66]

It appears that Ford enjoyed good interpersonal communication with staff members. He treated them well, with mutual respect. The environment encouraged open discussion. And perhaps more importantly, Gerald Ford enjoyed communicating and being with others.

Jimmy Carter

Jimmy Carter professed a love for people and a genuine concern for his fellow man. But Carter also shared personality characteristics of both Nixon and Johnson.

Carter very early decided to take some of the "talented Georgians" with him to Washington. He was well aware of the criticisms of Roosevelt, Truman, Kennedy, and others for appointing their "cronies" to White House positions. Carter decided, however, "without any doubt that my predecessors had chosen wisely. The selection of loyal and well-known associates is the result of a need for maximum mutual confidence and a minimum of jealousy and backbiting within a president's inner circle."[67]

Carter was especially close to Jody Powell, his press secretary. He relates that they had "long talks, and sometimes fierce arguments, hammering out decisions together."[68] Jody was allowed to criticize and help with all planning. Carter also exhibited concern for his staff's general welfare. According to Hamilton Jordan, after a few months in office, Carter called his staff together and told them not to work such long hours. They were instructed to pace themselves, lead more balanced lives, and spend more time with their families.[69]

But despite Carter's public professions and genuine concern for others, he seemed clearly to lack interpersonal skills. He never really let many people become close. He was, on a daily basis, somewhat detached. In the words of Theodore White, Carter "loved humankind — but he gave his love and affection to very few individual members of humankind. He was always remote and distant. . . . It is better for a sovereign to be feared than loved. Carter achieved neither."[70]

Carter acknowledged that he preferred receiving questions, suggestions, and advice in writing rather than short visits or oral discussions. Such an approach saved time and was more efficient. At the beginning, Carter did meet with his cabinet for a couple of hours every Monday so they could "get to know each other." Although Carter encouraged a "collegial" approach, he did not want cabinet or other meetings to become "bull sessions." Nevertheless, he "sometimes permitted people to come into a discussion just so they would not be embarrassed or upset about being excluded."[71]

Betty Glad argues that Carter really didn't have an inclination toward bargaining or compromise.[72] He simply preferred not to bargain but to give direction, provide solutions. He would often threaten congressional leaders of "going over their heads to the American people." But Carter was not successful with this strategy. He both alienated Congress and failed to mobilize the American people.

While Nixon was more closed, Kellerman describes Carter as an introvert.[73] He considered himself an outsider to Washington, to politics as usually practiced. Kellerman suggests that Carter's preference for jogging was because he had no friends to share in sport activities. Carter developed a skill in face-to-face encounters and negotiation but possessed no natural bent toward such activities.

The portrait we get of Carter is one who sincerely liked people but was uncomfortable in interpersonal situations. As a loner, he simply preferred solitude to being part of a group.

Ronald Reagan

At this writing, Ronald Reagan still has over two years remaining in office. While much has been reported about the Reagan White House, it is without benefit of historical analysis and hindsight. Nevertheless, we can make several observations about Reagan's interpersonal communication style. He appears to be somewhere between Presidents Truman and Carter. His view of the presidency influences his style of management. Reagan views himself, according to Lou Cannon, as "a leader, communicator, executive decision-maker, chairman of the board."[74] But he places a great deal of importance upon his staff. He sought aides who would suit his own personality and thus enable him to run the office without conflict or strain. Reagan required three broad characteristics. First, key staffers were to be close personal friends. Second, he demanded a unity of purpose and ideology for the administration. Finally, loyalty was essential.[75]

As a result, there is a mutual trust and respect between Reagan and key staff members. They are free to be honest and open and Reagan usually accepts the staff's recommendations without changes. He is confident that issues have been thoroughly discussed in a series of small groups. He favors these "back and forth" discussions rather than briefing papers. Reagan also encourages staff and cabinet members to comment or offer advice on areas outside their expertise.

The key to Reagan's interpersonal style is the relationship he has with close staff members. The personal favorite of both Reagans was Michael Deaver. He functioned as a conciliator, a facilitator, and message carrier. Reagan is quoted as saying, "He and I have been together for so long that I think I almost instinctively know how he will react. And he knows that. And so, he has put confidence and trust in me and others in our structure see that, I am able to cut out an awful lot of time."[76]

Thus, within Reagan's inner circle, one can enjoy access, openness, and reciprocity in all areas. He enjoys friends and is intensely loyal. Yet, to outsiders or larger groups, his natural reserve may seem standoffish.

CONCLUSION

Scholars and the public alike tend to ignore the interpersonal skills of presidents. We only focus on the public speaking and mass communication skills of presidential candidates. Yet, we argue that there is value in understanding the interpersonal skills of candidates. Good interpersonal communication skills will result in smoother staff operations, a better touch with reality, and a more loyal staff.

We have also noted that some presidents have satisfactory interpersonal relations. They develop a mutual trust and respect for others. Some presidents, however, are loners and find it difficult to establish or maintain interpersonal relationships.

The office places great stress and demands upon the occupants. Much of the communication within the White House is "instrumental" and directive in nature. Too little is aimed at fulfilling the needs of inclusion and affection.

We can surmise that our contemporary presidents, while largely excelling in public communication, severely lack interpersonal skills. They tend to be autocratic, introverted, and self-centered. We are also suggesting that the pattern of interpersonal communication of potential presidential candidates would reveal to voters how they would handle crises, to what extent they would isolate themselves from reality, as well as their potential success in dealing with Congress.

NOTES

1. Kathleen Verderber and Rudolph Verderber, *Inter-act: Using Interpersonal Communication Skills* (Belmont, CA: Wadsworth, 1977), p. 13.

2. Every book on interpersonal communication provides such characteristics with very little variation of concepts. See David Mortensen, *Communication: The Study of Human Interaction* (New York: McGraw Hill, 1972), pp. 13–21.

3. Dan Rothwell and James Costigan, *Interpersonal Communication: Influences and Alternatives* (Columbus, Ohio: Charles Merrill, 1975), pp. 20–21.

4. William Schutz, "The Postulate of Interpersonal Needs" in *Messages*, ed. Jean Civikly (New York: Random House, 1977), pp. 174–184.

5. Ibid.

6. See James David Barber, *The Presidential Character* 2nd ed. (Englewood Cliffs, NJ: Prentice-Hall, 1977); Fawn Brodie, *Richard Nixon: The Shaping of His Character* (New York: W. W. Norton, 1981); Eli Chesen, *President Nixon's Psychiatric Profile* (New York: Medallion Books, 1973); Alan Elms, *Personality in Politics* (New York: Harcourt Brace Jovanovich, 1976); Fred Greenstein, *Personality and Politics* (New York: W. W. Norton, 1975); Doris Kearns, *Lyndon Johnson and the American Dream* (New York: Harper & Row, 1976); and Theodore White, *Breach of Faith* (New York: Atheneum, 1975).

7. See Bruce Buchanan, *The Presidential Experience* (Englewood Cliffs, NJ: Prentice-Hall, 1978); Godfrey Hodgson, *All Things to All Men* (New York: Touchstone Books, 1980); Michael Novak, *Choosing Our King* (New York:

Macmillan, 1974); Terry Sanford, *A Danger of Democracy* (Boulder, CO: Westview, 1981): and Richard Watson and Norman Thomas, *The Politics of the Presidency* (New York: John Wiley & Sons, 1983), especially pp. 99–129.

8. Bobby Patton and Kim Giffin, *Interpersonal Communication In Action*, 2nd ed. (New York: Harper & Row, 1977), pp. 375–377.

9. For further explanation see Rothwell and Costigan, *Interpersonal Communication*, p. 13.

10. Ibid.

11. The basis of this discussion is provided in Freda S. Sathre et al., *Let's Talk*, 3rd ed. (Glenview, IL: Scott, Foresman, 1980), pp. 116–118.

12. In the foreword of Theodore Sorensen, *Decision-Making in the White House* (New York: Columbia University Press, 1963), p. xii.

13. As quoted in Dom Bonafede, "White House Staffing: The Nixon-Ford Era" in *The Presidency Reappraised*, ed. Thomas Cronin and Rexford Tugwell (New York: Praeger, 1977), p. 152.

14. Emmet Hughes, *The Living Presidency* (New York: Penguin Books, 1974), p. 139.

15. Clinton Rossiter, *The American Presidency* (New York: Mentor Books, 1960), pp. 122–124.

16. Hughes, *The Living Presidency*, p. 143.

17. George Reedy, *The Twilight of the Presidency* (New York: World Publishing, 1970), p. 85.

18. Ibid., p. 12.

19. Ibid., p. 23.

20. Hughes, *The Living Presidency*, p. 145.

21. Michael Medved, *The Shadow Presidents* (New York: Times Books, 1979), p. 352.

22. As quoted in Thomas Cronin, *The State of the President* (Boston: Little, Brown, 1975), p. 64.

23. Barbara Kellerman, "Introversion in the Oval Office," in *Presidential Studies Quarterly*, vol. 13, no. 3 (Summer 1983):383–399.

24. As quoted in Merle Miller, *Plain Speaking* (New York: Putnam, 1974), p. 355.

25. Margaret Truman, *Harry S Truman* (New York: William Morrow, 1973), p. 451.

26. Ibid., p. 451.

27. Ibid., p. 3.

28. Emmet Hughes, "Eisenhower's Personality and Politics" in *The Eisenhower Era*, ed. Paul Holbo and Robert Sellen (Hinsdale, IL: The Dryden Press, 1974), pp. 111–118.

29. Medved, *The Shadow Presidents*, p. 246.

30. Garry Wills, "The Kennedy Imprisonment," *Ladies and Gentlemen: The President of the United States* (New York: The Atlantic Monthly, 1984), p. 3.

31. Theodore Sorensen, *Kennedy* (New York: Harper & Row, 1965), p. 283.

32. Arthur Schlesinger, *A Thousand Days* (New York: Houghton Mifflin, 1965), p. 685.

33. Ibid., p. 684.

34. Sorensen, *Kennedy*, p. 262.

35. Ibid., p. 373.

36. As quoted in Schlesinger, *A Thousand Days*, p. 673.

37. Ibid., p. 687.

38. Sorensen, *Kennedy*, p. 374.

39. Jack Valenti, *A Very Human President* (New York: W. W. Norton, 1975), p. 97.

40. Rowland Evans and Robert Novak, *Lyndon B. Johnson: The Exercise of Power* (New York: The New American Library, 1966), pp. 412–413.

41. Kearns, *Johnson and the American Dream*, p. 175.

42. Ibid., p. 176.

43. Evans and Novak, *Johnson: The Exercise of Power*, p. 384.

44. George Reedy, *Lyndon Johnson: A Memoir* (New York: Andrews and McMeel, 1982), p. x.

45. Medved, *The Shadow Presidents*, p. 296.

46. Kearns, *Johnson and the American Dream*, p. 238.

47. Reedy, *Lyndon Johnson*, p. 6.

48. Merle Miller, *Lyndon* (New York: Putnam, 1980), p. 345.

49. For excesses see Reedy, *Lyndon Johnson*.

50. Ronnie Dugger, *The Politician* (New York: W. W. Norton, 1982), p. 21.

51. Reedy, *Lyndon Johnson*, p. 82.

52. Ibid., p. 82.

53. Dugger, *The Politician*, p. 12.

54. White, *Breach of Faith*, p. 108.

55. See Medved, *The Shadow Presidents*, p. 310.

56. See Chesen, *Nixon's Psychiatric Profile*, p. 106 and Brodie, *Nixon: The Shaping of His Character*, p. 464.

57. See John Ehrlichman, *Witness to Power* (New York: Simon and Schuster, 1982), pp. 111–112.

58. Chesen, *Nixon's Psychiatric Profile*, p. 94.

59. For list of sources see Kellerman, "Introversion in the Oval Office."

60. Ibid., p. 388.

61. Gerald Ford, *A Time to Heal* (New York: Harper & Row, 1979), p. 147.

62. Ibid., p. 148.

63. See Richard Reeves, *A Ford, Not a Lincoln* (New York: Harcourt Brace Jovanovich, 1975), pp. 18, 75 and Ford, *A Time to Heal*, p. 184.

64. As quoted in Reeves, *A Ford, Not a Lincoln*, p. 127.

65. Ibid., p. 187.

66. Medved, *The Shadow Presidents*, p. 341.

67. Jimmy Carter, *Keeping Faith* (New York: Bantom Books, 1982), p. 41.

68. Ibid., p. 43.

69. Hamilton Jordan, *Crisis* (New York: Berkley Books, 1982), p. 48.

70. Theodore White, *America in Search of Itself* (New York: Harper & Row, 1982), p. 225.

71. Carter, *Keeping Faith*, pp. 58–60.

72. Betty Glad, *Jimmy Carter* (New York: Norton, 1980), p. 420.

73. Kellerman, "Introversion in the Oval Office," pp. 394–395.

74. Lou Cannon, *Reagan* (New York: Putnam, 1982), p. 375.

75. Richard Nathan, *The Administrative Presidency* (New York: John Wiley & Sons, 1983), p. 75.

76. As quoted in Cannon, *Reagan*, p. 377.

READINGS

INTRODUCTION

Chapter 3 explored the interpersonal relationships of presidents and their staff. While public communication skills are most important, their communication skills behind closed doors, between individuals is equally important and revealing. The first essay looks at the relationship between Congress and the president. That relationship has both objective and symbolic significance. The essay argues that primarily because of the symbolic supremacy of the presidency, Congress continues to lose its policy-making initiative.

The second essay suggests a communication model of presidential power that identifies and emphasizes the dynamic, relational, and interactive dimensions of political power. The model also describes four orientations or styles of presidential power.

The final essay, utilizing the basic principles of transactional analysis, investigates President Carter's energy message to the public with his energy message two days later before a joint session of Congress. In the former, he spoke as "parent to child," in the latter as an "adult to adult." The authors suggest that the public's general mistrust and lack of confidence in politicians may be due to their failure to address the public from an adult ego state. Reasons as to why presidential rhetoric appears to be parental are also discussed.

POLITICAL SYMBOLISM: CONGRESS VERSUS THE PRESIDENT

Every organization of national importance is bound to have a good deal of symbolic significance. Objective importance tends to be accompanied by symbolic importance — although the opposite is not true. That is, it is possible for something to be symbolically important but objectively insignificant (the hula hoop is a good example), although symbolic importance often generates an objective significance. At any rate, Congress is important — both objectively and symbolically. On the symbolic level its most important role is as a symbol of the idea of rational debate, *the* pre-eminent idea buttressing the theory of democracy (for, unless you believe people are rational and can reach decisions by exchanging rational arguments, you have very little reason to believe in democracy). A secondary, but related, congressional symbol is as a watchdog over the presumed dictatorial bent of any power-hungry president.

Congress has always been self-consciously concerned with following rituals which emphasize the rationality of their debate, especially those symbols that achieve decorum through courtesy:

Senators bear ancient and honorific titles that date from the days of Rome's glory. Members of both houses are entitled to preface their names with the distinctive term "the Honorable." . . . The opening of each session is marked by impressive ritual, including a prayer. Members speak of one another as "the distinguished member" (or senator), no matter how undistinguished, and the tradition is that remarks on the floor are never addressed in a personal manner to another member. All members are expected to behave with proper decorum.

Other important symbols are used: no one except members and legislative staff (and, in the Senate, former members) is allowed on the floor. Few members may be on the floor at any particular time, and they may be inattentive, but they are expected never to walk across the front of the rostrum. Spectators in the gallery are not permitted to talk or applaud. And affront to "the dignity" of either house is potentially contempt of Congress. The national popular assembly seeks always to maintain the ritual appearance of dignity and thoughtful reflection, no matter what the facts of the moment, because they symbolize its important democratic role.[1]

This is not to say, of course, that members never break these rules, but when they do they tend to "play" with the rules even as they are breaking them, as when John W. McCormack, then Speaker of the House, said of

Representative H. R. Gross, an Iowa Republican, "I hold the gentleman in minimum high regard."

The second major congressional symbolic role, that of watchdog, is based somewhat on the first, for it assumes that while Congress can be rational an unwatched executive will engage in irrational behavior. That irrational and potentially power-hungry executive branch, then, must be checked and balanced by the rational branch, the body with a large enough membership that power is effectively dispersed.

Thus, when presidential power and rationality seemed to be getting out of hand in the 1960s, Senator J. William Fulbright, defending his attack upon President Johnson's use of troops in the 1966 Dominican Republic uprising, pointed out that ". . . a highly controversial policy was being carried out without controversy — without debate, without review, without the necessary calling to account which is a vital part of the democratic process."[2] Thus began the long, slow process of reinvesting the Congress with some vigor (some would say, with some guts), a process helped by the Nixon impeachment and that is still going on (some would say, that has since stalemated). And throughout this debate, through the Dominican crisis, the Vietnam war, the passing of the War Powers Act, the Nixon impeachment, the salient symbol has been accountability, the power of Congress to exercise its checking and balancing function.

Riding the wave of that symbol, Congress has won a few battles with the president. Every time Congress wins a battle somebody in the media announces that Congress has "reasserted" itself. Even on the surface this would appear to be false, following the time-honored definition of news being when a man bites a dog. If we ever reach the point when the Dan Rathers of the media world express surprise when the president wins an occasional battle you can then believe that Congress has reasserted itself. In the meantime, you will be better informed if you believe the depiction, in 1975, of political scientist Malcolm Moos: "What we have been witnessing in the past three administrations is a form of cannibalism — the executive devouring part of the legislative branch and perhaps, in addition, a few vital organs of the Constitution."[3]

It seems clear that the presidency has gained the upper hand over Congress. And it has done so, on the objective level, through taking over the congressional bailiwick, policy-making. But before we get into that, consider the symbolic supremacy of the presidency. As an indication, think of the field of political humor. We have a good deal of humor regarding specific presidents, but not about the institutional office — the presidency. And very often one of the points of presidential humor is that the president in question is not quite noble enough for the office. Was that not the point being made by those who repeated Johnson's contention that Gerald Ford was the only man alive who couldn't walk and chew gum at the same time? The point is that specific presidents, and their families, are fair game; the presidency itself is inviolate. Congress, on the other hand, is the butt of many jokes. This may be because of an inherent defect, as there is something ludicrous about the possibility of 535 people establishing policy (as anyone who has ever served on a five-person committee can understand). As Mark Twain once remarked, we'll never need comedians as long as we have the United States Senate. And who can forget those most classic Twain lines: "Reader, suppose you were an idiot. And suppose you were a member of Congress. But I repeat myself."[4]

How did Congress fall into such low repute? The Founders thought they had established a system in which the executive could not achieve supremacy. What happened? Let us start at the beginning.

> The United States Constitution is specific in its vesting of "all legislative powers herein granted" in the two houses of Congress. . . . Despite these clear constitutional assignments of legislative power, it has become customary to refer to the President . . . as the "chief legislator." Students will look in vain for amendments to the United States Constitution which expand the President's role in the legislative process. The only amendment affecting his power, the Twenty-second, restricts the President by limiting him to two terms. The grants of legislative authority to the President in the Constitution are few, though important: he shall make legislative recommendations to Congress, he may call special sessions, and he has the power to veto legislation (subject to overriding by a two-thirds vote in the Congress).[5]

The constitutional key to the growth of the presidency at the expense of Congress lies in that phrase about the president making legislative proposals to Congress. All presidents have done so, but it was not until the twentieth century that that part of the presidential "duties" became significant.

> Theodore Roosevelt started the practice of initiating a wide range of legislative proposals in messages to Congress, and Wilson dramatized his legislative recommendations by appearing personally before Congress to deliver them. Bills were drafted in the executive departments and forwarded without fanfare to Congress. Roosevelt and Wilson did not merely propose legislation; they recognized the need . . . "to push politely but relentlessly" for enactment of their proposals, and they did so by writing letters to

members of Congress, conferring with congressional leaders, and delegating members of the cabinet to lobby in caucuses and in the corridors of the Capitol.[6]

In Franklin Roosevelt's time, this meant a wide variety of special messages, followed up by drafts of Administration bills. Presidents Truman and Eisenhower added a further refinement to this procedure: a detailed and comprehensive legislative package presented at the start of each session of Congress.[7]

So the presidential dominance of legislation to which we are all now accustomed is of relatively recent vintage. More recent, certainly, than the president's symbolic supremacy. So other avenues for the emergence of both objective and symbolic prevalence must be explored. We will try to do this somewhat systematically by examining the nature of Congress, the nature of the presidency, the essential qualities of their interaction as well as electoral and attitudinal causes.

THE NATURE OF CONGRESS

One of the things about Congress that makes congressional dominance over the president difficult is that Congress is fragmented. There are two houses of Congress, each of which is ruled by small baronies controlled by committee chairmen, and there are 535 individuals vying for recognition. "The division of Congress that occasionally encourages each body to use strategies against the other permits the President to play one house against the other and frustrates the possibilities of members serving as leaders in proposing national policy."[8]

Just as it is impossible for either house of Congress to exert leadership, so centralization of leadership within each house is impeded by the relative autonomy of committees.

If the committee system, as a method for creating leadership and locating responsibility for policy making, is a method of cooperation among legislators, it on some counts aggravates the problem of achieving cooperation. It has not provided for cooperation among committees or among their chairmen. Jealous of their prerogatives, committee chairmen compel central leadership to come largely from the President.[9]

Compounding these organizational problems is the sheer glut of numbers in Congress — and the fact that all of these people are elected by

In an age in which national organizations of businessmen, workers, farmers, and professional people compel government to think nationally, congressmen [continue to] think locally. They are of course elected to represent an area, not a nation. Moreover, whereas executives and administrative leaders in government . . . tend now to come from metropolitan centers, a majority of congressmen come from small towns and rural areas.[10]

This localism (provincial chauvinism) means that Congress is not staffed for *national* decision-making; their various talents and predilections lie elsewhere.

Thus it is not surprising that Congress has given away much of its national policy-making authority. Nor is it surprising that the presidents, having tasted centralized power, have grappled for evermore control over national policy.

As government takes on new functions over the years, some of them, like monetary management, foreign aid, and space exploration, pose technical problems beyond the competence and time that Congress can bring to their solution. When Congress consequently delegates tasks to administrative officials, it further increases the influence of the President on policy simply because of his constitutional authority to supervise the administrators.

In addition, Congress has explicitly loaded onto the President increasing policy-making authority, as in requiring him to recommend to Congress a budget of proposed expenditures for each year. Other acts of Congress illustrate a deliberate expansion, step by step, of Presidential policy-making authority: the Railway Labor Act, Taft-Hartley Act, Employment Act, National Security Act, Atomic Energy Act, among others. Each of these instructs the President to take from Congress certain policy-making responsibilities.

Because leadership in Congress is fragmented through the committee system and because congressmen know that someone or some small group has to take responsibility for organizing a legislative program, congressmen have informally conferred on the President both the authority and the positive responsibility, to the near exclusion of any similar role for themselves, to propose major legislation. Clearly, presidential authority for legislative leadership is now well established.

The President also exercises extra-legal authority as leader of his party. That authority is conceded to him for various reasons. For one, he is the most effective spokesman of his party; what he says commands press coverage to a degree unmatched by the announcements of any other public official. And, again, just as Congress needs leadership, so does the party.

His control over patronage and appropriations, his powers of publicity, the range of favors he can grant, the difficulties he can throw in the way of a legislator's own bills — all rooted in presidential authority — give him indirectly still other powers in policy making. Consequently, he participates at all stages in legislative and administrative policy making. There is no field or phase of policy making into which he cannot reach. Through his broad formal and informal authority, he can always find leverage. President Johnson's announcement in the fall of 1967 of a freeze on certain categories of federal expenditure . . . was a tactic designed to push congressmen into supporting his proposal for a tax increase. The President had no authority to require congressional assent to his tax increase, but he had at hand a variety of methods of employing his other grants of authority to bring Congress around to his position.[11]

Having given away so much, Congress often looks silly in its attempts to regain lost power. We observe these efforts and are reminded of the classic farce: "A man in a telephone booth cannot reach his party, then cannot get his dime back, then finds the door stuck, and has to pound on it to be let out. This is comic frustration, a ludicrous display of ineffectuality by a powerful force. . . ."[12]

NATURE OF THE PRESIDENCY

If congressional policy-making reminds us of farce, presidential efforts seem fraught with drama — comedic or tragic, depending on your ideology. "President Nixon boasted of the drama and power that lie at his fingertips to an audience of southern Democrats at a White House dinner in November of 1972: 'I can walk into my office, pick up the telephone and in twenty minutes seventy million people will be dead.'"[13] Whether that frightens you because it is true or because of Nixon's lack of taste in bragging about it, the fact remains that

the power to conduct foreign policy is by its nature largely an Executive power. As the primacy of foreign relations as such has assumed dominating importance in all nations of the world, that fact alone has led to an enormous expansion of the Presidential power. This is particularly true where the nation's defense is concerned — and especially if a President places an over-emphasis on foreign policy at the expense of domestic policy.[14]

Even if the president does not overemphasize foreign policy, his centrality in foreign relations decision-making improves his power relations vis-à-vis Congress.

A foreign policy suited to meet the necessities of extended global interest demands centralization of power. But there is a "spill over" effect from foreign policy that touches other sectors of domestic life. As Felix Morley noted . . . : "The advocate of an aggressive foreign policy is . . . likely to be an advocate of centralization. For he cannot consistently urge that the Administration be untrammeled in its conduct of foreign relations yet subject to strict Constitutional checks and balances in its control over domestic activities. Conversely, the advocate of a limited foreign policy cannot consistently urge that the Executive should be given power to override local government in social issues. . . . One may support either the expansion or the limitation of Presidential power. To advocate both simultaneously is perilously close to double talk."[15]

The emergence of the United States as a major world power coincided, in this century, with the expansion of government activity in domestic affairs. Both increased the relative power of the president. Each time a new federal agency was established the executive branch had to hire more personnel. And each new employee started doing what all bureaucrats do — producing papers for research, studies, polls, analyses, speculations, and orders. This escalation of information has by now almost completely befuddled Congress. They cannot possibly cope with the information-gathering potential of the executive branch. In any executive-congressional struggle the information is on the side of the executive. And information is power. ". . . the congressional battleground is not without its experts on the side of Congres, but such skilled aides still lack the disciplined efficiency of the information-gathering corps supporting the executive. The development of a comparable corps that can keep information in the family is the key to congressional influence on policy making."[16] Without equal information Congress can regain neither literal nor symbolic equality. As long as executive secrecy, executive privilege, is accepted as normal and desirable, Congress is destined to be inferior in power to the president.

One measure of that power differential, as well as a source increasing the distance between them, is the president's publicity advantage over Congress. As long ago as 1908 an obscure political scientist named Woodrow Wilson commented, "That part of the government which has the most direct access to opinion has the best chance of leadership and mastery: and at present that part is the President."[17]

The only things that have changed since 1908 are that the president is more powerful, hundreds of press agents are now employed by the executive branch, and several new media of mass communication have been added to his arsenal. The result is that, as former Minnesota Senator

Eugene McCarthy has noted, "The Presidential press conference gets more coverage than a whole week of what happens on the Senate floor."[18]

Consider some figures. During his first 39 months in office, President Nixon spoke during prime-time television hours 31 times, while his congressional opponents appeared on television only three times, never during prime-time hours.[19] Because of this inequity:

> In 1970, Senator William Fulbright introduced a resolution amending the 1934 Communications Act to require television networks to "provide a reasonable amount of public service time" to members of the House and Senate to talk about "issues of public importance" at least four times a year. Network officials objected.[20]

Yet ". . . the networks have *never* denied a formal White House request for television time."[21] That is, all three networks have never denied a request at the same time; occasionally one or two have refused to supply the free time. But the president has always been given the requested time by at least one of the networks.

To the average citizen, watching television and generally not paying very close attention to the Washington scene, the implied message powerfully suggests that the views of the president are significant while those of Congress are not.

About the only possible congressional response to this executive monopoly of the airwaves is the congressional investigation. Yet you could count on one hand the investigations that have been carried live in the past 30 years, and it probably would not take all of the remaining fingers of both hands to list the investigations that have been covered *well* by the electronic media. In almost all executive-legislative controversies the chief executive can go over the heads of Congress and appeal directly to the people for support. Normally, all a belligerent Congress can do is delay action and hope the interest sparked by the president's appeal will die down before they have to face re-election.

NATURE OF THEIR INTERACTION

As if it were not enough that the contemporary natures of both Congress and the presidency favor the president, it is also true that the interactions between the two favor the executive.

As the presidential bureaucracy has grown, the overseeing responsibilities of Congress have increased proportionately. Legislative oversight of all those bureaus and agencies — policy review, budget hearings, personnel approval — now means that ". . . congressmen can find their hands full of work even without attending to policy at all."[22] It takes them so much time to find out what the executive branch is doing that they do not have any time left to legislate meaningful changes.

Time and timing are valuable commodities. The president, through control of much of the policy-proposing power, can control the timing of congressional consideration of policy. Since he is the boss of those around him, he can produce proposals on demand — timed to his own sense of political advantage. Congressmen, a bickering lot of 535 equals, cannot even control their own timing, much less materially affect that of the president.

Another area of interaction where the president has the advantage is in vetoing legislation. The veto is easy to initiate — the one man need merely say "no." To override the veto requires the votes of 290 representatives and 67 senators. Consequently, the success record of vetoes is impressive. Only about 3 percent of them are overridden.[23]

How do presidents achieve such fantastic levels of success? In addition to being aided by the two-thirds requirement to override, presidents rely on a number of other mechanisms — raw pressure applied to wavering party members, promises of support or retribution in upcoming elections, providing executive-controlled favors such as relocating government installations in return for votes. An example of the kind of thing possible even without these pressure tactics came when President Ford vetoed a $1.2 billion housing bill in June 1975. Immediately after he vetoed the bill, but before the Congress held the vote to override, ". . . the President ordered the immediate release of $2 billion for Government purchase of home mortgages at subsidized rates. . . . The release of the $2 billion in funds, previously authorized by Congress to purchase mortgages, [was] designed to blunt the effort in Congress to sustain the housing legislation over the President's veto."[24]

We need also consider the symbolic nature of the drama of the veto. When the president casts the veto his veto message always points out that he is acting to protect the general public against the greediness of some private interest. But when the Congress votes to override, that is seen as narrow politics because the two-thirds requirement inevitably means that an override vote has been achieved through political deals. If the president wins he is the hero because he stood up to a large group. A congressional win cannot make them heroes in the same way because a group of 535 cannot be perceived to have faced down the attempted victimage of one man. Actually, the president wins either way, for if the veto is sustained he is a hero and if he is overridden he is seen as the "victim" of the "bullies" who ganged up on him.

Clearly, in the interactions of Congress and the president the president has most of the objective power. And even when he loses, his symbolic power tends to increase.

But, you might ask, what about a big loss, like the one Nixon suffered at the hands of the Judiciary Committee when they voted the Bill of Impeachment? Did not that demonstrate the power of Congress over the president? Many people assumed that the major effect of the Watergate hearings was to tarnish Nixon and the presidency. Not true. Three institutions — the presidency, the Congress, and the media — were hurt, that is, lost legitimacy in the eyes of the public.[25] Only one of the three — the presidency — was purged (hence, cleansed). Thus, the long-run loss was to Congress and the press.

It will always be this way. When the people are suspicious of a president they can throw him out — and eliminate their suspicions at the same time. They cannot so revitalize Congress, thus the suspicion of that body can never be completely exorcised.

ATTITUDES: PART CAUSE–PART EFFECT

Indeed, attitudes do play an important role in determining both objective and symbolic power. Whether contemporary attitudes are the effect of the present power alignment or both cause *and* effect, there is no doubt but that they make it difficult for Congress to regain much of its power.

Congressional Attitudes

That is even true of congressional attitudes.

Since the turn of the century, congressional attitudes toward the role of the President have undergone a profound change. One senator described the senatorial mind at that time: "The most eminent senators would have received as a personal affront a private message from the White House expressing a desire that they should adopt any course in the discharge of their legislative duties that they did not approve. If they visited the White House, it was to give, not to receive advice."[26]

Present congressional attitudes are much different.

It was a senior Republican committee chairman who best exemplified the new attitude in 1953, when he told an Administration witness: "Don't expect us to start from scratch on what you people want. That's not the way we do things here — *you* draft the bills and *we* work them over." Neustadt has listed some practical reasons why congressmen consider presidential initiatives a service rather than a threat: "In practical effect they represent a means whereby Congress can gain from the outside what comes hard from within: a handy and official guide to the wants of its biggest customer; an advance formulation of main issues at each session; a work-load ready-to-hand for every legislative committee; an indication, more or less, of what may risk the veto; a borrowing of presidential prestige for major bills — and thus a boosting of publicity-potentials in both sponsorship and opposition."[27]

Presidential Attitudes

Presidential attitudes also have changed. The contemporary president tends to see himself as the *only* representative of all the people and to view his own election, especially if it approached landslide proportions, as a mandate to do whatever he wants. Congress is, in this view, something of a nuisance, an anachronistic holdover from an earlier, simpler time.

Compare, for instance, the turn-of-the-century notion of the president as a trustee or steward for the nation with the vast leadership orientation in Nixon's prescription that the president ". . . must articulate the nation's values, define its goals, and marshall its will."[28] When a leader decides that a people cannot determine their own values, define their own goals nor exercise their own will power we should not be surprised when that leader begins to appropriate to himself the trappings of the dictator. Such a view of the followers demands an authoritarian center.

Public Attitudes

Yet we have not experienced to date a public reaction to the domineering status and authoritarian activities of the presidency. Perhaps that is because our

> civics lessons taught admiration and respect to the easily understood and personalized President who represented a symbol of national unity and purpose. The symbolic function of the Presidency has well served civic educators who attempted to push assimilationist values to thirty-five million

immigrants, many of them possessing few of the original Anglo-American presuppositions about government.[29]

And, of course, part of the adulation of the president comes from the basic necessity to believe in *something*.

In a highly mobile mass society, the need to believe in something concrete becomes more acute. Most people do not want to see their views of public life which seem to have overarching value disparaged. Criticism becomes muted. The President has come to symbolize authority itself. As Dostoevsky's Grand Inquisitor noted, authority yields great relief from anxiety and uncertainty. Thus, Lyndon Johnson used to try to calm the nervous and vacillating multitude by exclaiming: "I'm the only President you've got."[30]

And what happens when "the only President we've got" dies?

The profound reaction of the American people to the death of an incumbent President gives empirical warrant to the suspicion that the President has become a national oedipal symbol. More than half a national sample of people polled after Kennedy's assassination reported personal bereavement. Fifty percent of the American people acknowledged that they wept. Forty-three percent could not eat, forty-eight percent reported insomnia and sixty-eight percent acknowledged a sense of nervousness and tension.[31]

Weeping, loss of hunger, insomnia, nervousness, tension — these are exactly the behavioral manifestations most of us suffer when a member of our own family dies. The conclusion that Americans think of the president as though he were a family member is difficult to escape; and the fact that we do not react in the same way to the death of a member of Congress goes a long way toward explaining the objective and symbolic power differential between the two branches of government.

Clearly, we identify with our presidents. "In 1945 a poll asked, 'In your opinion, who is the greatest person living or dead?' Roosevelt won an overwhelming first, Lincoln second, and Jesus Christ managed a meager fifteen point third place."[32] If that poll were repeated today there is but little doubt that the incumbent president would place first. That would be expected, yet many people would be surprised to discover that Richard Nixon would make a respectable showing, probably in the top five, certainly in the top ten.

If presidents tend to see themselves as the country, to confuse their own interests with the interests of the nation, this does not discomfit most people, for they share in the delusion.

> For Americans, the President becomes both the symbol of authority and the symbol of the nation. . . . So powerfully have these feelings developed by adulthood, normal and healthy citizens see themselves, their nation and the President as inextricably intertwined.[33]

Thus all the patriotism and reverence and hopefulness that the people feel for their nation comes to be felt also for the president. And this infusing of the president with the objective power of running the nation and the symbolic power of controlling our hopes for the future indeed makes the president what he is so often called: the most powerful man in the world.

> Through a constellation of forces, the President's symbolic function has been converted into the nation's symbol-making function. It is a significant transformation, for it gives the President the power to create — and create in his own image — the nation's deepest beliefs and most revered symbols. And whoever can control a nation's symbols can thereby control that nation.[34]

The president can control policy-making, and thereby determine what we can do. But that is a trifling power compared to his control of our symbols, for that allows him to determine what we can be.

NOTES

1.   Charles R. Adrian and Charles Press, *The American Political Process* (New York: McGraw-Hill, 1965), p. 406.

2.   Quoted in Larry L. Bradshaw, "The Genesis of Dissent," *The Southern Speech Communication Journal* 38 (1972):149.

3.   Malcolm Moos, "To Halt the March Toward Autocratic Government," *The Center Report*, February 1975, p. 10.

4.   Quoted in Marvin Kitman, "A Capitol Show," *The New Leader*, September 16, 1974, p. 25.

5.   Malcolm E. Jewell and Samuel C. Patterson, *The Legislative Process in the United States* (New York: Random House, 1966), p. 301.

6.   Ibid., p. 303.

7.   Ibid., p. 307.

8.   Adrian and Press, *The American Political Process*, p. 448.

9.   Charles E. Lindblom, *The Policy-Making Process* (Englewood Cliffs, NJ: Prentice-Hall, 1968), p. 68.

10.   Ibid.

11.   Ibid., pp. 71–72.

12.   Orrin E. Klapp, *Symbolic Leaders: Public Dramas and Public Men* (Chicago: Aldine, 1964), p. 204.

13.   James Nathan, "The Roots of the Imperial Presidency: Public Opinion, Domestic Institutions, and Global Interests," *Presidential Studies Quarterly* 5

(1975):65.

14.   Moos, "To Halt the March," p. 11.

15.   Nathan, "Roots of Imperial Presidency," p. 63.

16.   Adrian and Press, *The American Political Process*, p. 449.

17.   Quoted in Vukan Kuic, "Theory and Practice of the American Presidency," *Presidential Studies Quarterly* 5 (1975):55.

18.   Quoted in Moos, "To Halt the March," p. 11.

19.   Richard D. MacCann, "Televising Congress," *The American Scholar* 44 (1975):467.

20.   Ibid.

21.   Les Brown, "Political Access to Television: A Double Standard," *The New York Times*, October 26, 1974, p. 63.

22.   Lindblom, *Policy-Making Process*, p. 86.

23.   Jewel and Patterson, *The Legislative Process*, p. 309.

24.   James N. Naughton, "President Vetoes $1.2 Billion Bill for Aid to Housing," *The New York Times*, June 25, 1975, p. 1.

25.   Michael J. Robinson, "The Impact of the Televised Watergate Hearings," *Journal of Communication* 24 (1974):30.

26.   Jewell and Patterson, *The Legislative Process*, p. 304.

27.   Ibid., pp. 304–305.

28.   Quoted in Nathan, "Roots of Imperial Presidency," p. 63.

29.   Ibid.

30.   Ibid., p. 65.

31.   Ibid., p. 66.

32.   Ibid., p. 65.

33.   Ibid., p. 66.

34.   Moos, "To Halt the March," p. 10.

A COMMUNICATION MODEL OF PRESIDENTIAL POWER

How does the presidency of today differ from that of George Washington? Most scholars would reply that the office today is much more powerful. It directly affects every citizen, for the president is responsible for setting national policy and goals. In this complex world, nearly every presidential decision affects us economically and even psychologically. The office, if not the officeholder, enjoys a kind of worldwide prestige unknown in the days of George Washington. Clinton Rossiter, a noted presidential scholar, asserts "that the outstanding feature of American constitutional development has been the growth of the power and prestige of the Presidency."[1] The powers of the American presidency, both constitutionally and pragmatically, have been a subject of endless fascination and study to American political scientists.

Nearly all political scientists recognize that the presidency is both an institution and a role. As such, the presidency has a great deal of influence upon those who occupy the office as well as the general public. Historians, when studying the relationship between presidents and the presidency, usually focus on the growth of presidential power. Political scientists, specifically, tend to emphasize the individual president's use of power. Power, therefore, is viewed as the "heart" of the presidency or at least the "heart" of strong leadership. Scholars, in relation to the presidency, have been obsessed with the end result or product of power. Consequently, traditional political approaches to presidential roles or models are attempts to view the nature and functioning of presidential power. But in investigating power, one is led to many areas of study and questions. What is power? Where is power? How does one obtain power? When should one use power? Although all these questions deal with the "nature" of power, some scholars end up focusing on such diverse topics as: constitutional law, the nature of society, socialization, personality theory, management theory, persuasion, and decision-making.

Yet, the more presidential power is studied and analyzed, the more elusive it becomes. The formal powers granted in the Constitution are indeed negligible and recently Congress is even challenging these. Perhaps the greatest difficulty in understanding presidential power is the misconception that the exercise of power is the consequence of "rational" decision-making. The task, therefore, becomes simply one of identifying all the participants and influences that go into the process of decision-making. The illusion which results from such an approach tends to view decisions as choices among clearly understood alternatives made by knowledgeable actors. However, close examination of key historical presidential decisions tends to reveal a process earmarked by luck, accident, and general lack of information. The Cuban missile crisis is a prime example.[2] At the very least, the president should not be viewed as a "generalissimo" issuing a never ending series of commands and having them immediately obeyed.

For communication scholars, power is neither the "beginning" nor the "end all" of the study of relationships and institutions. Power is not a concrete, static entity. Rather, power results from interactions that possess unique characteristics and recognizable social features. Michael Korda seriously proclaims in his popular bestseller, *Power: How to Get It, How to Use It*, that "all life is a game of power."[3] Certainly, power is created through the process of social organization. Whether organizations are simply small groups, families, communities, or whole societies; the creation and use of power is at the core of social life. For Marvin Olsen, social activities that involve the use of power in social life are "politics." He defines politics as ". . . the total process through which social power is distributed and exercised, with particular emphasis on the making of collective decisions."[4]

Indeed, politics is how a president wins an election and governs a nation. As an occupant of a political office, a president must possess and exercise traditional politician's skills of communication and persuasion. According to Philippa Strum, "the essence of leadership is the formulation of new proposals and solutions and the persuading of the public to accept them."[5] Especially since Truman, presidents have been required to submit a plan for solutions to our national problems; to motivate and mobilize public support; and to convince Congress to act accordingly. This is no easy task. Godfrey Hodgson observes that "both the ceremonial prestige of the office and its institutional resources must be pressed into the service of what is an act of persuasion, not an act of imperial command."[6]

The presidency has become the focal point of our political system. This was not always the case. Early presidents seldom gave public addresses. Written statements served as notice of issue positions. Campaigns were conducted by the parties. Only a handful of people were knowledgeable and aware of public issues. Even fewer actually voted or participated in the electoral process. Today, presidential rhetoric and communication activities are a source of tremendous power; power to define, justify, legitimize, persuade, and inspire. Everything a president does or says has implications and communicates "something." A president surrounds himself with communication specialists. Every act, work, or phrase becomes calculated and measured for a response. Every occasion proclaims a need for utterance.

James Ceaser, with several other colleagues, argues that three factors have attributed to the rise of the "rhetorical Presidency."[7] The first factor is the modern doctrine of presidential leadership. The public expects a president to set goals and provide solutions to national problems. To be a "leader of men" is a cherished concept and a political expectation and, hence, a necessity for our presidents. The second factor giving rise to the rhetorical presidency is the development of the mass media. The mass media have increased the size of the audience, provided immediate access to the public, and changed the mode of communicating with the public from primarily the written word to the spoken word delivered in dramatic form. The final factor contributing to the supremacy of the rhetorical presidency is the modern electoral campaigns. Contemporary presidential campaigns require national travel, public performances, image creation, issue definition, and the articulation of problem solutions. A "common man" can become known and win an election. Competition for communication opportunities is great.

In this essay we will: investigate traditional orientations and perspectives of presidential power; consider the shortcomings of these orientations from a communication perspective; and present a communication model of presidential power which identifies and emphasizes the dynamic, relational, and interactive dimensions of political power. The model is both descriptive and prescriptive. Four orientations or styles of presidential power are identified. In short the model offers a comprehensive, systematic way to analyze presidential power from its creation, use, and consequences independent of individual presidential decisions. It should be noted from the outset that much of the model is not limited to presidential considerations but applicable to the nature of power in social life in general.

PERSPECTIVES OF PRESIDENTIAL POWER

Prior works mentioning presidential power usually emphasize one of three approaches.[8] A historical approach to presidential power views power as a consequence of individual presidents attempting to maximize their personal orientation to the office. Historians focus on individual influence, control of the country's destiny, and their capacity to draw talented men to their administrations. They rank each president based upon his attitude toward presidential power as specified in the Constitution.[9] For example, Madisonianism is based upon the constitutional theory of separation of powers and thus views presidential power as restricted, conservative, and literal. William Howard Taft serves as the best contemporary example of this "constitutional" orientation to presidential power. Hamiltonianism is based upon the constitutional theory of executive power and defines presidential power more broadly. This "stewardship" view is traced to Theodore Roosevelt who argued that the Constitution is not literal and requires a president to use good judgment in matters of interpretation to preserve the "democratic" interest of the Constitution. Jeffersonianism is the most liberal view of the office and espouses the need for strong leadership and constitutional "flexibility" in order to meet the ever changing demands of governing the nation. This "prerogative" power orientation came to full fruition under Franklin Roosevelt and clearly shaped the behavior of all succeeding presidents. Also, for the historical approach, electoral results, partisan politics, and mobilization of public opinion are key elements in studying presidential power.

Many political scientists prefer to focus on the formal powers of the office. Presidential power is a direct result of constitutional authority, congressional authority, and the system of checks and balances. Individual presidents are judged on the "quantity" of power exhibited ranging from crisis to crisis and administration to administration. Such an approach serves as an alarm system to presidential abuse of power and authority.

Within recent years, psychological orientations to power focus on leadership and personality factors. The concern here is on the characteristics that enable a president to persuade and influence Congress as well as the nation. This orientation probably began with the work of French and Raven in 1959.[10] They argued that power can be analyzed from two different perspectives: the behavior of the individual who "holds" power over others and the reactions of those who are subject to the use of power. They identified five "bases" of power: reward, coercion, legitimate, referent, and expert. Psychological theorists have developed personality models and typologies to establish criteria for evaluating presidential performance and attitudes toward the job. Some of the more familiar classifications include: authoritarian-democratic, open-closed, positive-negative, and active-passive. For psychologists, personality is a complex phenomenon comprised of many diverse elements such as how people adapt to their surroundings, express emotions, and relate to others. Insight into these aspects of behavior would not only explain presidential behavior but would also predict performance while in the office.

In the past, little attention has been given to the social scientific study of presidential power.[11] The above approaches primarily focus on the structural, theoretical, and mechanistic consequences of power. For the interactionist, power is a "quality" of interaction and not necessarily an entity. However, there have been three notable attempts of studying presidential power encompassing interactional elements.

Each "job" of the presidency, according to Rossiter, carries unique authority. By recognizing five "extra-constitutional" roles of the president, Rossiter effectively argued that presidential power had indeed expanded with the job. The major idea was that each role of the presidency is a source of power. Yet, most of the early books still emphasized the system of "checks and balances" which controlled presidential power. Rossiter was quick to identify ten elements that limit the power of the president which includes: a four-year term, no third term, Congress's ability to override vetos, frequent reports to Congress, various limits on power of appointments, Supreme Court decisions, various congressional authority, the federal administration and bureaucracy, the opposition political party, and simply world opinion.[12] But even Rossiter recognized that presidential power was more than simple "actions." For presidential power "operates within a grand and durable pattern of private liberty and public morality, which means that it operates successfully only when the President honors the pattern by selecting ends and means that are characteristically American."[13]

Richard Neustadt's classic, *Presidential Power*, was the first major work that emphasized the importance and role individual presidents have in developing power and influence.[14] His goal was to show how a president can become a powerful leader and what a president must do if he hopes to maintain influence over others. Neustadt believed "that the Presidency as an office is so weak that the President as a person has to watch every single choice he makes today, with particular concern for its effect on his prospective influence tomorrow."[15]

Presidential leadership, for Neustadt, "is not so much his own actions but his influence on the actions of others. Not what he does, but what he gets done, indicates his true powers."[16] Realistically, then, "presidential power is the power to persuade" and consequently is not guaranteed to any president. A president must, first, want to maximize his power and second, be willing to bargain and trade advantages.

A president's influence or power, according to Neustadt, comes from three sources. The first is from the bargaining advantages he has resulting from the office. Second, a great deal of influence comes from a president's professional reputation comprised of his willingness to use sanctions at his disposal. Finally, the public prestige of a president allows even greater latitude in expanding and developing influence. Ultimately, the interaction of the four variables of personality, experience, events and conditions, and vantage points determines a president's actual power.[17]

Neustadt's scheme is both content- and value-free. There is a heavy reliance upon presidential choices. Thus, the emphasis is still on rather concrete decisions and choices made by a president which fails to appreciate the nature of power from a communication perspective. Perhaps the closest analysis of presidential power that more fully recognizes its dynamic, process nature is rendered in a work by Myron

Hale. Hale distinguishes among presidential influence, authority, and power. Such a distinction is necessary, according to Hale, "in order not only to improve our understanding of Presidential politics, but to evaluate Presidential power and policy results."[18] For Hale, presidential influence is the encompassing term which is rooted in presidential authority. There are two types of authority. Institutional authority is founded upon the office as defined in the Constitution plus the status and prestige associated with the office. Personal authority is the development and maintenance of individual credibility. It is important to note, that while institutional authority is transferable, personal authority is not. In addition, the authority of a president, in either category, depends upon the acceptance of such authority as appropriate and legitimate. "If the President's behavior does not meet the normative expectations of the society, he may lose legitimacy. If the President loses legitimacy, authority will vanish, and with it political power."[19]

Hale's treatment of presidential power has several advantages. First, it emphasizes the dynamic, inherent nature of power rather than results or end products of power. Second, the approach recognizes the importance of interaction of the people with the office and the office with the people in the development of power. Third, Hale clearly distinguishes between the "power" of the office and the "power" of the officeholder. Finally, the model acknowledges the importance of public expectations in assessing presidential power.

THE PERCEPTUAL, RELATIONAL, AND INTERACTIVE NATURE OF POWER

Power is a relational phenomenon and not principally a psychological one. Power is created and exists resulting from social relationships. Individuals may possess unique strengths, knowledge, or skills, but these capabilities in no way constitute social power. Of course, one's personal characteristics can enhance power in a particular situation. The simple point is that power is something people participate in rather than something people react to.

There is a tremendous difference between, as recognized by Louis Koenig, an imagined presidency and the presidency of reality.[20] The imagined presidency possesses a great deal more power than the office really has or is available in any situation. "The imagined Presidency is a euphoric impression of its past, present, and future, and is grounded partly in reality and partly in fancy. It exaggerates the office's strength, encouraged by the substantial power it actually possesses, the prestige built in its past and the pomp that surrounds it."[21] Yet, perceptions often mean more than actual power or force. In the international climate, the perception of a leader's resolve can have a greater impact than the number of a nation's aircraft carriers. Hugh Sidey noted, in reference to the Iranian hostage situation of 1980, that "terrorist tactics can mock stockpiled nukes."[22] "The winning of the President's power," according to Theodore White, "lies in noise and clangor, the flogging of the emotions and the appeal to all the tribal pasts of America."[23]

The presidency simply is not as "powerful" as many citizens believe. An aide to President Truman is quoted as saying:

> The most startling thing a new President discovers is that his world is *not* monolithic. In the world of the Presidency, giving an order does not end the matter. You can pound your fist on the table or you can get mad or you can blow it all and go out to the golf course. But nothing gets done except by endless follow-up, endless kissing and coaxing, endless threatening and compelling.[24]

Richard Cheney, an advisor to several contemporary presidents concurs by stating that "there's a tendency for us to think, gee, the President has enormous power, that the people around him are powerful people, that they sit around all day and they wield something called power. Well, when you get there you quickly find that's not the case."[25]

This is best illustrated by the Cuban missile crisis. In early 1961, Kennedy talked about removing U.S. missiles from Turkey. In August 1962, he officially directed the missiles to be removed "immediately." Both the State and Defense Departments concurred. Of course, by October 1962, Kennedy was shocked to discover that the missiles were still in Turkey. Thus, perhaps one of the greatest problems a president faces is control of the ever-growing bureaucracy. Among the Congress, the bureaucracy, and special interest groups, the power of the presidency is far removed from the simple instruments of war.

From this discussion, the first important point to be made is that the perception of power implies an expectation of power. "Every expectation" argues Grant McConnell, "proclaims that he is a man of power, and at every point the expectation is itself a source of power."[26] Second, power is not simply a quality that a person possesses like brown hair and blue eyes. Rather, it is a relational phenomenon dependent upon citizen perceptions, history of the office, and personal development of mass perceptions of the power of the office.

For Richard Pious, presidential choices serve as the basis for presidential power. A president's use of his constitutional prerogatives sets the stage for congressional action and judicial interpretations. His "theory" of presidential power specifies that one should "concentrate on the constitutional authority that the President asserts unilaterally through various rules of constitutional construction and interpretation, in order to resolve crises or important issues facing the nation."[27] Such a theory, however, still lacks the dynamic personal development of "power." There is a confusion between substance of power and style of power. As McConnell observes, "while the appearance of power is sometimes mistaken for the substance of power, appearance can occasionally be useful substitute for reality and indeed may even become reality."[28] Different problems and skills involved in politics result in various presidential "styles" of power. Woodrow Wilson and John Kennedy emphasized appearances of leadership and moral appeals to the nation. In contrast, Lyndon Johnson relied on personal contact and pressure on individual congressmen for impact. Bryce Harlow, advisor to several contemporary presidents, recalls, "LBJ was the most forceful person in relationship to people that I have ever met or expect to meet. He could charm you, he could frighten you, he could buy you, he could seduce or induce, influence you in an incredible variety of ways that came to him automatically."[29] The key, perhaps, is knowing and utilizing the appropriate "style" to the problems of the times. The use of an inappropriate "style" could easily result in being perceived as weak, or mean, or compromising, etc.

Independent of styles is skill or the techniques used to develop styles. In the words of Wildavsky, "to meet the constitutional duties of the office as well as the strong expectations of others, Presidents must persuade, bargain, or coerce."[30] President Truman's famous retort about the power of the presidency is now classic among scholars: ". . . the principle power that the President has is to bring people in and try to persuade them to do what they ought to do without persuasion. That's what I spend most of my time doing. That's what the powers of the President amounts to."[31] For communication scholars, this is a key observation. Power, defined as the control of others, results from getting others to accept one's view and perspective of "reality." To do so, one must control, influence, and sustain one's own definition of the situation by "acting" which creates an image that ultimately leads others to voluntarily behave in the desired way. Persuasion involves awakening in an individual a voluntary inclination toward certain courses of action.

A president is required, in order to successfully persuade, to manipulate valued political symbols appropriate to our political culture. Our values and beliefs are identified, emphasized, and utilized in shaping a reality upon which to act. As Peter Hall succinctly states:

> The politician is potentially always on stage. Every aspect of his behavior can become part of a public performance which must be managed and controlled to mobilize support. Many of his activities will be essentially symbolic, i.e. for the purpose of creating the desired identity in order to draw the audience into *his* drama.[32]

The notion of presidential power is grounded in perceptions of power. Corresponding expectations are based on images of power created or "styles" that develop. But, essential to each of these steps of the process is interaction. Persuasion, bargaining, and coercion are all modes of interaction subject to various styles and approaches.

A COMMUNICATION MODEL OF PRESIDENTIAL POWER

Authority-Influence Continuum

Myron Hale's distinction between authority and influence is very valuable.[33] In the realm of politics, the concepts, however, exist as a continuum. The ultimate authority for the presidency is the U.S. Constitution which specifies rules and procedures for presidential duties and behavior. Although rather specific, the Constitution is subject to debate and varieties of interpretation. To simply define power as the effective use of authority is missing a tremendous point. If power is the "legitimate" use of authority, then what is "legitimate?" To Machiavelli, legitimate means to expand or increase power at all costs. Indeed, any "use" of power implies the personal, influence dimension. The "influence" aspect is the "how" to use power. Nicholas von Hoffman argues that "the more narrowly limited the power of the office, the more important the personality of the officeholder."[34] An individual is as powerful or powerless as they desire to be. Gordon Tullock concurs by arguing that real power is much more restricted than apparent power. "Real power is, by necessity, strictly limited, and its exercise requires hard and unremitting work. Apparent power on the other hand, can be substantially unlimited and can be more easily obtained."[35] But, of course, the perception of power with little or no legitimate authority to back it up is of little consequence as well as dangerous. Olsen correctly observes, "Social influence is an instance of power in which outcomes are not predetermined. Influence can only be attempted, not enforced, and its results are always problematic."[36]

In terms of the model, the first continuum is the authority-influence continuum (see Figure 3-1). Authority refers to the laws, statutes, or constitutions which prescribe duties, responsibilities, and behaviors of the president. Such documents legitimize one's action. The structure of an organization is one method of clearly delineating relative power and authority. Obviously, an individual may utilize organizational roles and status as resources for enhancing personal power and prestige. A difficult question becomes how do we tell whether a person is acting as a legitimate representative of an organization or acting as an independent agent attempting to increase or exercise interpersonal power and influence? Hence, the authority-influence dimension.

The influence element of the continuum refers to the overt attempts to increase relative power by relying on persuasive and bargaining skills and techniques. Other factors include public prestige and credibility.

Presidential leadership clearly involves aspects of both elements. Extremes in either case may be fatal. Watergate continually decreased Nixon's influence without decreasing his authority. The result, however, was an ineffective presidency. The secret is, perhaps, to reach a balance between the two extremes. Some scholars would argue that President

FIGURE 3-1

AUTHORITY
(constitutional, legalistic, prescribed)

INFLUENCE
(interpersonal, bargaining skills, personality)

Reagan found just the right niche in getting his tax cut proposal through Congress in July 1981.

Traditional views of political power are founded upon the notion that orders given by "the government" are legitimate because they are ultimately approved by the citizenry and are in accordance with the Constitution. But the enforcement of various governmental orders relies upon the psychological skills and techniques of "coercion," not ideas of legitimacy.

Openness-Secrecy Continuum

Equal access to information is vital to the functioning of a democracy. American society has gone to great lengths to protect its citizens' access to information ranging from the Revolutionary Bill of Rights to the more recent Freedom of Information Act of 1967. Dissemination of knowledge is required to insure a well-informed citizenry. Yet, within the realm of politics, information is indeed "power." Murray Edelman observes that "political beliefs and perceptions are very largely not based upon empirical observations or indeed, upon 'information' at all."[37] People receive information, change it, store it, pass it around, amplify it, and distort it. Political realities created may or may not be grounded upon facts. Hence, information becomes a valuable commodity both at the national level as well as the interpersonal level. Perry London argues that "every kind of information and every medium for communicating it is potentially useful as an instrument of control."[38] For him, control by information includes nearly all of the communication and persuasion methods that our society has traditionally regarded as legitimate ranging from propaganda to education.[39] Vital to persuasion is knowing how to use information that is relevant to another person's interests and goals.

For purposes of this model, the openness-secrecy continuum refers to the general use of information by a president as a method of control or inducing desired behavior (see Figure 3-2). The model recognizes that there exists a rather wide range of options between complete secrecy or complete disclosure of information which may be persuasively powerful. The control of information enhances one's problem-solving ability. Thus, this dimension refers to a president's general orientation to secrecy or openness in daily interaction.

Lyndon Johnson is most often cited as a president who frequently used secrecy as an instrument of control. Chester Cooper notes that Johnson's "compulsive secrecy was not so much a conscious conspiracy

FIGURE 3-2

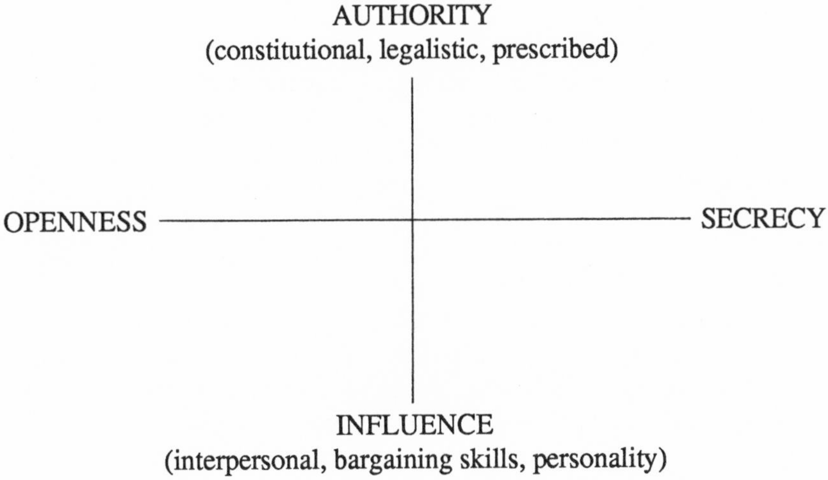

AUTHORITY
(constitutional, legalistic, prescribed)

OPENNESS ———————————————— SECRECY

INFLUENCE
(interpersonal, bargaining skills, personality)

as it was a reflection of the President's personal style — a style that favored a 'closed' rather than an 'open' system of policymaking."[40] Perhaps the real task for any president is to keep secrecy from becoming deception and honesty mere publicity. At either extreme the nation is subjected to coercion and not persuasion. This model, therefore, views information as a means of control and the degree or use of secrecy-openness is a characteristic technique of increasing or defining presidential power.

FOUR ORIENTATIONS TO POWER

With the two continuums intersecting, four orientations to presidential power may be identified (see Figure 3-3).[41] Each quadrant possesses unique characteristics, and heavy reliance upon any one of the orientations may be recognized as a president's "style" of power. Of course, presidents use all four orientations; each of which has advantages in specific situations. The model is flexible, therefore, by allowing analysis of specific presidential decisions and actions as well as in characterizing individual presidential performances.

"Constitutional"

Quadrant I of Figure 3-3 represents the "constitutional" orientation to power. In this mode, the president maximizes openness and legitimate authority. Power stems from the legal foundations of the institution. Questions of presidential power are observable and consequently clearly "right or wrong," "good or bad." Thus, actions are based upon constitutional, legal authority. This orientation views the powers of the presidency conservatively. The individual maintains a high belief in the rationality of the people. The president views his major role as one of management, providing directions for Congress and the public to follow.

Truman was certainly known for his directness and openness in dealing with public issues. He refused to isolate the decision-making process of the presidency from the public. He made great efforts to encourage public discussion and justify his positions. This approach was both his blessing and his curse. It served to both generate public support and create divisions of public opinion.

Jimmy Carter's presidency best exemplifies this orientation to power. He naively believed that if he effectively recognized and articulated a problem, subsequent corrective action and behavior would naturally

FIGURE 3-3

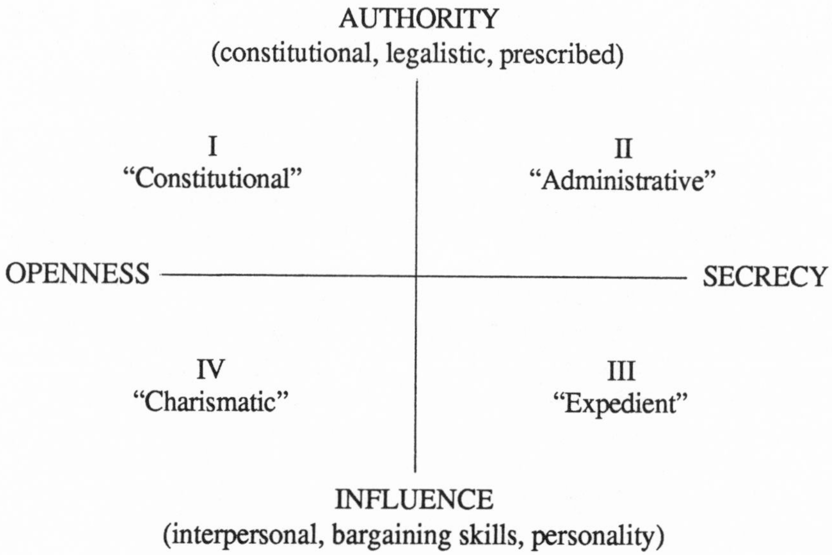

AUTHORITY
(constitutional, legalistic, prescribed)

| I | II |
| "Constitutional" | "Administrative" |

OPENNESS ——————————————————— SECRECY

| IV | III |
| "Charismatic" | "Expedient" |

INFLUENCE
(interpersonal, bargaining skills, personality)

follow. Carter's primary technique of persuasion was to shower the public and Congress with facts — facts that would lead to rational decisions and logical actions.

The limitations of this orientation are fairly obvious. There exists a lack of the ability to motivate and persuade the public and key individuals who surround the office. Both Truman and Carter had little tolerance for pampering legislative leaders. Indeed, Carter's failure to get his energy program passed by Congress is largely because of his failure to "wine and dine" key congressional leaders. James Barber argues that the primary reason Carter's legislative relations were often stormy was because of his refusal to "play the customary patronage and special privilege games."[42] Although he made many efforts to popularize the presidency, relate to the public, and strive for an "open" office, Carter's major fault lay not in his view of a "virtuous citizenry" but in his lack of understanding "of the constraints on the domestic presidency — from the Congress, the press, interest groups and abroad."[43] In short, according to Heineman and Hessler, the Carter presidency failed because "he could not join politics and policy."[44]

Thus, if the powers of the presidency are viewed conservatively, then available sanctions are limited as well. This orientation simply ignores the dynamics of the office. It treats the power of the institution as strictly, empirically defined ignoring the emotional, symbolic significance of the office. The presidency is more than a management office. To identify a problem, isolate the variables, and construct a solution is not the same as generating support, persuading a public of a law's necessity, and getting the legislation passed through Congress. Leadership, as a quality, differs from simple management. Because the office is "public," structure and legalistic formulations are of little consequence when attempting to gauge the "power" of the presidency.

"Administrative"

Quadrant II of Figure 3-3 represents the "administrative" orientation to power. Presidential actions are based on legitimate authority but generally surrounded by secrecy. The president has the authority to issue unilateral, nonreciprocal commands with government and fully expect them to be followed. What often results, however, is large scale bargaining among individuals positioned in the hierarchy of government. The key to this orientation is presidential bargaining. The president has authority to take specified actions but prefers to avoid publicity. The president utilizes the "machinery" of government to obtain the implementation of certain policies. Lines of organizational authority and hierarchy are maximized. This kind of power is no longer ideological but merely psychological relying upon both physical and psychological forces.

The goal here *is not deception* but efficiency and internal control. This orientation to power promotes operational efficiency through standardized administration thus ensuring internal control and coordination. During the Cuban missile crisis, President Kennedy heavily relied upon this orientation to power. There was never any doubt about his authority to handle the situation, but Kennedy severely limited the information concerning the crisis to both the American people as well as high ranking governmental officials. Even segments of the military were not fully informed when given commands of action.[45] Lyndon Johnson's secret ground war in Laos between 1963 and 1968 was also of this nature. But this orientation to power is not limited to crisis situations. The focus of the orientation, however, is upon efficiency and implementation. Laws and statutes may proclaim "equal opportunity employment" and nondiscrimination but how are these laws implemented and enforced? The denying of effective political participation of blacks certainly occurred after the passage of the Voting Rights Act. An agreement, of course, is only as "good" as the people who sign it. Information is a tool used in the bargaining process. This orientation is very similar to Neustadt's model of presidential power.[46] As already noted, he argued that the power to persuade lies in the ability to bargain. Abuse of his model may lead to the expedient orientation to power.

Hoover was not comfortable in public and actually detested the presidency's demand for dramatization.[47] "I have never liked the clamor of crowds," Hoover wrote. "I intensely dislike superficial social contacts. I made no pretensions to oratory. . . ."[48] He relied heavily on committees and endless meetings. His major asset was the mastery of information. Thus, Hoover's lack of enthusiasm for compromise, politics, and public drama resulted in his "administrative approach" to presidential power.

Ford's public performances and presentations, like Hoover, were less than inspiring. While president, he relied heavily upon the skills perfected as House Minority Leader: accommodation, compromise, and deal-making. He was most comfortable in giving freer rein to the federal bureaucracy. According to Philip Shabecoff, "Ford . . . shared more power with members of his cabinet than recent Presidents."[49] It is important to remember that although Ford relied upon the legal and institutional authority of his office for action, his "secrecy" resulted not from conscious attempts at deception but private processes of decision-making and policy implementation. Thus the secrecy dimension of the "administrative" orientation to power is one of style or method rather than intent.

"Expedient"

Quadrant III of Figure 3-3 represents the true Machiavellian perspective of power. The president attempts to maximize power at all costs. There is a heavy reliance upon secrecy and interpersonal skills of persuasion and bargaining. Presidential requests, actions, and behaviors go beyond legitimate authority. This approach, however, is rational because decisions are based upon cost-benefit analyses. Considerations may include questions of national security, domestic political environment, opponent strengths, or simply desires to conceal incompetence, embarrassment, or governmental inefficiency. Secrecy easily becomes deception and influence a matter of coercion. It should be emphasized that this orientation to power is not inherently bad; rather, it offers more opportunity for abuse. Power is a function of individual endeavors to maximize bargaining advantages including elements of public prestige.

Perhaps no president had a greater desire for power than Lyndon Johnson. But his quest for power was clearly pragmatic. Evans and Novak report Johnson telling a group of senators in 1966 that "they say Jack Kennedy had style, but I'm the one who's got the bills passed."[50] As Senate Majority Leader, Johnson soon realized that information was an *instrument* of power. According to biographer Doris Kearns, Johnson would create a "composite mental portrait" of every senator from a multitude of personal facts, gossip, and observations.[51] "Each encounter, whatever its purpose, was also a 'planned interview' in which Johnson probed, questioned, and directed the conversation according to *his* ends."[52]

Johnson's success in persuasion was because of his reliance upon intimacy and one-to-one interactions. Kearns provides a most interesting statement of Johnson revealing his attitude toward and importance of the interpersonal approach to persuasion.

> But you see, they never take the time to think about what really goes on in these one-to-one sessions because they've never been involved in persuading

anyone to do anything. They're just like a pack of nuns who've convinced themselves that sex is dirty and ugly and low-down and forced because *they* can never have it. And because they can never have it, they see it all as rape instead of seduction and they miss the elaborate preparation that goes in before the act is finally done.[53]

The "Johnson treatment" is defined by Barber as his "razzle-dazzle way of winning compliance, could mix verbal supplication, accusation, cajolery, exuberance, scorn, tears, complaint, the hint of threat with physical lapel-holding, shoulder massage, elbow and knee grabbing, fingerwagging, and nose thrusting — all at a whirlwind pace."[54] His techniques of persuasion were designed to confirm his power and control.

Johnson's legislative strategy consisted of five key components: knowledge of Congress as an institution, knowledge of congressional members, "consultation" with opinion leaders of Congress, formal "briefings" to congressional members prior to a key vote, and "intense" personal phone calls to members of Congress.[55] Notice that Johnson seldom resorted to generating public support for an issue. Johnson preferred private pressure in order to obtain desired results — whatever the methods. Thus, the preference for "secrecy" and maximizing personal influence.

But, as already noted, when personal influence wanes so does credibility and subsequent authority. This was the case for both Johnson and Nixon. As Johnson began to lose credibility on the Vietnam issue, his personal influence and authority also declined. For Nixon, the Watergate episode resulted not only in loss of personal influence and credibility but also, for the first time in our nation's history, jeopardized the institutional authority of the presidency. Thus, the "expedient" orientation to power is also the most dangerous for both the occupant and the office.

"Charismatic"

Quadrant IV of Figure 3-3 represents the "charismatic" orientation to power. The president's personality characteristics are key to his persuasive efforts. Information is not used as a weapon or bargaining tool. The individual has an attraction, affectivity, and identification that is most appealing and persuasive. Key interpersonal skills developed include the abilities to: create a sense of obligation and loyalty with those with whom the president interacts, foster unconscious identification with subordinates or ideas they profess, and create perceptions of dependence with those with whom he interacts. While Jimmy Carter avoided this orientation until the latter part of his presidency, Ronald Reagan began his presidency utilizing this style. Now, of course, it is evident that Reagan prefers the "administrative" style.

Since Franklin Roosevelt's time, the dramatization of the presidency has resulted in the emphasis of the charismatic rather than the administrative or constitutional basis of authority. Wilson was, perhaps, the first president to consciously pursue the charismatic orientation to power. As a scholar and historian, Wilson appreciated the constitutional and historic limitations of the office. His profound belief in democracy generated his continual desire to take "his case to the people." He preferred direct relations with his audience and disliked communicating with the public through the press.[56] Wilson wrote, as president, "I have no patience with the tedious toil of what is known as 'research'; I have a passion for interpreting great thoughts to the world."[57] The world, however, was less than enthusiastic toward some of his views on national issues. Nevertheless, he perceived the potential of the office in relating directly to the public for political support.

Of course, Kennedy is the best example of a contemporary president exhibiting this orientation to power. Camelot and Kennedy's legacy are well known. John Murphy writes that "Kennedy's personality, appearance, youth and style permitted him to mobilize latent American idealism in support of projects which were ethically correct and socially desirable."[58] But Kennedy was more than mere image. In his press conferences Kennedy impressed both the correspondents and the public with his depth of information, readiness to answer questions, and sense of humor. Kennedy combined both the authority of the office with personal influence. "Obviously, the more intense the positive identification," Hale argues, "the greater will be the influence of the President, and his access to the media more greatly facilitates the identification process."[59]

CONCLUSION

Power consists of potential (resources), action (behavior), and patterns of interaction (style). Power is a relative measure of an individual's potential to get others to do what the person wants them to do. Power-oriented behavior is the action taken by an individual whose purpose is to obtain, maintain, or increase their relative power.[60] A person's style or orientation to power consists of identifiable patterns of interactions involving the elements of information, position, and interpersonal skills.

Power is, of course, an inevitable element of politics. Someone must lead the nation, set priorities, and implement programs. Power is neither good nor bad. Philippa Strum makes an interesting observation.[61] Franklin Roosevelt had a great deal of power at the same time Adolph Hitler had a great deal of power. Thus, *how* power is achieved, maintained, and used is of prime importance. The danger, then, is not the "quantity" of power but the "quality" of power.

The somewhat speculative and conceptual model presented in this essay provides a framework for analyzing the dynamics of power rather than simply the resources of power. The model is flexible in allowing investigation of overall presidencies or specific presidential actions and decisions. At the very least, the model forces the scholar to recognize the importance of interaction when discussing the phenomenon of power in human society.

NOTES

1. Clinton Rossiter, *The American Presidency,* 2nd ed. (New York: Mentor Book, 1960), p. 79.

2. One of the best studies on the Cuban missile crisis that illustrates this notion is Graham T. Allison, *Essence of Decision* (Boston: Little, Brown, 1971).

3. Michael Korda, *Power: How to Get It, How to Use It* (New York: Random House, 1975), p. 3.

4. Marvin E. Olsen, *The Process of Social Organization* (New York: Holt, Rinehart, and Winston, 1968), p. 171.

5. Philippa Strum, *Presidential Power and American Democracy* (California: Goodyear Publishing, 1972), p. 25.

6. Godfrey Hodgson, *All Things to All Men* (New York: Touchstone Books, 1980), p. 21.

7. James W. Ceaser et al., "The Rise of the Rhetorical Presidency," in *Essays in Presidential Rhetoric,* ed. Theodore Windt (Dubuque: Kendall/Hunt, 1983), p. 7.

8. For a concise statement of these see Richard Pious, *The American Presidency* (New York: Basic Books, 1979), pp. 15–16.

9. Myron Hale, "Presidential Influence, Authority, and Power and Economics Policy," in *Toward a Humanistic Science of Politics,* ed. Dalmas Nelson and Richard Sklar (Lanham: University Press of America, 1983), p. 399.

10. J. French and B. Raven, "The Bases of Social Power," in *Group Dynamics: Research and Theory,* 3rd ed., ed. D. Cartwright and A. Zander (New York: Harper & Row, 1968), pp. 259–269.

11.   For classic psychological orientations see Harold Lasswell, *Psychopathology and Politics* (Chicago: University of Chicago Press, 1930); Edwin Hargrove, *Presidential Leadership: Personality and Political Style* (New York: Macmillan, 1966); James Barber, *The Presidential Character*, 2nd ed. (Englewood Cliffs: Prentice-Hall, 1977).

12.   Rossiter, *The American Presidency*, pp. 41–69.

13.   Ibid., p. 43.

14.   Richard Neustadt, *Presidential Power* (New York: John Wiley & Sons, 1980), pp. 28, 122.

15.   *Every Four Years: A Study of the Presidency* (Public Broadcasting Service, 1980), p. 45.

16.   Neustadt, *Presidential Power*, p. 2.

17.   See ibid.

18.   Hale, "Presidential Influence," p. 408.

19.   Ibid., p. 411.

20.   Louis W. Koenig, *The Chief Executive* (New York: Harcourt, Brace, and World, 1964), p. 5.

21.   Ibid., p. 5.

22.   Hugh Sidey, "Shadow Dancing with the World," *Times*, December 31, 1979, p. 20.

23.   Theodore H. White, *The Making of the President 1960* (New York: Atheneum, 1961), p. 371.

24.   Ibid., p. 367.

25.   *Every Four Years*, p. 45.

26.   Grant McConnell, *The Modern Presidency* (New York: St. Martin's Press, 1976), p. 82.

27.   Pious, *The American Presidency*, p. 16.

28.   McConnell, *The Modern Presidency*, p. 6.

29.   *Every Four Years*, p. 49.

30.   Aaron Wildavsky, *The Presidency* (Boston: Little, Brown, 1969), p. xi.

31.   As quoted in Rossiter, *The American Presidency*, p. 149.

32.   Peter Hall, "A Symbolic Interactionist Analysis of Politics," *Sociological Inquiry* 42 (1972):61.

33.   See Myron Hale, "Presidential Influence."

34.   Nicholas von Hoffman, *Make-Believe Presidents: Illusions of Power from McKinley to Carter* (New York: Pantheon Books, 1978), p. 225.

35.   Gordon Tullock, *The Politics of Bureaucracy* (Washington: Public Affairs Press, 1965), p. 131.

36.   Olsen, *Process of Social Organization*, p. 173.

37.   Murray Edelman, *Politics as Symbolic Action* (Chicago: Markham, 1971), p. 31.

38.   Perry London, *Behavior Control* (New York: Meridian Books, 1977), p. 36.

39.   Ibid., p. 27.

40.   Chester Cooper, *The Last Crusade: America in Vietnam* (New York: Dodd, Mead, 1970), p. 416.

41.   The idea of the Quadrants was stimulated by John Orman's *Presidential Secrecy and Deception: Beyond the Power to Persuade* (Connecticut: Greenwood Press,

1980) and his discussion of presidential secrecy and deception. The openness-secrecy dimension is borrowed from his work.

42. Barber, 2nd ed., p. 533.

43. Ben Heineman and Curtis Hessler, *Memorandum for the President* (New York: Random House, 1980), p. 51.

44. Ibid., p. 300.

45. For a complete account, see Allison, *Essence of Decision.*

46. See Neustadt, *Presidential Power.*

47. Barber, 2nd ed., pp. 69–72.

48. As reported in Barber, 2nd ed., p. 69.

49. Philip Shabecoff, "Appraising Presidential Power: The Ford Presidency" in *The Presidency Reappraised,* ed. Thomas Cronin and Rexford Tugwell (New York: Praeger, 1977), p. 32.

50. Rowland Evans and Robert Novak, *Lyndon Johnson: The Exercise of Power* (New York: New American Library, 1966), p. 2.

51. Doris Kearns, *Lyndon Johnson and the American Dream* (New York: Harper & Row, 1976), pp. 117–119.

52. Ibid., p. 117.

53. Ibid., p. 122.

54. Barber, 2nd ed., p. 79.

55. Richard Watson and Norman Thomas, *The Politics of the Presidency* (New York: John Wiley & Sons, 1983), p. 263.

56. Barber, 2nd ed., p. 59.

57. As reported in Barber, 2nd ed., p. 59.

58. John Murphy, *The Pinnacle: The Contemporary American Presidency* (Philadelphia: J. B. Lippincott, 1977), p. 199.

59. Hale, "Presidential Influence," p. 424.

60. See John Kotter, *Power in Management* (New York: AMACOM, 1979) for a clear distinction among power, power-oriented behavior, and power dynamics. Although an applied book for managers, his distinctions are developed well.

61. Strum, *Presidential Power and American Democracy,* p. 21.

TA AND POLITICAL RHETORIC: A NEW CONSIDERATION ON THE ISSUE OF PUBLIC TRUST

On August 15, 1973, Richard Nixon noted that Watergate "has come to mean a whole series of acts that either represent or appear to represent an abuse of trust."[1] In the wake of Watergate, the presidential election of 1976 demanded an honest, open, and value-oriented campaign. All the candidates emphasized moral and ethical considerations. Perhaps the most successful candidate in this realm was Jimmy Carter.

President Carter nurtured an image of being a "populist" president. The media aided this image by showing Carter as a man of the people with little pretense who indeed identifies with the common man. But the rhetoric of President Carter failed to live up to this common man image. His public discourses were often patronizing, over simplistic, evaluative, and obviously not so structured as to be speaking to an audience of "equals." This becomes vividly apparent when comparing President Carter's energy message to the public with his energy message two days later before a joint session of the United States Congress. In the former case, he spoke as "parent to child"; in the latter case, as an "adult to adult."

Traditional approaches to these addresses would emphasize the factor of audience adaption as the key influence in determining their structure. Our concern, however, is an attempt to isolate the motives behind Carter's choices of audience adaptation. In doing so, our analysis focuses on three related assumptions. Most of President Carter's addresses aimed at the general public were of a "parent to child" nature as expressed in transactional analysis terms. Second, the public's general mistrust and lack of confidence in politicians may be due to the politicians' failure to address the public from an adult ego state. Finally, the American presidency has undergone an expansion of domestic power and authority. This escalation of presidential power has altered the nature of political rhetoric encouraging the superior, parental tone.

The purpose of this essay is to consider some of the dimensions of the assumptions stated above plus encourage the application of transactional analysis principles to the realm of public discourse. Such an application proves beneficial in ascertaining a speaker's true motive or attitude toward his or her role and the general public.

TRANSACTIONAL ANALYSIS

Transactional analysis, specifically, describes a system or method of group treatment of psychotherapy.[2] Its theoretical constructs are also useful for studying dyadic relationships within organizations as a method of analyzing problems of communication.[3] Eric Berne, who developed transactional analysis, believed that people are basically okay. In addition, he believed that people could control or change their behavior if indeed they possessed enough awareness about the nature of their behavior. Thus, transactional analysis serves as a simple model whereby individuals may gain such personal awareness and hence effect behavior change.

Transactional analysis is increasing in popularity. It is being applied whenever people interact including such diverse fields as criminal justice, education, management, literature, advertising, and communication.[4]

Each individual is comprised of three ego states: adult, parent, and child. The adult ego state may be defined as the "verbal and nonverbal behavior oriented toward reality."[5] The "adult" behaves much like a computer in "gathering, processing, storing and recalling information."[6] This ego state may be characterized by rationality and the absence of emotion. Decisions are arrived at by the calculation of estimates and probabilities.

The parent ego state is the "verbal and nonverbal behavior learned from and modeled after one's parents."[7] This ego state reflects two dimensions: nurturing behaviors and critical behaviors. Nurturing behaviors may be characterized by showing concern, being protective, loving, or helping. Critical behaviors are characterized by being punitive, evaluative, condescending, authoritative, or dictatorial.[8] These behaviors are reflected in statements such as "You're a winner," "You're beautiful," "I love you no matter what"[9] or "You must," "You should," "Don't."[10] The "parent," then, is a collection of pre-recorded rules for living.

Finally, the child ego state may be defined as the "verbal and nonverbal behavior based upon early childhood memories and experiences."[11] A "child's" behavior may be characterized as being creative, imaginative, impulsive, unthinking, and fun-loving. Such behavior is reflected in statements as "I want what I want when I want it" or "try and make me."[12]

All conversations or verbal exchanges are a series of transactions. These transactions can be adult to adult, adult to child, adult to parent, parent to parent, parent to adult, parent to child, child to parent, child to adult, or child to child.[13] Transactions that are not complementary or of the same ego state usually result in a breakdown of communication. It is this dimension that is most apropos to our consideration.

ANALYSIS

As already stated, the parent ego state is usually characterized by exhibiting nurturing or critical behavior. President Carter's April 18, 1977, energy address to the American people over radio and television reflected both qualities.[14] He was pointedly critical of our selfishness and wastefulness of energy. He continually reminded us that "Each American uses the energy equivalent of 60 barrels of oil per person each year. Ours is the most wasteful nation on earth. We waste more energy than we import."[15]

His aggravation was expressed by threats of "punishment" if we did not alter our behavior. President Carter outlined explicitly our "punishment" if we failed to act by facing, ". . . an economic, social, and political crisis that will threaten our free institutions."[16] Economically, ". . . we will spend more than $550 billion for imported oil by 1985 — more than $2,500 for every man, woman, and child in America."[17] In addition, ". . . our factories will not be able to keep our people on the job with reduced supplies of fuel."[18] Socially, "we will not be ready to keep our transportation systems running . . ." and "we will feel mounting pressure to plunder the environment."[19] Politically, "we will live in fear of embargoes."[20]

President Carter went to great lengths to educate us regarding the problem of energy and assured us that even though his actions may be "painful," such "sacrifices" were necessary for our own betterment.

> I can't tell you that these measures will be easy, nor will they be popular . . . I am sure each of you find something you don't like about the specifics of our proposal. It will demand that we make sacrifices and changes in our lives. To some degree, the sacrifices will be painful — but so is any meaningful sacrifice. It will lead to some higher costs, and to some greater inconveniences for everyone.[21]

In educating us so that ". . . the people understand the seriousness of the challenge and are willing to make sacrifices," Carter developed a simple explanation for a very complex problem. In fact, he took us back 200 years into history to explain the trends of fuel consumption ranging from the use of wood to coal to oil and natural gas.

President Carter's solution to the energy problem was expressed in terms of principles and goals. The specific mechanics of how these principles and goals were to be achieved were not disclosed. Thus, only the structure of the solution was provided.

The tone of this address was one of reprimand and chiding thus reflecting mainly a parent ego state. In addition, Carter exhibited elements of authoritativeness as well as possessiveness. He sought to complement the assumed child ego state of the public by countering their impulsive and unthinking nature with simplistic parental explanations and portrayal of a bleak future. However, two days later when President Carter addressed a joint session of Congress on the same topic, his tone and approach reflected more the adult ego state.[22]

While both addresses were persuasive, the one before Congress was less instructional and informational. Carter spent less time attempting to convince the audience that a problem existed and more time dealing with rational, concrete action to be taken. In this address, President Carter had received information, computed probabilities, and was attempting to deal objectively with reality. While doing so, Carter referred to the congressmen as partners, equals, and did not rely upon threats to sanction their cooperation. Rather, he relied upon intelligence and reason.

From the very beginning of the address, President Carter made clear his view of partnership with Congress in handling the problem.

> In the months ahead, we must work together even more closely, for we have to deal with the greatest domestic challenge our nation will face in our lifetime. We must act now together, to devise and to implement a comprehensive national energy plan to cope with a crisis that otherwise could overwhelm us.[23]

He even acknowledged Congress's influence on his legislative proposals. "Your advice has been an important influence as this plan has taken shape. Many of its proposals will build on your own legislative initiatives."[24]

At times Carter is possessive of the American people and states that he, along with Congress, will save the people in this crisis. "None of our people must make an unfair sacrifice. None shoud reap an unfair benefit."[25]

The structure of the Congressional address is much more organized than his previous address to the U.S. public. Once revealing his five categories of proposals, President Carter proceeded to fully describe in great detail their functions and implications. He clearly stated his purpose and major topics to be dealt with.

> Tonight I want to outline the specific steps by which we can reach those goals. The proposals fall into these central categories: conservation, production, conversion, development and fairness, which is a primary consideration in all our proposals.[26]

In addition, throughout the address Carter's transitions were clearly articulated such as "Our fourth strategy is to develop permanent and reliable new energy sources."[27]

The nature of each proposal was specifically detailed. For example, rather than simply stating that an excise tax should be levied on autos that do not meet federal mileage standards, Carter stated:

> The tax will start low and then rise each year until 1985. In 1978, a tax of $180 will be levied on a car getting 15 miles per gallon, and for an 11 mile-per-gallon car the tax will be $450. By 1985 on wasteful new cars with the same low mileage, the taxes will have risen to $1,600 and $2,500.[28]

Such a lack of specificity in Carter's address to the nation is most noticeable when comparing the two addresses.

Finally, in speaking to Congress, Carter used more neutral words such as "proposal," "recommend," "our," "we," etc. Thus, President Carter's address before Congress is more of adult to adult — equals who are responsible for solving the people's problem of energy. The address is earmarked by rationality, objectivity, and clear decision-making.

IMPLICATIONS

The use of transactional analysis in this way presents several interesting considerations. Transactional analysis theory states that if exchanges are not complementary or of the same ego state, effective and productive communication ceases. The transaction described in President Carter's first address to the public resembles theoretically the dyadic "counter-transference" crossed transaction. Such crossed transactions whereby the general public expects elected officials to discuss vital national issues openly, rationally, and objectively but who are addressed as naive "children" lacking the intelligence and ability to handle full disclosure of matters may indeed result in mistrust and hence avoidance of political communication. From this observation one may speculate, then, that perhaps the best way to restore the public's confidence in elected officials is for them to respond to the public's questions and need for information by addressing them as fellow adults.

The problem, however, may be greater than that implied. During the 1976 presidential campaign Carter was perceived as "one of us" and perhaps his greatest appeal was that he had never been part of the Washington scene. By midterm, however, Carter's popularity dropped (*Newsweek,* November 7, 1977, p. 75). This fact leads one to question, among other things, the nature of the office of the presidency. Specifically, is it the office of president that dictates the nature and relationship of the president with the public? There is some indication that this is the case.

Several political scholars believe that the nature of the American presidency has undergone a change which was vividly magnified under the tenure of Richard Nixon. However, as early as 1970 George Reedy warned of "the twilight of the presidency."[29] Reedy labeled the presidency as "The American Monarchy" and recognized that "the essence of Presidential leadership is the mechanism by which the chief executive has a monopoly on authoritative answers to crucial questions in a context of uncertainty."[30]

Perhaps an even stronger statement of this belief is expressed by Arthur Schlesinger.[31] He maintains that the president, in modern history, has gained a great deal of power. "In recent years the imperial Presidency, having established itself in Foreign affairs, has made a bold bid for supremacy at home."[32] According to Schlesinger, if the president has the powers of life-and-death decisions abroad, how could he be expected to restrain from gathering such powers at home? Thus, the office itself has taken the parental role of absolute, unlimited power hence providing national direction and manipulation.

The personality and nature of the individual president must not, however, be ignored. Woodrow Wilson believed that one who is to be president should be ". . . a man who understands his own day and the needs of the country, and who has the personality and the initiative to enforce his views both upon the people and upon Congress."[33] In doing the above, however, a president may select one of several leadership types.[34] As "conservator" the president is the guardian of the existing order and as such, would be expected to behave as a parent. In the "protective" leadership type, the chief executive provides security against external danger to society's survival. Protection, again, is a function of being a parent.

It is generally agreed that the Nixon administration abused the public's trust. Yet, Nixon viewed the public's trust as demanding strong leadership and direction. An advisor to Nixon wrote in a memorandum in 1967 that "Potential presidents are measured against an ideal that's a combination of leading man, God, father, hero, pope, king with maybe just a touch of the avenging furies thrown in."[35] Nixon clearly believed this philosophy. In a campaign speech on the nature of the presidency on September 19, 1968, Nixon stated that a president "has to take *hold* of America before he can move it forward. . . . He must articulate the nation's values, define its goals and marshall its will."[36]

For Nixon, then, the question becomes simply one of providing what the people want and expect. He is not alone in this belief. James Barber believes that Americans look at the presidency

> in the propensity of children who want to believe the President is a good man, that people turn to the President for a sense that things will be all right; that in the midst of trouble is a core of serenity, and that our ordinary ease will be sustained.[37]

Regardless of the cause of the nature of present-day presidential rhetoric, the question of the public's trust and confidence in elected officials is of prime importance. This analysis identifies the potential problem as one of communication breakdown or barrier. To overcome this barrier, the public must become once again, a part of the national decision-making process.

CONCLUSION

The basic principles and concepts of transactional analysis may be applied to a public rhetorical situation which may reveal a speaker's true attitude toward his role or audience. Upon consideration of President Carter's energy address to the nation and his energy address two days later before a joint session of Congress, the former communicative transaction is of a parent to child nature while the latter reflects an adult to adult exchange. It was suggested that the public's general mistrust and lack of confidence in politicians may be due to the politician's failure to address the public from an adult ego state which may be characterized by full, objective, and complete discussion of the major issues of today. Reasons as to why presidential rhetoric appears to be parental were also investigated. The overall analysis suggests that the role of the office of president may need reappraisal in order to instigate effective change.

NOTES

1. Frank Mankiewicz, *Perfectly Clear* (New York: New York Times Book, 1973), p. 1.
2. Eric Berne, *Principles of Group Treatment* (New York: Oxford University Press, 1966) and *Transactional Analysis in Psychotherapy* (New York: Grove Press, 1961).
3. Gerald Goldhaber, *Organizational Communication* (Iowa: W. C. Brown, 1974).

4.   Gerald and Marylynn Goldhaber, *Transactional Analysis: Principles and Applications* (Boston: Allyn and Bacon, 1976), p. viii.

5.   Ibid., p. 6.

6.   Ibid., p. 35.

7.   Ibid., p. 6.

8.   Ibid., p. 35.

9.   Claude Steiner and Carmen Kerr, *Transactional Analysis Made Simple* (Berkeley: RA Press, 1971), p. 2.

10.   Leonard Campos and Paul McCormick, *Introduce Yourself to Transactional Analysis* (Berkeley: Transactional Pubs, 1972), p. 1.

11.   Gerald and Marylynn Goldhaber, *Transactional Analysis*, p. 6.

12.   Campos and McCormick, *Introduce Yourself*, p. 1.

13.   Ibid., p. 5.

14.   Jimmy Carter, "President's Proposed Energy Policy," *Vital Speeches of the Day* 43 (1977):418–420.

15.   Ibid., p. 419.

16.   Ibid.

17.   Ibid.

18.   Ibid.

19.   Ibid.

20.   Ibid.

21.   Ibid., p. 420.

22.   Jimmy Carter, "The Moral Equivalent of War," *Vital Speeches of the Day* 43 (1977):420–423.

23.   Ibid., p. 420.

24.   Ibid., p. 421.

25.   Ibid., p. 423.

26.   Ibid., p. 421.

27.   Ibid., p. 423.

28.   Ibid., p. 421.

29.   George Reedy, *The Twilight of the Presidency* (New York: New American Library, 1970).

30.   Ibid., p. 111.

31.   Arthur M. Schlesinger, Jr., *The Imperial Presidency* (Boston: Houghton Mifflin, 1973).

32.   Ibid., p. viii.

33.   Woodrow Wilson, "The President's Role in American Government," in *The Power of the Presidency*, ed. Robert Hirschfield (Chicago: Aldine, 1973), p. 89.

34.   Louis Koenig, *The Chief Executive* (New York: Harcourt, Brace and World, 1964), p. 189.

35.   Joe McGinniss, *The Selling of the President 1968* (New York: Pocket Books, 1970), p. 19.

36.   Richard Nixon, "Campaign Speech on the Nature of the Presidency," in *The Power of the Presidency*, ed. Robert Hirschfield (Chicago: Aldine, 1973), p. 165.

37.   James Barber, "Man, Mood, and the Presidency," in *The Presidency Reappraised*, ed. Rexford Tugwell and Thomas Cronin (New York: Praeger, 1974), p. 206.

Chapter 4

INTRAPERSONAL COMMUNICATION DIMENSIONS OF THE AMERICAN PRESIDENCY

> To venture causes anxiety, but to not venture is to lose one's self. . . . And
> to venture in the highest sense is precisely to become conscious of one's self.
>
> Sören Kierkegaard

When does an individual become president of the United States? For most Americans, an individual becomes president upon taking the oath of office. Yet, does merely taking the oath of office make someone a "president" in the fullest sense of the word? The purpose of this chapter is to explore the intrapersonal nature of the presidency. More specifically, we will focus on the interaction of the office with the officeholder and the resulting realities of that interaction. Such an investigation requires considering presidential roles, role expectations, and the subsequent adaptation of "self" to the presidency. Herzik and Dodson somewhat recently asserted that "the relationship between the President and the public's expectations of his roles and responsibilities is a relatively unexplored topic in the Presidential studies literature."[1] Equally important, the expectations of the public in the pre-governing period are also lacking theoretical treatment.[2] In this chapter we will systematically address both dimensions.

Any discussion of expectations that surround the presidency naturally leads to the consideration of how individual occupants of the office fit into the already established and defined role. But, as nearly all scholars recognize, there is no apprenticeship of training an individual may obtain in preparation for the presidency. There is no convenient book or guide that provides a detailed step by step analysis of the requirements and demands of the office. As Theodore White observes, the office is

". . . defined not so much by law as by the nature of men and the pressures of history."[3] Thus, what separates a good president from one not so good is the ability to perceive the office and "become" president.

When viewing the interaction of the office with the individual officeholder, three dimensions of the interaction emerge:

1. The individual begins a process of evaluating "self" against the perceived demands and expectations of the office.
2. The process of adapting oneself to the office is often long and painful, involving essentially three phases.
3. There are distinct and possibly harmful consequences of the transformation process of "becoming" president, as exemplified in the experiences of Johnson, Nixon, and Carter.

INTRAPERSONAL COMMUNICATION DEFINED

Intrapersonal communication is perhaps the most fundamental and basic form of all communication experiences. It is simply the process of communicating with ourselves. It is rather obvious to assert that before we can *share* "meanings" with others (that is, the process of articulating a belief, attitude, value, or felt need) we must first *create* "meanings" for ourselves. The distinction, however, is not quite that simple because as we communicate with others we are simultaneously communicating with ourselves.

The human being is constantly active in a process of self-determination and self-modification. Our view of the human being is of an organism that confronts its world with a "mechanism" for making self-evaluations. For us, the mechanism is a product of "self," "role," and interaction. The "self" is a social object that one shares with others in interaction. An individual comes to know self in interaction with others and the self is isolated, interpreted, and defined socially. As an object, therefore, "self" can be modified, evaluated, and reinforced. The notion of self-interaction emphasizes the dynamic nature of self and the importance of communication. William James stated that "a man has as many social selves as there are individuals who recognize him and carry an image of him in their minds."[4]

Thus, at the heart of intrapersonal communication is the concept of "self": how the self is created, modified, and maintained through social interaction. We define "self" in four ways. First, there is the self we think we are. We actively select, define, and interpret roles to play everyday.

This process provides us, upon reflection, a rather distinct self-concept. Second, most of us also can identify a self we would like to become. This imagined self provides an ideal basis for how we hope others will view us and the model for the self we hope to become. Third, and more difficult for most of us to articulate is the self others think we are. However, most of our reactions and role selections are based upon how we think others view us. Our goal is always to confirm, deny, or modify how we think others perceive us. If all these "selves" were the same, human relations would be easier. Finally, our physical and mental capabilities provide a rough framework for the creation of self.

George Mead argued that the self emerges in three separate, sequential phases.[5] He called the phases "play," "game," and "the generalized other." As a child progressively goes from one stage to another, the child is better able to differentiate self from others. In the "play" stage, the child can only handle one role. However, in the "game" phase, multiple roles are identified but not combined into a consistent symbolic perspective. Implicit rules appropriate to various role sets are recognized. Imitation becomes the primary means of acquiring a role. It is in the last phase, "the generalized other," that an individual actively interprets one's experiences with others. Here the individual is capable of separating self from the outside community. One is able to clearly see self in terms of the moral and symbolic expressions of others. Through role playing we become conscious of the rules that govern how we communicate, what we communicate, and behavior associated with specific roles. We develop the ability to respond to situations on the basis of what we believe to be appropriate and what others think of us.

In actuality, then, the self is a set of roles that a person may assume in a variety of social situations. The presidency, as a role set, involves the process of symbolic role-taking behavior by anyone who pursues the office. This process involves the ability to view the office as one imagines other people would view the office. Any candidate's communication behavior is greatly influenced by the candidate's perception of how the public perceives the office. They become concerned with self-images based on what they imagine others think of their behavior.

From this discussion, four characteristics of self may be identified.[6] First, the self is a process and not merely some entity. As a process, behavior includes: "carving out a line of action that mediates between one's impulses and the expectations of the social environment; observing and responding to one's own and other's behavior; adjusting and directing one's subsequent behavior on these two bases."[7] Second, the self is reflexive. One may define, modify, and evaluate one's own behavior. Third, the self involves various attitudes that dictate behavioral expectations as well as proper responses to situations. Finally, related to the previous notion, the self is the primary means of social control. "To have a self is to internalize the attitudes of the community and hereby to control one's own behavior in terms of those attitudes."[8] Hence, social control is self-control.

PRESIDENTIAL ROLES

Most all political scientists recognize that the presidency is both an institution and a role. As such, the presidency has a great deal of influence upon those who occupy the office as well as upon the general public.

Political roles are not concrete, static entities. Rather, they are ideas about what people expect to do in certain situations as well as what others expect them to do in certain situations. While the concept of role does deal with behavior, it *is not* the activity of behavior itself. The distinction between what individuals think they should do and what in fact they do should not be ignored. As Norton Long notes:

> The actors in the world of politics are neither the rational calculators of economic man nor the uncultured savages of Hobbe's state of nature but are born into a political culture, albeit frequently an ambiguous one, and are socialized to a range of response patterns that may be invoked by diverse stimuli. With this equipment, they confront a reality that seems to each public, one-dimensional common sense but, in fact, through the differing glasses that it is viewed, presents widely differing perspectives.[9]

Political actors, therefore, possess a "repertory of responses" or roles. Upon any stimulus, the appropriate role behavior is a product of what the actor perceives the defined role to be which also fulfills the expectations of the public. "The existence of these patterned sets of roles is part of the technology of the political culture and permits the actors to function with the same ease as a ballplayer playing his position."[10]

Thus, roles (political or otherwise) are comprised of internal and external elements.[11] The former consists of the individual's own perception of what a task demands and how to fulfill it; the latter are the expectations and orientations of members of society. However, as Haight and Johnston point out:

The division into roles can be deceptive . . . and one must never forget the fact that one man plays all the parts. The President can never separate his problems and divide them into preconceived categories for decision. Each decision will involve the President as a whole man, and he will need in some manner to accommodate several often conflicting roles in order to determine a course of action.[12]

Edward Corwin was the first to mention presidential roles as sources of power.[13] A president's power is based upon five constitutional roles: chief of state, chief executive, chief diplomat, commander-in-chief, and chief legislator. These roles are roughly analogous to the various areas of responsibilities outlined in the Constitution.

Clinton Rossiter, building on Corwin's analysis, argues that an additional five extra-constitutional roles must be recognized: chief of party, protector of the peace, manager of prosperity, world leader, and voice of the people.[14] Rossiter, as Corwin, believes that the source of presidential power lies in the combination of various roles. Rossiter, at least, recognizes the "expanding" nature of the presidency. Extra roles result from the growing activities of a president plus the growing expectations of the public. As Myron Hale succinctly states, "roles became obligations and duties, as each role becomes a Presidential responsibility."[15] When speaking of presidential roles, most scholars cite Rossiter's classic *The American Presidency*. Hence, the list of roles is fairly constant. Yet, as the functions or duties of the presidency grow, so do the roles. As the various tasks become more complex, numerous roles may be required to carry out one function. However, a president who creates additional roles which add to his power without a public mandate to do so may be "over-personalizing" the office to a dangerous extent.

ROLE EXPECTATIONS

A "role set" is a set of "behavioral relationships that exist between positions."[16] Borden, Gregg, and Grove argue that there are two kinds of role sets: traditional role sets and unique role sets.[17] Traditional role sets refer to institutionalized relationships such as husband and wife, lawyer and client, etc. These role sets provide general guidelines for behavior. Traditional role sets serve primarily task-maintenance functions. Unique role sets refer primarily to person-maintenance functions. Thus, traditional role sets provide already established interaction patterns and set up general expectations of the participants.

Certainly, the American presidency has established a rather clear traditional role set. The title of president implies more than simply a job description. To know that a person is president is to know in a very general way how the individual is likely to behave and how others will behave toward the individual. The title not only provides a means for anticipating a range of behaviors, but also confines the range of behaviors possible. Thus, behavioral expectations and restrictions are attached to all social positions. Richard Rose notes that "empirical investigation usually reveals that leaders are often constrained by the expectations of their followers and in some cases compelled to follow their followers or risk deposition as leader."[18]

Cronin recognizes that a basic tendency of Americans is to believe in great personages, ". . . that someone, somewhere, can and will cope with the major crises of the present and future."[19] Within our society, the presidency fulfills this need and becomes the symbol of our hopes. Presidents are much more likely, historically, to be placed on a pedestal rather than under a microscope. Although the tendency is acknowledged by political scientists, Cronin insists that political scientists have ". . . usually not read in such meaning, or at least have not infused their view of the Presidency with connotations of a civil religion."[20] Consequently, to simply speak of presidential functions in no way adequately describes what the presidency "really is."

Emmet Hughes, in *The Living Presidency*, states that a president faces two constituencies: "the living citizens and the future historians."[21] This certainly is not an easy task. Nearly all scholars agree that any American president inherits a vast, complex set of role expectations. "The fact that there are many roles involved in the most important political office gives a politician the discretion of deciding which to emphasize and which to ignore. He can, at the least, choose what he ignores."[22] But such a choice is not a one-way street. Just as political roles create public expectations, expectations can create political roles. As Murray Edelman perceptively notes:

> Expectations also evoke a specific political role and self-conception for those individuals who accept the myth in question: the patriotic soldier whose role it is to sacrifice, fight, and die for his country; the policeman or National Guardsmen whose role it is to save the social order from subhuman or radical hordes.[23]

For Edelman, the degree of attachment to a political myth and the role it creates plus the fervor with which the role is acted out depend upon "the degree of anxiety the myth rationalizes, and the intensity with which the particular expectations that form the central premise of the myth is held."[24] When Alfred de Grazia speaks of "the myth of the President," he is referring to "a number of qualities [that] are given to every President that are either quite fictitious or large exaggerations of the real man."[25] He further notes that "the myth is not alone the property of the untutored mind, but of academicians, scientists, newspapermen, and even Congressmen."[26]

Thus, the office of the presidency has grown because of interaction; interaction of the office with the public and the public with the office. As public expectations increase, so does the job. Concurrently, as the job is expanded, so are public expectations.

The already noted contemporary growth in public expectations of the presidency seems directly related to the growth of mass media. Because twentieth-century presidents have been able to speak directly to the public through electronic mass media rather than having to rely upon the nineteenth-century intermediaries — party bosses — they have tended to encourage the public to identify directly with them. This has given them more power, while underlining the power of the parties. Political promises, once the province of the often corrupt political bosses, have by now become almost exclusively the responsibility (and burden) of the presidents.

Theodore White asserts that, especially since 1960, our idea of government consists of promises — promises to take care of people, the cities, the sick, the old, the young. According to White, "by 1980 we had promised ourselves almost to the point of natural bankruptcy."[27] Consequently, the public has responded by holding the president accountable for meeting various demands. David Easton has identified two types of expectations that citizens have of political leadership.[28] One focuses on the office and the other focuses on the individual who holds the office. Thus public expectations are vast and complex. Upon investigating the research on presidential and public expectations, Herzick and Dodson conclude that indeed "a consensus does exist concerning public expectations of the President — a consensus focused around general traits of personality, leadership, and individual virtue."[29]

The simple truth is that the nation expects more from the president than either his authority or his power allows him to provide. In fact, about 75 percent of the American people, when questioned, admit that their expectations are unfairly high.[30] One man simply cannot keep the economy at a high level, decrease unemployment, and stop inflation. No man can guarantee, in this world, a life of peace, contentment, and security. As Sidney Hyman notes: "He does not have God's autonomous powers to make mountains without valleys as the mood strikes him."[31] Consequently, "the difference between what some of us imagine the Presidency to be and what it really is leads to disappointment, frustrations, and attack."[32] Thus, expecting the impossible from a president inevitably leads to disappointment in his performance.

But disappointment in presidential performance is not the only consequence of false expectations. False expectations also encourage presidents to attempt more than they can accomplish in any term of office. Thus, false expectations invite presidents to overpromise and overextend themselves. This, in turn, creates the need for image-making activities. Such activities, in some cases, become the major task or work function of an administration. Soon, the emphasis, out of necessity, becomes style over substance. As Cronin argues,

> The public-relations apparatus, not only has directly enlarged the Presidential work force but has expanded public-relations expectations about the Presidency at the same time. More disquieting is the fact that, by its very nature, this type of press-agentry feeds on itself, and the resulting distortions encourage an ever increasing subordination of substance to style.[33]

PRESIDENTIAL ROLES CREATED AND PERMEATED

Political roles, although undergoing constant modification, exist prior to any political event. Politicians, however, do not consciously decide each morning during what parts of the day they will act as statesman, administrator, or partisan vote-getter. Yet, as already argued, public expectations of behavior and performance are rather clearly defined. Such expectations develop over time and consequently are slow in changing. Because political roles are fairly well defined, they are learned by politicians through the process of socialization. New legislators soon learn what roles are appropriate in various situations.

Role-taking, according to Edelman, is action.[34] It is both behavioral and observable. The process of role-taking by politicians directly influences the behaviors of officeholders by revealing public expectations and hence expected behavior. Edelman succinctly explains the process as follows:

> Through taking the roles of publics whose support they need, public officials achieve and maintain their positions of leadership. The official who correctly gauges the response of publics to his acts, speeches, and gestures makes those behaviors significant symbols, evoking common meaning for his audience

and for himself and so shaping his further actions as to reassure his public and in this sense "represent" them.[35]

This process of role socialization, argues Rose, is "emotionally intense and highly compressed in time; it is the chief means by which people fit and are fitted into place in established institutions."[36]

One of the major points to be made in discussing the paradoxical nature of the presidency is that the expectations and functions of the office are often competing, conflicting, and contradictory. Role conflicts are essential elements of political life. Role conflicts occur "when contradictory types of behavior are expected from a person who holds different positions or when contradictory types of behavior are expected within one role."[37] A successful politician, therefore, is one who can handle role conflicts. Unfortunately, depending upon one's view, when a discrepancy develops between individual preferences and institutional role expectations, it is more often the individual who changes. For Richard Rose, the best measure of a politician's greatness is his ability to create new roles for an established office.[38] In fact, Rose views such an ability as one attribute of charismatic leadership.

Politics is primarily symbolic activity which touches the lives of a significantly large number of people.[39] Such activity has a unique and often profound meaning because, in the words of Kenneth Burke, man is uniquely "the symbol-making, and symbol-misusing animal."[40] Political reality, the implications and consequences of which are felt and observable, is conveyed through the creation of "significant symbols." Images of politics are largely, therefore, symbolic. The degree to which images of politics are useful and gratifying, according to Nimmo, is related to three factors:

> First, no matter how correct or incorrect, complete or incomplete may be one's knowledge about politics, it gives that person some way of understanding specific political events. . . . Second, the general likes and dislikes in a person's political images offer a basis for evaluating political objects. . . .Third, a person's self-image provides a way of relating one's self to others.[41]

Political images, then, are beneficial in an individual's evaluating and identifying with various political leaders, events, ideas, or causes.

Many attitudes about the presidency stem from messages received in childhood about the virtues of various presidents. Studies continually find that the president is ordinarily the first public official to come to the attention of young children.[42] Long before children are informed about the specific functions of the presidency, they view individual presidents as exceptionally important and benign. Easton and Hess found that children, stressing personal characteristics, see the president as honest, wise, helpful, powerful, good, and benign.[43] Such attitudes probably result from parents omitting negative aspects of the political world from the children plus the general tendency of children selectively to perceive more supportive characteristics of individuals in a wider environment. Even in 1973, at the height of the Watergate episode Greenstein found "numerous idealized references to the President."[44] Thus, esteem and respect for the office independent of the occupant, are established at a rather early age.

Such orientations to the presidency in adolescence have a profound influence on later attitudes. When political assessments of adult life conflict with earlier child attitudes, psychologists argue that the longest held attitudes would most likely dictate the response given.[45] Thus, even though adults are aware of the faults of the political system, they continue generally to respect the presidency above all other institutions.

Since World War II, every year seven or eight of the ten most admired men and women are involved in national politics. And the president, regardless of performance, is among them.[46] Doris Graber, in a study designed to analyze images of presidential candidates in the press during campaigns, found that citizens tend selectively to extract information about a president's personal image that is beyond the media content, while ignoring issue elements.[47] Therefore, apparently, citizens perceive and evaluate a president as a person rather than his policies and skill in office. According to Greenstein, when people are asked to indicate what they like or dislike about a president, they usually cite aspects of personal image.[48]

A presidential campaign emphasizes the childhood visions and qualities of the office. Hence, campaigns themselves perpetuate the mythic and heroic role demands of the office. To mobilize a nation is indeed a somewhat mysterious process. For McConnell it is the essential dimension of the presidency; that is, because the presidency is the central "national symbol," only the president can give substance and purpose to the nation itself.[49] The process of selecting a president is important and vital. Campaigns may best be characterized as noisy, disorderly, contentious, and even absurd. "The gap between the indignity of the process and the grandeur of the end is enormous."[50] Yet, the process allows the opportunity of assessing and projecting of presidential qualities upon the candidates.

From this perspective an election is seen not simply as a reflection of the preference for one individual over another. Rather, it is a composite of all the individual desires, hopes, frustrations, and anger of citizens encompassing an infinite number of issues or concerns. However chaotic, the process has value. As McConnell notes:

> Purists may well wish for more graceful campaigning, and more incisive and intellectually elevated debates. Quite possibly, however, achieving these desirable conditions might rob the process of much of its vitality and leave the ultimate winner with no accurate sense of the temper of the American people. A Presidential election is, above all, articulation of the mood of the electorate.[51]

By inauguration day a candidate has emerged as president. A tremendous transformation, at least in the eyes of the public, has occurred. Americans want and even need to believe that the common man they elevated to the presidency is a "Lincolnesque" bearer of infinite wisdom and benevolence. The perceived qualities are confirmed as soon as the candidate takes the oath of office.

IMPLICATIONS

The intrapersonal communication dimensions of the American presidency are complex. The office has a clear, historical impact upon each officeholder. Every American, from seven to seventy, has a list of criteria for what makes a "good" president. Yet, when consulting the ultimate authority, Article II of our Constitution, which delineates the functions and duties of the president, one notices how short, sketchy, vague, and trivial the description of the office appears. The presidency is indeed a very real office with an elected official, space, desks, and staff, yet it remains elusive and undefined. The presidency is the work of the presidents. Expectations (both their own and those of the citizens) are created through their rhetoric, use of symbols, rituals, and sense of history.

The "political self" must be isolated, interpreted, and defined socially. The political self involves continual mediation between one's own impulses and the expectations of others. Each president confronts the role and must adapt to the office.

From this discussion, several elements of the interaction of the office with the officeholder are emphasized. First, clearly the presidency, as an office, has profound influence upon any occupant. Each president must become an "object" subject to self-evaluation, assessment, and comparison. In becoming president, an individual must respond to self, as well as public expectations and perceptions of the office. This often requires adoption of certain perceived qualities and characteristics, a process that occurs over a period of time. Thus, as a result of interacting with the public, historical expectations, and individual views of the office, the person "becomes" president.

While the process of becoming president is intriguing, it forces us to consider the function and nature of political campaigns. Campaigns serve to *define* acceptable role behavior. But perhaps more importantly, they serve to confirm, for both the candidate and the public, that the individual running for office meets our role expectations and is "right" for the job.

Today, political consultants are the "king makers" of politics and are at the very heart of our electoral process. Their primary purpose, according to Nimmo and Combs, is to communicate "political celebrities" much like the Hollywood star system and movie gossip magazines.[52] Consequently, politicians have become fantasy figures and symbolic leaders because they are shown to represent not only issues positions but values, lifestyle, visions, and glamour.

Our electoral process, therefore, contributed greatly to the development of today's "political celebrity." Americans have historically believed that our democratic political system allows the best, most qualified individual to rise from the masses to lead the people, representing their collective hopes and desires as well as reflecting their values.[53] To succeed, politicians must honor this illusion and demonstrate that they indeed meet the role demands and expectations of the public.

Of course, another important factor is the public's dependence upon the mass media for political information. Few citizens experience the process of politics by direct participation. Thus, political realities are mediated through group and mass communication activities.[54] Thomas Patterson, who conducted a detailed study of presidential campaigns, concludes that "it is no exaggeration to say that, for the large majority of voters, the campaign has little reality apart from its media version."[55] The ultimate danger of media consultants, according to Herbert Schiller, is that by "using myths which explain, justify, and sometimes even glamorize the prevailing conditions of existence, manipulators secure popular support for a social order that is not in the majority's long-term interest."[56]

Meeting public expectations is itself a complex and difficult task. As already noted, we prize the notion of a common man, "one of us" leading his fellowmen. But our presidents certainly *have not* been common men.

There are three basic legal qualifications for becoming president of the United States: a natural born citizen, at least 35 years of age, and a resident of the United States for 14 years. These qualifications are rather simple and nondiscriminating. But even a casual reflection upon those who have held our highest political office reveals how "uncommon," nonrepresentative presidents are of the general population.[57] Four American families alone produced eight presidents, namely, John Adams, John Quincy Adams, James Madison, Zachary Taylor, William Henry Harrison, Benjamin Harrison, Theodore Roosevelt, and Franklin Roosevelt, and four presidents came from prominent political families, namely, John Tyler, Franklin Pierce, William Taft, and John Kennedy. When considering the income and occupation of the parents, at least half of the presidents came from the upper socioeconomic class. All American presidents have a European lineage and 34 of the 39 had ancestors from the British Isles. Although all the presidents, with one exception, have been Protestant, most have been Episcopalian, Presbyterian, and Unitarian rather than from the more numerous Methodists or Baptists. Twenty-four of the presidents (62 percent) have come from only five states: New York, Ohio, Virginia, Massachusetts, and Tennessee. Thirty-four states have never had a resident become president. All but nine of our presidents (30 out of 39) not only attended college but most attended prestigious private institutions, whereas in the general public, only 22 percent of men 25 years or older have four years or more of college. Sixty-two percent of our presidents were trained attorneys. Law is certainly a high prestige occupation. In the general public, however, only 16 percent of the population are employed in professional occupations. Thus, our presidents have tended to be white, members of a "high status" Protestant denomination, born to a relatively prosperous family whose ancestors came to America from the British Isles, well-educated at prestigious private institutions, and have tended to practice law.

But belief in the myth that any citizen may become president of the United States becomes a paradox in that, once elected, we demand uncommon leadership, great insight, a vast knowledge from our presidents. This paradox is, perhaps, most critical to the success of a president in terms of his transition from candidate to president.

President Carter nurtured an image of being a "populist" president. Presenting himself as a common man and a man of the people, was clearly at the heart of both his campaign strategy and presidential behavior. Once elected, however, citizens criticized Carter's lack of "presidential" behavior, dress, and demeanor. As Kathy Smith observes, in addition to "*who* to represent" a president must concern himself with "*how* to represent" the public.[58] Thus, if a candidate acts "too presidential" and not "folksy" enough he may indeed alienate the voters and lose the election. Conversely, if a president acts "too folksy" and not "presidential" he may well lose the confidence of the voters. The suggestion is that as candidate for the presidency an individual must demonstrate commonalities with the electorate. As president, the individual must demonstrate elements of strength, genius, and sophistication.

The candidacy and presidency of Jimmy Carter provide insight into the role transition.

Carter as Presidential Candidate

Nearly all presidential candidates make overt attempts to appeal to the common man or average citizen. Such attempts of audience adaptation and identification are well-known, expected, and widely accepted political campaign techniques. Carter's presidential campaign of 1976 is well known to most communication scholars. Presenting himself as a "common man" and a "man of the people" was clearly at the heart of his campaign strategy. James Wooten noted that Carter "worked hard at establishing himself in the eyes of the public as a common man, just another American hired to do a particular job."[59]

Early in the Carter campaign, Jerry Rafshoon realized that the typical 30- and 60-second political commercials would be insufficient to present Carter as an average citizen. They decided, therefore, to use a five-minute format.[60] Rafshoon reasoned that "TV gives Carter the opportunity to comfort the voter in the same type atmosphere in which he campaigns."[61] Carter was presented shaking hands and talking with voters in a "cinema verite" style as if the television audience were seeing Carter in person.

Both verbally and nonverbally, Carter's commercials reinforced the "common man" theme. Visually, Carter was shown in open-collar sport shirts or plaid work shirts standing by a split-rail fence or in the fields picking peanuts. His theme was twofold: a citizen president and a government "as idealistic, as decent, as competent, as compassionate, as good as its people." In one ad Carter stated,

I think it is time to have a non-lawyer in the White House for a change. Somebody that's had to work with his hands. Somebody who has had to run a complicated business. Somebody who has actually had to manage the affairs of a large government as I have in my own state.[62]

Throughout the entire campaign, Carter effectively portrayed himself as "one of us." The evening news showed candidate Carter humbly carrying his own garment bag over his shoulder.[63] He told us that he preferred to be called "Jimmy" and that he too, like the rest of us, had "lust in his heart."

Carter effectively articulated the traditional values of "an average American citizen." Carter's campaign rhetoric reflected how Americans wanted to conceive of themselves and the myth they wanted to live by. Johnstone argues that "a vote for Carter became for us a symbolic repossession of the virtues that we need to see in ourselves."[64] Carter's campaign slogan, "a government as good as its people" focuses attention on the above notion. Johnstone concludes:

His discourse, consequently, did more than present an image of himself; it developed and presented an image of *our*selves. Whereas both Ford and Carter told us that *they* were honest, competent, compassionate, etc., Carter carried the idea further. He told us what *we* were. Beyond this, he told us that he derived his own wisdom, compassion, and competence *from us*. *We* become the subject-matter of Jimmy Carter's discourse, and we were persuaded to reaffirm our faith in ourselves by acting for him.[65]

Several scholars have made the same observation. This idea is also clearly represented in the campaign ads. Richard Katula examined the ads of both Carter and Ford for leadership appeals.[66] He found that Ford's ads were dominated by the pronoun "he" while Carter's relied heavily on the pronoun "we." Thus, "Carter's approach elevated people to the status of co-leaders."[67]

Patrick Devlin argues that Carter's final television ads were a rather drastic departure from his earlier ones. He began speaking directly to the voter rather than being shown speaking to a group of people. "These new ads," Devlin posits, "sought to make him appear more Presidential by communicating to a compassionate yet forceful leader image."[68] Devlin concludes that

one clear impression from viewing the spots sequentially from the beginning of the primary campaigns to the end of the general election is that the personable candidate (that is, Carter) became more presidential and the presidential candidate (that is, Ford) became more personable.[69]

While clearly a successful strategy, Carter did not maximize the strategy upon his inauguration.

Carter as President

From the beginning, in both words and deeds, Carter made many efforts to reinforce the notion of "common man" serving as president. At his inauguration, Carter wore a blue business suit rather than the traditional morning coat and top hat. He insisted upon taking the oath of office as "Jimmy Carter" rather than as "James Earl Carter, Jr."

Perhaps the most dramatic event that signaled a change in presidential style was Carter's inaugural walk down Pennsylvania Avenue to the White House. While Senator William Proxmire suggested to Carter that a walk from the Capitol to the White House would serve as a good example to reinforce the nation's physical fitness program, Carter reveals in his memoirs that:

> Later, however, I began to realize that the symbolism of our leaving the armored car would be much more far-reaching than simply to promote exercise. . . . I felt a simple walk would be a tangible indication of some reduction in the imperial status of the President and his family. . . .Besides, I wanted it to be a dramatic moment.[70]

Carter not only knew what he wanted to do in terms of redefining the presidency but also he realized the value and impact of symbolic acts. Carter relates his desire to have "populist" inauguration festivities that would mirror the style of his campaign and administration.[71] Rosalynn Carter's decision not to purchase a new gown for the inaugural ball was a "symbolic and sentimental decision of ours."[72]

Carter prohibited the traditional playing of "Hail to the Chief" upon his arrival before groups, required his staff to drive their own automobiles rather than chauffeur-driven limousines, and barred security men from opening doors for him.[73]

But Carter went beyond aspects of personal treatment to signal to the public that he was a president of "the people." Carter sold the presidential yacht *Sequoia*, turned in 29 presidential planes, sent Amy to a public school, still carried his own baggage on trips, and told Barbara Walters, on a nationally televised program, that blue jeans were his "normal attire" at the White House and Rosalynn often in the evenings wore only her bathrobe.[74] The president held "town meetings" and spent some nights on the road in the modest homes of local citizens. His "fireside chats" were carefully produced to reflect the desired "common man" image. As Carter described his first such chat on the energy problem, "wearing a cardigan sweater, I sat by an open fire in the White House library on the night of February 2, 1977, and outlined as clearly as possible what we needed to do together."[75]

Carter's purpose was clear. He writes:

> Although we altered little in the White House itself, I wanted to make some basic changes in how a President lived and governed. In addition to the gesture of walking down Pennsylvania Avenue, I tried in my ways to convince the people that barriers between them and top officials in Washington were being broken down. A simpler lifestyle, more frugality, less ostentation, more accessibility to the press and public — all these suited the way I had always lived.[76]

But, did it work?

Carter's Failure

After only 90 days in office, Carter's popularity had risen 20 points in the polls.[77] In July 1977, Carter received a 64 percent positive rating on the question of restoring public confidence in government. Just one year later, however, Carter received a 63 percent negative response to the same question.[78] For Victor Lasky, the Carter presidency began "with a series of public relations gestures which for a time, added considerably to the President's popularity" but ended with a president "who demonstrated so quickly an inability to conduct even the simplest affairs of state."[79]

It is not our purpose to document the failures of the Carter presidency. There is evidence to suggest, however, that the public soon resented and rejected Carter's attempts to reduce the perceived stature and dignity of the presidency. Carter did not endear himself to the public. In fact, "among the people there seemed to be a huge emotional void about the President. He was neither loved nor hated, neither greatly admired nor deeply distrusted."[80] Part of the reason may well lie in the question, why should we pay deference to or give loyalty to someone no better or worse than ourselves? Carter, much too late, realized this fact. In his memoirs he writes:

> However, in reducing the imperial Presidency, I overreacted at first. We began to receive many complaints that I had gone too far in cutting back the pomp and ceremony, so after a few months I authorized the band to play "Hail to the Chief" on special occasions. I found it to be impressive and enjoyed it.[81]

But the correction of the "overreaction" was too little and too late. In the 1980 campaign Ronald Reagan's bearing and smooth handling of the media made him seem a regal alternative to the "too plain" man from Plains.

It is tempting to compare the Carter presidency with the Truman presidency. Indeed, there are many similarities. Both were Democrats, Baptists, hard-working small businessmen from small towns. The question arises, if the populist orientation worked for Truman, why did it fail for Carter? In this regard, there are four considerations. First, the "populist" presidency of Truman *did not* work. The press and the public lost confidence in Truman. It is only somewhat recently that Truman has been classified as a "near-great" president. Second, the modern presidency, beginning with Franklin Roosevelt, is a different institution from that of earlier days. America is no longer an isolated, agrarian society. Our president must meet with other kings and rulers of other nations. The office embodies the hopes, desires, dignity, and wealth of our nation. The office, in becoming more powerful, is both our administrative office and our ceremonial office. The modern presidency possesses a unique ceremonial dimension that earlier presidencies did not possess. Third, Barbara Kellerman argues that "all politicians must have at least some minimal skill at ingratiating themselves with, and appealing to, unfamiliar others."[82] Carter's skill in this area was minimal and he "derived no pleasure from interpersonal activity that involved more than a handful of intimates, and [he] regarded interaction with others as a means to an end rather than an end in itself."[83] Kellerman posits that, as an introvert, Carter "assumed the guise of the populist to counter his perception that among the in-crowd he would find few friends. . . . Consciously, Carter the outsider saw himself as better than those inside."[84] Finally, then, perhaps Carter's "populism" was not real and the public sensed its phoniness or perhaps Carter tried too hard to convince the people that he was ordinary and common. With Truman, although the people rejected him, his commonness and unpretentiousness were sincere.

Although it may seem that we have broadened our concern in this chapter beyond a consideration of intrapersonal communication, it should be understood that such broadening was done in order to get at the components of the intrapersonal. For intrapersonal communication, what we tell ourselves to do and be, is determined by what others (directly and through societal role-setting) tell us to do and be. Since we are not privy to the actual conversations of presidents with themselves, we must guess at those conversations by noting what the presidential roles are, how the public responds to specific presidents playing specific roles, and, especially any resultant changes in presidential behaviors. That is the only route, short of psychoanalysis to trace the relationship between presidential intrapersonal communication and presidential job performance. For if there is a gap between presidential style and substance, promise and performance, its roots are firmly in the dimensions of intrapersonal communication behaviors. The roles of "leader," "manager," and "campaigner" are distinct and very different. To succeed in one does not guarantee success in the others. It is difficult and unrealistic for any person to be all things to all people. With this understanding, we can better judge the candidates running for office.

CONCLUSION

Intrapersonal communication is the basis for all communication endeavors. It involves the concepts of "self," "roles," and "social interaction." The presidency is an office consisting of ever-accumulating functions, roles, obligations, and expectations. As individuals interact with the office, roles develop. The roles not only constrain individual behavior but also help create expectations of specific behavior. As expectations grow, so does the job. The public's perceptions of the office are institutionalized into models, myths, history, and textbooks. Unrealistic demands force candidates to rely upon style over substance and image over issues. A presidential candidate and president must appear active, moral, common, smart, etc. But "appearances" are deceiving and, as shown, even paradoxical. Each occupant must demonstrate that he possesses the qualities required and desired by the public. Presidential elections become, therefore, contests for symbolic legitimation.

NOTES

1. Erick Herzik and Mary Dodson, "The President and Public Expectations: A Research Note," *Presidential Studies Quarterly*, vol. 12, no. 2 (Spring 1982):172.

2. Ibid., pp. 168–169.

3. Theodore H. White, *The Making of the President 1960* (New York: Atheneum, 1961), p. 367.

4. William James, "The Social Self," in *Social Psychology Through Symbolic Interaction*, ed. Gregory Stone and Harvey Farberman (Mass.: Ginn-Blaisdell, 1970), p. 374.

5. George H. Mead, *Mind, Self, and Society* (Chicago: University of Chicago Press, 1972), pp. 135–222.

6. These characteristics are based on those provided by Robert Lauer and Warren Handell, *Social Psychology: The Theory and Application of Symbolic Interaction* (Boston: Houghton Mifflin, 1977), pp. 67–70.

7. Ibid., p. 67.

8. Ibid., p. 68.

9. Norton Long, "The Political Act as an Act of Will," in *The Political Vocation*, ed. Paul Tillett (New York: Basic Books, 1965), p. 179.

10. Ibid., p. 179.

11. For a good concise discussion of these two dimensions see Fred Greenstein, "What the President Means to Americans: Presidential 'Choice' Between Elections" in *Choosing the President*, ed. James D. Barber (Englewood Cliffs: Prentice-Hall, 1974), pp. 121–147.

12. David Haight and Larry Johnston, *The President: Roles and Powers* (Chicago: Rand McNally, 1965), p. 366.

13. Edward S. Corwin, *The President: Office and Powers*, 3rd ed. (New York: New York University Press, 1948), pp. 20–23.

14. Clinton Rossiter, *The American Presidency*, 2nd ed. (New York: Mentor Book, 1960), pp. 28–37.

15. Myron Hale, "Presidential Influence, Authority, and Power and Economic Policy" to be published in a *Festschrift* in honor of Francis D. Wormuth. The selection is also contained in the author's forthcoming book on "The President and the Policy Process," p. 10.

16. Don Faules and Dennis Alexander, *Communication and Social Behavior: A Symbolic Interaction Perspective* (Mass: Addison-Wesley, 1978), p. 67.

17. As stated in ibid.

18. Richard Rose, *People in Politics: Observations Across the Atlantic* (New York: Basic Books, 1965), p. 110.

19. Thomas Cronin, *The State of the Presidency* (Boston: Little, Brown, 1975), p. 34.

20. Ibid.

21. Emmet J. Hughes, *The Living Presidency* (New York: Penguin Books, 1972), p. 26.

22. Rose, *People in Politics*, p. 111.

23. Murray Edelman, *Politics as Symbolic Action* (Chicago: Markham, 1971), p. 55.

24. Ibid.

25. Alfred deGrazia, "The Myth of the President" in *The Presidency*, ed. Aaron Wildavsky (Boston: Little, Brown, 1969), p. 50.

26. Ibid.

27. Alvin Sanoff, "A Conversation with Theodore H. White," *U.S. News and World Report,* July 5, 1982, p. 59.

28. David Easton, *A System Analysis of Political Life* (New York: Wiley, 1965), pp. 273–274.

29. Herzik and Dodson, "The President and Public Expectations," pp. 172–173.

30. *Every Four Years: A Study of the Presidency,* Public Broadcasting Service, 1980, p. 17.

31. Louis W. Koenig, *The Chief Executive* (New York: Harcourt, Brace and World, 1964), p. 6.

32. Ibid.

33. Thomas Cronin, "The Presidency Public Relations Script" in *The Presidency Reappraised,* ed. Rexford Tugwell and Thomas E. Cronin (New York: Praeger, 1974), p. 168.

34. For a good discussion of political role-taking see Murray Edelman, *The Symbolic Uses of Politics* (Urbana: University of Illinois Press, 1964).

35. Ibid., p. 188.

36. Rose, *People in Politics,* p. 99.

37. Faules and Alexander, *Communication and Social Behavior,* p. 71.

38. Rose, *People in Politics,* p. 114.

39. For such an orientation to political behavior see Dan Nimmo, *Political Communication and Public Opinion in America* (California: Goodyear Publishing, 1978).

40. Kenneth Burke, *Language as Symbolic Action* (Berkeley: University of California Press, 1966), especially pp. 3–24.

41. Nimmo, *Political Communication,* pp. 227–228.

42. Greenstein, "What The President Means to Americans," pp. 121–147 and Fred Greenstein, "Popular Images of the President," in *The Presidency,* ed. Aaron Wildavsky (Boston: Little, Brown, 1969), pp. 287–295.

43. David Easton and Robert Hess, "The Child's Political 'World,'" *Midwest Journal of Political Science,* no. 3 (August 1962):241–242.

44. Greenstein, "What the President Means to Americans," p. 134.

45. Willam Mullen, *Presidential Power and Politics* (New York: St. Martin's Press, 1976), p. 114.

46. Bruce Campbell, *The American Electorate* (New York: Holt, Rinehart, and Winston, 1979), p. 78.

47. Doris Graber, "Personal Qualities in Presidential Images, The Contribution of the Press," *Midwest Journal of Political Science* 16 (February 1972):142.

48. Greenstein, "Popular Images of the President," p. 292.

49. Grant McConnell, *The Modern Presidency* (New York: St. Martin's Press, 1976), p. 19.

50. Ibid., p. 21.

51. Ibid., p. 39.

52. Dan Nimmo and James Combs, *Mediated Political Realities* (New York: Longman, 1983), p. 96.

53. See Robert E. Denton, Jr., *The Symbolic Dimensions of the American Presidency* (Prospect Heights: Waveland Press, 1982).

54. For a detailed discussion of "mediated political realities" see Nimmo and

Combs, *Mediated Political Realities.*
55. Thomas Patterson, *The Mass Election* (New York: Praeger, 1980), p. 3.
56. Herbert Schiller, *The Mind Managers* (Boston: Beacon Press, 1973), p. 1.
57. For a good discussion of backgrounds of American presidents see Richard Watson and Norman Thomas, *The Politics of the Presidency* (New York: John Wiley & Sons, 1983), especially pp. 99–116.
58. Kathy Smith, "Harry Truman: Man of His Times?" *Presidential Studies Quarterly,* vol. 13, no. 1 (Winter 1983):70–80.
59. James Wooten, *Dasher: The Roots and Rising of Jimmy Carter* (New York: Warner Books, 1978), p. 361.
60. As reported in Patrick Devlin, "Contrasts in Presidential Campaign Commercials of 1976," *Central States Speech Journal,* vol. 28, no. 4 (Winter 1977):243.
61. Ibid., p. 244.
62. As reported in ibid., p. 238.
63. Victor Lasky claims that after the cameras recorded his carrying his garment bag, "the bag was quickly taken from him by an aide once the cameras were turned off; and most of Carter's luggage was processed the usual way." *Jimmy Carter: The Man and the Myth* (New York: Richard Marek, 1979), p. 270.
64. Christopher Johnstone, "Electing Ourselves in 1976: Jimmy Carter and the American Faith," *Western Journal of Speech Communication* 42 (Fall 1978):242.
65. Ibid., p. 245.
66. Richard A. Katula, "Media Rhetoric in the Presidential Campaign of 1976" (Paper presented at the Eastern Communication Association Convention, New York, March 1977), p. 9.
67. Ibid., p. 9.
68. Devlin, "Contrasts in Presidential Campaign Commercials," p. 245.
69. Ibid., p. 246.
70. Jimmy Carter, *Keeping Faith* (New York: Bantam Books, 1982), p. 18.
71. Ibid., p. 24.
72. Ibid., p. 25.
73. See ibid., especially pp. 24–26 and Lasky, *Jimmy Carter,* pp. 315–317.
74. Lasky, *Jimmy Carter,* pp. 313–318.
75. Carter, *Keeping Faith,* p. 93.
76. Ibid., p. 26.
77. Lasky, *Jimmy Carter,* p. 320.
78. Ibid., p. 16.
79. Ibid., p. 11.
80. Ibid., p. 389.
81. Carter, *Keeping Faith,* p. 27.
82. Barbara Kellerman, "Introversion in the Oval Office," *Presidential Studies Quarterly,* vol. 13, no. 3 (Summer 1983):383.
83. Ibid., p. 383.
84. Ibid., p. 391.

READINGS

INTRODUCTION

Chapter 4 investigated the intrapersonal communication dimensions of the presidency. Such an investigation considered the concepts of self, roles, and public expectations in relation to our chief executive. The first essay traces the process of individual transformation from candidate to president and how the office impacts the psyche of the officeholder.

The second essay analyzes the rhetoric of Richard Nixon. The authors argue that there is an inordinate amount of predictability inherent in President Nixon's rhetoric and politics. The predictability is predicated on his personalization of the office and concepts of leadership.

The final essay explores the citizen dilemmas of who is the best candidate and who one should vote for. The essay provides a methodology for the citizen-critic revolving around the biographical dimensions of personality orientation, views of leadership, personal and political ideology, epistemology, and hierarchy value structure. Ultimately, the framework provides a way to discover not just what a candidate says but why he says it.

ON "BECOMING" PRESIDENT OF THE UNITED STATES: THE INTERACTION OF THE OFFICE WITH THE OFFICE HOLDER*

The "self," as already noted in the chapter, is a social object that one shares with others in interaction. It comprises the individual's view of himself in all the various statuses and roles which dictate one's behavior toward all of the objects of one's experience. A "political self," then, refers to an individual's view of oneself in the single-role of political actor or one's package of orientations regarding politics. One's self is isolated, interpreted, and defined socially. An individual's perception of the political role consists of all the norms established socially resulting from interaction. One's political self becomes a separate object for investigation. As an object, the self can be modified, evaluated, and reinforced. The political self, as a process, involves continual mediation between one's own impulses and the expectations of others. A political self arises from political socialization. Political socialization, as noted earlier, is a process of adopting and adapting the self to the actions of others through role-taking.

Political learning may be characterized as interpersonal, accumulative, and adaptive.[1] As interpersonal, it requires recognizing, evaluating, and defining self from the perspectives of others. As accumulative, political learning occurs in stages (that is, pretending and imitating). Political learning is adaptive resulting from the capacity to change self depending on political environment, beliefs, values, and expectations.

The presidency is certainly a grand office. The civil service job classification is Executive I. In addition to a salary of $200,000 and $50,000 for expenses, the officeholders have Air Force One, twelve Boeing 707's, eight VH-3 helicopters, and specially constructed Lincoln Continentals at their disposal. The White House grounds have 30 gardeners who maintain the outside and more than that number who maintain the house itself. The president also has access to Camp David which is run by 150 Naval personnel. Can such a job not have a profound impact upon the individual occupant? Presidential advisor Richard Chaney thinks not:

*Originally published as part of Robert E. Denton, Jr., "On 'Becoming' President of the United States: The Interaction of the Office with the Office Holder," *Presidential Studies Quarterly,* vol. 13, no. 3 (Summer 1983):367–382. Reprinted with permission.

I can't think of a recent time when a man became President and didn't have it have some kind of an impact on his ego. You know, all of a sudden there are hundreds of people willing to wait on you hand and foot and do whatever needs to be done. Helicopters, Air Force One, Limousines, Secret Service Agents, cheering multitudes and "Hail to the Chief" — you'd have to be less than human not to respond to those kinds of trappings that go with the office. And it does, I think, affect people.[2]

Most recent scholars have been quick to recognize that the office has a tremendous impact upon the occupant. As president, one becomes ennobled despite past failures or preparation for the job. Presidents become captives of campaign illusions of self grandeur. According to Reedy, "a President would have to be a dull clod indeed to regard himself without a feeling of awe. The atmosphere of the White House is calculated to instill in any man a sense of destiny."[3] The president walks where Jefferson walked, sleeps where Lincoln slept, writes on Wilson's desk, and dines where the Roosevelts dined. The president becomes the personification of the people. "The President becomes the nation" as Reedy observes, "and when he is insulted, the nation is insulted; when he has a dream, the nation has a dream; when he has an antagonist, the nation has an antagonist."[4]

Thus, the environment of the presidency is one of adulation, respect, awe and near-divinity. When such an environment affects the individual, it also affects job performance. Most alarming, for Reedy, is that "virtually all the information [President Johnson] received was presented by people who desired to retain his favor."[5] The central question becomes, therefore, what can a president do to resist the idolatry and respect for a national symbol?

Recent scholars have been more concerned with the impact of certain personalities upon the office. Perhaps the first person to evaluate systematically the impact of the office upon individuals was Bruce Buchanan.[6] He posited:

1. there is an essential, trans-historical presidential experience, capable of influencing *any* incumbent, and tending to influence most of them in characteristic ways,
2. the origins of this common experience are essentially constitutional . . . over years sedimentary accretion of additional formal and informal functions and expectations for which the presidency is now held accountable,
3. the experience of concern is essentially psychological: a fourfold "environmental press" created and sustained by the role requirements of the presidency.

For Buchanan, the core or generic functions of the office include: symbol, policy advocate, mediator, and crisis manager. These four functions "virtually guarantee recurring and consistent kinds of personal exposures for the President" which "are the brute realities with which he must contend."[7] These exposures or pressures include: frustration, dissonance, deference, and stress. Because the president is ego-involved, such exposures affect job performance as well as the individual psyche. It is helpful to consider briefly each of these "pressures" in order to more fully appreciate the impact of the office upon the occupant's "self."

Stress results from the role requirements of mediator and crisis manager. These roles may be characterized as being unpredictable, physically wearing, and emotionally draining. Buchanan argues that the exposure to stress, which is chronic and intense, results in threat to self-concept, decline in performance and effectiveness, physical deterioration, psychological disorientation, and formalistic management system employment.

Deference results from the symbolic nature of the office. Our majestic treatment of presidents causes status inequality, inflation of self-concept, and distorted perception of external events. Such exposure manifests distortion of social comparison processes, "over identification" with the office, and misinformed decisions. A president easily incorporates the trappings, powers, and prerogatives of the presidency into one's self-definition. Every president is treated as if uniquely gifted and wise. In such a world, "reality" is very difficult to assess.

Presidents are exposed to dissonance mainly resulting from the policy advocate and symbolic functions of the job. Presidents are constantly pressured to misrepresent or distort themselves to various national constituencies. Such a continual pressure causes further misrepresentation, erosion of truth norms, and self-delusion. Consequently, lying and misrepresentation (that is, as in Watergate, Gulf of Tonkin incident, etc.) become accepted practices.

The role of policy advocate, according to Buchanan, produces continual frustration. The impact of such exposure is revealed in increased preoccupation with personal success and survival as well as concern for prevailing over the opposition. Frustration manifests itself in threat of self-concept, arrogation of power (for example, misuse of CIA and FBI), plebiscitary presidency (for example, discrediting press and Congress) and provocation of confrontation (for example, Roosevelt's attempted stacking of the Supreme Court or Nixon's refusal to cooperate in Watergate proceedings).

The key to handling the exposure to stress, deference, dissonance, and frustration, according to Buchanan, is to have a good self-concept and high self-esteem. He posits that "Presidents lacking in self-esteem are more likely to display variants of the "undesirable" behavior than Presidents possessed of high self-esteem."[8] We disagree somewhat with this conclusion. Most presidents behave as president based on their own perceptions of presidential behavior. If they perceive the office as all powerful, they will try to become all powerful. Each president confronts the "role" and must adapt to the office. This "transformation" is readily noticeable in presidential memoirs and writings. One notices, first, a comparison process whereby the individual assesses his capabilities of *being* president. Next, one finds considerable speculation as to the awe when one *is* president. Finally, as a result of interacting with the public, historical expectations, and individual views of the office, the person *becomes* president.

Potential presidents must at some point assume their perceived role of the presidency. "When playing at being someone else," Hugh Duncan argues, "the self realizes its own nature at the same time it realizes the nature of the person whose role is being played."[9] Arthur Schlesinger recognized this phenomenon in John Kennedy. Schlesinger suggests that Kennedy's writing of *Profiles In Courage* aided in defining his "political self" and working out the continual dilemma of political means versus political ends.[10] Schlesinger writes:

> Gradually there evolved a sense of his own identity as a political man, compounded of his growing mastery of the political arts and, even more, of his growing understanding that, for better or worse, his public self had to be faithful to his private self.[11]

An integral part of this process is recognizing the public's expectations of the role. The eventual "presidential self" includes all the subjective thoughts, feelings, and needs which are associated with the role. Naturally, therefore, presidents consciously and unconsciously set the scenes to create preferred images in their interactions with others. As Schlesinger relates, "Every politician has to fake a little, and Kennedy was a politician determined to become President. He was prepared to do many things, to cut corners, to exploit people and situations, to 'go, go, go,' even to merchandise himself."[12]

Perhaps the most profound recognition of the importance of establishing a "presidential image" was that made by Lyndon Johnson upon the death of John Kennedy. Johnson realized that the first impression of his presidency would be most critical. Although Johnson had been a senior senator and vice-president, meetings with old acquaintances and political allies must reflect a "presidential tone." Kearns writes:

> He knew they were looking at him afresh; he knew they would be thinking what he would have been thinking on seeing an old friend or an associate suddenly become President. The initial definition of the situation would provide the basis for all future meetings.[13]

Carter, in his memoirs, details his attempt to create a new or different "presidential image." He tried to reflect a more simple, frugal, and less ostentatious lifestyle. Perhaps his most symbolic populist gesture was his inaugural walk from the Capitol to the White House. Carter recognized the symbolic value of the event.

> I wanted to provide a vivid demonstration of my confidence in the people as far as security was concerned, and I felt a simple walk would be a tangible indication of some reduction in the imperial status of the President and his family. . . . .Besides, I wanted it to be a dramatic moment.[14]

Carter's goal was to convince the public that the barriers between them and top government officials were being removed. Yet, the transformation failed. A president must be "presidential."

A clear, systematic process of transformation from candidate to president appears in nearly every presidential biography. Carter serves as a good example. The origins of Carter's decision to run for president are somewhat hard to pinpoint. According to Carter, it was a combination of conscious and subconscious reflection.

> I think it just evolved, probably without my being aware of it at all, until at some point or another I entertained the idea, probably for just a split second and probably without realizing I had, and then it probably occurred again, this time maybe for a little longer than the first, and also probably without my actual conscious realization that it was there, until finally when I acknowledged that it was there, I couldn't remember when it wasn't there.[15]

Carter speaks rather specifically about his assessing and comparing his qualities for the presidency in 1975. In doing so, Carter becomes an object unto himself for evaluation and possibly adaptation.

> I have always looked on the Presidency of the United States with reverence and awe, and still do. But recently I began to realize that the President is just

another human being. I can almost remember when I began to change my mind and form this opinion. . . . Then during 1971 and 1972 I met Richard Nixon, Spiro Agnew, George McGovern, Henry Jackson, Hubert Humphrey, Ed Muskie, George Wallace, Ronald Reagan, Nelson Rockefeller, and other Presidential hopefuls, and I lost my feeling of awe about Presidents.[16]

In relaying the same sentiments at a press conference in Little Rock, he added, "I didn't feel inferior anymore. I feel that I am as qualified to be President as any one of them."[17]

Interestingly, Carter openly admits how difficult it was to play the role of self-assured candidate early in the campaign. In a 1974 interview with Robert Turner of the *Boston Globe*, Carter observed that "the main difficulty I had to overcome was embarrassment, telling folks I was running for — you know, for President."[18] But during the course of the long campaign, Carter did become the self-assured candidate. As James Wooten observed:

And it soon became clear that, although his repeated self-assurances of victory were psychological crutches for him, they were also more. He believed them, by God, believed them when no one could or would or should, believed them fervently and passionately and probably more deeply than anyone who had ever had the temerity to tell himself that he really ought to be President of the United States.[19]

By June of 1976, not only was Carter "good" at playing the presidential candidate role but was conscious of the fact that he was attempting to fulfill a role image. When asked in an interview if he ever plays a role, Carter responded, "I'm sure I do."[20]

Once elected, Carter, as all presidents, responded with a sense of awe and humility. The office, he stated, "calls more for humility than pride, more for reflection than for celebration."[21] But becoming president is a tough task and certainly does not result by taking the oath of office. For Carter, our national and international problems compounded almost weekly. Inflation, unemployment, and intense special interests groups were immune to anything his administration attempted to do. Salt II, Cuba, the Middle East, Afghanistan, and Iran all provided "crises" of leadership and tough decisions. By November 1979, Hugh Sidey had noticed a difference in Carter. He had "become" president, even though some argued much too late. Sidey noted:

President Carter looks different. Older, gaunter, grayer, tireder. All that is true. But it is something else. . . . They have asked themselves exactly what it is — the intensity in the eyes, or the mouth line, or the fractional shift in his jaw set? ... But from both the White House and beyond there is testimony that he is more of a President. ..."He is challenged from within and from without," ... But what is less important is through some alchemy of these past weeks Jimmy Carter has joined the Presidential club, likes it there, and wants to stay there badly enough to change himself. We all benefit.[22]

Gerald Ford, in his memoirs, *A Time To Heal,* reveals very much the same process. During the spring and summer of 1973, Ford's aides would comment on the eventuality of his becoming president but Ford said he "brushed it off, partly because (he) didn't want to believe it."[23] But when Alexander Haig confronted Ford with the "new evidence" revealed in the tapes of June 23, 1972, Ford had to start assessing his capabilities for the office. He was forced to become an "object" for comparison and evaluation.

For several minutes after Haig left, the implications of our conversation weighed heavily on me. Nixon was going to leave one way or the other. The only questions were when and how. And I was going to become President — a job to which I'd never aspired.... I'm not the kind of person who is torn by self-doubt, and I had no doubts about my ability to function well in the office.[24]

After evaluation and often adaptation, acceptance follows. Presidents react according to self-perception of the office as well as public expectations of the office. When Nixon told Ford of his decision to resign, Ford reportedly responded, "Mr. President, you know that I'm saddened by this circumstance. I would have wanted it to be otherwise, but I am ready to do the job and think I'm fully qualified to do it."[25] Upon leaving the White House after the above exchange, Ford writes, "Nor did I glance at the Secret Service agents accompanying me because I was afraid my feelings might show. I stared ahead at the car, and I wanted the agents to open the door as soon as possible so I could climb inside. I needed to be alone."[26] Likewise, Ford felt a sense of awe and the imposing nature of the office upon inauguration.

As I waited for the proceedings to begin, I felt a sense of awe. It was different from the feeling I'd had when I took my oath as a member of Congress in 1948 or even as Vice President in 1973. At this historic moment, I was aware of kinship with my predecessors. It was almost as if all of America's past Presidents were praying for me to succeed.[27]

Despite Nixon's subsequent "overidentification" with the office, he too initially had doubts.

> As I anticipated becoming President, I found that I was awed by the prospect but not fearful of it. I felt prepared. I had the advantage of experience and of the detachment that comes from being out of office. The "wilderness years" had been years of education and growth.[28]

But as the rest, he also became convinced of his ability to meet the challenges of the office.

> I had no illusions about either the difficulty of the challenge or about my ability to meet it. I felt I knew what would *not* work. On the other hand, I was less sure what *would* work. I did not have all the answers. But I did have definite ideas about the changes I felt were needed.[29]

Of course, we are not privileged to have Kennedy's reflections on becoming president. However, Schlesinger notes that Kennedy's transformation from candidate to president in relation to self-confidence encompassed more than a year.

> What one noticed most was the transformation of Kennedy himself from the vigorous but still uncertain figure of early September to a supremely assured and powerful leader. . . . He had changed somewhat physically in this year and a half. The face was more lined and furrowed; the features were heavier, less handsome but more powerful. The first eighteen months is always the period of Presidential definition, and for Kennedy the succession of crises had tied an already disciplined personality ever more irrevocably to the responsibilities for which he held himself accountable to the future.[30]

Ronald Reagan, of course, has not written his presidential memoirs. Nor have historians attempted to seek out the "real" Reagan. Nevertheless, there is evidence to support the notion that Reagan too had to grapple with the nature of the office before it became as comfortable as an "old shoe."

By 1980, Ronald Reagan had been running for president a very long time — at least since 1966.[31] This may indeed be why his transition was so normal, natural. Presidential campaigns force candidates continually to assess their capabilities, image, and to define their object of desire. As Godfrey Hodgson argues,

> The distinction between being a President and being a Presidential candidate has been progressively rubbed away. The Presidential election campaign is no

200 / PRESIDENTIAL COMMUNICATION

longer simply the way a President is chosen. It has come to influence the
kind of man who is chosen, the men and women he surrounds himself within
the White House, their priorities as they look out at the world from there and
their whole style of operating.[32]

Thus, Reagan's major confrontation and interaction with the office of
president had occurred long before the inauguration of 1980.

But Reagan was more fortunate than most contemporary presidential
candidates. From 1954 to 1962, Reagan was a touring spokesman for
General Electric.[33] He toured more than 100 company plants talking to
workers in rather formal settings. This provided a unique opportunity for
Reagan to develop a public speaking style, image, and confidence. With
no electoral or editorial restrictions, Reagan was free to develop and
express his philosophies of government, work, and American life. His
most popular speech during this period, although controversial to General
Electric, was developed in 1960 entitled "Encroaching Government
Control."[34] For two years Reagan continued his verbal attack on the
workings of the federal government. The General Electric tours, then,
proved to be an effective political training ground for Reagan. Edward
Langley perceptively describes Reagan's transformation during the years
of touring:

But gradually, and only he knows precisely when, he came to share the middle
American views of his audiences. Reagan, then as now, was a consummate
crowd-pleaser who loved the applause and the interplay with his listeners.
Eventually, from whatever mixture of performing instinct and new
conviction, he started taking his audience's opinions for his own, and telling
them what they wanted to hear.[35]

In only four years after the tours, Reagan was governor of California. He
entered public life as an already successful and practicing politician.

According to White, Reagan's decision to run for president was made
only two weeks after becoming governor.[36] But his weak attempt in
1968 was premature by Reagan's own admission. Cannon reports that
Reagan felt a sense of relief when Nixon was nominated and later
confided to Michael Deaver that he was not ready to be president at that
time.[37] Since that time, Reagan has not publicly doubted his ability to be
president. Upon becoming president, Reagan "seemed more contented
than excited."[38] Perhaps he had run for the office too many times, given
too many speeches, was too old to get overly excited about the challenges
ahead. More likely, however, Reagan's self-assessment and examination
of the office occurred many years before his inauguration. As Cannon

observes, "The novice President knew more than the novice governor or the novice Presidential campaigner had known."[39] Elizabeth Drew, however, noted a change between candidate Reagan and President Reagan. "There is a certain dewiness to every new President — even a sixty-nine year old one. Reagan is more relaxed than he was during the campaign, and shows a certain charm that he did not allow himself to display then."[40]

But some of our presidents did not have the luxury of months of campaigning to evaluate and adapt themselves for the job of president. Tragedy demanded immediate assessment and instant acceptance. Truman, after suddenly being told of Roosevelt's death, relates "During those first few hours, painful as they were because of our tragic loss, my mind kept turning to the task I had inherited and to the grave responsibilities that confronted our nation at that critical moment in history."[41] Johnson articulately states the immediate role requirements of suddenly becoming president.

> Most of all I realized that, ready or not, new and immeasurable duties had been thrust upon me. There were tasks to perform that only I had the authority to perform. A nation stunned, shaken to its very heart, had to be reassured that the government was not in a state of paralysis. I had to convince everyone everywhere that the country would go forward, that the business of the United States would proceed. I knew that not only the nation but the whole world would be anxiously following every move I made — watching, judging, weighing, balancing.[42]

It is interesting to note how former presidents recall the first time being addressed as "Mr. President." Nearly all of them emphasize the special quality of the moment and their cognizance of its implications. John Mitchell was with Nixon when the networks began declaring Nixon as the winner of the presidential race. Nixon recalls:

> I put a hand on John Mitchell's shoulder and said, "Well, John, we had better get down to Florida and get this thing planned out." Before Mitchell could respond, tears welled up in his eyes. He said very quietly, "Mr. President, I think I'd better go up to be with Martha." This was a doubly moving moment for us both. It was the first time that anyone addressed me by the title I had just won.[43]

At the hospital in Dallas, Assistant Press Secretary Malcolm Kilduff addressed Johnson as "Mr. President." Johnson writes, "This was the first time anyone had called me that and I must have looked startled; I certainly felt strange."[44] Carter concurs by writing, "Even though I had been preparing to be President, I was genuinely surprised when in the benediction, the Bishop referred to 'blessings on President Carter.' Just the phrase, 'President Carter' was startling to me."[45]

Presidential memoirs, similarly, express the forbidding, isolating nature of the office. Even among the closest of friends, the presidency imposes and invades upon any relationship. When Johnson's friends stood up upon his arrival on Air Force One, the event signaled a profound change to Johnson.

> It was at that moment that I realized nothing would ever be the same again. A wall — high, forbidding, historic — separated us now, a wall that derives from the office of the Presidency of the United States. . . . To old friends who had never called me anything but Lyndon, I would now be "Mr. President." It was a frightening disturbing prospect. I instinctively reached for Lady Bird's hand for reassurance.[46]

Eisenhower touchingly recalls,

> My first full day at the Presidential desk — my old friend General Omar Bradley, then chairman of the Joint Chiefs of Staff, phoned me. For years we had been "Ike" and "Brad" to each other. But now, in the course of our conversation, he addressed me as "Mr. President." Somehow this little incident rocked me back on my heels. Naturally, I knew all about Presidential protocol, but I suppose I had never quite realized the isolation that the job forces upon a man.[47]

For Truman, the enormous responsibilities of the office contributed to the isolation of the job. "No one who has not had the responsibilities can really understand what it is like to be President, not even his closest aides or members of his immediate family. There is no end to the chain of responsibility that binds him, and he is never allowed to forget that he is President."[48] Carter echoes this sentiment by writing, "although I was surrounded by people eager to help me, my most vivid impression of the Presidency remains the loneliness in which the most difficult decisions had to be made . . . I prayed a lot — more than ever before in my life."[49]

NOTES

1.   Dan Nimmo, *Political Communication and Public Opinion in America* (California: Goodyear Publishing, 1978), pp. 313–314.

2.   *Every Four Years: A Study of the Presidency,* Public Broadcasting Service, 1980, p. 5.

3.   George Reedy, *The Twilight of the Presidency* (New York: World Publishing, 1970), p. 15.

4.   Ibid., p. 16.

5.   George Reedy, "On the Isolation of Presidents," in *The Presidency Reappraised,* 2nd ed., ed. Thomas Cronin and Rexford Tugwell (New York: Praeger Publishers, 1977), p. 194.

6.   Bruce Buchanan, *The Presidential Experience* (Englewood Cliffs: Prentice-Hall, 1978).

7.   Ibid., p. 18.

8.   Ibid., p. 138.

9.   Hugh Dalziel Duncan, *Symbols in Society* (New York: Oxford University Press, 1968), p. 19.

10.   Arthur Schlesinger, *A Thousand Days* (Greenwich: Fawcett, 1965), p. 100.

11.   Ibid., p. 101.

12.   Ibid., p. 113.

13.   Doris Kearns, *Lyndon Johnson and the American Dream* (New York: Harper & Row, 1976), p. 180.

14.   Jimmy Carter, *Keeping Faith* (New York: Bantam Books, 1982), pp. 17–18.

15.   James Wooten, *Dasher: The Roots and Rising of Jimmy Carter* (New York: Warner Books, 1978), p. 296.

16.   Jimmy Carter, *Why Not the Best* (New York: Bantam, 1975), pp. 158–159.

17.   Robert L. Turner, *"I'll Never Lie to You:" Jimmy Carter in His Own Words* (New York: Ballantine Books, 1976), p. 63.

18.   Ibid., p. 3.

19.   Wooten, *Dasher,* p. 21.

20.   Turner, *"I'll Never Lie,"* p. 65.

21.   Ibid., p. 2.

22.   Hugh Sidey, "The Presidency: Change in the Set of the Jaw," *Time,* Nov. 12, 1979, p. 26.

23.   Gerald Ford, *A Time to Heal* (New York: Harper & Row, 1979), p. 5.

24.   Ibid., p. 5.

25.   Ibid., p. 28.

26.   Ibid., p. 30.

27.   Ibid., p. 40.

28.   Richard Nixon, *The Memoirs of Richard Nixon* (New York: Grosset and Dunlop, 1978), p. 361.

29.   Ibid., p. 361.

30.   Schlesinger, *A Thousand Days,* pp. 11 and 609.

31.   Theodore H. White, *America in Search of Itself* (New York: Harper & Row, 1982), p. 241.

32.   Godfrey Hodgson, *All Things to All Men* (New York: Simon and Schuster, 1980), p. 211.

33.   See Lou Cannon, *Reagan* (New York: Putnam, 1982), pp. 72–108 and Ronald Reagan and Richard Hubler, *Where's the Rest of Me?* (New York: Dell Publishing, 1965), pp. 298–312.

34. Edward Langley, "How the Star Changed His Stripes," *Politics Today,* Jan. 1980, p. 44.

35. Ibid., p. 44.

36. White, *America,* p. 244.

37. Cannon, *Reagan,* p. 164.

38. Ibid., p. 303.

39. Ibid., p. 306.

40. Elizabeth Drew, *Portrait of an Election* (New York: Simon and Schuster, 1981), p. 346.

41. Harry S Truman, *Memoirs: Years of Decisions,* vol. 1 (New York: Doubleday, 1955), p. 11.

42. Lyndon B. Johnson, *The Vantage Point* (New York: Holt, Rinehart, and Winston, 1971), p. 12.

43. Nixon, *Memoirs,* pp. 333–334.

44. Johnson, *Vantage Point,* p. 11.

45. Carter, *Keeping Faith,* p. 22.

46. Johnson, *Vantage Point,* p. 13.

47. Dwight D. Eisenhower, "Some Thoughts on the Presidency," in *The Power of the Presidency,* 2nd ed., ed. Robert Hirschfield (Chicago: Aldine, 1973), p. 118.

48. Truman, *Memoirs,* p. 1.

49. Carter, *Keeping Faith,* pp. 61–62.

THE RHETORICAL PREDICTABILITY OF RICHARD M. NIXON*

"Enigmatic," "isolated," "cool," "insensitive," these are the words that political observers utilized as they searched for the "real" Richard Nixon. What has become "real" for us in our study of the man is the inordinate amount of predictability inherent in Mr. Nixon's rhetoric and politics. We are working on the hypothesis that President Richard Nixon, to a great extent, was predictable, first, because he so clearly and fully personalized the presidency, and, second, because of his concepts of leadership.

*Originally published by Ruth M. Gonchar and Dan F. Hahn, "The Rhetorical Predictability of Richard M. Nixon," *Today's Speech* (now *Communication Quarterly*) 19 (1971):3–13. Reprinted with permission.

PERSONALIZING THE PRESIDENCY

Perhaps because it eluded him for so long, Richard Nixon held a highly personalized view of the presidency. All presidents personalize their historic role, but few have been quite as personal about it as Richard Nixon. Nixon became what he was merely elected to represent. In a way this intense identification is analogous to what Wendell Johnson called "ventriloquizing": to speak as if with the voice of another.[1]

Politically, there is ample evidence of personalization. Nixon was the only president ever to have named a foreign policy after himself — the Nixon Doctrine. The Monroe and Truman Doctrines were personalized long after they were enunciated, and then not by Monroe and Truman. Traditionally, U.S. presidents traveling abroad present world leaders with gifts of crystal. On his trip to the Vatican, Nixon gave the Pope not a piece of crystal, but a photograph of the Nixon family. Nixon's belief in "taking government to the people" was commendable; yet it was not government or the presidency that Nixon brought to the people, but himself.

Rhetorically, personalizations permeated Nixon's utterances. From his inaugural address, in which personalization flourished,[2] to his 1970 Report to the Congress on Foreign Policy,[3] in which Nixon quoted himself 33 times and the rest of the published world only four, to his April 30, 1970 Cambodian address,[4] in which he justified the invasion in terms of his own political future — becoming a one-term president — and identified his own "humiliation," his own role as a "pitiful, helpless giant" with the nation's, personalization abounded. To Nixon, the nation and the president were one. From his inaugural address, when he said, "I speak from my own heart, and the heart of my country . . ."[5] to his defense of himself in the Watergate controversy, in which his personal defense was couched in terms designed to appear as though it was the presidency he was defending, the Nixonian confusion between himself and the office always was apparent.

Any threat to Nixon, the office of the presidency or the United States of America was, *ipso facto*, a threat to the other two. Because of this triple-threat perception, any threat was critical (a crisis). Thus, implicitly, we were lucky to have as president one who understood that crises are "exquisite agony," "life's mountaintop experiences,"[6] engaging all of man's talents. His list of crises facing the nation included Vietnam, of course, but also the American city, welfare, civil disorder, inflation, unemployment, crime, housing, pollution, inadequate education, and a crisis of the spirit. In what way was Nixon different from those politicians who would have labeled these as "problems" rather than "crises?" Put another way, what sort of person perceives the world in crisis/non-crisis proportions? First, it is a person who has accepted the Judeo-Christian two-valued orientation, the consequences of which have been well documented by general semanticists. Second, it is a person who has perverted this judgmental system by using it for descriptive purposes. Third, it is a person who, by combining judgment and description, eliminates the possibility of not taking action, for only a weakling would refuse to take action in the face of a crisis.

Personalization contributed also to Nixon's concern for the way in which history would record his presidency. He called himself a "student of history" and as such was particularly sensitive to the historical implications of his actions. "Historical" references punctuated his rhetoric. From the personal letter of peace to Ho Chi Minh which Nixon revealed during his November 3, 1969 address: "Let history record that at this critical juncture, both sides turned their faces toward peace rather than toward conflict and war."[7] Later in the same speech, Nixon concluded: "Let historians not record that when America was the most powerful nation in the world we passed on the other side of the road and allowed the last hopes for peace and freedom of millions of people to be suffocated by the forces of totalitarianism."[8]

One other observable personality characteristic served to intensify Nixon's personalized presidency. An excessive sensitivity to criticism led Nixon to react rigidly and predictably to attack. Personal criticism is difficult for anyone to accept, but particularly difficult for an elected official who views his popular mandate as an absolution from error. Nixon reacted predictably to all forms of criticism, rigidly denying even the smallest personal contribution of error.

That Nixon was overly sensitive to criticism is undeniable. Even he understood this — after the Checkers Speech, he said: "We [Pat and himself] had both become perhaps overly sensitive, even when we were subjected to the standard attacks which a public figure must expect with regard to his personal affairs."[9] That his response was unvarying is observable. When Nixon ordered U.S. troops into Cambodia, he was criticized for disregarding congressional advice and consent. Confronted with this criticism, Nixon denied error, and administrative spokesmen, labeling senatorial censure as "a partisan Democratic attack on Nixon" (and note the personalization here), concluded: "It is not the proper posture for anyone to correct the President of the United States."[10] Rather than admitting his "Manson blooper" was a mistake and retracting it, Nixon pleaded journalistic misinterpretation. When Supreme Court nominee Clement Haynsworth, accused of suspicious "financial manipulations," asked Nixon to withdraw his name, the president refused, and instead held a press conference in which he denied his nominee's guilt and his own selection error. A similar denial accompanied the Carswell defeat.

The relationship between Nixon's denial response pattern and his personalized presidency is evident. Because an attack on the competence of his Supreme Court nominees, for example, was viewed as a personal attack against him, Nixon felt the need to deny.

CONCEPTS OF LEADERSHIP

Each man who assumes the presidency plays the role in keeping with his own conception of leadership. In *Six Crises* and subsequent speeches and addresses, Nixon revealed his concept of consummate leadership — his leadership ideology.

Nixon said that to be great, a leader must be a "big man in big affairs."[11] To him, "big affairs" meant the global arena — international diplomacy. To this end, Nixon presented himself as an expert in foreign policy. It was not surprising, therefore, during the 1968 presidential campaign, that Nixon announced he would be his own secretary of state. Nor was it unexpected that the Nixon Doctrine was a personalized directive on foreign policy.

Strength was a second characteristic of Nixon's leadership ideology, and one of the marks of strength, he thought, is action. Nixon insisted, ". . . it isn't enough just to be for peace; one must also do something about it."[12] Strong leaders do not tarry with indecision; they weigh the alternatives and then choose a line of action. One would doubt, therefore, if Nixon's "option papers" included a "no-action option" or a "sit tight" strategy on the supposition that political crises often clear of their own volition. No, Nixon's belief in action as symbolic strength, and inaction or flight from action as inherent weakness were at the very heart of his beliefs. Weakness, after all, is not the American way. Strength through action, the ability to face the challenge, to work hard, to take the responsibility, to deserve success because you've earned it, these are the characteristics of American stick-to-itiveness. Why, every heartland fifth grader knows that the last four letters of American spell "I can."

Is action the more difficult of the paths to follow? Yes. Action is strength and strength in leadership is "right," and the right path, according to Nixon, is the more difficult. Thus, the argument in his

October 7, 1970 "Proposal for Indochina Peace" may be summarized. "To accomplish any task, to solve any problem, there are many alternatives. All of them, except the one Nixon has chosen, are wrong. How does he know he has chosen the right path? The right path is always difficult; all paths but one are easy; he has chosen the difficult path; he has chosen the right path."[13] Critics also noted this same difficult-is-right orientation in his November 3, 1969 address: "He contrasted the easy way with the right way, as though the right way could never be easy, or that his way was right because it wasn't easy."[14] Nixon's references to his difficult, thus right, actions permeated his speeches: May 14, 1969:

> I know that some believe I should have ended the war immediately after the inauguration by simply ordering our forces home from Viet Nam. This would have been the easy thing to do. It might have been a popular move. But if I had done so, I would have betrayed my solemn responsibility as President of the United States.[15]

November 3, 1969: "I have chosen this second course [Vietnamization]. It is not the easy way. It is the right way."[16] Degree of difficulty, of course, was only one way Nixon justified the "rightness" of his actions. Later we will discuss three more: importance, selflessness, and good results.

Once committed to an action a strong leader will see it through to the end, Nixon believed. Long before he was forced to "step down" he saw resignation under fire as an admission of guilt. Before President Johnson announced he would not run for re-election, Nixon commented: "I can't see this man, who is very competitive, end his political life by running away from the last contest."[17] A change in course had to be resisted because it implied error; error is a sign of weakness, and we already know Nixon's opinion of weakness. But there is a further reason that Nixon held so strongly to his "never retreat" belief. He said in *Six Crises* that a decision to act must be preceded by "a necessary period of indecision, of doubt, and soul-searching," after which a leader "resolves that his cause is right and determines that he must fight the battle to the finish."[18] Once Nixon perceived his action as "right" (the implication here being that "right" equals "moral"), it would have been immoral to surrender. Exemplary of his "never retreat" position was the Haynsworth nomination debate, during which an administrative aide confided: "Nixon's going over the hill with this one." The identification between retreat and immorality was paramount in Nixon's conception of leadership. Nixon's reaction to attack (prior to Watergate) was predictable: he saw his action through regardless of opposition, evidently judging retreat as more deserving of censure than defeat.

Rhetorically, the decision not to back down manifested itself in counter-attack. Nixon rationalized this approach: "I don't think anybody ever is as good on the defense as on the offense, but when anybody attacks, I believe the way to answer is not simply to defend, but to take the offensive. . . ."[19] However, Nixon's belief in counter-attack conflicted with another portion of his leadership concept — "coolness under fire," although he was never a cool leader in crisis. His presidential rhetoric was filled with "coolness" reminders, as if saying "cool" would help him in staying "cool." The "rule" which he said he followed was "When the action is hot, keep the rhetoric cool."[20] Eulogizing Eisenhower, Nixon offered this praise: "No matter how heated the arguments were, he was always the coolest man in the room. . . . He restored calm to a divided nation."[21]

Even the physical aspects of "cool" concerned Nixon. Prolific perspiration plagued him throughout his political career. From 1960, when he discovered the effects of exudation on ethos, to his November 3, 1969 Vietnam address, when the cameras caught him furtively sideswiping a droplet of sweat as it inched mercilessly down his upper lip, Nixon took precautionary measures to effectuate his "literal cool." For example, to lessen the amount of perspiration created by the heat of television cameras, when he was giving a televised speech from the White House he had the room cooled to 40 degrees before the speech began. Even so, of course, by the time he was 15 minutes into the speech the room would be over 70 degrees — and President Nixon would begin sweating.

Nixon operated "in cool" only at such times as he controlled the situation. Somehow, controlling the situation and controlling himself became inseparable. What resulted was ideological dissonance between coolness and counter-attack. Nixon counter-attacked when he perceived a crisis situation beyond his control. It was at such times when he was in greatest danger of "blowing his cool." Witness, for example, Nixon's statement about the Senate after its rejection of Supreme Court nominee Carswell. Having lost control of the appointment process, Nixon charged the senators with "vicious assaults," "racism," "hypocrisy," and "malicious character assassination."[22]

To obviate the possibility of losing control in a crisis situation, Nixon included thorough preparation among his criteria of ideal leadership. There is, of course, a close connection between thorough preparation and hard work; and hard work, as everyone knows, is a virtue in the Puritan ethic. Ethics are justificatory. Thus, Nixon frequently used thorough preparation when justifying policies and actions. From his 1971 state of the union message: "Based on a long and intensive study with the aid of the best advice obtainable, I have concluded. . . ."[23] From his "New Proposals for Indochina Peace": "After considering the recommendations of all my principal advisors, I am tonight announcing. . . ."[24] The evidence examined, the options analyzed, a leader will never be caught off guard by his opponents. However, conflict arose here because of another of Nixon's criteria of leadership excellence — concentrating on one issue at a time. It is difficult to deal with one issue while remaining thoroughly prepared on all others, and "lesser issues" have a way of developing into "greater issues" when ignored. The Carswell nomination offers a perfect example. Carswell's name was placed in nomination on the assumption that the Senate, after rejecting Haynsworth, would confirm anyone short of Chairman Mao. Too late did Nixon realize that defeat of his second nominee was imminent. What was Nixon doing during the long debate on Carswell? Why didn't he publicly support his nominee? His concentration had shifted from Carswell and Capitol Hill to Communism and the invasion of Cambodia.

Nixon's final criteria for leadership was the achievement of public repect. As his one-time advisor, Robert Finch, said of him: "He's lost the syndrome of 1960 and 1962. He doesn't want to be loved; he's not looking for adulation the way he used to; it's a case of cold respect; he wants respect. . . ."[25] Arguing against proposals for the withdrawal of troops from Vietnam, Nixon asserted: "We would plunge from the anguish of war into a nightmare of recrimination. We would lose respect for this nation, respect for one another, respect for ourselves."[26]

This need for respect may explain Nixon's deployment of Spiro Agnew; with Agnew taking the rhetorical low road, Nixon was supposed to be able to remain cool and "above" gritty politics. Eisenhower had utilized Nixon in precisely the same manner. But, unlike Eisenhower, Nixon found it difficult to sustain this high road approach, and threw himself into the political arena when he saw time growing short and victory out of reach, as he did during the 1970 congressional campaign.

RHETORICAL PREDICTABILITY

What, then, can we predict about the rhetoric of a man who inhabits a world filled with threats and crises, a man who approaches these crises from a two-valued orientation, a man who is action-oriented? What can we predict about the rhetoric of a man who wants to be a big man in big affairs, strong, cool, thoroughly prepared, and thoroughly respected by both contemporaries and historians? Indeed, what can we predict about the rhetoric of a man who confuses himself with his office and the country he leads and who is so sensitive to criticism as to deny all error? Most obviously, we can predict that such a man will devote his rhetoric to justifying his actions and himself.

Justification of Action

When justifying actions, Nixon equated right with morality. He believed that if he could prove his action was right, that would prove it moral as well. How did Nixon justify the "rightness" of his actions rhetorically? He did so by demonstrating that they were important, difficult, selfless, and/or had good results.

The first justification was importance. Nixon characterized the importance of his actions with superlatives. In his 1971 state of the union address, he called his six major proposals, "six great goals," and described one of them as "historic in scope and bold in concept." Referring to his welfare proposal, Nixon approvingly quoted "many observers" as saying it was "the most important piece of domestic legislation proposed in the past fifty years. . . ."[27] It is not difficult to predict that Nixon ascribed importance to his actions; what else would we expect from a person whose concept of leadership demanded that he be a big man in big affairs? Nixon endowed even relatively mundane occurrences with history-making significance, labeling them "firsts." We have heard this called "The Making of a Precedent."[28] From Nixon's toast to the president of Indonesia: "I realize that the position I am in is a unique one, one that will not come again . . . since I am the first American President ever to pay a state visit to Indonesia, the next American president who comes here will not be in the position I presently find myself in."[29] This concern for precedence was only a part of his larger concern for the way in which history would record his personalized presidency. Frequently, he argued the acceptance of his proposals on the basis of their place in history: "So let us approach these six great goals with a sense, not only of the moment in history, but also, of history itself."[30]

Because of Nixon's leadership concept that right decisions are always difficult to make, we can predict a second justification of his actions. Called "The Most Difficult Decision," it describes a resolution in terms of its formidability, and formidability, in turn, heightens a decision's importance. He hailed his own "New National Health Strategy," saying: "It will not be easy for our nation to achieve this goal."[31] His decision to enter Cambodia was characterized inevitably as "difficult." When Nixon said that he had made a difficult decision, he was not talking about the decision-making process as such. What he meant was that, having gone through a period of indecision and soul-searching, he had arrived at a moral decision, one that ignored political expediency.

The third Nixonian justification was selflessness. Nixon's need for respect precipitated this justification. He believed a leader is respected who puts aside personal gain and acts for the good of the nation — a selfless leader for a selfless nation. And so, actions of Nixon's America were pictured as having been taken without ulterior motives, and this somehow proved that the actions were right. All of our wars had been right because we fought "selflessly and for no gain."[32] Why, then, did we fight them? Because ". . . the mantle of leadership fell on American shoulders not by our desire and not for the purposes of conquest."[33] And what did we hope to achieve? ". . . nothing — nothing but the right for everyone to live and let live."[34] When Nixon applied this selfless view to the war in which he was involved, his rhetoric became almost Churchillian: ". . . never in history have men fought for less selfish motives — not for conquest, not for glory, only for the right of a people far away to choose the kind of government they want."[35] It is this view of the selflessness of our actions which made it impossible for Nixon to conceive of anyone disagreeing with our objectives; so it is predictable that throughout Nixon's speeches he would assert that we agree on the ends and only disagree on the means. The ends are selfless, on that there can be no disagreement.

Nixon's final justification of action was "good results." Good results stem from thorough preparation: if a leader prepares his actions thoroughly enough, the results cannot be bad. Here is also the rhetorical manifestation of Nixon's need to deny error. How could he be guilty of error if his actions netted such good results? But the problem for the analyst, and the great advantage for Nixon, is that *any* result was a good result. Did we miss the "Headquarters for all Communist activity in Viet Nam" during the Cambodian incursion? No matter. We captured mounds of rice and guns. Did the raid to free P.O.W.'s fail? No matter. It lifted the morale of the prisoners and of their wives here at home. James Wechsler, noting Nixon's tendency to find good results in all of his actions, predicted how Nixon would have reported the fiasco of the Bay of Pigs Invasion had he been president at that time:

Do not be misled by Communist claims that our Bay of Pigs operation was a failure. Certain of the objectives achieved cannot be divulged now for reasons of military security; but I can tell you now that our intelligence reports reveal that our action has been a major blow to the morale of the Castro regime, greatly strengthened the chances for an early liberation of Cuba and once again convincingly demonstrated to the world that the United States will not tolerate subversive infiltration of this hemisphere.[36]

What Wechsler zeroes in on in this frighteningly excellent parody is that Nixon always could find "good results" even in cases of total "failure." Nixon believed, "We often can learn more from a program that fails to achieve its purpose than from one that succeeds. If we apply those lessons, then even the 'failure' will have made a significant contribution to our larger purposes."[37]

Thus, Nixon justified all of his actions rhetorically. All actions have some importance, so he could emphasize that. Or he could stress the difficulty of the action, or how selfless we were in taking it. Or, finally, he could either find good results or suggest that some unseen good results emanated from the action. It was a very neat rhetorical package — but Nixon did not rely on it alone. He so personalized the office of president that he was never sure whether an attack was directed to his executive action or to himself, so he also justified his role.

Justification of Role

Because Nixon personalized the presidency, he found he could justify himself by demonstrating that he was fulfilling the requirements of his office. On what basis were requirements of his office determined? On the basis of Nixon's personalized leadership concepts. He fulfilled his role because he had constructed it to fit himself.

Nixon's justification of his own role took any one, or any combination, of the following "I am the president" forms: (1) I want nothing for myself (a selfless leader is respected); (2) But I am concerned and working hard (hard work is a virtue and so justificatory); (3) I will act (action is strength); (4) I have the best information (a good leader is thoroughly prepared); and (5) I will take the responsibility (good leaders do not shirk their responsibilities; they face the challenge).

"I am the president" pictured Nixon's motives as selfless and thereby morally justified. Because he felt the need to erase past accusations of political opportunism and also to gain respect, Nixon constantly reminded us of his personal selflessness in statements like "The crowds weren't cheering me, they were cheering America,"[38] and "Whether I am a one-term President is insignificant. . . ."[39] This latter statement, of course, is predictable presidential rhetoric, and we have never believed it. Indeed, there is nothing more political than a president's pretensions at being above politics, for he intends for us to reward him handsomely for his apolitical stance at that most political of all sites, the voting booth.

Because the Puritan ethic projects hard work as virtuous, hence moral, the second "I am the president" posture pictured Nixon as concerned and hard-working. It was predictable that Nixon seldom would let pass an opportunity to remind us of his dedication. Even before he took office, he said, he had launched an "intensive review of every aspect of the nation's Viet Nam policy."[40] After being in office four months, he alleged ". . . nothing has taken so much of my time and energy as the search for a way to bring lasting peace to Vietnam."[41] A year later, when the agony of war was escalated by the Cambodian invasion, Nixon's efforts also had increased: ". . . I have been working 18, 20 hours a day, mostly on Viet Nam, trying to bring these men home."[42] It may seem inconceivable that a president could concentrate his energies so completely on one problem when so many are facing him, but Nixon's notion of leadership required him to focus on "one issue at a time." Thus, in this case the two leadership concepts reinforce each other.

Nixon's basic belief in action *per se* and his further belief that action is both a sign of strength and "right" form the basis of the third "I am the president" justification. "I will act" manifested itself in Nixon's use of personal pronouns. Two predictions can be made here. First, since Nixon saw foreign policy as more important than domestic policy, he would employ more personal pronouns in foreign policy speeches than in domestic addresses. Evidence bears this out. We examined ten speeches, five devoted to foreign policy, five to domestic affairs. We correlated length of speeches and audiences addressed. For example, we compared a 4,000-word television address to the nation on Vietnam to a 4,000-word address to the nation on the new welfare plan; a 2,500-word speech to the nation on Vietnam and a 2,500-word speech to the nation on the worth of a dollar. In every case, the foreign policy speeches contained many more "I" references than the domestic addresses. In the two examples specified here, Nixon use "I" 95 times in his November 3, 1969 Vietnam speech and only 40 times in his August 8, 1969 welfare plan address. Similarly, Nixon's April 30, 1970 Vietnam speech contained 44 "I" references while his October 17, 1969 worth of a dollar address contained 25 "I" usages.[43] Second, since Nixon wanted to be viewed as a "big man in big affairs" who was not afraid to take action, the personal pronoun "I" generally was followed by action, proposal, or warning verbs, while "We" pronouns were used in the subordinate position of carrying out or in the receptive position of reaping the benefits of the "I" actions. From his April 30, 1970 address on Vietnam: "The action I take tonight is essential if we are to accomplish that goal."[44] The formula, then, was: "I act, and we receive the benefits of my actions."

The fourth "I am the president" form, called the "Worldly-Wise" approach, a favorite of Lyndon Johnson's, was Nixon's reminder that as president he was better prepared than anyone to see the picture and take appropriate action, not only because he had done much work, but because he had sources available to no one else. Responding to a question about secret government reports on the dangers of the SST, Nixon explained: ". . . I have satisfied myself, after a long deliberation, and considering both of these reports, that the arguments with regard to the environment could be met, that this prototype should be built."[45]

The final "I am the president" justification is not just the last but the culmination of the series. Examine the relationship between "I take the responsibility" and the preceding forms. Because Nixon wanted nothing for himself, his willingness to take the responsibility was meant to be seen as a magnanimous gesture. The fact that he had expended so much effort made his responsibility-taking seem reasonable. Likewise, since the act was Nixon's, it follows that the responsibility ought to have been his, and since the action was based on information that only he had, only he could have been responsible. We have been presented with the image of a "big man in big affairs," taking decisive actions, assuming burdensome responsibilities. Behind the "I take the responsibility" image, however, was a no-risk reality. As we discussed earlier, Nixon's actions could never fail because he could always find a "good result." Therefore, to take responsibility for such actions left him accountable only for success. So, predictably, Nixon announced, ". . . I made this decision. I take the responsibility for it. I believe it was a right decision. I believe it will work out. If it doesn't, then I'm to blame."[46] He even could spell out in what way he was to be held responsible: ". . . if I fail to do so [end the war], I expect the American people to hold me accountable for that failure."[47] Nixon felt free to personalize because he knew his *assertion* of responsibilities could not lead to the *assumption* of responsibility.

To this point we have dealt with the rhetoric of justification — the approach Nixon utilized to support all his actions. We turn now to an examination of the rhetoric of vindication — the approach Nixon employed when his policies were criticized. We already know that Nixon was so sensitive to criticism as to deny all error. Therefore, it is no surprise that the rhetoric of vindication had these two components: (1) there is no error in my policies, and (2) if my policies have not come to fruition, the blame lies elsewhere. Since these components are interwoven in his rhetoric, we will not artificially divide them here.

Nixon's two-valued orientation, evident in his crisis/not-crisis world view, was responsible for the either-or format of his error-denying rhetoric. We call the rhetoric "Divide and Conquer"; Vice-President Agnew called it "Positive Polarization." It combines what we have labeled as "The Dread Alternatives" variant with a "Straw Man" attack. Not only did this combination enable Nixon to deny policy error, it did so by distorting his opponent's projected position, thereby preempting the rational middle ground.

Nixon first identified three or four paths which his thorough preparation and private sources demonstrated were open to him. He then negated all but the last, indicating as he did that these unacceptable, dread paths were the alternatives suggested by "them," the amorphous enemy, his critics. Nixon negated, first, by the use of a "Straw Man," distorting his critics' position beyond the latitude of acceptance for the nation's majority, and, second, by predicting the terrible consequences that would accrue from accepting those alternatives. His critics' position radicalized and his crystal ball having revealed the dread effects of those alternatives, Nixon then concluded that the path he had chosen was the right path because it was the only viable one available. His action was vindicated.

The "Dread Alternatives" variant developed from an earlier Nixon posture — the "Either-Or Option." In his November 3, 1969 Vietnam speech, Nixon presented two alternatives for ending the war: "their" way — immediate, precipitant withdrawal without regard to the effects of that action, or Nixon's way — gradual withdrawal and Vietnamization.[48]

Since Nixon personalized the presidency so that he saw himself and the nation as one, he predictably would deny error by referring to his support among the patriotic Silent Majority. This support undermined his critics by calling their patriotism into question. In his June 3 Indochina speech, Nixon said:

> In seeking peace let us remember that at this time only this Administration can end the war and bring peace — and the greater the support the Administration receives in its efforts, the greater the opportunity to win that just peace we all desire.[49]

The formula here was: since we all want peace, and since only I can achieve peace, anyone who opposes me is unpatriotic.

A more specific use of the Silent Majority is the "Out of the Mouths of Babes" variant.[50] It was Nixon fortuitously happening upon members of the Silent Majority who offered him gems of wisdom which coincidently supported his policies. From that same June 3 address: "I was talking with a union leader from New York. His son died in Vietnam this past February. He told me that, had we moved earlier into Cambodia, we might have captured the enemy weapon that eventually killed his son."[51] Here was proof that the nation's majority agreed with him. His action was vindicated. While it was predictable that Nixon would call on the patriotic Silent Majority for support, it was not predictable in what manner he would do so, whether generally asserting that they backed his policy or specifically quoting one of their members.

The complement of "Out of the Mouths of Babes" is the "I would never have said that Myself" variant, in which Nixon reported the attacks the Silent Majority had made against his critics. "When I say I inherited this war, I want to point out that I am actually quoting what others say. I'm not going to cast the blame for the war in Vietnam on either of my predecessors."[52] Nixon disassociated himself from the statement by indicating that he personally did not hold with this view, but the jury was not instructed to disregard the testimony. The variant allowed Nixon to vindicate his action without having to specify blame. We just knew that blame lay elsewhere.

Shifting blame also was the goal of Nixon's "you too" defense. If he was in error, well then, so were his predecessors. When Nixon said, "The problem existing in communicating with students is not new — it existed in other Administrations,"[53] he was saying, in effect: Don't blame just me; Truman, Kennedy, and Johnson had the same problem, and I inherited it from them. His action was vindicated; the blame fell elsewhere.

CONCLUSION

We should like to conclude with two observations. First, the personalization, leadership concepts, and resulting rhetoric we have hurriedly outlined here are not unique to Richard Nixon. Our point is not that Nixon was unique, but that he was predictable. Which leads to our second point: if Nixon were predictable, it may also be that other leaders are predictable, and that rhetorical analysis can provide the insights we need to uncover those predictabilities.

NOTES

1. Wendell Johnson, *People in Quandaries* (New York: Harper, 1946), p. 65.
2. Robert L. Scott, "Rhetoric that Postures: An Intrinsic Reading of Richard M. Nixon's Inaugural Address," *Western Speech* 34 (1970):47ff.
3. Richard M. Nixon, "United States Foreign Policy for the '70's," in *Setting the Course, The First Year: Major Policy Statements by President Richard Nixon,* ed. Richard Wilson (New York: Funk and Wagnalls, 1970), pp. 400–484.
4. Richard M. Nixon, "The Situation in Southeast Asia," Radio and Television Address, April 30, 1970.
5. Richard M. Nixon, "The Inaugural Address," in Wilson, *Setting the Course,* p. 7.
6. Richard M. Nixon, *Six Crises* (Garden City: Doubleday, 1968), p. xxviii.
7. Richard M. Nixon, "To the Great Silent Majority," in Wilson, *Setting the Course,* p. 24.
8. Ibid., p. 30.
9. Nixon, *Six Crises,* p. 137.
10. Clayton Fritchey, "Sovereign Law," *New York Post,* August 21, 1970, p. 39.
11. Nixon, *Six Crises,* p. xxvi.
12. C. L. Sulzberger, "Mr. Nixon in the Mirror," *The New York Times,* March 10, 1971, p. 43.
13. Dan F. Hahn, "Old Rhetoric in Old Bottles," *Speaker and Gavel* 8 (1971):71.
14. Lynn Hinds and Carolyn Smith, "Rhetoric of Opposites," *The Nation,* February 16, 1970, p. 173.
15. Richard M. Nixon, "The Terms of Peace," in Wilson, *Setting the Course,* p. 12.
16. Richard M. Nixon, "To the Great Silent Majority," in ibid., p. 28.
17. M. B. Schnapper, *Quotations from the Would-Be Chairman Richard M. Nixon* (Washington: Public Affairs Press, 1968), p. 46.
18. Nixon, *Six Crises,* pp. 20–21.
19. Earl Mazo, *Richard Nixon: A Political and Personal Portrait* (New York: Harper & Row, 1959), p. 267.
20. Richard M. Nixon, "News Conference on Foreign and Domestic Matters," *The New York Times,* May 9, 1970, p. 8.
21. Richard M. Nixon, "Farewell to an Old Friend," in Wilson, *Setting the Course,* p. 389.
22. Richard M. Nixon, "Statement on High Court," *The New York Times,* January 23, 1971, p. 12.
23. Richard M. Nixon, "State of the Union Message," *The New York Times,* January 23, 1971, p. 12.
24. Richard M. Nixon, "New Proposals for Indochina Peace," in Wilson, *Setting the Course,* p. 18.
25. Theodore H. White, *The Making of the President, 1968* (New York: Pocket Books, 1969), p. 166.
26. Richard M. Nixon, "Address by the President," *The New York Times,* April 8, 1971, p. 6.

27.   Richard M. Nixon, "Hunger Must Be Banished" (Remarks by the President at the White House Conference on Food, Nutrition, and Health, Washington, D.C., December 2, 1969).

28.   Joseph Albright, "The Making of a Precedent," *Newsday*, March 7, 1970, pp. 9W–11W.

29.   Ibid.

30.   Richard M. Nixon, "State of the Union Message," p. 12.

31.   Richard M. Nixon, "A New National Health Strategy," *The New York Times*, February 19, 1971, p. 16.

32.   Richard M. Nixon, "Interview with C. L. Sulzberger," *The New York Times*, March 10, 1971, p. 14.

33.   Ibid.

34.   Ibid.

35.   Nixon, "Address by the President," p. 6.

36.   James A. Wechsler, "All Famous Victories," *New York Post*, November 27, 1970, p. 55.

37.   Richard M. Nixon, "People Must Be Given a Chance," in Wilson, *Setting the Course*, p. 43.

38.   Nixon, "New Proposals for Indochina Peace," p. 18.

39.   Nixon, "The Situation in Southeast Asia."

40.   Richard M. Nixon, "Vietnam Speech," in Wilson, *Setting the Course*, p. 13.

41.   Ibid.

42.   Nixon, "News Conference on Foreign and Domestic Matters," p. 8.

43.   Nixon, "To the Great Silent Majority"; Richard M. Nixon, "We Must Have a New Welfare Plan," in Wilson, *Setting the Course*, pp. 49–59; Nixon, "The Situation in Southeast Asia"; Richard M. Nixon, "The Worth of a Dollar," in Wilson, *Setting the Course*, pp. 118–124.

44.   Nixon, "The Situation in Southeast Asia," p. 4.

45.   Richard M. Nixon, "News Conference," *The New York Times*, December 11, 1970, p. 32.

46.   Nixon, "News Conference on Foreign and Domestic Matters," p. 8.

47.   Nixon, "Vietnam Speech," p. 19.

48.   Nixon, "To the Great Silent Majority," p. 28.

49.   Richard M. Nixon, "Address to the Nation on the Situation in Indochina," *The New York Times*, June 4, 1970, p. 180.

50.   Garry Wills, *Nixon Agonistes: The Crisis of the Self-Made Man* (Boston: Houghton Mifflin, 1970), p. 144.

51.   Nixon, "News Conference on Foreign and Domestic Matters," p. 8.

52.   Richard M. Nixon, "News Conference on Foreign and Domestic Matters," *The New York Times*, April 30, 1971, p. 18.

53.   Richard M. Nixon, "President's News Conference on Foreign and Domestic Matters," *The New York Times*, July 31, 1970, p. 10.

RHETORICAL BIOGRAPHY: A METHODOLOGY FOR THE CITIZEN-CRITIC*

In 1956 candidate Adlai Stevenson pre-empted the last five minutes of one of the "I Love Lucy" shows to present a paid political advertisement. One of the responses he received from the public was a telegram reading, "I like Ike and I Love Lucy. Drop dead." While many of us can identify with this animosity toward political ads, tuning out all such advertising would not seem to be a proper response. Rather, the viewer needs to examine those ads to determine the validity of the claims therein. Our purpose in this essay is to provide the citizen-critic with a methodology of candidate analysis which will allow somewhat more sophisticated and creative responses to candidate presentations.

The conventional approach of the citizen-critic is to ask, "What did the candidate say, and do I agree with him?" There are many problems with this approach — the candidate may not be saying what he really believes, he may have stated his "position" in such a vague way that we are led to think he agrees with us when he really does not, he may change his mind after he is elected. However, the most important drawback of this approach to candidate evaluation stems from the nature of our political system, the fact that we have elections every four years whether we need them or not. By that we mean that our elections are determined by the calendar rather than by the emergence of important issues. Thus campaigns involve debate about whatever issues are lying around when the calendar indicates it is time for another election. The problems this situation creates for the citizen-critic are twofold: (1) none of the issues being debated may be important to his own life so he may have no reason to get involved in the campaign, and (2) the positions taken on these issues may not provide the citizen-critic with many clues about the orientations of the candidates toward issues which will surface in the next three and one-half years.

Frequently, the citizen-critic, recognizing the inadequacy of issue analysis, turns to biographical characteristics to help him decide his vote. His question then becomes, "What kind of man is the candidate and is he similar to me?" And so religion becomes an important criterion, as do

---

*Originally published by Ruth M. Gonchar and Dan F. Hahn, "Rhetorical Biography: A Methodology for the Citizen-Critic," *The Speech Teacher* Speech Communications Association, 22 (1973):48–53. Reprinted with permission.

nationality, sex, and age. None of these is sufficient grounds, we feel, upon which to base a vote.

What is proposed in the remainder of this essay is a methodology which attempts to answer the question: Why did the speaker do what he did in the speaking situation? We suggest five biographical dimensions which can provide the critic with information with which he can begin to search for causality, and determine a more sophisticated basis for his vote. They are: (1) personality orientation; (2) views of leadership; (3) personal and political ideology; (4) epistemology; and (5) hierarchy value structure. The five dimensions are not mutually exclusive; they are interactive. They overlap and are designed that way purposely.

PERSONALITY ORIENTATION

The personality dimension deals with the candidate's orientation toward his own life. Barber and Lasswell both have developed detailed personality classifications to aid the citizen-critic.

Barber suggests the possibility of utilizing two sets of characteristics — active vs. passive and positive vs. negative — to evaluate a candidate.[1] Thus, if the candidate urges active government involvement in the issues confronting the nation now, he is likely to do so for future issues. The approach is not fool-proof, of course, but it is one piece of evidence the citizen-critic can utilize in predicting the future behavior of the candidates.

Harold Lasswell sets forth a psychological methodology for studying the compulsive and dramatizing characteristics of politicians. The compulsive political character

> relies upon rigid, obsessive ways of handling human relations. . . . The dramatizing character may resort to traces of exhibitionism, flirtatiousness, provocativeness, indignation; but in any case all devices are pivoted around the task of "getting a rise out of" the other person.[2]

While we would recommend that any interested citizen-critic should read this approach, it does seem to require relatively inaccessible psychological data.

Information which *is* accessible, however, can be utilized by the citizen-critic to discover the speaker's self-image (through what he says about himself and others he admires) and its relation to his public image (what others say about him; how well his actions fit his self-descriptions). This may lead the critic to identify the candidate vis-à-vis a "hot" or "cool" personality* and cause him to consider the conflict that may occur when the "cool" public image of a speaker confronts his "hot" self-image. When Edmund Muskie, widely perceived as calm and dispassionate, broke down crying on the steps of the Manchester *Union-Leader*, voters had to attempt to determine whether a President Muskie would react "coolly" or "hotly" to difficult events.

The critic should consider also the symbols with which the candidate's image is identified. Those symbols are likely to be reinforced in his speeches. The candidate who flaunts his patriotism through excessive identification with the American flag is more likely to take the "my country, right or wrong" approach — an approach less likely to lead him to solve problems than the more calm, "my country, when right to be kept right, when wrong to be put right" orientation.

The citizen-critic should determine whether the candidate personalizes his actions, whether he views himself as the personification of the people he represents, and when he "ventriloquizes" (that is, speaks as with the voice of another).[3] Each of these orientations will affect the speaker's rhetoric. Further, the critic should attempt to discover the needs of the speaker's personality — whether deference, safety, income, or power[4] — and whether these needs are sought to overcome low self-esteem or to enhance prestige. Moreover, the personality orientation of a candidate will be reflected in the manner in which he reacts to calm and crisis situations. Does the candidate define his environment in "either-or," "calm-crisis" terms? If he does, can predictions be made about the two-valued orientation of his arguments? How does the speaker differentiate between "work" and "play?" Is "play" a part of the candidates's personal vocabulary, or does his "Puritan ethic" proscribe play? Can the candidate admit error? Could he, like John Kennedy, acknowledge the Bay of Pigs invasion as a personal blunder, or would he, like Richard Nixon, attribute his "Manson blooper" to journalistic misinterpretation?

Finally, the citizen-critic should examine the candidate's personality orientation in relation to his operational style. A candidate who is personally a "loner" may adopt an aloof operational style; a more

---

*By "hot" personality we mean a person who is excitable, flamboyant, dramatizing. Typical of this style in politics: George Wallace. By "cool" personality we mean an individual who is deliberate, calm — a delayed reactor. Adlai Stevenson may be the political paradigm of this style.

gregarious speaker may enjoy a tangled and turbulent operation. Almost without question, a candidate's operational style will be manifested in his rhetoric — in his choice of arguments and wording. From these clues, the citizen-critic can make some assumptions about whether the candidate will seek (and follow) advice or whether he will "go it alone" and run the risk of making the kind of strategic and moral mistake that Nixon did in his support of the Pakistan dictatorship.

VIEWS OF LEADERSHIP

When the critic begins to examine a candidate's view of ideal leadership, he should try to discover whether the speaker has constructed his ideal to agree with his own leadership abilities, or whether he has conceived the ideal first and then attempted to fashion his leadership skills and image in its likeness. The citizen should identify the characteristics of that ideal leader-image. Is it a realistic image or one based on a folklore "hero-myth" ideal? Thomas Cronin has analyzed as unrealistic and infeasible the "textbook president," the all-knowing, wise, good, and kind president.[5] The chief executive who tries to live up to this image may find himself frustrated in his attempts, as was President Nixon when he tried to exert moral leadership by taking a stand on the New York State abortion controversy. The president who translates the folklore myth of the presidency into the specifics of everyday behavior may adjust more easily to his leadership role. Such a president would exert religious influence simply by going to church; a "textbook president" would have church services broadcast from the White House. Either way, the folklore myth of leadership will find its way into the speaker's rhetoric; and the more strongly he holds to the ideal myth, the more apparent will be its verbal manifestations.

When analyzing a candidate's view of an ideal leader, the citizen-critic will want to determine whether the candidate is an action-leader (one who operates from a position of strength) or a compromise-leader (one who sees his task as mediation). A candidate who conceives of his ideal leader as an action-taker, a gambler, may utilize the rhetorical strategy of prediction as a demonstration of this leadership characteristic.[6] Only a gambler would predict the outcome of issues yet unresolved. A speaker who visualizes his ideal leader as a mediator or compromiser may symbolize his image rhetorically by the use of carefully-reasoned argument. A speaker who views innovation as a leader's most outstanding attribute may attempt consciously to find new solutions to problems, even while risking condemnation from his critics for speculation and whimsy.

A candidate's view of ideal leadership may be influenced by his power position. A candidate in a power-*seeking* position may conceptualize his leadership image differently than he would were he in a power-*holding* position. A power-holder, through his actions and rhetoric, seeks to reinforce his followers and prevent slippage; a power-seeker uses rhetoric to advertise his position and gain recruits.

Finally, the critic should watch for conflict between a speaker's idealized view of leadership and his self-image or public image. The critic who can determine which image is altered and the method by which the conflict is abated may gain insight into the candidate's overall view of leadership. This analysis is likely to be most helpful to the citizen-critic who has a clear view of the qualities an ideal leader should possess. The development of such a view will be based upon attitudes toward democracy, dignity and freedom for the individual, and the role of politics in solving what the citizen-critic perceives to be societal problems.

PERSONAL AND POLITICAL IDEOLOGY

A critic examining a speaker's personal and political ideology might begin by characterizing his "God-Man" dichotomy. A member of the Far Right, for example, whose God approximates the wrathful, fear-evoking God of the Old Testament, and who views man as untrustworthy and evil would tend to rely on appeals to fear because they mirror his ideology structure.[7] Similarly, a humanitarian ideology might be reflected by use of "love" or "brotherhood" appeals in a speaker's rhetoric.

A critic might expand the God-Man dichotomy into an exploration of optimism-pessimism as a component of the candidate's personal ideology. Not only might this component influence the rhetorical style of the candidate generally, it might go so far as to affect the manner of metaphor the speaker might employ. Metaphors of the sea, for example, often are used by speakers who see society imperiled and are pessimistic of the future,[8] while the candidate who relies heavily on mechanical metaphors when describing human activity might be giving away his own tendency to manipulate people.

At this point the citizen-critic can move to the candidate's political ideology and the effects this ideology may have on his rhetoric. Three variables come to mind immediately in relation to political ideology, although there are many more: orthodoxy, aristocracy, and territory.

Orthodoxy compares what a speaker holds to be right, correct, or true with what society has accepted as right, correct, or true. Specifically, the citizen can attempt to determine whether the candidate is merely mouthing these beliefs or whether he conducts his life on the basis of them. A candidate may regard preservation of the democratic process as a cardinal plank in his political ideology — or he may support democratic principles only until political efficacy suggests it would be to his advantage to sidestep the difficulties inherent in democracy in favor of the simplicity of the authoritarian approach. Similarly, the critic can analyze his candidate's orthodoxy in terms of violence/nonviolence, attack/defense, etc. It might be helpful if the citizen-critic could identify initially what authorities the speaker reveres and what authorities he discards. Knowledge of this sort could provide the citizen with an understanding of the speaker's rhetorical use of expert and prestige sources. It could also lead to a discovery of the candidate's "enemies," and what ideology they represent.

Aristocracy refers to the way in which a speaker divides the populace into elite and masses. Here the critic will want to ascertain the candidate's ideological alignment on the social continuum. If he identifies with the elite or strives to enter the elite circle, his selection of rhetorical strategies will be influenced by his desire for elitist acceptance. Conflict may be generated within a speaker if he desires elitist stature while deriving his power from the masses.

By studying the candidate's references to territory, the critic can discover whether the speaker's ideology is representative of local, regional, national, or international attitudes. When a candidate is seeking the White House, he normally attempts to speak to (and for) all the citizens. Regional candidates and those with specialized audiences (laborers, farmers, etc.) usually do not stand much chance of being elected. Even Richard Nixon's speeches on behalf of the "silent majority" were greeted with a degree of suspicion and hostility on the grounds that a candidate who has ignored or attacked part of the citizenry during the campaign is not likely to be able to achieve unity once elected.

EPISTEMOLOGY

What does epistemology have to do with rhetorical biography? It is not enough for the citizen-critic to analyze a speaker's use of logic and evidence. He must understand the bases upon which a candidate abstracts knowledge, knows what he knows. Any citizen studying a speaker of the Far Right, for example, must consider Far Right epistemology: "God cannot be known empirically, i.e., through the senses; He can be known only through faith; the human who so knows Him also knows God's truth; faith leads to knowledge."[9] Once it is recognized that the epistemology of speakers of the Far Right is based on "God's truth," the relationship between their epistemology and their primary forms of argument can be understood:

> The "Communism as cancer" metaphor, which Edwin Black contends is endemic to the Far Right, grows out of the philosophic God-Devil conflict in which the Right sees itself ordained by God. The Bible, metaphoric throughout, also may influence the Far Right to choose this convenient argument form (convenient because their faith-based ideology cannot be proved by reference to reality).[10]

Epistemology concerns itself not only with whom the candidate accepts as valid sources for his knowledge, but how the candidate abstracts that knowledge. The citizen who perceives in a candidate a decision-making style which limits the free flow of information and knowledge has a basis for his vote beyond the candidate's stand on particular issues.

HIERARCHY VALUE STRUCTURE

The citizen-critic will want to discover a candidate's hierarchy value structure because it will provide him with insight into the candidate's priorities. Lasswell identifies a value hierarchy for the political man: power, first, then respect, affection, rectitude, well-being, wealth, enlightenment, and skill;[11] his political man accentuates power in relation to all the other values. The critic should ask whether the candidate is seeking power for instrumental or consummatory purposes. Does he rely on legitimate, coercive, referent, or expert power? If the candidate seems to be seeking power for his own use, the citizen would want to find out what happens to the man when he faces situations which cannot be solved through power. Is his resultant action and rhetoric tinged with frustration?

A candidate's value hierarchy is not easy to discover. It seems to be the most elusive of the dimensions when it comes to gathering specifics. Here are questions, the answers to which the citizen may find useful. Is the candidate's loyalty to traditional *friends* stronger than his loyalty to traditional institutions? Does he balance the weight of one citizen against society? If the citizen-critic answers these first two questions affirmatively, he might conclude that the candidate values the importance and uniqueness of the individual equally with the worth of society. If the answers are negative, however, the citizen might begin to worry about the degree of freedom which would remain if that candidate were elected.

The critic may want to discover the candidate's value hierarchy in reference to responsibility. Will he as an individual assume when necessary the collective responsibility of a society? His acceptance of societal responsibility should surface almost immediately in his rhetoric; again, the citizen has to know his own value-choices in order to utilize fully this information.

Of course, one of the most logical questions the citizen-critic can ask is, what does the speaker view as moral and immoral within his value structure? If he defines an issue in terms of its morality and immorality, he has, in effect, closed off debate on all but the moral dimension. What values, moral or immoral, does the speaker associate with such things as retreat and defeat, for example? If the speaker values defeat as less damning than retreat, the citizen can expect a reflection of this aspect of the value hierarchy in the speaker's rhetoric, as well as in his actions. The citizen is then in a position to evaluate the candidate according to his own attitude toward the "damn the danger, full speed ahead" approach to problem-solving.

CONCLUSION

The foregoing methodology is only a beginning, with the five dimensions offering a framework for the citizen-critic's analysis. The methodology uses as its primary resource the creativity of the critic; it is designed to encourage creativity rather than cripple it, to generate insight rather than paralyze it. Because it is an outline, the product of the methodology will not be the same for any two people; but it does provide the citizen-critic with a way to get "behind" what a candidate says in order to discover *why* he says it.

NOTES

1. James David Barber, "From Passive-Positive Taft to Active-Negative Nixon," *The Washington Monthly,* October 1969, pp. 33-42.

2. Harold Lasswell, *Power and Personality* (New York: Viking, 1948), p. 62.

3. Wendell Johnson, *People in Quandaries* (New York: Harper, 1946), p. 65.

4. Harold Lasswell, *Politics: Who Gets What, When, How* (New York: Meridian, 1958), p. 13.

5. Thomas Cronin, "Everybody Believes in Democracy Until He Becomes President" (Paper presented at Symposium on "Mr. Nixon and the Presidency," University of Pittsburgh, March 18, 1971).

6. Ruth M. Gonchar and Dan F. Hahn, "The Rhetorical Predictability of Richard M. Nixon," *Today's Speech* 19 (1971):3–13.

7. Dan F. Hahn and Ruth M. Gonchar, "Studying Social Movements: A Rhetorical Methodology," *The Speech Teacher* 20 (1971):44–52.

8. Michael Osborne, "The Rhetorical Metaphor in Criticism" (Unpublished paper, Department of Speech and Drama, Memphis State University), p. 5.

9. Hahn and Gonchar, "Studying Social Movements," p. 49.

10. Ibid.

11. Lasswell, *Power and Personality*, p. 18.

Chapter 5

SMALL GROUP COMMUNICATION DIMENSIONS OF THE AMERICAN PRESIDENCY

> Indeed, if the president is to shape and not just rail against or ride with events in the 1980's ... [he] must be the central organizing intelligence of his administration: and that requires a vision, a mental strength and a procedural discipline — a political, substantive and managerial sense — that has been all too rare in our chief executives.
>
> Ben Heineman and Curtis Hessler

It is true that we elect one person as president of the United States. Our Constitution and heritage reject the notion of a council of state or a parliamentary collective administration. The president is responsible, at least in the minds of the public, for all the government does and fails to do. But, of course, no one person can singly manage the vastness of our government. In 1939 the Brownlow Commission recommended the creation of a White House staff to assist the president in simply dealing with the vast federal bureaucracy.[1] The report of the commission proclaimed that "the president needs help. His immediate staff assistance is entirely inadequate. He should be given a small number of executive assistants who would be his direct aides in dealing with managerial agencies and administrative departments of government."[2]

Today, the institutionalized presidency is comprised of numerous small groups whose tasks include organizing the bureaucracy, formulating policy and issuing recommendations, as well as providing information and advice for presidential decision-making. Our system of government is, by definition, a process and a team effort. Although decision by committee is slow and cumbersome, it is the essence of democratic government. In this chapter we will discuss the nature and importance of small group communication as it relates to the presidency.

SMALL GROUP COMMUNICATION DEFINED

Groups are an important part of our lives and are probably the oldest form of social organization. They are pragmatic (that is, accomplish things, make decisions, have a purpose, etc.) and psychologically satisfying (that is, meet needs of belonging, security, self-esteem, etc.). Ronald Applbaum and his colleagues define group communication as "two or more persons who are interacting with one another in such a manner that each person influences and is influenced by each other person."[3] Group communication implies that the interaction is face to face, task oriented, structured, and involves the process of decision-making or problem solving. There are several important characteristics of group communication.

1. Group communication occurs within a well-defined context and socio-system. There are many elements of influence within a group discussion: members, attitudes, attraction, social pressures, agendas, status, identification, etc. And all of the various elements are interactive and mutually influencing the nature and outcome of the discussion.
2. Group communication is dynamic and "process" oriented. A group, especially if it meets over a period of time, is in a continual process of changing, altering, and influencing members.
3. Group communication, because it usually is structured, has rather clearly defined leadership and membership roles. There are both explicit and implicit rules, procedures, and regulations influencing member behavior, group outcomes, and the nature of interaction.
4. Group communication is rather complex. There are many variables that influence the group members and the nature of the interaction. All the various dimensions and elements mutually influence each other and operate simultaneously.

Many of these factors will be discussed in greater detail.

Group communication, especially in terms of decision-making, is purported to have several advantages.[4] Some scholars argue that groups arrive at better decisions than individuals because groups possess more information and resources than individuals and members are stimulated by the presence of other members. In addition, group decision-making allows for greater understanding of issues by the collective membership and results in a more unified and stronger commitment to the ultimate group decision. Finally, groups can be more productive than individuals because they allow for division of labor of various tasks.

But there are weaknesses to the group communication process. Although groups may be more productive, there is no guarantee that the ultimate decision may be better or more rational than an individual decision. Group communication takes time, can be wasteful and even unsuited for some tasks. Some individual members may suppress convictions, feel threatened, or continually generate conflict. Groups also tend to reach decisions in "spurts" often failing to question the "rush toward consensus."

Formats of Group Communication

There are many different types of groups: social, casual, appointed, elected, task, policy, fact-finding, to name only a few. In addition to several types of groups, there are also several common formats of group communication. They differ in degrees of formality, control, and privacy. *Round table* discussions are the most private and least structured of group discussion formats. There is no audience and group members are free to discuss and express their views. A *panel* discussion, however, is held before an audience and comprised of "experts" who freely express views and arguments relevant to the assigned topic. No final consensus or decision is required. The *forum or symposium* is the most structured and public of all the discussion formats. Here group members provide public statements in sequential order and the audience is free to ask questions. Again, no final consensus or decision is required.

Phases of Group Communication

It was in 1933 that John Dewey, in his book *How We Think*, provided the "philosophical framework" of the discussion process.[5] He identified five steps: defining the problem, analyzing the problem, proposing solutions to the problem, testing the solutions, and selecting the single solution. Today, however, communication scholars would argue that groups really don't make decisions. Rather, because of the interdependence of all the variables involved in the process of discussion, decisions emerge from the group discussion. Realities are created and significance assigned to various facts that influence decisions.

Aubrey Fisher recognizes four phases of the process of decision emergence.[6] In the orientation phase there is a great deal of socializing, roles are defined, and basic member attitudes are shared. In the conflict phase coalitions emerge, problems and issues are identified, and arguments of proposals are rendered. Conflict dissipates, however, in the emergence phase and outcomes become more clear. Finally, in the reinforcement phase decisions are confirmed, bridges mended, and commitment to outcome increased.

Roles and Group Communication

Because group communication is structured and purposeful, there are several roles members fulfill. Social roles are those where members act as negotiators, arbitrators, encouragers, and are concerned with group cohesiveness. Task roles are those where members initiate action, seek information and opinions, coordinate and orient discussion. Of course, leadership roles are, perhaps, the most complex. Group leaders can be appointed, emerge, or obtain the position because of unique traits, skills, or desirable characteristics.

Communication scholars identify several types or styles of leadership. Authoritarian or autocratic leaders are usually perceived as less desirable. Such group leaders rely upon rewards and punishments to keep fellow members in line and tend to make all decisions. In contrast, a laissez-faire style of leadership exercises a minimal amount of control over the group members. They function primarily as information givers. The democratic leader is described as one who seeks opinions, ideas, and suggestions from group members as well as encourages maximum participation. The permissive leader is one Halbert Gulley describes as left of democratic.[7] The leader encourages spontaneity and serves more as a director of traffic than a guide. The group tends to be more social than task oriented. The supervisory leader is, in comparison, to the right of democratic. The leader exercises more control and keeps the group on the assigned topic. Efficiency is the main concern of the leader.

With these general definitions and characteristics of group communication, it is useful to investigate in greater detail the role and function of group communication within the institutionalized presidency.

PRESIDENTIAL DECISION-MAKING

As already noted, the institutionalized presidency is a collectivity of groups that function as the eyes, ears, and often the brain of the president. Some presidential decisions are large, some small. But regardless of scope, Theodore Sorensen argues that "White House decision-making is not a science but an art. It requires, not calculation, but judgment."[8] The reason that few decisions are clear-cut is because at the heart of all decisions is conflict — conflict among various groups, philosophies, or policies.

For most major policy decisions there are eight rather distinct steps in the decision-making process:[9]

1. agreement on the facts,
2. agreement on the overall policy objective,
3. precise definition of the problem,
4. canvassing of all possible solutions,
5. list all possible consequences that would follow each solution,
6. recommendation and final solution choice,
7. communication of solution selection,
8. provision for execution of selection.

Each of these steps may require inter- and intra-group meetings. The degree of presidential involvement depends upon the style and choice of the occupant.

Recently, scholars are recommending a type of "collegial" decision-making process for a president.[10] Here the president functions as the hub of the wheel and advisors function as the spokes. Information and advice flows to the president from several sources rather than a strict, hierarchical, bureaucratic process. Presidents Roosevelt, Truman, Kennedy, Johnson, and Carter used primarily this approach.

Ben Heineman and Curtis Hessler posit that the presidents of the 1980s "must be the central organizing intelligence of their administration."[11] They call a "strategic presidency" one that does not just exercise but *shares* influence and responsibility with other key actors in the administration, depersonalizing the office to ensure that all important decisions do not flow directly to him or from him alone.[12]

Ryan Barilleaux, however, takes exception to the growing endorsement of "collegial" decision-making. He concludes that "even an energetic and highly motivated president would be unable to use it as a general decision mechanism."[13] Upon reviewing Kennedy's Bay of Pigs decision-making process, the epitomy of a collegial approach, Barilleaux finds several serious problems. First, the demands on a president's time and attention for effective group process becomes unrealistic. It is difficult for a president to have active participation in all phases of the group decision process. Second, because of a president's lack of involvement in all phases of the decision-making process, there is an absence of routine oversight. The lack of control reduces the ability to ensure that ideas or solutions presented are the best alternatives. The possibility for idea refinement and redefinition is greatly reduced. Finally, the personality, charisma, and position of a president may overwhelm group members. Advisors may be less than honest and may not challenge the president's position. Thus, the president's presence could limit debate and group dynamics. To avoid this problem, Sorensen reports that Kennedy often asked the National Security Council to hold preliminary meetings without him to ensure more honest debate and discussion. In addition, Kennedy often just listened without revealing his personal opinions or impressions.[14]

But even Sorensen acknowledges the difficulty of group decision-making.[15] Many members of the president's staff are more concerned with personal images than issues. Group recommendations tend to "emphasize consensus rather than content, unanimity rather than precision, compromise rather than creativity."[16] Groups, because of the diversity of egos and motives of various members, allow more "leaks" and the "airing of dirty laundry" than private presidential decision-making.

The nature and effectiveness of White House decision-making, like that of all groups, depends upon the style of leadership of the president. How they view their role in the process, the public mandate, and the commitment toward specific policy all influence how a president utilizes his staff. In addition, presidents differ greatly in expertise, motivation, and social skill that also influences the workings of groups in the White House.

Dan Nimmo claims that political leaders have several common tendencies.[17] Leaders gain satisfactions from being part of a group; are more intense in holding values; possess more beliefs about the group and its relation to other groups and issues; are less likely to change their values or positions due to pressure; are more likely to make decisions based on prior beliefs, attitudes, or values; and are certainly more issue-oriented. But these tendencies endorse strong leadership. In fact, few

Americans desire an impartial, laissez-faire style of leadership. When it comes to crisis or policy decisions, most Americans would probably favor an authoritarian style. Americans generally favor the view of Theodore Roosevelt that "in a crisis, the duty of a leader is to lead — and not to take refuge behind the generally timid wisdom of a multitude of counsellors."[18]

Kennedy especially wanted to obtain information and views of all sides of an issue. He preferred a series of meetings on an issue and would often end meetings without expressing his view or making a decision in order to keep his options open as long as possible. Kennedy encouraged informality and flexibility in discussion. Large public meetings, he believed, were largely unproductive and thus he preferred small sub-groups of larger groups such as the National Security Council rather than the full cabinet. Kennedy valued small group discussions to the extent that he would often have meetings going on simultaneously and would make periodic appearances to "see how things were going." For example, the morning of the Cuban missile crisis, Kennedy also met with a panel on mental retardation, disaster relief for storm-ravaged Oregon, and with astronaut Walter Shirra.[19]

Reagan's decision-making style is very different from that of Kennedy. Reagan does not like getting involved in the details of an issue. Nor does he like open conflict or heated discussion among his staff. Reagan looks for philosophical consistency in decisions and will rely upon his instincts more than staff analyses.[20]

The more public, announced White House meetings serve very different functions. They are often staged to increase public confidence that some issue or topic is receiving presidential attention.[21] They may also increase staff member morale. But more importantly, public meetings stimulate public discussion and the airing of various views on a subject.

Although it is often difficult to assess the specific impact or frequency of small group discussions upon the ultimate policy decisions of any administration, it is clear that through White House group discussions, issues are defined, positions formulated, and decisions made. The potential problems of the group decision-making process are, however, no different than with any other group. The success of the group decision-making process depends greatly upon the leadership style of the president.

PRESIDENTIAL CABINET

The presidential cabinet is probably the most recognized "small group" of the institutionalized presidency. But the Constitution made no provisions for a cabinet. The term was first used by newspapermen in the 1790s during the Washington administration. The old Articles of Confederation had provided "Heads of Departments" and thus the cabinet evolved from this concept. It received official status by Congress in 1798 and was described as "the great council of the nation."[22] Early cabinet members served as the president's staff: they answered mail, helped formulate legislation, prepared speeches, and even acted as tour guides.[23] Actually, the Reorganization Act of 1939 reduced the power of cabinet members by providing a personal, presidential staff. Many of the functions provided by cabinet members were replaced by staff members. Early cabinet members were personal acquaintances of the president. In the nineteenth century, however, members were increasingly appointed as a political reward or to represent a particular political interest or group. As cabinet members were no longer personal friends or acquaintances of presidents, presidents began to formulate advisory groups consisting of non-cabinet members. As Gordon Hoxie observes, Andrew Jackson had his "Kitchen Cabinet"; John Tyler, his "Virginia Schoolmasters"; Grover Cleveland, his "Fishing Cabinet"; Theodore Roosevelt, his "Tennis Cabinet"; Warren Harding, his "Poker Cabinet"; Herbert Hoover, his "Medicine Ball Cabinet"; and Franklin Roosevelt, his "Brain Trust."[24]

Thus, cabinet members are appointed and serve at the pleasure of the president. The president has no constitutional obligation to convene, consult, or follow the cabinet's advice. It is, as with all groups, up to the president (or leader) to determine *how* to use the cabinet. And, indeed, there has been great variation among the presidents.

At least in theory, the cabinet can serve as a sounding board, an advisory body, a forum for debate, or as a source of innovation.[25] Members could fulfill several roles or orientations. They could represent certain groups or issue positions, mirror presidential concerns, or be good problem solvers.

Eisenhower institutionalized the presidential office and restored the "collegiality" of the cabinet.[26] He made the cabinet an official part of the chain of command. The cabinet under Eisenhower met regularly and were formal gatherings where department heads presented position papers. The president created the position of Cabinet Secretariat who prepared the agenda for the weekly meeting, logged decisions, and followed up on decisions. Eisenhower wanted the body to serve as more than advisors.[27]

It is interesting to note that although Kennedy recognized the value of the group decision process, he did not perceive the collective cabinet as a valuable decision-making group. Arthur Schlesinger reports Kennedy stating to John Sharon on one occasion that "Cabinet meetings . . . are simply useless. Why should the Postmaster General sit there and listen to a discussion of the problems of Laos?"[28] Under Kennedy the cabinet as a whole met infrequently. Members would submit weekly reports detailing activities and proposals. When the cabinet did meet, Kennedy would listen to presentations and ask pertinent questions. He expected precise statements and presentations. He would summarize the key points and generally end the meeting. Kennedy used cabinet meetings, therefore, as sources for information. In staff meetings he would solicit debate and conduct brainstorming.

Rather than using cabinet meetings as sources for information, Johnson would use them as opportunities to express his desires and tasks for the members to execute. All information, policy formation, and decisions came from the White House staff. Johnson wanted obedience and loyalty from cabinet members. Any unauthorized statements or leaks would result in the cancellation of pet projects.[29] The Johnson cabinet, then, contributed little to policy formation and decision-making.

Such an approach to the cabinet has become the rule rather than the exception. Reagan, upon the idea of Edwin Meese, created seven Cabinet Councils each focusing on specific subject areas: economic affairs, commerce and trade, food and agriculture, human resources, natural resources, legal policy, and management and administration. During the first 18 months in office, over 200 issues were considered using the Cabinet Councils.[30] Without doubt, as Richard Pious observes, the cabinet is used more for "public relations symbolism than substantive governing."[31]

Ironically, each modern president upon election has proclaimed the goal of making the cabinet an important and vital part of the administration. Soon, however, presidents become disillusioned with their effectiveness. Cabinet members become more loyal to departments than the president as a simple matter of survival within their own departments. Competition and conflict develop among departments. Soon, cabinet members realize that their main function is to run their departments rather than formulate policy. Strong presidents tend either to dominate or ignore their cabinets. Thus, the cabinet today is not a vital part of the institutionalized presidency. Its importance and role depends solely upon the chief executive.

We must acknowledge some remorse upon the current ineffective use of the cabinet. We concur with Hoxie in recognizing the need for both a strong, experienced White House staff and a dynamic cabinet. "With the growth of government and the complexities of presidential responsibilities, it is imperative that Cabinet and staff have an effective relationship."[32]

PRESIDENTIAL PRESS CONFERENCES

According to our definition and discussion of group communication, today's presidential press conferences are not appropriate for the category. Early press conferences, however, were informal small group discussions. There were recognized rules and decorum.[33] Reporters were given several options during a conference. Some statements could be quoted verbatim and attributed to a president or a top official. Statements "not for direct quotation" could be reported and the source identified but only paraphrased. Information could be reported but the sources not identified in "background only" statements. Finally, remarks "off the record" were for reporter's general knowledge and not to be reported in any form.

Press conferences, however, have always served to influence public opinion. Although Franklin Roosevelt was the first to permit spontaneous questioning, staff members still attempted to plant special questions with receptive newsmen. Truman liked press conferences but always performed poorly. Eisenhower allowed cameramen to film press conferences but they were edited before being shown on television. He was faulted for providing shallow answers to most questions. Kennedy enjoyed press conferences and allowed live television coverage. Press conferences were a way to inform and educate the public. For Kennedy, they also demonstrated wit, intelligence, and mastery of information. Johnson avoided formal press conferences. He would even announce press conferences at the last possible minute, usually on weekends, making issue research for reporters very difficult. With the introduction of the "opening statement," the free exchange and discussion of issues were no longer an aspect of the press conference. Television, more than anything else, contributed to the drastic decrease of the frequency of press conferences and the attempt of control by presidents.

It is not our purpose to analyze the nature of presidential press conferences. We do suggest, however, that they did provide a small group forum for discussion of public issues. The extent to which they are now forms of public opinion manipulation is discussed in great detail in the explication section on "What Did Nixon Say and When Did He Say It?"

CONCLUSION

In this brief overview of group communication, we have attempted to demonstrate the importance and prevalence of its activity in the presidency. Designated groups within the White House formulate policy, reach decisions, and handle crises. Their success, like all groups, depends upon the leader. Most of the problems and failures of such groups, we would argue, rests on the lack of understanding of group dynamics and communication skills. Ironically, a strong president may be the least effective user of group communication. We also suggest that analyses of presidential decision-making and policy implementation must consider dimensions of group communication.

Variables and skills of effective group communication may be difficult to assess but vital to the functioning of the presidency and, consequently, the nation.

NOTES

1. Richard Pious, *The American Presidency* (New York: Basic Books, 1979), p. 243.

2. As quoted in ibid., p. 243.

3. Ronald Applbaum et al., *The Process of Group Communication* (Chicago: SRA, 1974).

4. Halbert Gulley, *Discussion, Conference, and Group Process* (New York: Holt, Rinehart, and Winston, 1968), pp. 20–42.

5. See John Dewey, *How We Think* (Boston: D. C. Heath, 1933).

6. Aubrey Fisher, *Small Group Decision Making* (New York: McGraw-Hill, 1974), pp. 168–173.

7. Gulley, *Discussion, Conference,* p. 179.

8. Theodore Sorensen, *Decision-Making in the White House* (New York: Columbia University Press, 1963), p. 10.

9. Ibid., pp. 18–19.

10. See Roger Porter, *Presidential Decision Making* (New York: Cambridge University Press, 1980); Alexander George, *Presidential Decisionmaking in Foreign*

Policy (Boulder, CO: Westview Press, 1980); and Ben Heineman and Curtis Hessler, *Memorandum for the President* (New York: Random House, 1980).

11. Heineman and Hessler, *Memorandum for the President,* p. xviii.

12. Ibid., p. xvii.

13. Ryan Barilleaux, "Kennedy, The Bay of Pigs, and the Limits of Collegial Decision Making" in *The Presidency and National Security Policy,* ed. Gordon Hoxie (New York: Center for the Study of the Presidency, 1984), pp. 207–222.

14. Sorensen, *Decision-Making in the White House,* p. 60.

15. Ibid., pp. 60–63.

16. Ibid., p. 61.

17. Dan Nimmo, *Political Communication and Public Opinion in America* (Santa Monica, CA: Goodyear, 1978), p. 35.

18. As quoted in Sorensen, *Decision-Making in the White House,* p. 83.

19. Theodore Sorensen, *The Kennedy Legacy* (New York: Macmillan, 1969), p. 168.

20. See George Church, "How Reagan Decides," *Times,* December 13, 1982, pp. 12–17.

21. Thomas Cronin, *The State of the Presidency* (Boston: Little, Brown, 1975), p. 178.

22. Gordon Hoxie, "The Cabinet in the American Presidency, 1789–1984," *Presidential Studies Quarterly,* vol. 14, no. 2 (Spring 1984):214.

23. Doris Kearns, *Lyndon Johnson and the American Dream* (New York: Harper & Row, 1976), p. 243.

24. Hoxie, "The Cabinet," p. 215.

25. As suggested in Pious, *The American Presidency,* p. 240.

26. Hoxie, "The Cabinet," p. 223.

27. Pious, *The American Presidency,* p. 182.

28. Arthur Schlesinger, Jr., *A Thousand Days* (Boston: Houghton Mifflin, 1965), p. 688.

29. Kearns, *Lyndon Johnson,* p. 244.

30. Hoxie, "The Cabinet," p. 226.

31. Pious, *The American Presidency,* p. 240.

32. Hoxie, "The Cabinet," p. 228.

33. Richard Watson and Norman Thomas, *The Politics of the Presidency* (New York: John Wiley & Sons, 1983), p. 185.

READINGS

INTRODUCTION

Chapter 5 investigated the institutionalized presidency which is comprised of numerous small groups whose tasks include organizing the bureaucracy, formulating policy, and issuing recommendations. Also, the reality of the office is that occupants must continually appeal to very specific public groups.

The first essay looks at Jimmy Carter's controversial interview in *Playboy* magazine during the 1980 presidential campaign. The authors suggest that the remarks were totally appropriate for the intended audience but were problematic when revealed to a larger, national audience. The pervasive nature of today's mass media virtually makes it impossible for presidential candidates to mold their remarks for a specific audience. As a result, political rhetoric becomes even more general and noncommittal.

The second essay focuses on Richard Nixon's press conferences. The way Nixon obverted them and the techniques he used to frustrate reporters are identified. The authors suggest, in terms of small group communication, that Nixon's press conferences were not a forum for the discussion of public issues.

The final essay looks at John Kennedy's call for a change in the nature of the national dialogue in an address at Yale. He wanted to replace the old ideological debate with a technocratic one. His attempt, however, was unsuccessful.

THE DILEMMA OF MULTIPLE AUDIENCES: CARTER'S *PLAYBOY* INTERVIEW

The presidential campaign of 1976 will undoubtedly be recorded as one of the most unique and exciting campaigns of our modern history. Within the shadows of Watergate, the presidential election provided a close and nearly classic electoral contest. The primaries were marked by intense rhetoric and masterful strategies on both sides. In addition to the historic debates, the election campaign resulted in numerous "heresies" and states of naiveté.

Perhaps one of the most interesting rhetorical events of the campaign was Jimmy Carter's interview in *Playboy* magazine.[1] The November 1976 article was the result of five hours of interviewing by Robert Scheer given over a three-month period.[2] Journalists traveling with Carter had known of the interview for several months.[3] Carter was questioned on such substantive topics as,

> Vietnam, prayer, Chile, the rigors of campaigning, Kissinger, his relationship with his wife, his role in Georgia politics, the judges he would appoint, civil rights, homosexuality, the media, corporations, taxes, the right of reporters to protect their sources, blue laws, religion, victimless crimes, his relationship to his sister Ruth's "faith-healing," Lyndon Johnson, how he felt about his son Jack fighting in the war, his friendship with Hunter Thompson, his meeting with Bob Dylan and how it came about, William Calley, and My Lai, health care legislation, the number of women on his staff, the pressures of the White House, Robert Shrum's attack on him, the allegation that he is fuzzy and the possibility of his own assassination.[4]

None of these, however, created a stir.

What did stimulate controversy was Carter's use of the words "screw" and "shack up" while revealing that he too, like other humans, has "looked on a lot of women with lust," thus having ". . . committed adultery in (his) heart many times."[5] This revelation by Carter opened himself to ridicule and serious questions about his judgment. As a rhetorical event, the critic must also question Carter's modes of expression, consistency of assumptions, and the relationship between those assumptions and the values espoused by society.[6]

Traditional criticism of this event, while recognizing the obvious paradoxes created, would too quickly dismiss Carter's rhetorical strategies of persuasion as logically inconsistent with his prior statements of being a "Christian," lacking appropriate "style" and "eloquence," and countering the values idealized in our society. Such a conclusion would indeed fail to recognize clearly Carter's purpose and evaluation of the rhetorical event. We posit that by applying Kenneth Burke's concept of the pentad to both the immediate rhetorical event and the broader societal exposure of the event, the critic may more clearly assess the wisdom in Carter's rhetorical strategy. More specifically, it is from the broad societal perspective that reveals the potential problems and paradoxes of the *Playboy* interview. Thus, from a dual pentad perspective, one may better perceive Carter's motives and strategies which successfully fulfilled his purpose in the immediate context (that is, readers of *Playboy*), but caused him problems when applied to a new audience or rhetorical situation (that is, general society).

METHOD

Burkean criticism, in a broad sense, is based upon specified assumptions and certain key concepts. The basic assumptions are that man, as a rational animal, is a symbol-using animal which distinguishes him from other animals and that man uses symbols "rhetorically" in communication to control and make sense of his world. Burke's key concepts evolve from the central questions: How are language and motives related? How does man use language rhetorically to create his symbolic world? How does man use language to communicate with others to fit himself and his motives into that symbolic world?[7] In answering these basic questions, Burke developed the concepts of motive, "the negative," ambiguity, identification, transcendence, and the pentad.

Each of these concepts enables the critic to judge the appropriateness and adequacy of the description of "reality" the speaker has presented. Almost any behavior, because of the ambiguity of language, can be rationalized or justified by appealing to a motive which is simply a linguistic label for a situation.[8] Persons have a large number of ways to define or describe their environment symbolically. Thus, it is the ambiguity of language that enables persons to create their own symbolic realities into which they can best fit themselves.[9] However, conflict may occur if "symbolic realities" greatly differ. It is only when people *think* there is common ground that they may live in cooperation. Every time a speaker "identifies" with the audience, he or she seeks to reduce ambiguity and use language to communicate motivational meanings.[10] In communicating, we also "transcend" to higher planes of meaning that enable us to overcome differences. For instance, all persons agree that there should be law and order, but they may disagree on many specific laws. Thus, both "identification" and "transcendence" are used in communication to reduce that ambiguity of language and hence, ensure cooperation.

Finally, Burke has developed a dramatistic model of approach to man's communicative behavior. It contains five elements and is called the pentad.[11] The five elements are: the scene (the environment in which behavior occurs), the act (the behavior itself), the agent (the action), the agency (the means or methods by which the act is carried out), and the purpose (the motive assigned to the agent's act). For the critic, the pentad may be used as a means of examining how the speaker has attempted to reconstruct the audience's view of reality. It is with these concepts of Burkean rhetorical criticism that we approach Carter's interview.

ANALYSIS

Applying Burke's dramatistic pentad is valuable in realizing the full scope of Carter's rhetorical behavior. The pentad is valuable not only in applying it to Carter's behavior in the interview, but also to the broader societal context in which the interview was only a small part. In doing so, one becomes aware of two essential things. First, Carter's assessment of the immediate rhetorical event was largely accurate and reflects considerable judgment in fulfilling the rhetorical requirement of the event. Second, several rhetorical dilemmas emerge as a result of the interview being directed to a different audience than that intended. Both of these dimensions become clear upon analysis.

The scene of Carter's interview was the campaign trail of 1976. The "interviews" totaled five hours and were given over a three-month period. Some of the interview sessions were as short as half an hour while others were somewhat longer. They occurred between campaign stops aboard the candidate's plane with the exception of the last session which took place at Carter's home in Georgia.[12] The act was the actual "interviews" given by Carter to Scheer. The agent was Carter who performed the act. The agency, or means by which the act was carried out, was Carter making sound or speech. Finally, the purpose of the act was to "assure *Playboy*'s presumably hedonistic readers that (Carter's) own preference for marital fidelity has not given him a holier-than-thou attitude."[13] By this categorization of the immediate rhetorical behavior, we see that the scene is dominant. For it is only by it being an election year and campaign that the act of granting an interview to *Playboy* could exist in relation to fulfilling the *purpose* of gaining the votes of the "liberal" readers of *Playboy* by easing their fear of a "religious fanatic" becoming president. The scene of the act determined the purpose of the act and to a large extent, the act itself. "Insofar as men's actions are to be interpreted in terms of the circumstances in which they are acting, their behavior would fall under the heading of a 'scene-act ratio.'"[14] Thus, in the immediate rhetorical behavior, the scene is dominant.

Within this realm of analysis, Carter's rhetorical choices appear justifiable. To win elections, obviously, one needs to obtain votes. In close elections a candidate must not ignore perceived "blocks of voters." As a result of the publicity about Carter's "religion," it was feared that some "liberal" voters would reject Carter on this issue alone. Carter's choice of the medium and the message was thus pragmatic. Hamilton Jordon, Carter's campaign manager, commented prior to the release of the interview, "We wouldn't do it if it weren't in our interest. It's your readers who are probably predisposed toward Jimmy — but they may not vote at all if they feel uneasy about him."[15]

Clearly Carter adapted to his audience. In addition to using a recognizable medium of his targeted audience, Carter attempted to create a sense of "identification" with his audience. As already noted, identification serves to unify or create common ground between individuals. It is by identifying common references that ambiguity is reduced. In the interview, Carter seeks identification two ways. First, by use of the words "screw" and "shack up" Carter's language is intended to be in line with that of the readers'. Expressions more formal would not have been consistent in terms of the audience, medium, or stated purpose of the interview. Second, Carter created identification with the audience by the example he gave. Clearly Carter's admission to lusting in his heart portrayed him to the readers as a "normal healthy American male." Carter's distinction with the audience (that is, "saved" not by moral performance but by "grace" of God's forgiveness) would not have been understood if he had not first of all created a sense of commonality with the audience. In doing so, the audience should have been more predisposed to listen to his arguments.

What about Carter's arguments and logic? Here, too, little fault may be found. Carter's purpose was to persuade the readers that his religious beliefs would not make him excessively self-righteous or puritanical. In fact, his beliefs dictate the opposite: humility and forgiveness. Carter's illustration comes straight from the Bible in the collection of scripture comprising The Sermon on the Mount which appears in Matthew 5. The point Carter was attempting to make really had nothing to do with lust, sex, or adultery. He was trying to explain justification by grace alone which is founded in the Protestant Reformation and Luther.[16] His example to illustrate this Christian doctrine was one easily understood by the readers of *Playboy*.

> I try not to commit a deliberate sin. I recognize that I'm going to do it anyhow, because I'm human and I'm tempted. And Christ set some almost impossible standards for us ... I've looked on a lot of women with lust. I've committed adultery in my heart many times. This is something that God recognizes I will do — and I have done it — and God forgave me for it.[17]

One is hard pressed to find religious scholars who disagreed with the accuracy of Carter's scriptural interpretation. Dr. William Wolf, professor at the Episcopal Divinity School in Cambridge responded, "It sounds to me like good theology and good honest human experience brought together."[18] Gerald Sherry, editor of San Francisco's *Catholic Monitor* stated, "I think he was trying to explain Christian ideas on promiscuity. If anything, he showed himself much less arrogant than Ford ... Carter was being truthful with all due humility."[19] Even Carter's own pastor, Reverend Edwards of Plains Baptist Church, commented, "I have no particular objections to it ... but I would have used other words to describe the same thing."[20]

As a result of the application of Burke's pentad to this rhetorical event, several things become obvious. The nature of Carter's motive is clearly revealed. The rhetorical choices made to fulfill the purpose of the event were consistent with traditional concerns with audience adaptation. In addition to a good selection of medium to reach his targeted audience, Carter's examples and language related to his audience well. Finally, Carter's interpretation of the scripture was accurate. Norman Mailer, in a subsequent article in the Sunday *New York Times Magazine* wrote, "It was said from duty, from the quiet decent demands of duty, as if he, too, had to present his credentials to that part of the 20th century personified by his interviewer."[21] To that end I believe Carter was successful in a large part because of the rhetorical choices utilized.

One may gain another perspective of Carter's rhetorical event by applying the pentad to the larger situation. In doing so, the paradoxes of the situation become clear. The scene was the United States complete with societal norms, values, and traditions. The act was the publishing of the interview in *Playboy* magazine. The agent of the act was *Playboy*'s publishers. The agency or the methods of fulfilling the act was print or the collective contents that comprise the magazine. In this consideration, the purpose of the act or the motivation of the act stemmed primarily from economic and profit considerations. *Playboy* was aware of the "newsworthiness" of the interview. Barry Golson, assistant managing editor of the magazine who joined Scheer for the final interview, phoned portions of the story to Judy Woodruft of NBC urging her to pass it on to the "Today" show. In fact, the magazine issue hit the stands about a month early.[22] In this case, the act of publishing the interview structures or influences the remaining four elements. In short, they relate directly to the act. Thus, the act is dominant rather than the scene.

From this perspective we see several paradoxes develop. Society in general avoids open and public discussions about sexual behavior. Any revelation by Carter in this area was destined to create controversy. Martin Mary, of *Christian Century*, publicly mused:

> What if you'd said, "Let me confess. I have *killed* people. Jesus' standards are very high. He says, 'Whoever hateth his brother, is a murderer,' and I've had my bad days." You know what would have happened. You would not have heard a word of criticism. Hating isn't such a big deal.[23]

Daily we are told that the moral standards of our nation are declining while sexually explicit films continue to break box office records. Some observers contend that we have grown comfortable as a nation with our own hypocrisy.[24] William Miller best summarizes the irony of the event.

> The cynical urban world that created *Playboy* magazine and keeps it going and writes for it and advertises in it and shares its vulgar world view and helps it reach 40 million people then turned and criticized Carter for frankly answering the questions of its interviewers.[25]

Thus, the first major paradox revealed by viewing the larger pentadic structure resulted from societal attitudes toward the public discussion of sexual behavior.

Also significant in arousing controversy were the statements contrast to the "moral," "Christian," "born again" image Carter had created. As a result, the statements were characterized as "curious intermingling of pulpit and lockerroom language . . ." and "undeacon-like idiom."[26] Carter had nurtured an image of an "outsider" who would "never tell a lie" and *practiced* the principles of Christianity. This perceived image magnified the impact of the medium as well as the message. For Meg Greenfield, of *Newsweek* magazine, Carter's ". . . re-creating himself as an eccentric, a stranger to common experience, a man whose 'we' becomes increasingly unfamiliar and uncomfortable in its implications ...." opened himself up for attack.[27] Thus, the contrast between Carter's image and the message conveyed in *Playboy* resulted in the irony that as "... informed an exposition of Christianity as you can find from any American politician got turned clear around into something offensive exactly to the people who should have been most deeply impressed by it."[28]

Finally, most Americans have a unique perception of the office of president. Aspirants to that office, while allowed to campaign as one of "us," must be above the petty attitudes and behavior of the common man. With the release of Nixon's White House transcripts, many Americans were upset that the president of the United States would use, even in private, such profane language. Lyndon Johnson, also, has been criticized for his perceived crudeness in speech and behavior. From this standpoint, the interview was seen as a political mistake. Robert Byrd of West Virginia, Senate Democratic leader, publicly pondered why Carter granted the interview originally.[29] Political columnists and reporters criticized Carter "... not for committing a sin but for making a mistake, which in their eyes is far worse. It wasn't that he lacked moral integrity but that he wasn't prudent, calculating, smart in his own interest."[30]

From the broader pentad the potential problems of the interview are evident. For society in general, Carter misjudged the audience. The medium and word usage are counter to the norms and values (real or perceived) publicly espoused by the public. Carter's rhetorical choices were inappropriate for the larger audience. His purpose was largely negated by the interview when viewed from this perspective alone.

CONCLUSION

Carter's interview in *Playboy* magazine stimulated a great deal of controversy. The medium and the message appeared to contradict the "image" portrayed to the public. Thus, Carter's modes of expressing consistency of assumptions, and the relationship between those assumptions and the values espoused by society were questioned. By applying Burke's pentad to the immediate and broader rhetorical event, one is better able to view the full scope of Carter's rhetorical choices. In the former, the choices were accurate in relation to the targeted audience. In the latter, the choices reflect poor judgment from a "political" pragmatic viewpoint. Thus, this dual perspective better enabled one to perceive Carter's motives and strategies which successfully fulfilled his purpose in the immediate context but caused problems when applied to a new audience. This distinction, we believe, is important.

The pervasive dimensions of today's mass media virtually make it impossible for a presidential candidate to mold his or her remarks for a *specified* audience. The candidate must create messages designed to appeal to the "average," "lowest common denominator." The mass media produce the requirement that candidates be able to speak to several audiences simultaneously. This new requirement restricts a candidate's rhetorical choices in terms of examples, illustrations, and even persuasive strategies. As a result, political rhetoric may become *even more* general, noncommittal, and lacking in specificity. The world of high-powered publicity is capable of revealing truth as well as creating distortion. The critic must painfully be aware of the influence of the mass media on every address. Such awareness requires special consideration of a speaker's motive and rhetorical choices as influenced by the media. The distinction between the media as the primary intended channel of the message versus the media as an "accidental" transmitter of a message is of prime importance. It is within this context that the problem of multiple audiences is magnified.

NOTES

1. "Playboy Interview: Jimmy Carter," *Playboy,* Nov. 1976, pp. 63–86.

2. "Trying to be One of the Boys," *Time,* Oct. 4, 1976, p. 33.

3. "Bowdlerizing Jimmy," *Time,* Oct. 4, 1976, p. 71.

4. William Lee Miller, "Defending Carter's Heresies," *New Republic,* Oct. 9, 1976, p. 17.

5. "Playboy Interview: Jimmy Carter," p. 86.

6. For a statement of the dimensions about which a critic must make evaluative judgments, see Barbara and Henry Ewbank, "The Critical Statement," *Central States Speech Journal* (Winter 1976):285–294.

7. Leonard C. Hawes, *Pragmatics of Analoguing* (Reading: Addison-Wesley, 1975), p. 48.

8. Kenneth Burke, *Permanance and Change* (Los Altos: Hermes, 1954), pp. 29–30; see also Kenneth Burke, *Language as Symbolic Action* (California: University of California Press, 1952), pp. 3–25.

9. Kenneth Burke, *A Grammar of Motives* (Englewood Cliffs: Prentice-Hall, 1945), pp. 3–20.

10. Kenneth Burke, *A Rhetoric of Motives* (New York: George Braziller, 1950), p. 21.

11. Kenneth Burke, *Grammar of Motives,* pp. xv–xxiii.

12. "Playboy Interview: Jimmy Carter," p. 63.

13. "Trying to be One of the Boys," p. 33.

14. Kenneth Burke, "Interaction: Dramatism," *International Encyclopaedia of Social Sciences* (New York: Macmillan, 1968), p. 447.

15. "Playboy Interview: Jimmy Carter," p. 64.

16. Miller, "Defending Carter's Heresies," p. 18.

17. "Playboy Interview: Jimmy Carter," p. 86.

18. "Trying to be One of the Boys," p. 33.

19. Ibid., p. 34.

20. Ibid., p. 33.

21. Ibid.

22. "The Great Playboy Furor," *Newsweek,* Oct. 4, 1976, p. 70.

23. Martin Mary, "About That Interview," *Christian Century,* Oct. 6, 1976, p. 847.

24. Meg Greenfield, "Carter's Real Blunder," *Newsweek,* Oct. 11, 1976, p. 120.

25. Miller, "Defending Carter's Heresies," p. 19.

26. "Trying to be One of the Boys," p. 33.

27. Greenfield, "Carter's Real Blunder," p. 120.

28. Miller, "Defending Carter's Heresies," p. 18.

29. "Trying to be One of the Boys," p. 34.

30. Miller, "Defending Carter's Heresies," p. 19.

WHAT DID NIXON SAY AND WHEN DID HE SAY IT? PRESIDENTIAL PRESS CONFERENCES AND PRESS SECRETARY BRIEFINGS

> Democracy . . . requires rituals as much as any other form of government and the televised news conference serves the purpose. . . . In a process which purports to be the supreme form of communication between a President and his people, the presentation has become the dominant factor. Performance, in a theatrical sense, rides roughshod over content. For all the public learns about a chief executive's thinking, the newsmen might as well sit in the front lobby and dutifully file the press releases handed out by the press office. . . . What has really happened is that a device universally hailed as a boon to communication has become a one-way street. It is the means by which a man can conduct a monologue *in* public and convince himself that he is conducting a dialogue *with* the public.[1]

A description of Richard M. Nixon's press conferences? No. An analysis of Lyndon Johnson's press conferences by Johnson's former press secretary, George Reedy.

But Richard Nixon's press conferences could easily have been confused with Johnson's, although Nixon's dislike for the press itself and press conferences and his belief that the press disliked him was, perhaps, more intense than Johnson's. The distaste that Richard Nixon exhibited toward press contacts was neither unprecedented nor partisan. "In fact, a careful study has turned up only one President who did not at some time engage in an open fight with the media. He was William Henry Harrison, who died after a few weeks in office."[2]

Our purposes in this essay, then, are to identify the similarities between Richard Nixon's press conferences and those of previous presidents and to analyze the unusual distinctions.

No president has liked the idea of press conferences. One modern response to that dislike has been to avoid holding them. From F.D.R. to Nixon the number of press conferences steadily decreased. Compared to Franklin Roosevelt, who scheduled 150 press conferences in his first two years as president, and who continued at the rate of more than one a week thereafter, Truman scheduled 94 in his first two years in office, Eisenhower held 58, Kennedy, 46, 50 for Johnson, and Nixon, 17. Significantly, Nixon held only 12 press conferences in the 24 months between May 1971 and May 1973, the critical Vietnam war and Watergate scandal period.[3]

While no president has liked the idea of meeting the press, some, like Roosevelt and Kennedy, have done well in press conference situations, probably because such situations tend to reflect the personality orientations and rhetorical abilities of the president. For John Kennedy, particularly, ". . . the conferences offered a showcase for a number of his most characteristic qualities — the intellectual speech and vivacity, the remarkable mastery of the data of government, the terse, self-mocking wit, the exhilarating personal command."[4]

Lyndon Johnson did not relish the idea of press conferences either. But he enjoyed sparring and he had a flair for the dramatic. Combined together, these two personality characteristics helped Johnson to overcome his "dread of televised news conferences" and he usually ended each conference with a distinct improvement in his "public image."[5] "The relationship between the press and any President usually turns more on the personality of the chief executive than the collective personality of the reporters, which changes little from Administration to Administration."[6]

Richard Nixon did not like press conferences, nor did his relatively cold personality orientation adapt to the form or rise to the drama. And because of his limited rhetorical talents in the press conference situation, he did not excel at it. It is easy to understand why Richard Nixon held fewer press conferences during his six years in office than any other president in a comparable period of time. His distrust of the media, stemming from his earliest days in politics — the Voorhis election and the

Hiss case — led him to ignore the critical White House press corps. His double isolation from the press — the press corps from himself and himself from direct observation of the news or press interviews — will be discussed later in relation to his methods of obverting the press conference. But the dual purposes of the presidential press conference obviously were ill-suited to Richard Nixon: (1) to keep the president accountable for his actions to the American people; and, (2) to keep the president informed through the questions asked of him since they reflect often what is critical in the news.[7] It was no wonder that Nixon feared press conferences and avoided them when he could.

If general dislike is one similar reaction presidents have to press conferences, their attempt to exert control over press conferences is another. Control of press conferences is not a difficult maneuver for a president. He schedules them, he limits the time allotted to them (generally 30 minutes or less), he chooses the reporters who will question him (by recognizing some and not others), and he can filibuster to run out the clock if he thinks he is in trouble.

> The President dominates the scene completely. The lead questions are easily predictable. The "follow up" questions — the kind that narrow down generalizations or pinpoint evasions — are nearly impossible in a situation where 200 to 400 correspondents are clamoring for recognition and where time is limited. Any President who has done his homework will emerge unscathed, with a generality for the "tough" questions and a rebuff for the "impertinent" questions.[8]

Some presidents have even controlled what questions will be asked, by what reporters, and in what order; there are indications that both Johnson and Nixon attempted such control on one or two occasions, but rarely were such controls necessary.[9]

In instances where a president wanted to avoid a direct question, he would make statements at the beginning of the press conference with a stipulation that he would answer no questions about the opening statement.

> Thus, the day of the elections last [November, 1970, Nixon] met newsmen in front of his secluded White House-By-The-Sea in San Clemente and said, in effect, the elections were a great success for my party. No questions. Or in Dromoland Castle near Limerick, Ireland . . . Nixon stood before a microphone and said, my show-the-flag tour of the Mediterranean was a great success. No questions. In Denver . . . Charles Manson is guilty. No questions.[10]

The similarities between Richard Nixon's presidential press conferences and his predecessors' are far outweighed by the differences which distinguish them. For one, Nixon avoided the press and the press conference and instead invented multiple means to obvert them: (1) top-level briefings for news executives — led by Nixon himself, the briefings included senior members of the administration, including Henry Kissinger; (2) briefings on legislative proposals for reporters around the country by administration teams; (3) special mailings to editorial writers, radio and television station news directors, and writers who focus on particular issues; (4) direct appeals to the public through presidential television addresses or televised "news conversations" that Nixon could control; (5) a removal of the White House press corps to the West wing of the White House, away from the Oval Office so that White House pressmen could not observe who was seeing the president; (6) briefings of press representatives at the summer White House in San Clemente and in New Orleans and Chicago for regional news executives;[11] (7) unleashing Vice-President Spiro T. Agnew when Nixon wanted to pummel the press into silence; and (8) the development of a two-man press office. This two-man press office was composed of Herb Klein, who functioned in four work categories: providing public relations advice for high-level officials; enhancing the reputation of the Nixon administration; serving as "spokesman to the hinterlands press"; and helping capital newsmen obtain information;[12] and Ronald Zeigler, who functioned as representative of the president. A charming, inexperienced press secretary, Zeigler had the ability "to anesthetize the nastiest newsman."[13]

The two-man press office, designed as a tactic to avoid press conferences and the press corps itself, had several other implications for the rhetorical critic interested in identifying the differences in Nixon's handling of press contacts.

For one thing, in many respects Ron Zeigler was a carbon copy of his master when it came to tactics, strategies, and style. Compare a Zeigler daily press briefing with a Nixon press conference and the similarities are highlighted. "Nobody wants to know what Ron Zeigler thinks about anything," he told *Time* magazine, "the worst thing a press secretary can ever do is shoot from the hip. . . ."[14] Notice the similarity to Nixon's directive that words were weapons to be chosen carefully: "I know from experience that when a President speaks . . . it is for keeps. He doesn't get a second chance. He can't call a bullet back after he shoots from the hip."[15] Even their "apologies" for error, while rare in either Zeigler's or

Nixon's rhetoric, were similar. Zeigler's apology to Woodward and Bernstein, replete with modifiers: "I think we would all have to say, and I would be, I think, remiss if I did not say, that mistakes were made during this period in terms of comments that were made, perhaps."[16] And here is Nixon's apology to the press in response to a question concerning his Manson, My Lai, and Angela Davis pre-trial faux pas: "I think sometimes we lawyers, even like doctors who try to prescribe for themselves, may make mistakes. And I think that kind of comment probably is unjustified."[17]

Perhaps it is true that "every President, in reality, is his own press secretary."[18] It certainly accounts, in part, for the difficulty of the job all presidential press secretaries face:

> The problem for all of them, the one that is apparently built into the position, is the need to balance what they conceive their job to be against what the President often perceives as their proper role. For most of the Presidential press secretaries have seen themselves as dispensers of information, conduits between "the man" in the White House and the press. Presidents, however, often see their press secretary somewhat differently, viewing him as a public relations man, hawking the President's line.[19]

But Ron Zeigler had an even more difficult job. Press secretary to a president who disliked and mistrusted the press, Zeigler had to accept strategies given him to cope with an increasingly hostile press community. A 16-member professional relations committee of the National Press Club, an institution known for its conservatism, issued a report in June 1973 charging the Nixon administration with

> an unprecedented Government-wide effort to control, restrict, and conceal information to which the public is entitled. Ronald Zeigler as White House press secretary, particularly during the Watergate disclosures of the past year, has misled the public and affronted the professional standards of the Washington press corps.[20]

But the telling point regarding Zeigler's acceptance of Nixon strategies appeared toward the end of the report: "The White House press secretary has been reduced to a totally programmed spokesman without independent authority or comprehensive background knowledge of administration policies. Rather than opening a window into the White House, the press secretary closes doors."[21] As *Newsweek* put it:

> Zeigler's role as front man has been custom-tailored for a remote President who prefers dealing with the press as formally — and as little — as possible.

Critics charge Zeigler with failing, as one newsman defines it, "to let the President know how bad things were" on issues like Watergate. Yet the press secretary reflects a White House-wide conviction that media criticisms are capricious, self-serving and generally best ignored.[22]

That Nixon appointed an inexperienced, 29-year-old as press secretary was looked upon by some of the press corpsmen as a debasement of the office itself. Initially, Zeigler's title was to be "press assistant," a further denigration of the office — and the press. "The ultimate goal may be achieved," Bill Gill noted, "a single, unified voice of government, speaking in near choral harmony to spread the administration's party line — and — no questions, please!"[23]

One strategy of all public relations experts, including presidents and their press secretaries, evasion, was raised to such a level of art form by Zeigler that the press corps christened what he did "Zeigling." For instance, when Zeigler was asked, in February 1971, whether a Laotian incursion was planned, he replied, "The President is aware of what is going on in Southeast Asia. That is not to say anything is going on in Southeast Asia."[24] His withdrawal of a previous explanation by labeling it "inoperative" is now classic doublespeak. Zeigler's "Zeigling" may have peaked in the following White House briefing session:

Q. Who told the President and who did he ask?
A. This is something, Bob, I just can't get into because of the situation that we face, but there was no question about the fact that the President and others of us who were here during this period of time were under the understanding that, first of all, the President did ask for an investigation and was informed by individuals that his investigation was taking place and that the information he was provided was the fact of the matter. Now, as to how this information was provided to the President, it came in various ways and as I said, I am not prepared to get into a detailed discussion of that at this time.[25]

Notice the two references to "time" in the above quotation. A sophisticated doublespeak speaker will always leave himself an out and "time" is a good legal excuse. Another doublespeak example: "Q. What is the purpose, Ron, of the cabinet meeting? A. The purpose is to meet with members of the cabinet."[26] And again: "Q. Are we in direct contact, or any kind of contact, with the insurgent groups in Cambodia? A. I am going to answer your question by saying not to my knowledge, and I would add to that by saying that we are not."[27]

Common sense tells a critic that there should be a basic distinction between a presidential press conference and a press secretary briefing for the press corps. The first, as indicated earlier, has two purposes — to keep the American people informed and up to date on presidential action, and to keep the president informed by the questions pressmen ask. The purposes of the press secretary briefings, on the other hand, should be to dispel rumors, to correct errors in yesterday's press clippings, and to inform the press of upcoming issues of imminent concern, to name a few. The rhetorical critic, therefore, would expect the daily press briefing to be, in form, strategy, and style, nothing like the presidential press conference. Perhaps it is here that the Nixon administration differed most dramatically from its predecessors. The same form and strategies Nixon utilized in his own press conference rhetoric appeared in Zeigler's daily briefings.

Robert Walters identified eight distinct techniques that Zeigler used to frustrate newsmen.[28] (1) The Broad — and Meaningless — Statement:

> At the close of the March 21, 1973 briefing, one reporter innocently asked: "What is the President working on today?" Replied Gerald Warren [Deputy press secretary, who was handling the meeting that day], "He has the schedule that you know of, and he will be in discussion with staff members, on other matters. I don't have anything to isolate for you at this briefing."[29]

That was the day, March 21, which Nixon was later to claim was the first time he had ever been told that Watergate reached into the heart of his staff system. (2) The I'll-Try-to-Find-Out ploy. Taken directly from an earlier Nixon "I didn't do it, but I'll find out who did," the I'll-try-to-find-out ploy let Zeigler appear to be cooperating while avoiding the responsibility for answering the difficult or embarrassing question. (3) The I-Stand-on-my-Previous-Answer answer:

> It isn't unusual for a press spokesman to refer reporters to an earlier statement, but for more than a year after the Watergate break-in, the White House was referring reporters to previous answers which (a) could not be easily located, (b) were not responsive to the question, (c) had been totally discredited by subsequent developments, or (d) were pious but non-specific statements issued periodically by the President in his feeble effort to stay ahead of the scandal.[30]

Here is Zeigler's use of the technique:

> Q. Ron, is the President convinced that no persons employed in the White House last July and August were engaged in political espionage?
> A. We have responded to questions such as that previously, and I stand on those answers.

Q. When did you respond to them, Ron? Would you mind repeating the answers?

A. Over the last three months.

Q. Would you mind repeating the answer?

A. I will answer your questions by saying I stand on what I have said.

Q. When, Ron?

A. Over the course of the last three months.[31]

(4) The I-Would-Not-Join-You-in-the-Gutter response. Similar to the Nixon "I would not dignify that with a response" syndrome, Zeigler adopted it for the press briefings. Here is an example from the April 2, 1973 briefing:

Q. Ron, yesterday Senator Weicker of the Republican Party accused one of the President's top aides, Robert Haldeman, Bob Haldeman, of having knowledge of political espionage and sabotage. Does the White House have any comment on that?

A. We do not intend to discuss these issues on television shows, at press conferences, or by overstatement on our part. It is our feeling that there is a fair way to proceed and an orderly and judicial way to proceed with the examination of this matter.[32]

It will immediately be noted, of course, that the I-Would-Not-Join-You-in-the-Gutter response inherently involves gutter-sniping, for it implies that the "other fellow" is in the gutter without in any way substantiating the implied assertion.

(5) The Wild-Goose Chase. Harry Truman had a famous sign on his desk which stated, "The buck stops here." This was not the philosophy of the Nixon administration. If anything, their sign read, "the bucks stop here." Passing the buck from the Nixon White House staff to the Committee to Re-elect the President (CREEP) was an example of a masterful use of the Wild-Goose Chase tactic. Any of us who have ever been bucked from one department of a bureaucracy to another in search for an answer to our questions understands the process. By withholding information, by misdirecting your critics, a politician can send potential opponents on a chase after information and thereby deny him the means to oppose.

(6) No Comment. Perhaps the most "forthcoming" of the tactics, it is equally the most frustrating. Witness the following exchange between a member of the press and Deputy Press Secretary Gerald Warren:

Q. Jerry, is it still the White House position that no members of the staff were involved in any way in the Watergate incident?

A. I have nothing to add to what has been said before and I have no comment on that this morning.
Q. Does what has been said before still stand?
A. I just have no comment this morning.[33]

While Nixon was not found using this specific language in his press conferences, his "No Questions" was the presidential equivalent.

(7) The Carefully-Constructed Deception. The Nixon administration utilized this useful tactic during the buildup of troops in Vietnam, when in response to the question, "How many American troops are in Vietnam?" the administration gave that figure only, omitting thousands of Navy personnel in ships offshore, support personnel at bases in adjacent countries, and even those troops then en route to the scene but not yet actually *in* Vietnam. Here is the Carefully-Constructed Deception tactic at work in the Watergate scandal:

Q. Has the President asked for any resignations so far, and have any been submitted or on his desk?
A. I have repeatedly stated, Helen, that there is no change in the status of the White House staff.
Q. But that was not my question. Has he asked for any resignations?
A. I understand your question and I heard it the first time. Let me go through my answer. As I said, there is no change in the status of the White House staff. There have been no resignations submitted.[34]

Zeigler insisted on answering a question that had not been asked, that is, "Has there been any change in the status of the White House staff?" When pressed finally he answered one question that had been asked — "Have any resignations been submitted?" — but never answered the central question, "Has the President asked for any resignations?"

And, finally, there is (8) The Lie. While we now know that Richard M. Nixon lied continuously and consciously to the American people for over two and a half years during the Watergate period, it is less common knowledge that his press secretary lied to the press on a regular basis. When caught in such lies, Zeigler calmly replied, "That statement is inoperative." Such language gives the critic a sure clue to the mentality of the person who uses it, for such a person obviously perceives language not as a vehicle for telling truth or lies, but as a tactical weapon which either works or doesn't. The press was not entirely misled; Clark Mollenhoff challenged the "inoperative" statement immediately, when he exploded: "Do you feel free to stand up there and lie and put out misinformation and then come around later and just say it is all inoperative: That is what you are doing. You are not entitled to any credibility at all when you do that."[35]

What are we to conclude about the press conference and the press secretary briefing during the Nixon years? Like everything else in the Nixon administration, they were warped to fit the needs of corrupt men. But they were warped right under the noses of the most astute political observers in the country, the White House press corps. That should lead the rhetorical critic to advocate a serious shift in format and tactics in both the presidential press conference and the press secretary briefings.

NOTES

1. George Reedy, *The Twilight of the Presidency* (New York: World Publishing, 1970), pp. 164–166.

2. George Reedy, "Some Questions for the President," *The New York Times*, January 6, 1971, p. 37.

3. Arthur M. Schlesinger, Jr., *A Thousand Days* (Boston: Houghton Mifflin, 1965), p. 717.

4. St. Louis *Post–Dispatch*, November 22, 1970, p. 1.

5. Reedy, *Twilight*, p. 164.

6. Robert Semple, "Nixon Tries Some New Approaches to the Press," *The New York Times*, September 4, 1970, p. 4.

7. Stuart H. Loory, "The Adversaries," *The New York Times*, May 10, 1973, p. 41.

8. Reedy, *Twilight*, p. 162.

9. Ibid. See also Richard Halloran, "Nixon's Strategy for Reaching Public Largely Bypasses Washington Press Corps," *The New York Times*, August 24, 1970, p. 18.

10. Stuart H. Loory, "Nixon's News Conference: Pablum for Permissivists," *The Village Voice*, December 24, 1970, p. 3.

11. Halloran, "Nixon's Strategy," p. 18.

12. Bob Wilson, "Klein and Zeigler: Nixon's PR Men," *Freedom of Information Center, Report #244*, School of Journalism, University of Missouri at Columbia (June 1970):3.

13. Semple, "Nixon Tries New Approaches," p. 3.

14. *Time*, October 10, 1969, p. 14.

15. Richard Nixon, *Six Crises* (New York: Pyramid Books, 1968), p. 389.

16. *Newsweek*, May 14, 1973, p. 75.

17. Richard Nixon, "Press Conference on Foreign and Domestic Matters," *The New York Times*, August 18, 1973, p. 17.

18. Reedy, *Twilight*, p. 87.

19. Martin Arnold, "A President's Troubled Spokesman," *The New York Times*, August 6, 1973, p. 33.

20. Cited in John Herbers, "New Zeigler Job; More Authority or Less?" *The New York Times*, June 14, 1973, p. 14.

21. Ibid.

22. *Newsweek*, p. 75.

23. Bill Gill, "Richard Nixon as News Editor," *The Quill*, March 1973, p. 9.

24. *Newsweek*, p. 75.

25. Cited in Alexander Cockburn, "It Might Be Said that in Some Respects This Article is About White House Misspeak," *The Village Voice*, June 14, 1973, p. 5.

26. Ibid.

27. Ibid.

28. Robert Walters, "What Did Zeigler Say, and When Did He Say It?" *Columbia Journalism Review* (September/October 1974):30–36.

29. Ibid., p. 30.

30. Ibid., p. 32.

31. Ibid.

32. Ibid., p. 33.

33. Ibid., pp. 33–34.

34. Ibid., p. 34.

35. Ibid., p. 35.

IDEOLOGY VERSUS TECHNOLOGY: JOHN F. KENNEDY AND THE NATIONAL DIALOGUE

When John F. Kennedy took office in 1961 the country was mired in a recession. Unemployment was high and growing; the economic growth rate was low and stagnant. Seventeen months later, when he traveled to New Haven, Connecticut, to give the commencement address at Yale University, the economy had improved, but it was still sluggish. Neither the rate nor the extent of the improvement was satisfactory to President Kennedy. So, despite the actual and projected budget deficits, he had proposed a tax cut to pump more dollars into the economy, a cut that was being resisted by those who believed fiscal soundness required a balanced budget and by those who feared the deficits combined with an increase in the money supply would initiate a new round of inflation.

His immediate purpose in his address at Yale, then, was to calm the business community about the economic steps of his administration and to school the nation in what was to be called the "New Economics." The speech, however, was designed not merely as a rebuttal of his critics. Rather, an attempt was made to lead the public to shrug off the old questions about governmental size, fiscal integrity, and economic confidence and adopt a new, more pragmatic, approach wherein the national debate concerning any proposal about an arena of governmental concern would be "approached on its own merits and in terms of specific national needs."[1] In short, President Kennedy argued that the old ideological debate should be replaced with a technocratic one.

To bolster his contention that this change in the national dialogue was needed, he labeled the old debate style "mythic" and "political" and argued that old myths could not cope with new realities. It was, on the surface, a brilliant stratagem for defusing the debate and recasting future argumentation into forms more advantageous to the Kennedy administration. But it did not work — the speech ". . . received a cold response from business, and the tax cut the President sponsored did not receive Congressional approval until after his death. . . ."[2]

The question we face is the straightforward pragmatic one: Why? That is, beyond the anti-change forces found in any society, beyond the specific forces in this society arraigned against this specific change, was there anything in the speech itself that militated against its acceptance? Did Kennedy undermine his own case?

We argue that the speech, though brilliant in concept, in execution fell short of the mark in three ways. First, even though Kennedy, as president, wanted to lead the people to a new debate, a new kind of debate, he was betrayed by his own basic political nature: he could not help but make a political argument even as he was calling for an end to political argumentation. Second, his expressed concern for the health of the national dialogue, however sincere in his mind, seemed like just another way of making his political argument. Third, his whole position was based upon a myth about the end of ideology which neither audience nor opposition accepted.

THE POLITICAL ARGUMENT

Rather than attempt an examination of all the political argumentation in the speech, it will suffice to demonstrate that in the three areas he identified as unduly burdened with political (ideological, mythological) argumentation, he himself engaged in political argument.

The first "myth" he identified was that ". . . government is big, and bad — and steadily getting bigger and worse." Here Kennedy admitted that government was getting bigger, but argued that it was not "growing relatively bigger." In fact, he said, "If we leave defense and space expenditures aside, the Federal Government has expanded less than any other major sector of our national life. . . ."

Note here that Kennedy did not address the "myth" he identified. That is, the ideological "myth" in question is premised on the old assumption that "the government that governs least, governs best." Kennedy ignored that premise. Further, he engaged in political argumentation by ignoring even the thrust of the question in changing the charge from "government is getting bigger" to "government is getting *relatively* bigger." Then, he moved even further from the original question by omitting space and defense expenditures from his calculations. In short, having defined as "mythic" the idea that government was getting bigger, he was faced with the fact that the assertion was true. So he dodged the question by asking a new one: Is the government getting bigger at a faster or slower rate than the rest of the economy? Then he found he could not handle the question even in that form unless he omitted space and defense from his calculations. It was a clever ploy, and it may have convinced many in his audience that the government was not growing at an unreasonable rate, but it certainly did not prove that the original assertion about the government getting bigger was a myth.

It probably is the case that the real "mythic" element in the original proposition concerned the formulaic assumption that bigger equaled worse. So Kennedy attacked that idea with the assertion that while size *can* bring dangers, it also can bring benefits. As a specific example, he pointed out that ". . . in 1961, in support of all university research in science and medicine, three dollars out of every four came from the Federal Government," yet American scientists had not been hampered by undue governmental control.

This was an adroit example to utilize before a university audience, but it obfuscated as much as it clarified. For instance, before government became the primary patron of research, where had the research monies come from? Had those monies been adequate? Did governmental support merely supplement the old supplies or supplant them? That is, were there more monies or merely new sources? Were we better off? As to the question of control, there were additional queries. Given that decisions about what research to fund always provides the donor with a substantial degree of control, was this an arena in which the government should have been involved? Was it reasonable to assume that such control could not be bent to the ideological predilections of the party in power?

Even if Kennedy's points could have been proven — namely, that the research dollars were needed and that government patronage had brought with it absolutely no controls — all of that still begged the question of whether research in science and medicine was an area in which our constitutionally limited government ought to have been engaged. Those who ideologically opposed such government ventures would have found Kennedy's arguments about benefits beside the point, another example of his political argumentation.

The argument that big government is bad government is a philosophical position that carries with it a series of assumptions about legitimate and illegitimate spheres of governmental activity. Proving that government interference in an illegitimate sphere is beneficial does not prove that such activity is legitimate. If anything, it proves that the speaker is applying the wrong criteria. Workability, practicality, and desirability, persuasive though they may be, do not "get at" the question of legitimacy any more than the health or happiness of a baby prove that it is legitimate. In both cases, the key question is parentage, and in the case we are concerned with the only recognized parent is the Constitution. Kennedy's opponents thought that if the Constitution says that support of research is a legitimate government activity, it is legitimate; and, if the Constitution forbids or is mute on the question, it is illegitimate. Kennedy did not address this question, opting instead implicitly to support a position that constitutional muteness is no bar to government activity and to make a political argument about the desirability of the activity in question. Obviously, such an approach had no chance of persuading his opponents.

The second arena in which President Kennedy made a political argument was in fiscal policy. He labeled as "myth" the position that ". . . deficits automatically bring inflation," and contended that "a more sophisticated view" would recognize that was not always the case. What made his argument political was that he overstated his opposition's position as an absolute rather than as a tendency. Undoubtedly there were some people who assumed a one-to-one correlation between deficits and inflation, but the economists who take part in national debates about fiscal policy normally are more sophisticated than that. What they argue is that, absent any correcting mechanism elsewhere in the economic policy, deficits *tend* to create inflationary pressures. Thus, their own tendency is to attack any proposed deficit as inflationary. By overstating their position, Kennedy really was setting up a straw man. He did a good job of defeating that straw man by demonstrating that deficits have not *always* brought inflation. But the straw man, the myth he attacked, was not what his opponents believed — thus destroying it did not eliminate their opposition.

Likewise, Kennedy oversimplified his opponents' position on the national debt. He stated it correctly enough: that the debt ". . . is growing at a dangerously rapid rate." The key word in the assertion is "dangerously," but Kennedy chose to ignore that word. A debt is "dangerous," of course, in proportion to income. Kennedy started to answer the question that way when he said, ". . . both the debt per person and the debt as a proportion of our gross national product have declined sharply since the Second World War," but he failed to indicate how "dangerously" in debt we might have been at the close of World War II, or if the decline were sufficient to take us out of the "dangerous" category.

Rather, at that point in the argument Kennedy chose to drop the question of the relationship of the debt to income and to substitute the question of the rate of the debt increase in comparison to the increase in private debt and state and local debt. Those comparative percentage increases — 8 percent for the national government, 305 percent for private debt, 378 percent for state and local debt — were impressive, but the percentages were meaningless in terms of the question of danger.

A simple example will demonstrate the meaninglessness of those impressive percentages. If today you are in debt by $1.00 and you borrow $350.00, you will have increased your debt by 350 percent, yet you still may not be in financial trouble. If, on the other hand, you are $100,000 in debt and borrow an additional 8 percent, putting you $108,000 in debt, that might be the proverbial straw that finally destroys the camel. The question about the danger of increasing debts is not the increase in percentage points over previous debts, or the comparison of your increase to somebody else's increases, but your total debt relative to your total income. In shifting away from that central question, President Kennedy strove to make the whole question of the danger of debts a mythic one and to confuse the debate by introducing irrelevant statistical comparisons. His opponents were not fooled. Neither were they converted nor mollified. President Kennedy did not end the old political debate; he continued it.

In the final arena which he attacked, economic confidence, President Kennedy again undermined his call for a new nonpartisan debate by making a political argument. The "myth" he was attacking here was that any economic downturn was the result of ". . . a lack of confidence in the national administration." He did a good job of demonstrating the "mythic" elements of that belief by pointing to historic examples where recession came despite full business confidence in the administration in power — 1929, 1954, 1958, 1960.

He also made a logical argument when he pointed out that business, labor, and government are all major factors in the economy and a lack of confidence in any one of the three could have deleterious effects on the economy. However, he undermined his own logic of the tri-partite "cause" by asserting the necessity of centralized management, or what he called "... the sensible and clearheaded management of the domestic affairs of the United States." Further, he then asked two questions which demonstrated the centrality of governmental decisions to the economy:

> First, how can our budget and tax policies supply adequate revenues and preserve our balance of payments position without slowing up our economic growth? Two, how are we to set our interest rates and regulate the flow of money in ways which will stimulate the economy at home, without weakening the dollar abroad?

In short, after logically contending that economic confidence depended upon the actions of three parties, he asserted the intention of one of those three parties, the government, to manage the economy through budget policy, tax policy, and interest rates. The help of the other two was not requested. In fact, the only request was the implied one that they each shoulder some of the blame for any resultant lack of confidence. Is it any wonder they did not applaud his position?

Likewise, is it any wonder that his call for an end to political debate was not heeded? If, for the moment, we were to consider political argumentation ritualistic, we would conclude that President Kennedy had engaged in the ritual of political argumentation even as he called for it to end; his opponents, recognizing the requirement of obligatory responses in all dialogic rituals, responded to his contentions. And the argument went on, the ritualistic dialogue continued. Kennedy could not stop it because he could not step out of it himself.

THE NATIONAL DIALOGUE

While President Kennedy expressed concern for the health of the national dialogue, and perhaps sincerely felt that the dialogue was off-base and debilitating, his discussion of it in this speech seemed like special pleading, another way in which he was making a political argument.

If Kennedy had not made a political argument he might have been persuasive with his myth-realities dichotomy. For instance, it clearly is the case that our economy is so complicated that the relation between deficits and inflation is unclear. But it also is the case that the relation between deficits and employment is unclear. Yet Kennedy had proposed a tax cut, which would have increased the deficit, in order to stimulate employment. In arguing in a partisan way for that proposal he lost the possibility of an across-the-board analysis of economic myth. Thus it was special pleading when he identified his opposition's position as myth and his own as reality.

In fact, that same problem ran throughout the speech. All the ideas he identified as "mythic" were ideas of his opponents; all "realities" were supportive of his programs. Objectively, it is unlikely that the only people utilizing myth would be on the other side. And even if that were true, it would be unpersuasive to say so in a speech purporting to lay the groundwork for a more responsible debate with those same opponents. Surely someone truly interested in shifting the tone and techniques of a debate could find at least one token example of his own mistaken mythic thinking.

Without such self-effacing, the whole myth-realities structure came off as just another portion of the political argumentation, another way to say "I'm right and they're wrong." The absence of any ameliorative identification of mythic thinking on Kennedy's side made the whole myth-realities structure of the speech merely a clever method of political definition, perhaps even name-calling. As such, rather than raise the level of national debate to a stress on realities, it lowered it to gutter-sniping, calling into question the president's own motivation as well as his commitment to healthy dialogue. What was presented as a way of improving the debate had become a mechanism to obliterate the opposition.

If we accept for a moment the idea that the opposition's positions really were based on myths (using "myth" now as psychologists and sociologists use it, rather than just a synonym for "error" as Kennedy employed it), we find that myths are used by the individual to define and advertise self.[3] To denigrate or deny those mythic roots, then, is to destroy the person — an almost literal "tearing out of roots" which symbolically kills the believer. We argue that Kennedy, under the guise of calling for a new level of debate, attempted to obliterate his debating opposition by defining them in such a way that would have foreclosed their participation in a rational debate.

Additional support for this position can be found in Kennedy's characterizations of his opponents and their debating positions. He labeled his opponents' positions as "truisms," "stereotypes," "stale phrases," "prefabricated ... interpretations," "illusion," "platitude," "noise," "irrelevant," "misleading," "traditional labels," "worn out slogans," "political," and "sterile acrimony." His own rhetoric and positions, by contrast, he labeled "new," "essential confrontations with reality," "truth," "careful," "dispassionate," "ways to separate false problems from real ones," "honest assessment," "sophisticated," "sensible," "clear-headed," "technical," and "sober."

Again, we find a clear dichotomy — all evil was on the other side, all good was on Kennedy's side. The national dialogue was polluted because of *"their* stale rhetoric and illusory ideas." And again we conclude that no one seriously interested in reforming the national debate would locate all error in the opposition. Thus, Kennedy's structuring of this speech around the call for an end to "political" debate was just a ruse, a method of continuing the political debate while enhancing his own presidential image of being above such bickering.

THE END OF IDEOLOGY

Finally, we want to suggest that Kennedy's Yale speech was a failure because his whole position was based upon a myth about the end of ideology which neither audience nor opposition accepted.

It is well to keep in mind that although Professor Daniel Bell had published a persuasive book in 1960 on "the end of ideology" in which he had argued that since the close of World War II political ideas had lost their power to influence American society, that thesis had not greatly affected political thinking in 1962.[4] Conservatives were gearing up for a 1964 run at the presidency under the Goldwater banner and liberals were, if somewhat reluctantly, beginning to line up behind President Kennedy. If political ideology had died, its practitioners had not gotten the word.

President Kennedy, surrounded by academics from Harvard and Yale, apparently had heard of the Bell thesis. Or perhaps the projected technocratic replacement for ideology, "a 'technocratic consciousness' with which the corporate order and its symbols of authority might be newly legitimated,"[5] fit the Kennedy penchant for realism, efficiency, and toughness[6] better than did the old ideological model. At any rate, the key word in the ideology of technology, "efficiency," also was the key word in Kennedy's decision-making.[7] The problem-solving approach recommended by Kennedy in this speech obviously was not the technocratic model. When Kennedy said, "The central domestic issues of our time . . . relate not to basic clashes of philosphy or ideology but to ways and means of reaching common goals," he was endorsing a technologically guided society.

His most obvious embrace of the technocratic approach came late in the speech when he argued, "What is at stake in our economic decisions today is not some grand warfare of rival ideologies which will sweep the country with passion but the practical management of a modern economy. What we need is not labels and cliches but more basic discussion of the sophisticated and technical questions involved in keeping a great economic machinery moving ahead." That is why Kennedy concluded that the problems of the 1960s demanded "technical answers, not political answers." It will be noted that throughout the speech the words "technical" and "sophisticated" tended to be used together, indeed, seemed to be interchangeable.

But if Kennedy saw the technological approach as sophisticated, what he did not see were the drawbacks of it. As Alvin Gouldner has concluded, "A technocratic model . . . which sees technicians dominating officials and management, and which sees the modern technologically developed bureaucracy as governed by an exclusive reliance on a standard of efficiency is a fantasy, a utopia, an ideal type."[8] As for Kennedy, it was a trap. For obeisance to efficiency can foreclose the logically prior questions, "efficiency at doing what?" "and at what cost in other spheres?" These questions cannot be answered technologically; they can be addressed only by ideological groundings outside the technical system.

Yet Kennedy's reliance upon the technological approach often led him to ignore those logically prior questions. For instance, after the Bay of Pigs invasion, Kennedy ordered General Maxwell Taylor to ". . . take a close look at all our practices and programs in the areas of military and para-military, guerrilla and anti-guerrilla activities . . ." and ". . . give special attention to the lessons which can be learned from recent events in Cuba."[9] As Garry Wills comments, "An investigation of the meaning of the Cuban invasion might have called into question the very notion of paramilitary assaults on other governments. Kennedy's instructions precluded that. The question was not whether Americans should acquire a guerrilla-warfare capability but how America might do so efficiently."[10]

In like manner, in this speech Kennedy called for an end to political (that is, ideological) debate because to him any question about what the government *should* be doing was mythic; to him, the only significant question was how we could most efficiently accomplish what we were then trying to do. That was the technical question, the sophisticated question. Rather than a debate between politicians concerned with shoulds and whys, he wanted a discussion between technocrats concerned with hows and wheres and whens.

But he could not get that change; indeed, such a change could have come only after agreements at the "ought" and "why" levels. His opposition, and the American people, had not reached consensus on those questions, thus Kennedy's attempt to move "beyond" such questions to the "sophisticated, technological" questions was doomed. You cannot switch to a discussion of how to accomplish a goal until you have established whether that is the goal that ought to be pursued.

CONCLUSION

In summary, Kennedy's call for a change in the nature of the national dialogue went unheeded because he presented a political argument even as he called for the end of such argumentation, because his myth-versus-realities structuring of the speech was merely more political argumentation, and because he tried to move from an ideological to a technical debate before the needed ideological consensus had been reached.

It is tempting to conclude that after this speech President Kennedy had not only a Harvard education and a Yale degree but a good grounding in the College of Hard Knocks, but that is not clear. That is, it is not clear that he did not go to his grave believing that the great ideological questions had been solved, leaving only technological and managerial decisions to be engineered — and the myths of the rest of us to be eradicated.

NOTES

1. John F. Kennedy, "Commencement Address at Yale University, June 11, 1962," in *Spoken Arts Treasury of John F. Kennedy Addresses,* ed. Arthur L. Klein (New Rochelle, NY: Spoken Arts, 1972), pp. 63–70. All subsequent quotations from this same source.

2. William E. Leuchtenburg, "Introductory Remarks," in *Spoken Arts Treasury,* ed. Arthur L. Klein (New Rochelle, NY: Spoken Arts, 1972), p. 63.

3. Jerome S. Bruner, "Myth and Identity," in *Myth and Mythmaking,* ed. Henry A. Murray (Boston: Beacon Press, 1968), pp. 276–287.

4. Daniel Bell, *The End of Ideology* (Glencoe, IL: The Free Press, 1960).

5. Alvin W. Gouldner, *The Dialectic of Ideology and Technology: The Origins, Grammar, and Future of Ideology* (New York: The Seabury Press, 1976), p. 250.

6. Garry Wills, "The Kennedy Imprisonment," *The Atlantic Monthly,* February 1982, pp. 52–66.

7. Ibid.

8. Gouldner, *Dialectic of Ideology,* p. 257.

9. Wills, "Kennedy Imprisonment," p. 54.

10. Ibid., p. 55.

Chapter **6**

MASS COMMUNICATION DIMENSIONS OF THE AMERICAN PRESIDENCY

Societies have always been shaped more by the nature of the media by which men communicate than by the content of the communication.

Marshall McLuhan

Television, either directly or indirectly, regulates our work, sleep, play, sex, and even, as Donna Cross observes, our bathroom habits.[1] Water pressure dips dramatically during commercials and between television programs. In fact, the water department of Lafayette, Louisiana, reported that during the first showing of the television program "Airport," from the time the bomb exploded to the end hardly anyone left their television sets. But after the show, over 20,000 people flushed 80,000 gallons of water nearly at the same time, causing a 25-pound drop in water pressure.[2]

It should not be surprising, therefore, that the mass media have become vital instruments and tools of politicians and elected officials to govern our nation. In this chapter we will investigate the role of media in politics and especially the importance of the media to the creation, sustenance, and maintenance of presidential influence in our society.

THE NATURE OF MASS COMMUNICATION

In many ways the mass media have become the central nervous system of our society. Traditionally, scholars have recognized four basic functions of the mass media: information dissemination, persuasion (both commercial and political), entertainment, and cultural transmission.[3] Mass communication has several distinctive characteristics.[4] In our country, the mass media are commercial. They are simply economic, capitalistic industries which are essential parts of our total economy. The audience of the mass media is large, anonymous, and most often heterogeneous. The messages are transient, rapidly transmitted, and provide no opportunity for immediate feedback. And the sources of the messages of mass communication are institutions, impersonal, and by nature financially able to hire highly trained specialists to write and produce the messages we consume.

These characteristics provide insight into how mass communication differs from other forms of communication. In addition to much larger audiences and reduced opportunities for feedback, there is greater competition for receiver attention because of channel noise (that is, situational and contextual) and message repetition. Speed and accuracy of message transmission are not only major differences between mass communication and other forms but also are advantages of mass communication.

Scholars and lay people alike recognize the social power of mass media.[5] The media can quickly and efficiently attract, focus, and direct attention to social problems. In addition, the media can serve as channels for public persuasion and mobilization. In mobilizing groups or "kinds of public," the media also help sustain them and their causes. In doing so, the media confer status and legitimacy to groups, issues, or ideas. Increasingly, the media are recognized for providing psychic rewards and gratifications. While these powers are rather positive and beneficial, there are some less attractive powers or influences. In the 1960s, Marshall McLuhan observed that "the public, in the sense of a great consensus of separate and distinct viewpoints, is finished. Today, the mass audience (the successor to the 'public') can be used as a creative participating force. It is, instead, merely given packages of passive entertainment."[6] The media have an impact upon feelings and emotions as well as influence the beliefs, attitudes, and values of individuals. As a result, the media can influence individual and group behavior.

Thus, mediated communication is a unique form of communication. It differs significantly from other forms of communication. In addition, mass communication has become an integral and essential form in our society. Its role and influence in the political process are equally important.

MASS MEDIA AND POLITICS

Robert Denton and Gary Woodward argue that the mass media influence American politics in three principle ways.[7] First, the mass media collectively exert a considerable influence in determining the agenda of topics for public discussion, debate, and action. Not only is there a limit to the number of issues, topics, etc. that should or can receive public attention, but the selection of specific concerns increasingly lies with the mass communication industries rather than with citizens or public officials. It is difficult for politicians to initiate, establish, or maintain social agendas without the help and participation of the mass media industries. Politicians most often find themselves in the role of responder rather than initiator of public issues.

Certainly related to the above notion, the media give form and substance to world events. They construct our political realities, telling us who is good or bad, right or wrong, strong or weak, just or unjust. Media "snapshots" of the world become the "album" of both our knowledge and memories of the outside world. In addition to telling us *what* to think about, the media also tell us *how* to think. With the reporting of the facts comes a subsequent judgment. There is always a conclusion, point, or reason for a presentation, but there is little or no time for synthesis or analysis. Awareness is valued more than understanding. It is also rather ironic, despite the perception of an adversarial relationship with government officials, that governmental officials benefit more from mass media presentations than outsiders or critics of elected officials. In a study by Leon Sigal, government officials provided 75 percent of all news stories and less than 1 percent of all news stories were based on reporters' own analyses.[8] In addition, 90 percent of the stories were based on messages of key actors in the stories. Seldom do politicians speak for themselves. Reporters act as narrators and interpreters assessing the motives or consequences of political actors or events. And political realities are constructed to conform to the demands of the medium, demands that seem best satisfied by melodrama. Melodramatic images of foolishness, villainy, and heroes are common. The themes used to outline many stories are constant: the triumph of the individual over adversity, justice winning over evil, redemption of the individual through reform, and the rewarding of valor or heroism.

Finally, the media reduce abstract or ideological principles to human, personal components. Political issues and actions are linked to individuals. We have choices not among policies but between actors. Victims, villains, and heroes are easier to identify and address than issues, causes, or ideas. Television is especially a "personalistic" medium. With television the presenter dominates. It is a medium for actors and animate objects. To some extent, the personalizing nature of the mass media has contributed to the decline and lack of interest in party organizations and smaller political jurisdictions.

In essence, the mass media have changed politics in two significant ways. First, the nature of political participation has changed. As McLuhan early observed, "a new form of 'politics' is emerging and in ways we haven't yet noticed. The living room has become a voting booth."[9] Second, the content of politics has changed. Few citizens learn about politics through direct experience. Our political knowledge, as already noted, is mediated. And the mediated process, according to Dan Nimmo and James Combs, results "as much in the creation, transmission, and adoption of political fantasies as realistic views of what takes place."[10] Again, McLuhan addressed this point years ago. He argued that television was too "cool" to handle properly hot issues and sharply defined controversial topics. "As a cool medium TV has, some feel, introduced a kind of *rigor mortis* into the body politic. It is the extraordinary degree of audience participation in the TV medium that explains its failure to tackle hot issues."[11] Thus, politics becomes an activity of style over substance, image over reality, melodrama over analysis, belief over knowing, awareness over understanding.

MASS MEDIA AND THE PRESIDENCY

It is through the mass media that we come to know our presidents. And with the frequency of appearance we have come to know our presidents intimately. Any piece of information about the president, no matter how trivial or private, is newsworthy, ranging from Carter's hemorrhoids to Reagan's more serious colon cancer surgery.

Roderick Hart and several colleagues have identified six perspectives from which various groups of citizens view the presidential relationship with the mass media.[12] The "no bias" perspective maintains that the media merely pass along what the president says with no interpretation or bias. Despite contentions to the contrary from those in the news business, few scholars or even the general public believe this perspective.

The "liberal bias" perspective, vigorously argued by Vice-President Spiro Agnew in 1972, is still prominent today. The argument contends that the media are controlled by liberals who are far from objective in their presentations. In fact, some argue that the media only address liberal concerns, issues, candidates, or policies. Thus, those who accept this perspective believe conservative positions not only receive little serious attention but in fact receive negative treatment in the media. Today there are several networks whose primary purpose is to counter the perceived liberal bias, such as CBN, USA, or the PTL networks, to name only a few.

Ironically, however, an effective argument can be made that there is a "conservative bias" in the primary relationship between the president and the press. The basis for the belief in a conservative bias of the media lies in media support of corporate capitalism and other status quo positions. By extension, then, the media support presidential efforts of fiscal conservatism and, through their support of the status quo, are essentially anti-liberal in their orientation.

The fourth orientation, "presidential bias," holds that the media are really captive to the presidential office. Presidents have almost immediate and unlimited access to the media and thus the national audience. And when considering the efforts of the White House staff to control media events and image, it is nearly impossible to truly counter the powerful stronghold the president has over the media.

The "organizational bias" perspective provides a more sociological explanation of presidential-press relations. The emphasis of this perspective is on the power of the mass media organizations, a power that supposedly is great enough to allow the media to dictate what is covered and how material is presented. Even the geographic location of news organizations in New York and Washington is said to greatly influence the treatment and selection of stories.

The final perspective, the "rhetorical bias," posits that all mediated messages are formulated based upon recognized rules. These accepted "rules" conform to media requirements of presentation and dictate the style, form, and even content of news presentations.

Regardless of the nature of the relationship between the press and the president, they each desperately need the other. In the 1960s televised coverage of the presidency and political campaigns became a primary occupation of the news media. Since that time "image," "audience share," "targeting," "packaging," "teleprompter," and a host of others have become a part of the political lexicon. Presidents and potential presidents, since Theodore Roosevelt turned the White House into the "bully pulpit," need to link their public persuasive efforts with the media. But today, the media equally need presidential "bits" of exposure and information to satisfy the public's curiosity and preoccupation with our chief executive. And the White House provides many services for the press. It provides background briefings, "off the record" comments, transcripts, daily handouts, and grants access and interviews.

The result of this symbiotic relationship is a constant battle of presidential access and control. To use a medium effectively implies control, planning, and proper execution. For presidents, each category is a challenge, struggle, and process of adaptation. Perhaps the greatest challenge is to control news coverage to ensure that it is favorable to the incumbent. The president's press secretary is the immediate link with the press. Although his function is to serve as a conduit of information, he must attempt to control the agenda as well as what is said and is not said. There are, of course, several ways a president can attempt to control or at least coordinate news coverage. News or information favorable to the president is released from the White House whereas less favorable news is left unstated or released from other departments. All interviews and statements are channeled through one source, thus insuring control and consistency over content. Timing and managing of releases are also important techniques of news control. News items are often released in time to receive coverage on the evening news but not early enough to allow much time for full development or rebuttal. In addition, the releasing of two major stories in the same day is avoided. In a more active sense, presidents are always attempting to set the nation's agenda and goal priorities, creating "pseudo-events," and taking every opportunity to "plug" administration accomplishments, thus infusing the news with self-serving commercials.

Presidential press conferences, an obvious way for presidents to address the public, have become more and more problematic for officeholders to manage. Consequently, each president tends to have fewer and fewer. Franklin Roosevelt held about seven a month. Ronald Reagan held only seven his first year as president.[13] Today, press conferences are much more public and formal. There is little true interaction and every president is aware that answers often receive replay several times, sometimes for several days. Modern presidents have tried a wide variety of tactics in order to reduce the risk associated with televised press conferences. Presidents Johnson and Nixon attempted to plant favorable questions among the reporters to insure opportunities for presenting their views. In addition, Nixon used a blue curtain as a backdrop and got rid of the lectern to give a more calm, candid, and informal look to the press conferences. In April 1984, Reagan changed the location of his televised press conferences. He now stands before an open doorway in the East Room of the White House that reveals a long, elegant corridor. The cameras record a majestic setting and a stately exit that dramatizes the importance of the office. Additionally, President Reagan requires the press members to raise their hands to be recognized, symbolically converting the reporters into schoolchildren.

To further insure their success in the age of media politics, presidents and candidates have to rely upon the help and advice of consultants. They have become the new power in American politics. By 1950, advertising agencies handled most presidential electoral campaigns. But by 1970, most campaigns were directed by independent, individual political media specialists who coordinated the activities of media, advertising, public relations, and publicity. They understand both the new technologies and the unique requirements of campaigning. There are several reasons why officeholders and candidates need the service of consultants. First, the modern campaign is a complex endeavor, requiring highly specialized tasks such as advertising, research, and fundraising. It is unrealistic to expect candidates to have the technical expertise or the time to manage these activities in addition to campaigning or governing. The electoral process itself also places unique requirements upon candidates and campaigns. Direct voter contact is simply not possible and media coverage is, as already noted, the only exposure the average citizen has to the candidates. And consequently, the special requirements of the mass media have increased the need for consultants. To use a medium requires knowledge of the medium — its strengths, weaknesses, and nature. The growth of political consultants is directly related to the growth of the mass media and communication technologies. And finally, consultants are needed today because of what Sidney Blumenthal calls "the permanent campaign."[14] Governing the nation has become a perpetual campaign where public support is constantly being sought.

Presidents have even had to adapt their language and speaking style to the requirements of the media, making sure they provide the ten-second answer designed to fit the demands of a news story. As Hart observes, "radio and television have changed how our presidents talk. The president in our living rooms bears only partial resemblance to the president speaking in the courthouse square."[15] Presidential discourse has become less personal, more simple, and less passionate. The personal stamp is gone and the human touch is media-created.

Media have changed the way presidents govern and must govern. They dictate the form and consequently the content of issues and policies. The mass media become the primary link to the public. Cross posits that many of our earlier presidents probably would not have succeeded in today's media world.[16] Consider Washington's wig and false teeth; Lincoln's unpleasant looks and high pitched voice; Grant's alcoholism; or

Franklin Roosevelt's wheelchair. Even in presidential newscasts, conflict and drama are the key elements of presentation and the commentators are the stars.[17] At best, according to Hart, the media gives us a one-dimensional presidency. "It presents our presidents to us in their Sunday best but without their souls or feelings."[18]

MASS MEDIA AND PRESIDENTIAL CAMPAIGNS

Much has been written about political campaigns. And few would argue with Thomas Patterson's assessment that "today's presidential campaign is essentially a mass media campaign."[19] We take issue with the basic assumption that political campaigns do not play a significant role in election results. Too much research has focused on voter conversion. Such research tends to ignore the long-term, subtle, and cumulative effects of politics and campaigns. Campaigns, in a broad sense, are complex exercises in the creation, re-creation, and transmission of significant symbols through communication. Communication activities are the vehicles for action. Samuel Becker characterizes our communication environment as a "mosaic."[20] The mosaic consists of an infinite number of information "bits" or fragments on an infinite number of topics scattered over time and space. In addition, the "bits" are disorganized, and exposure is varied and repetitive. As these "bits" are relevant or address a need, they are attended. Thus, as we attempt to make sense of our environment, our current state of existence, political bits are elements of our voting choice, world view, or legislative desires. As voters, we must arrange these bits into a cognitive pattern that comprises our mosaic of a candidate, issue, or situation. Campaigns, then, are great sources of potential information and contain, however difficult to identify or measure, elements that impact upon decision-making. Information bits can replace other bits to change or modify our world view, attitudes, or opinions.

It is important, however, to recognize the differences between news and politics. The mass media are first of all businesses. They require audiences in order to make money and turn a profit. Ratings are of great concern to news personalities and news programming is very expensive. At best, secondarily are news organizations concerned about political values or issue dissemination. Thus, politicians and journalists have separate and distinct motives. Second, as already noted, the media dominate the creation of political agendas — not the politicians. For example, in the 1984 presidential campaign, the Geraldine Ferraro tax case dominated all newscasts and newspaper coverage for days. "No policy issue during the entire campaign," according to Thomas Patterson and Richard Davis, "commanded this level of news attention. Indeed, policy issues usually were not mentioned in the headlines or covered for more than a day or two consecutively."[21] Finally, the media have unique requirements that dictate how issues and candidates are treated. Television prefers, in order to hold viewer attention, personalized drama, action, conflict, and immediacy. A "horse race" is more appealing than a landslide; an individual is more appealing than an issue; the deviant or novel is better than the everyday or normal.

But just as the press and presidents need each other in nonelection years, they need each other even more so during campaigns. For journalists, elections are great news events; for campaigners they provide a way to reach the voters and obtain office. The importance of the media in campaigns has especially increased since political parties have declined in influence, the number of primaries have increased, and the campaign finance law of 1974 has restricted individual financial gifts.

So what are the effects of today's media campaigns and presidential elections? The classic "limited effects model" of campaign communication research has dominated scholars' views of campaign effects for nearly 40 years. The model was originally based upon data from the 1940 elections presented by Lazarsfeld, Berelson, and Gaudet in *The People's Choice*.[22] They found that most voter decisions were based upon attitude predispositions, group identification, and interpersonal communication. Thus, mediated messages would contribute little to the actual conversion of voters favoring one candidate over another. Today, however, scholars are now recognizing the variety of factors that influence voter preferences. The "uses and gratifications model" of campaign effects is increasing in popularity. This model basically argues that campaign effects upon voters depend upon the needs and motivations of the individual voter. Voters may turn to campaign messages for information, issue discussion, or pure entertainment.[23] There are a variety of motives, therefore, for exposure to campaign communication.

At the very least we can assert that the role of the mass media has caused quantitative and qualitative changes in presidential elections.[24] From a quantitative perspective, there are simply more campaign messages than ever before in the form of news coverage, debates, political advertising, and pseudo-events. Qualitative changes are equally as noticeable. Campaigns have become more sophisticated and slick, utilizing media techniques of presentation. Political strategy consists of market groups rather than geographic groups. And the entire campaign process has become depersonalized.

While folk wisdom holds that one effect of the media has been that candidates' messages have changed from issue and policy concerns to those of image and personality, that is a misleading oversimplification. After all, the candidates still talk about issues and policy, so, in a sense, the content is the same. But there are media-created differences. For one, if you place a contemporary campaign speech beside one of 50 years ago you find that the contemporary speech is much shorter, probably only about one-third as long, and it is comprised of much shorter paragraphs. The longer paragraphs of yesteryear contained arguments, attempts to convert the audience; contemporary short paragraphs contain assertions and conclusions, attempts to give the audience a position to identify with while simultaneously providing a 10- to 20-second pithy "bit" for the evening news. Additionally, some contemporary campaign speeches are given purely to establish image. When a liberal gives an anti-war speech to the American Legion convention or a conservative attacks welfare programs at a meeting of the NAACP, neither expects to convert the audience. Rather, the speeches are given for image reasons, to prove their courage, to prove that they can stand up to those opposed to their positions, to prove they are not wishy-washy. Thus, while the messages of modern campaigners have not changed from issues to images, the structures of the messages and the motivations for them have. Electioneering politicians no longer try to convert through argumentation; rather, they attempt to say something we in the audience can identify with, to project an image by what they say, to communicate something about their personalities by the audiences they choose to address.

Other specific media impacts also can be identified. The early stages of the nominating process are so unstructured that the press and media presentations can have great flexibility in structuring and defining political contests and issues. Thus, the media's greatest opportunity to influence the outcome of an election or campaign is in the primary period.[25] However, David Weaver and his colleagues report that in this early period only those truly interested in politics or the election pay any attention to media coverage.[26] Thus, the media's greatest opportunity to influence the outcome of an election or campaign is when the majority of the audience is paying the least attention. In addition, Thomas Patterson and Robert McClure even question television's ability to transmit a candidate's image to the general public.[27] They also argue that political ads contain much more issue content than network newscasts. Weaver and his colleagues concur and assert that "despite large amounts of available information, most people learn very few dimensions of the candidate's image and even fewer aspects of issues."[28] Most political learning is that of awareness about issues without recall of relevant facts. Most news stories go unnoticed or are simply forgotten.

Thus, rather than talking about media manipulation, it is better to describe media influence as that of orchestration. To assert that the news media have no influence or impact is naive. But to assert that the news media "make or break" a campaign is equally misleading. We do think, however, that political campaigns have adjusted to the technical demands of the mass media. Presidential campaigns have changed drastically since 1952.

CONCLUSION

We began this chapter recognizing the fundamental impact of the mass media upon our society. We now conclude with a cautionary note. The mass media, television specifically, not only changed the form, practice, and content of politics in America but also dictate the *type* of president we will have in the future. The marriage of politics and media started as one of convenience. It is difficult, at this point, to see who benefited most from the arrangement. Few desire a divorce of the two. Perhaps the most we can ask for is mutual respect and understanding.

NOTES

1. Donna Woolfolk Cross, *Media-Speak* (New York: Mentor Books, 1983), p. 2.
2. As reported in ibid., p. 2.
3. These functions were first recognized by Harold Lasswell, "The Structure and Function of Communication in Society," *The Communication of Ideas*, ed. Lyman Bryson (New York: Institute for Religious and Social Studies, 1948).
4. Kathleen Jamieson and Karlyn Campbell, *The Interplay of Influence* (Belmont, CA: Wadsworth, 1983), pp. 3–8.
5. See Dennis McQuail, "The Influence and Effects of Mass Media" in *Media Power in Politics*, ed. Doris Graber (Washington, D.C.: Congressional Quarterly, 1984), p. 50.
6. Marshall McLuhan, *The Medium is the Massage* (New York: Bantam Books, 1967), p. 22.
7. Robert E. Denton, Jr. and Gary Woodward, *Political Communication in America* (New York: Praeger, 1984), see chap. 6, especially pp. 146–162.

8.   As reported in Lance Bennett, *News: The Politics of Illusion* (New York: Longman, 1983), pp. 53–54.

9.   Marshall McLuhan, *Understanding Media* (New York: New American Library, 1964), p. 22.

10.   Dan Nimmo and James Combs, *Mediated Political Realities* (New York: Longman, 1983), p. xv.

11.   McLuhan, *Understanding Media*, p. 269.

12.   Roderick Hart, Patrick Jerome, and Karen McComb, "Rhetorical Features of Newscasts About the President," *Critical Studies in Mass Communication*, vol. 1, no. 3 (September 1984):261–284.

13.   As reported in George Edwards, *The Public Presidency* (New York: St. Martin's Press, 1983), p. 112.

14.   See Sidney Blumenthal, *The Permanent Campaign* (New York: A Touchstone Book, 1982).

15.   Roderick Hart, *Verbal Style and the Presidency* (Orlando, FL: Academic Press, 1984), p. 54.

16.   Cross, *Media-Speak*, p. 205.

17.   Hart et al., "Rhetorical Features of Newscasts About the President," pp. 261–284.

18.   Hart, *Verbal Style and the Presidency*, p. 54.

19.   Thomas Patterson, *The Mass Media Election* (New York: Praeger, 1980), p. 3.

20.   Samuel Becker, "Rhetorical Studies for the Contemporary World," in *The Prospect of Rhetoric*, ed. Lloyd Bitzer and Edwin Black (Englewood Cliffs, NJ: Prentice-Hall, 1971), p. 21–43.

21.   Thomas Patterson and Richard Davis, "The Media Campaign: Struggle for the Agenda," in *The Election of 1984*, ed. Michael Nelson (Washington, D.C.: Congressional Quarterly Press, 1985), p. 119.

22.   P. Lazarsfeld, B. Berelson, and H. Gaudet, *The People's Choice* (New York: Columbia University Press, 1984).

23.   For a full explanation of this approach, see R. Sanders and L. Kaid, "An Overview of Political Communication Theory and Research, 1976–1977," in *Communication Yearbook II*, ed. Brent Rubin (New Brunswick, NJ: Transaction Books, 1975), pp. 375–389.

24.   The broad changes are discussed by Richard Joslyn, *Mass Media and Elections* (Reading, MA: Addison-Wesley, 1984).

25.   See Donald Mathews, "The News Media and the 1976 Presidential Nominations," in *Race for the Presidency* (Englewood Cliffs, NJ: Prentice-Hall, 1978), pp. 56-57 and David Weaver, Doris Graber, Maxwell McCombs, and Chaim Eyal, *Media Agenda-Setting in Presidential Election* (New York: Praeger, 1981), p. 74.

26.   Weaver et al., *Media Agenda-Setting*, p. 26.

27.   Thomas Patterson and Robert McClure, *The Unseeing Eye* (New York: Paragon Books, 1976), pp. 22-23.

28.   Weaver et al., *Media Agenda-Setting*, p. 42.

READINGS

INTRODUCTION

Chapter 6 reviewed the impact of the mass media upon the American presidency. The first essay focuses on President Reagan's 1982 strategies to avoid a midterm debacle at the polls. The authors argued that Reagan utilized four basic strategies: consulting with world leaders, manipulating domestic issues, emphasizing accomplishments, and using administration surrogates.

The second essay looks at President Carter's 1980 state of the union address. It provided an opportunity for Carter to reestablish his sense of confidence and leadership. The address failed and the essay suggests several reasons for the "rhetorical" failure.

The final essay looks at President Johnson's 1965 state of the union address. In contrast to Carter, Johnson defined and united the nation. His address was successful. Johnson maintained the citizens' sense of community and, at the same time, rationalized future policies and action.

ON AVOIDING THE OFF-YEAR DEBACLE: REAGAN IN THE 1982 ELECTIONS

In 1980 Ronald Reagan captivated his way to the White House by employing a rhetorical strategy relatively common to challengers, the "politics of optimism."[1] The tactic affords candidates the freedom to criticize the policies of the incumbent while emphasizing the very real possibility of a better tomorrow. Once in office, Mr. Reagan retained his optimistic outlook and it became eminently successful in helping him propel through Congress domestic programs and tax cuts while simultaneously increasing military spending. The combination of these diverse acts was supposed to "power America to economic recovery and cure inflation without serious pain or economic dislocation."[2]

However, as 1982 began, everything began to unravel for the president. The program cuts not only had hurt large pockets of individual citizens, they also had reinforced the image of him as uncaring or insensitive to the needs of most Americans — without noticeably improving the economy. Moreover, the tax cuts had hurt the economy without perceptively improving the income of most citizens, while the massive increases in military spending were straining the economy without buying the worldwide respect Mr. Reagan had promised his approach to national defense would bring. And perhaps most ironic of all, a conservative president with a bare majority in the Senate and only a compromise majority in the House, a man who had run for the highest office against "the spenders" in Washington, was headed into a congressional election year projecting deficits of $423 billion over the next three years. "The candidate who pledged in the closing weeks of his campaign that his economic program would give the country 'a balanced budget by 1983 and possibly by 1982,' [stood] to become the nation's biggest-ever deficit spender."[3]

Problems continued to plague the president throughout the winter and spring. His job rating fell below 50 percent, lower than any other president after just one year in office.[4] His Justice Department decided to give tax breaks to racist schools.[5] The Vatican accused him of misquoting Pope John Paul on the wisdom of the administration's Poland policy.[6] Most of the major conservative groups which had worked so hard for his election began to attack him for appearing to have abandoned the causes he had been elected to promote,[7] while the Soviets said he was a warmonger, and European allies called him a waffler.[8] And so it went through the early months of 1982. As De Lawd said in *Green Pastures*, "Even bein' God ain't no bed of roses."

By March, Mr. Reagan had dropped another six points in the polls,[9] and Senator Robert Packwood, chair of the Senate Republican Campaign Committee, attacked him for visualizing America as "basically white, male and protestant."[10] In what is now an almost ritualized presidential response to public disenchantment and accusation, Mr. Reagan attacked the media. In an interview he said reporters should "trust us, and put themselves in our hands" when they have "sensitive information" so that he would be able to explain to them why they should not publish it.[11] But the strategy faltered when the president, while speaking in Oklahoma City, complained "of newscasts that dwell on the plight of the jobless in 'South Succotash' and wrongly [accused] a partially paralyzed welder from Virginia of receiving disability benefits not due him."[12] In considering the administration's ploy of using the media as scapegoats, one journalist wrote, "We know that a TV comedy or drama series is in trouble when the writers whip up a wedding or a childbirth for one of the continuing characters. We know an administration is in trouble when it starts blaming TV news for the nation's woes."[13]

Finally, by the end of September, the president's troubles multiplied when, in spite of overt attempts to prevent it, major anti-abortion legislation was defeated and his veto of a $14.1 billion spending bill was overridden by Congress. And by the middle of October, just three weeks before the election, unemployment reached a level not known since 1940 (11 million Americans were out of work, almost a million more than the month before and 3 million more than a year before) and a virtual two to one majority of the public rejected President Reagan's repeated assertion that they were "better off today" than they were when he took office in January of 1981. Although Mr. Reagan retained personal popularity as a "nice guy," the results of the *Washington Post*-ABC News poll revealed that 57 percent of those interviewed said that "things in this country have gotten pretty seriously off on the wrong track."[14]

One of the reasons for the seriousness of the president's problems was the timing. They occurred not only in a midterm election (a competition traditionally perceived as a referendum or rejection of the current administration), but in an election year relatively unique in two important respects. First, barring no unusual events (such as the announcement of the increase in unemployment to over 10 percent), Republican candidates, particularly those in House races, were expected to fare pretty well because the party was prepared to wage history's most expensive midterm campaign. In fact, the Republican party, with $146 million, had eight times as much money as did the Democratic party. But second, the election was to focus not on the more glamorous Senate, but on the House where the president, in order to maintain his "revolution" needed, at least, to retain the "shaky working coalition" which had allowed him to win so many close votes.

Thus, in the largest sense, the 1982 midterm elections only added to Mr. Reagan's troubles. At first, through the spring primary campaigns, the president made an attempt to ignore the "political goings-on," endorsing only one primary candidate in the whole country. He even failed to endorse a former member of his staff, Jeffrey Bell, who consciously "sought to make the race a referendum on Reagan and his programs."[15] In this sense, Reagan was employing a traditional strategy of incumbency, "creating/maintaining an above the political trenches image." However, by the middle of September, the president appeared to have changed his overall posture and began campaigning vigorously for selected candidates, primarily in the South and Southwest, and, less prominently, in the Midwest. Moreover, the focus of his effort was not only the House but the Senate. Obviously, Mr. Reagan had exchanged one incumbency strategy, being above politics, for another, using the prestige of the office to campaign.

Normally, sitting presidents have an enormous amount of political power, in part because of the many rhetorical strategies available to them. In addition to the important symbolic dimensions of the office, according to Judith Trent and Robert Friedenberg in the book *Principles and Practices of Political Campaign Communication*, there are no less than 11 "pragmatic strategies" that can be utilized, running from "creating pseudo-events" to riveting media attention to escalating the rhetorical elements of a "foreign policy problem so that it becomes an international crisis." Of these 11 strategies, President Reagan made extensive use of four in his attempt to avoid an off-year debacle at the polls. The remainder of this essay will be devoted to an examination of Mr. Reagan's use and/or misuse of those four strategies.

INCUMBENCY STRATEGIES

Russell Baker claims, "There is a fairly rigid schedule governing the conduct of Presidents when things aren't working. . . . In Phase 1, troubled Presidents spend a year blaming the previous Administration for the country's troubles. When this wears thin they move into Phase 2 by blaming the press. In Phase 3 they soar over oceans to faraway lands to be photographed looking vital and glamorous."[16] While we will eventually deal with all three of Baker's phases, we start with Phase 3 because it came so early in the campaign year.

Strategy 1: Consulting/Negotiating with World Leaders

Consulting with other leaders about global problems may allow a president to take public attention away from more pressing and difficult domestic problems. Additionally, they may help to create a statesmanlike rather than a strictly political image.

In June, during the first set of state primary campaigns, Mr. Reagan, in an effort to build his credentials as a world leader, turned his back on domestic politics with a ten-day trip to Versailles, London, Rome, Bonn, and West Berlin. With less than subtle clues, the purpose of the trip was not only to smooth over the serious problems between the United States and its NATO allies, but to smooth over the president's political problems at home by showing that he was a statesman, a world leader. In Mr. Reagan's case, the trip was especially important because of the widespread idea, both in Europe and in the United States, that he possessed a "remarkable lack of sophistication about foreign policy issues."[17]

In spite of White House hopes that the president's trip would provide unlimited media spectaculars to take America's mind off its economic problems, Mr. Reagan's trip was less than triumphant. The media reported that he almost fell asleep during a meeting with the Pope and during lunch with the Italian president. Queen Elizabeth was reported to have been annoyed with White House demands for a food taster, as well as with the persistent media instructions given to her. Moreover, the NATO leaders were unable to agree on many substantive issues; England appeared to avoid Reagan's plea for restraint in the war with Argentina; a full-scale anti-Reagan riot took place in Berlin; and the president was upstaged on American television news every night by the Israeli march on Beirut and the war in the Falklands. In other words, the president's first attempt to be viewed as a world leader was hardly an unqualified success.

The second attempt to employ the strategy differed slightly in that the president did not embark on another diplomatic trip, but used international events to divert attention from his $100 billion tax bill. This time, just as the fall congressional campaigns were beginning, he used national television to call for a "fresh start" in the Middle East by endorsing "full autonomy under some form of Jordanian supervision for Palestinians living in the Israeli-occupied West Bank and Gaza strip."[18]

Finally, and in perhaps the most direct use of the strategy, the president suspended Poland's most-favored-nation status within a day of the government's announcement that unemployment had risen to 10.1 percent. Concomitantly, his weekly radio broadcast of that week was changed suddenly from a discussion of growing unemployment in the United States to a talk about his sanction against Poland — a safe topic, one unlikely to arouse significant opposition in or out of Congress, but which was guaranteed to capture media attention during the first few days of the unemployment storm.

Strategy 2: Manipulating the Economy and Other Important Domestic Issues

Since the biggest Reagan legislative victories as president have been in the economic sphere, and since Reaganomics have not yet proven successful, it is no surprise that one of his major efforts in staving off a Democratic onslaught has been to attempt to structure citizen perceptions of the economic situation.

For the first six months of 1982, that perceptual struggle vacillated between Baker's Phase 1 and Phase 2, that is, between blaming the previous administration and blaming the press. The problem with blaming the previous administration, as Reagan found out, is that in recent years there has been a reciprocal relation between rising unemployment and lowering inflation, and vice versa. Thus, if the president took credit for lowering inflation, he was not well-positioned for blaming Carter for rising unemployment. Yet this was what he tried to do.

When the finger pointing seemed not to be working, President Reagan adopted a more clever ploy: in May, he quit blaming Jimmy Carter directly and started blaming "40 years of economic mismanagement."[19] A president can be held accountable if he does not fairly soon remedy the ills wrought by his predecessor, but when those ills have been building up through the last seven of his predecessors he can be given a little more time.

And the tactic seems to have worked. In July, Richard Wirthlin, the president's pollster, was able to report to him that there was a "surprisingly large pool of patience" around the country concerning his economic programs, with about 60 percent of the public still expecting it to take another year for "Reaganomics" to work.[20] And in mid-October, White House Chief of Staff James Baker said, "We have come out of this thing reasonably well."[21] In short, the "we need more time" argument seems to have succeeded.[22]

In addition to arguing for more time, and urging the public to "stay the course," the president abandoned the supply-side premises and altered the course by instituting some new taxes. And, in arguing for that change, he continued to try to shape economic perceptions. For instance, denying that his tax proposal could be labeled "the greatest single tax increase in history" (although it was), he suggested "it could be called the greatest tax reform in history."[23]

Another perceptual manipulation in that pro-tax speech came when the president argued that his program, in place only ten months, had brought the prime rate from 21.5 percent to 14 percent.[24] The manipulation, of course, has to do with causality. That is, as more of us became unemployed and thus bad credit risks and as more businesses failed, the banks became more cautious with their lending policies. "As banks become more cautious about lending, they in effect make more money available — and cheaper — for those they are still willing to do business with."[25] In short, if the August decline in the prime interest rates was to be credited to Reaganomics, the credit went to the negative aspects of it, the effects it had had upon rising unemployment and increasing business failures.

Likewise, when the president went on national television in October and pointed to the bullishness of the stock market as indicative of the success of his policies, he was manipulating economic perceptions.[26] The alternative, and more reasonable, explanation is that the stock market soared because the Federal Reserve Bank pumped up the money supply because it feared additional major business collapses.[27]

However, a president's power to mold public opinion is so strong that most of the public probably believed that positive aspects of President Reagan's policies indeed had been responsible for the dropping interest rates, as well as for the bullishness of the stock market.

But the president was not satisfied with just trying to structure economic perceptions. In case that strategy failed, he also was busy obscuring the centrality of economics with other issues. This effort started early in July with Reagan aides blitzing reporters "with phone calls aimed at generating news stories to the effect that Mr. Reagan's bowing to Congressional demands to cut aid to El Salvador by $20 million was, in fact, a major victory for the Caribbean Basin Initiative."[28]

Probably the most well-known of Reagan's election-year diversions was his support for a constitutional amendment requiring a balanced budget. Even his Conservative supporters were upset with the blatant "politicalness" of it. The New York Daily News called it "cynical" and asked, "where does he get off trying to rewrite the Constitution to require future administrations (not his own, mind you) to live with a fiscal straitjacket that would never fit around his bulging budget?"[29]

Additional parts of Reagan's "smokescreen" to obliterate economic concerns came in September, when the president returned to two concerns dominant in the 1980 campaign, abortion and school prayer, which one White House official dubbed "motherhood and apple pie to this Administration."[30] In October the president added a drive against crime, especially drug-dealing.[31] Translated, all of these noneconomic issues demonstrate that, with an election coming up, "the President is trying to please the radical right, his base of support, by showing that he's one of them — that Ronald Reagan *is* still a Reaganite."[32] For nearly two years the president had focused on economic issues and avoided the social ones, as though his 1980 winning coalition had been brought together by supply-side economics. But with a congressional election approaching, he returned to those social issues, perhaps recognizing that his was more a cultural than an economic coalition. They were shelved, only to be trotted out again in 1984.

Strategy 3: Emphasizing Accomplishments

One of the hallmarks of incumbency campaign rhetoric is the delineation of accomplishments. In the largest sense, the incumbent uses accomplishments as a kind of accountability to the voters for the way in which time has been utilized. Normally, the strategy is pretty matter-of-fact. The incumbent simply lists all that he has accomplished, the specific campaign promises which have been fulfilled, and outlines future goals which will be possible if the administration is victorious. The undertaking becomes a bit more complicated, however, where there have been few major accomplishments or when the dominant objective has not been achieved.

In instances like this, as in 1982, the incumbent is forced into one or more variations of the strategy, such as making minor accomplishments appear more important than they are, changing the dominant objective of the administration, announcing that there has not yet been enough time for the administration's plan to have succeeded, finding a scapegoat on whom to place blame, or even denying that problems are problems.

As the 1982 mid-term elections rolled around, Mr. Reagan found himself in the unfortunate position of having failed in what he had claimed was his number one priority, turning the nation's economy around. Thus, throughout 1982, he tried out each of the tactics — at times championing his success with Congress on the tax bill or his Mid East peace initiative; at other times returning to his concern for social values (a tactic that faltered after Congress defeated the anti-abortion legislation); blaming first Jimmy Carter, which was soon followed by blaming 40 years of Democratic mismanagement and overspending; and, finally, allowing that his economic program simply needed more time. At times, it seemed that the president deserved a special chutzpa award as he casually told audiences that his administration had succeeded in reducing inflation and interest rates, thus making dramatic progress on two of the three economic problems, or that the 99 million-plus Americans who were working were a lot better off than they had been in many years. But perhaps Mr. Reagan's most important use of the strategy was in his firm resolve to simultaneously acknowledge and deny that the problems were all that serious. As is frequently the case, perhaps a political cartoon captured best the major thrust of the president's strategy when it pictured Reagan as a medieval night watchman, shouting, "It's almost midnight, it's an election year, the Middle-East is still a mess, our economic indicators are down . . . and all's well."[33]

Strategy 4: Use of Surrogates

Although the mid-term elections have been important to most incumbents and their administrations, few have put their reputations on the line to the extent that the Reagan administration did throughout the summer and fall of 1982. Not only did the president himself campaign every week from Labor Day to Election Day, he made extensive use of another staple of incumbency, official surrogates.

Under a program called "Surrogate 82," which was coordinated by the Republican National Committee, all cabinet officers (except those prevented by law) were asked by the White House to give 15 days of their time to campaigning. For example, Commerce Secretary Malcolm Baldrige campaigned in five midwestern states and in one two-day period appeared at 15 separate events to help Republican candidates. Treasury Secretary Donald Regan made six trips in September, while Agriculture Secretary John Block helped 14 Republican candidates in eight states during the same period. Interior Secretary James Watt campaigned almost exclusively in the West, David Stockman in New Jersey, West Virginia, and Michigan. Housing and Urban Development's Samuel Pierce campaigned in South Carolina, Maryland, Michigan, and New Jersey, and Energy Secretary James Edwards made 14 trips to such oil states as Texas. The only cabinet members who did not join the campaign were Education's Terrel Bell, who was to leave his post in January, and Labor Secretary Raymond Donovan, who was too much of a political liability even to speak for Republican candidates in his home state of New Jersey. But of all the Reagan team, the surrogate who was used the most was George Bush. The vice-president made appearances on behalf of more than 140 Republican candidates, and helped raise over $18 million for the Republican National Committee.[34]

Thus, the president and his administration broke precedents — not in the use of surrogates — but in their extensive employment of the strategy. Apparently, the risks of the strategy were far outweighed by the importance of the goal — preserving a coalition which would provide the only possibility of continuing the "great revolution."

CONCLUSION

Obviously, as the election results of 1984 attest, Mr. Reagan persevered. And did so, principally, by utilizing well the incumbency strategies. But it is possible to make judgments about how well a strategy is enjoyed even without knowing the responses of the target audience. Thus, we offer the following conclusions.

We adjudge Strategy 1, "consulting/negotiating with world leaders," to have been a failure. Mr. Reagan was too inept on his ten-day trip, too ineffectual in stopping the Falklands War and the Israeli invasion of Lebanon, and too obviously motivated by domestic politics in his suspension of Poland's most-favored-nation status for these activities to have had a positive effect on his image and thus on voters' intentions.

Strategy 2, "manipulating the economy and other important domestic issues," seems to have been a partial success. He apparently did convince many people that his programs were working better than they really were, and that all that was needed was more time. More importantly, the fact that the president was speaking out on the economic issues relieved Republican House and Senate candidates from the necessity of doing so. Thus, they could focus their campaigns on noneconomic issues to an extent that would have been impossible if Reagan had not been taking the heat on the economic issues himself.

On the other hand, Mr. Reagan's stress on noneconomic issues such as abortion probably hurt more than they helped because the Far Right element who care so deeply about such issues have nowhere to go but to the Republican party anyway, whereas reminding moderates and liberals of his attachment to these extreme conservative causes probably cost the president's party some votes. Additionally, the flip-flopping from economic to cultural issues may have been perceived as a desperate search for "the" issue rather than merely an attempt to touch as many bases as possible.

Strategy 3, "emphasizing accomplishments," we see as a solid plus for Reagan. Despite the fact that the economy has worsened in the last two years, despite the fact that it took the president many months of trying various tactics before he encountered the "need for more time" argument, despite the suspiciousness with which Americans have come to view political argumentation, we think that President Reagan not only salvaged "accomplishments" where the rest of us saw only failure, but that he was able to convince enough voters that the election day carnage was kept to a minimum.

Finally, we see the "use of surrogates" mostly as a failure, despite the brilliance with which it was organized, partly because the Reagan administration really does not have any brilliant spokesmen and partly because every time Vice-President Bush spoke of the economic situation the local media reminded the audience that in 1980 Bush had called it "voodoo economics," and many repeated the line emanating out of Washington, D.C.: "Reaganomics is giving voodoo a bad name."

In general, then, we think that President Reagan handled the rhetorical strategies of incumbency pretty well. It took him a long time to settle on a tactic, but once he did so he handled it in precisely the professional way we have come to expect from "the great communicator."

NOTES

1. Hedrick Smith, "How Reagan Rode Out 1981," *The New York Times Magazine*, January 10, 1982, p. 83.

2. Ibid.

3. Ibid.

4. Adam Clymer, "Reagan Pace in Poll is Lagging Carter's: Rating Below 50%," *The New York Times*, January 10, 1982, p. 20.

5. Tom Wicker, "Where the Buck Stops," *The New York Times*, January 19, 1982, p. A27.

6. "Vatican: Prez Misquoted Us," *Daily News*, January 21, 1982, p. 2.

7. "President Warned by Conservatives," *The New York Times*, January 22, 1982, p. A20.

8. James Reston, "Reagan and His Critics," *The New York Times*, January 24, 1982, p. E19.

9. Louis Harris, "Prez Poll Accentuates Negative," *Daily News*, March 1, 1982, p. 16.

10. "Reagan's Concept of America Hurts Party, Packwood Says," *The New York Times*, March 2, 1982, p. D22.

11. James A. Wechsler, "Reagan vs the Media," *New York Post*, March 17, 1982, p. 35.

12. Howell Raines, "Can Reagan Change His Tactics to Suit the Season?" *The New York Times*, March 21, 1982, p. E4.

13. Tom Shales, "Reagavision: The Battle Continues," *The Los Angeles Times*, March 26, 1982, part VI, p. 17.

14. Barry Sussman, *Cincinnati Enquirer*, October 14, 1982, p. A1.

15. Patrick Clark and Sam Roberts, "GOP Moderate Defeats Former Reagan Aide," *Daily News*, June 9, 1982, p. 5.

16. Russell Baker, "The Big Scene Steal," *The New York Times*, June 12, 1982, p. 31.

17. Jack Germond and Jules Witcover, "Tour Won't Distract People from Woes," *Cincinnati Enquirer*, June 9, 1982, p. C15.

18. Howell Raines, "Reagan Urges Link to Jordan and Self-Rule by Palestinians," *The New York Times*, September 2, 1982, p. A1.

19. Wallace C. Peterson, "Economic History, As Reagan Tells It," *The New York Times*, May 9, 1982, p. E21.

20. "Reagan Pollster Finds Public Patience with Economic Policy," *The New York Times*, July 31, 1982, p. 8.

21. Niles Lathem, "GOP — Jobless Storm Won't Snow Us Under," *New York Post*, October 25, 1982, p. 14.

22. At a point after it became obvious that Reagan's program was going to produce giant deficits, but before he had decided to push for a new tax bill, the president devoted one of his regular Saturday radio shows to defending the deficits. He asked, "What is the difference whether the government has to borrow the money from the people and take it into government, out of private circulation, or take it out of circulation by taxes? Either way, the people are without the money." (Lars-Erik Nelson, "How Can Ronnie Keep 'Em Down on the Farm?" *Daily News*, February 10, 1982, p. 34.)

 At the macroeconomic level Reagan's position may make some sense. But at the microeconomic level it is nonsense, as this anlaysis filed from Des Moines, Iowa demonstrates: "The difference between borrowing and taxing ought to be clear. The government has to pay interest, over $100 billion this year, on its borrowing. Instead of taxing his rich friends, Reagan is borrowing from them — paying them for the use of their money to help run the government. It's out here in Iowa that ordinary people pay the price for that policy." (Ibid.) Hence, while the "we need more time" ploy may have worked, the argument itself is suspect.

23. Ronald Reagan, "Transcript of the President's Televised Speech on Tax Policy," *The New York Times*, August 17, 1982, p. D16.

24. Ibid.

25. "Analysts Expect Still More Cuts in Prime," *New York Post*, August 17, 1982, p. 44.

26. Ronald Reagan, "Transcript of Reagan's Speech to Nation on G.O.P. Policy and the Economy," *The New York Times*, October 14, 1982, p. B14.

27.   Lars-Eric Nelson, "And They're Laughing At Us," *Daily News*, October 20, 1982, p. 32.

28.   Howell Raines, "Reagan Strategy Seems to Avoid Economic Policy," *The New York Times*, July 22, 1982, p. B6.

29.   "A Political Balancing Act," *Daily News*, July 21, 1982, p. 27.

30.   Tom Wicker, "Reagan's Apple Pie," *The New York Times*, September 10, 1982, p. A23.

31.   Ronald Reagan, "Text of President's Speech on Drive Against Crime," *The New York Times*, October 15, 1982, p. A20.

32.   Wicker, "Reagan's Apple Pie," p. A23.

33.   Oliphant, Cartoon, Hamilton and Fairfield, *Ohio Journal News*, October 15, 1982, p. A4.

34.   Ann Devroy, "Cabinet Hitting Campaign Trail," *Cincinnati Enquirer*, October 11, 1982, p. A1.

ANATOMY OF AN ENIGMA: JIMMY CARTER'S 1980 STATE OF THE UNION ADDRESS*

In his 1980 state of the union address, President Jimmy Carter said that the state of the union was bad because the state of the world was bad. Thus, if America were to put her own house in order it would be necessary to be tough with the Soviet Union — and that would help put the world in order. But, he suggested, it would not be easy.

Neither was the rhetorical situation faced by Carter an easy one to modify. Given public cynicism about government generally, Carter's own lackluster performance in office and the ways the news media portray the modern presidency (and the effects of such protrayals on public opinion), Carter was in need of a rhetorical miracle. The 1980 state of the union speech did not provide one. This essay will be devoted to a discussion of the above mentioned factors affecting Carter's popularity and to a demonstration of how, through a series of rhetorical errors — including the use of absolutes and superlatives, internal contradictions, argumentative deficiencies, stylistic problems, and a lack of toughness — Carter failed to mitigate them.

*Originally published by Dan F. Hahn and Justin Gustainis, "Anatomy of an Enigma: Jimmy Carter's 1980 State of the Union Address," *Communication Quarterly*, vol. 33, no. 1 (Winter 1985):43–49.

CARTER'S PROBLEMS

One of the biggest problems that Jimmy Carter faced in his attempts to create and implement policy was public cynicism about government performance. In 1958, during the latter part of Dwight Eisenhower's administration, 60 percent of Americans surveyed indicated that they were "trusting" of government; only 11 percent saw themselves as "cynical." By 1978 opinions had shifted drastically. Only 19 percent of Americans who were questioned regarding their opinions about government described themselves as "trusting"; a characterization of "cynical" was given by 52 percent.[1]

Of course, not nearly all of this decline in trust could be blamed on Jimmy Carter. The Vietnam War and the Watergate scandal had been primary culprits. But Carter had been unable to reverse the trend, at least partially because of his own ineptness, including his rhetorical weaknesses.[2] His plan for a tax rebate had been abandoned because of "changed circumstances"; he characterized his energy program as the "moral equivalent of war" and then saw it mangled by a Congress dominated by his own party. And, although Carter described America's power as "second to none," it apparently was insufficient to deter Iranian militants from taking U.S. diplomats hostage.[3]

Thus, due partly to a general cynicism about government and partly to a specific cynicism that Jimmy Carter was not up to the job, the American people did not trust their president to lead them out of the international wilderness. *Time* magazine pointed out that many Americans felt Carter had been "too soft" in dealing with Iran; the number expressing dissatisfaction had risen from 27 percent in December 1979 to 44 percent by the end of January.[4] A writer for the *Washington Post* noted that "for most of Carter's presidency, it appeared that the country basically did not give a damn."[5] In fact, Lewis Lapham contended that Carter had been elected not to lead but to "perform the rites of purification":

He had a talent for telling fairy tales and cautionary stories, and most people didn't expect him to do much of importance. By electing him President, the country thought it had declared a four-year holiday, saying in effect that after the trouble caused by Richard Nixon it might be nice not to have any President at all. It was enough that Mr. Carter merely existed, a passive and ceremonial figure, representing noble or democratic states of feeling, making occasional well-photographed gestures signifying his earnest and life-long commitment to truth, liberty, justice, beauty, equality and the flag.[6]

Carter's task was further complicated by the ways in which modern Americans tend to view their presidents in the latter stages of their administrations. Just as the presidential "honeymoon" (that period immediately following the inauguration when the president's popularity reaches great heights, almost irrespective of his actions) is a recognized phenomenon, so too is the fact that presidential popularity inevitably declines over time, and reaches its lowest levels during the final two years of the president's term of office.[7]

The state of the union address is, of course, broadcast live on television and radio during prime time, and this massive public exposure represents the final monkey wrench that was waiting to drop into Jimmy Carter's machinery. As Grossman and Kumar point out, "The President and his aides know that a public judgment of his commitments will be made on the basis of what he says in [the State of the Union] address." There is a "public expectation that the President show himself as a policy leader. . . ."[8] The extensive media coverage that the president receives in the modern world has created a series of extremely high expectations for his performance, both rhetorically and otherwise. And, since these expectations are so unreasonably high much of the time, presidents often fail to meet them; their standing in public opinion often suffers as a result.[9] Jimmy Carter was no exception. The situation he faced in January 1980 called for a tough-minded and emotionally stirring piece of rhetoric. As will be shown below, the speech that was given failed to meet these criteria.

CARTER'S ERRORS

Despite the problems just outlined, the situation faced by Jimmy Carter as he prepared his state of the union address did not lack for opportunities. With the Iranian takeover of the U.S. embassy in Teheran and the Soviet invasion of Afghanistan, Carter was given a chance to move away from symbolism toward action, while concomitantly moving up in the estimation of his countrymen and thus in the polls. The people could now find out if the man they had elected was the right answer to the "Why Not the Best?" question or if "Wee Jimmy" (as James Reston called him) was as ineffectual as his critics had been charging. The 1980 state of the union speech was one of the first indications of Carter's response to the situation presented to him by the Iranians and the Soviets. It was his chance to convert to toughness, to shed his "Mr. Nice Guy" image and demonstrate that he was the right man for the job, both then and for the next four years. To use terms first employed by Bitzer, Carter was faced with a rhetorical situation, the exigencies of which were modifiable if only he could find the right rhetoric.[10]

While Carter's failure to win reelection nine months later can be taken as indicative of his failure to convert his opportunity into votes, it remains to be demonstrated whether any of that failure can reasonably be ascribed to weaknesses in the speech. The assessment argued here is that the speech, while one of Carter's better efforts, did contain a number of tactical errors. It was not a giant failure in the "wrong content at the wrong time by the wrong spokesman" mold, but there were a number of deficiencies which, added together, undermined his attempt to portray himself as the right man saying what needed to be said in the exigencies existing at the moment. Then too, as suggested earlier, he had other problems to overcome — those involving high public expectations of presidential media performances and the low public opinion that often afflicts presidents toward the ends of their terms.

One error committed by Carter in his state of the union address concerned his use of absolutes and superlatives. Americans have come to expect some exaggerations from politicians, of course, but those who understood that Afghanistan had already been a puppet of the Soviets for several years may have detected a poor fit between Carter's announcement that henceforth the United States was going to "face the world as it is" and his description of the Soviet use of troops to consolidate her hold there as "this latest Soviet attempt to extend its colonial domination of others."[11]

Carter's most famous superlative in the address was his contention that the Soviet invasion was "the most serious threat to the peace since the second world war." Senator Edward Kennedy, Carter's major opponent within his own party, took issue with that assertion, asking, "Is it a graver threat than the Berlin blockade, the Korean war, the Soviet march into Hungary and Czechoslovakia, the Berlin wall, the Cuban missile crisis, or Vietnam?" and concluding, "Exaggeration and hyperbole are the enemies of sensible foreign policy."[12] In short, Carter's superlatives undermined his assertion of fealty to the facts and brought into question his ability to assess the world realistically.

The superlatives might, however, have been seen as justifications for a rough stand, and Carter did make some major forays into toughness, saying, "The United States will not yield to blackmail," and "The Soviet Union must pay a concrete price for their aggression," and, most notably, in laying down a new Persian Gulf doctrine: "Any attempt by an outside force to gain control of the Persian Gulf will be regarded as an assault on the vital interests of the United States of America. And such an assault will be repelled by any means necessary, including military force."

But Carter also undermined his new toughness in two ways. First, he interlaced his speech with calls for caution and restraint — talk of avoiding bloodshed in Iran and observing the "mutual constraints" of the SALT treaties, as well as exercising restraint in the use of military force. The situation, Carter said, called for "careful thought," "steady nerves," "resolute action," "consultation," "close cooperation," "national will," and "diplomatic and political wisdom." If we define "tough talk" as "strong language in support of polar positions," the Carter language does not qualify.[13] Although the positions taken by Carter with respect to the Soviet Union may have been tough, the toughness was undermined by his vacillating language. This contrast was not, apparently, lost on the president's men. One of Carter's aides, after the speech had been given, described it as "forcefully ambiguous."[14]

The second way in which Carter watered down his earlier tough rhetoric probably had its root in political considerations. He could not, after all, allow the new crises to be seen as undermining his previous three years in the presidency. So, in the latter half of the speech Carter emphasized the necessity of continuing his policies, from stressing human rights in international relations to cutting bureaucratic paperwork here at home. In nine of the 11 references to his earlier policies, he even employed the phrase, "we will continue," so that it would be obvious that his administration had been on the right track all along.

But the implied contradiction was obvious. If Carter had been on the right track, then why did these crises develop? Or, conversely, since the world had moved into a crisis situation, why should the old policies be continued? Either way, the call for continuation of the policies seemed to conflict with the announcement of new crises demanding new policies. While that conflict may have been more apparent than real, and while restraint may have been the best course of action (given the nature of the Iranian and Afghanistanian crises), the fact remained that the *seeming* contradictions between the international exigencies and Carter's solutions made him appear weak and passive at precisely the moment when he needed to be perceived as tough and active. As Schumacher observed, "Critics say the statements [in the state of the union address] represent not evolution but inconsistent lurching from crisis to crisis."[15]

As a final demonstration of this "lack of fit," one may compare the first few paragraphs of the speech with the last few. In the introduction, Carter laid out the problems: "turmoil," "strife," "change," "challenges," "terrorism," "anarchy," "attempted subjugation," "international terrorism," "military aggression," and "threats to peace." And, in the conclusion, he provided his vision of America's future: "strong," "free," "at peace," "with equal rights," "jobs," "good health," "good education," "a clean and bountiful life," "secure," with "justice, tolerance and compassion." The formidable challenges depicted in the beginning of the speech were countered, not with a tough new foreign policy, but with the mushiness of the American dream. Carter had lapsed from national leader to national dreamer.

Another type of lapse by Carter might be called "argumentative inadequacy." When putting forth a new policy, a president normally is expected to argue for it, to give reasons why it should be adopted. Such argumentation need not be highly detailed, but it should be easy to follow. Causes and effects need to be clearly related. The nature of the change, and the reasons for it, should be persuasively stated. And, if possible, the dovetailing of the new policy with American experience and values should be demonstrated.

In his state of the union address, Jimmy Carter did very few of these things. He did establish a need for change, and he did announce a new doctrine. But he did not demonstrate how or whether the new doctrine would work, nor did he place it in the framework of past American policy.

Rather, perhaps because his own thought processes were honed by his engineering years, Carter tended to provide lists and leave the listeners to establish the relationships and rationales on their own. Thus, in this speech, he presented seven lists: a list of three basic developments that created the contemporary challenges, a list of five goals that he would continue to pursue, a four-part historic list of U.S.-Soviet confrontations organized by decades in chronological order, beginning with the 1940s, a list of six ways in which the United States will continue to work for world peace, a list of five actions that will be undertaken to strengthen the national economy, a list of eight visions of the U.S. future, and a list of three things that all Americans could do together to make these visions realities.

In no case were Carter's lists expanded upon, defended or in any way argued for in subsequent paragraphs; in only one instance, in reference to the need to continue supporting human rights in international relations (point four of list four) was an item on one of the lists argued for within the confines of the list-making. In short, his lists consisted of 33 unsupported assertions and one supported one. Whether these 34 items were meant to be the meat of his argument or mere byproducts offered as addenda to the argumentation found in the other paragraphs is unclear.

What is clear is that the lists were undemonstrated assertions, unsustained arguments, and unpersuasive rhetorical artifacts. They failed to show Carter as a strong leader.

Other indications of Carter's rhetorical softness may also be found in the address. His stylistic choices in describing the Soviet invasion are indicative. Carter characterized the invasion 17 times in the address. At the beginning, he employed angry language: "massive Soviet troops are attempting to subjugate . . . Afghanistan" and an "act of military aggression." This tough line continued through the ninth and tenth characterizations, with references to "this aggression" and "their aggression." But, by the twelfth mention, Carter had toned down to "Soviet invading forces in Afghanistan" and the final three references were considerably less hostile. They were as follows: fifteenth — "Soviet troops in Afghanistan"; sixteenth — "The Soviet effort to dominate Afghanistan"; and seventeenth — "The Soviet Union is now attempting to consolidate a strategic position." Rather than build to any kind of climax, Carter chose a style that unwittingly echoed his tendency to take hard positions and then back away from them when pressed by opponents.

More important than his rhetorical softening in depicting the Soviet invasion of Afghanistan was Carter's lack of toughness when making demands of enemies. To Iran he said, "If the American hostages are harmed, a severe price will be paid." The message to the Soviets was "While this invasion continues, we and the other nations of the world cannot continue business as usual with the Soviet Union." While on the surface both of these appear to be tough messages, they contain identical softnesses — namely, the implication that if the perpetrators will stop now, all will be forgiven. If the Iranians returned the hostages they would not be punished for their "international terrorism," and if the Soviet Union withdrew from Afghanistan, the United States would overlook her "military aggression." Further, there was no indication in the speech that the implied conditions would be withdrawn the next week, or at any other time. Carter did not draw a line in the dirt and tell the bullies not to cross it; rather, the message was that he would yell at them and threaten them until they chose to stop — then, everyone could kiss and make up. It would be difficult to imagine a less powerful message.

It is true that Carter did flex some policy muscles to support his blustery threats, but they were mostly symbolic (even if Carter did refer to them as "stiff economic penalties on the Soviet Union"). The totality of these supposedly potent penalties took up one short paragraph:

I will not issue any permits for Soviet ships to fish in the coastal waters of the United States. I've cut Soviet access to high technology equipment and to agricultural products. I've limited other commerce with the Soviet Union, and I've asked our allies and friends to join with us in restraining their own trade with the Soviets and not to replace our own embargoed items. And, I have notified the Olympic Committee . . . that neither the American people nor I will support sending an Olympic team to Moscow.

All told, then, the "penalties" were really quite mild. In response to armed aggression, the administration said, in effect, that the Soviets could not fish in our pond, buy our expensive toys, eat at our table, trade in our stores, or play with our children. In fact, a case could be made that the Carter response was so soft that Reagan was able to soften his pro-military force stance enough to escape his "trigger-happy" image and still come off much tougher than the incumbent.

CONCLUSION

To the extent that a specimen of rhetoric may be measured by its effects, Jimmy Carter's 1980 state of the union address was a failure. It did not convince the Iranians to return the hostages, did not influence the Soviets to withdraw from Afghanistan, and did not persuade the American people that Jimmy Carter was tough enough to be allowed to direct America's fight against her enemies for another four years.

Thus, several months later, amid the wreckage (both literal and figurative) of the abortive attempt by U.S. commandos to rescue the hostages from Iran, a widely held conclusion was that the episode was "just the sort of tragically flawed comedy of errors the public had come to expect from its president — a nice try, too bad the little guy couldn't pull it off."[16]

NOTES

1. R. Harwood, H. Johnson, and N. Lemann, "1980; On the Eve," in *The Pursuit of the Presidency, 1980*, ed. R. Harwood (New York: Berkeley Books, 1980), pp. 3–62.

2. Dan F. Hahn, "The Rhetoric of Jimmy Carter, 1976–1980," *Presidential Studies Quarterly* 14 (1984):265–288.

3. E. J. Walsh, "Carter," in *The Pursuit of the Presidency*, ed. R. Harwood (New York: Berkeley Books, 1980), pp. 232–252.

4. "In a Fiercely Hawkish Mood," *Time*, February 11, 1980, pp. 22–23.

5. M. Schram, "Carter Speech: Outflanking, Undercutting Rivals," *The Washington Post*, January 25, 1980, p. A22.

6. L. H. Lapham, "King Frederick's Mules," *Harper's*, March 1980, p. 18.

7. Thomas E. Cronin, "The Presidency and Its Paradoxes," in *The Presidency Reappraised*, 2nd ed., ed. Thomas E. Cronin and R. G. Tugwell (New York: Praeger, 1977), pp. 69–85.

8. M. B. Grossman and M. J. Kumar, *Portraying the Presidency: The White House and the News Media*, (Baltimore: Johns Hopkins University Press, 1981), p. 239.

9. Thomas E. Cronin, *The State of the Presidency*, (Boston: Little, Brown, 1975), p. 109.

10. L. F. Bitzer, "The Rhetorical Situation," *Philosophy and Rhetoric* 1 (1968):1–14.

11. Jimmy Carter, "Transcript of President's State of the Union Address to Joint Session of Congress," *The New York Times*, January 24, 1980, p. A12. All subsequent quotes from the speech from this source.

12. Edward Kennedy, "Transcript of Kennedy's Speech at Georgetown University on Campaign Issues," *The New York Times*, January 24, 1980, p. A13.

13. Dan F. Hahn, "The Semi-tough Language of the 1980 Presidential Campaign," *The Pennsylvania Speech Communication Annual* 38 (1982):41.

14. "Carter Takes Charge," *Time*, February 4, 1980, p. 14.

15. E. Schumacher, "For Carter, A Shift in View on Russians," *The New York Times*, January 24, 1980, p. A13.

16. Walsh, "Carter," p. 236.

ARCHETYPE AND SIGNATURE IN JOHNSON'S 1965 STATE OF THE UNION*

David Zarefsky has written of Lyndon Johnson's administrative and rhetorical successes:

> All told, eighty-nine major Administration bills were passed in 1965 alone, with the only major two defeats being Congress' refusal to repeal right-to-work laws or to grant home rule to the District of Columbia. Given the circumstances of divided or nonexistent constituencies coupled with potentially hostile opposition, the President's rhetorical success in gaining acceptance of his Great Society program is all the more impressive.[1]

---

*Originally published by Dan F. Hahn, "Archetype and Signature in Johnson's State of the Union," *Central States Speech Journal* 34 (1983):236–246. Reprinted with permission.

Without denying either Johnson's law-making record or the potential and real minority opposition to many of his programs, this essay will be devoted to demonstrating that the discontinuity between President Johnson and the American constituency was considerably smaller than Professor Zarefsky has implied.

All presidents, of course, search for arenas of continuity between their own desires and those of their constituency. All search for points of valuative consensus and the acceptable language in which to relate those points of consensus to their own policies and actions. To make the case that President Johnson accomplished this purpose, I shall rely somewhat upon the concepts of archetype and signature as interpreted by Anthony Hillbruner in his analysis of President Nixon's second inaugural.[2] Archetype, the voice (beliefs) of the community, and signature, the voice (beliefs) of the speaker, interact in successful rhetorical transactions. But to isolate these structures of belief and see their confluence, it is necessary to analyze the historic community beliefs and the speaker's biography,[3] for only then can we understand the ways in which speaker and audience are captured and meshed in the text of the address.

This archetype-signature approach allows the critic to explore presidential sociocultural reinforcements — the community-building and maintaining aspects of the presidency. Presidential discourse, the signature, makes concrete in particular situations the community valuations, the archetypes. To both maintain citizens' sense of community and rationalize policies and actions, presidents must speak in common idioms. Such language, then, functions both (epideictically) to praise the community standards and (enthymematically) to employ the standards to rationalize political action.

The archetype and signature approach normally works well in analyzing inaugurals, because that is where the new president attempts to put his "stamp" on the office and thus demonstrate how his administration ought to be seen as a manifestation of the national will that elected him. Yet, if we apply the methodology to the rhetoric of President Johnson we find that the appropriate speech was not the inaugural address of January 20, 1965, but his state of the union message of January 4, 1965. Always impatient, President Johnson did not wait for his inaugural to announce the major themes of his program. Though he already had been president for over 13 months, he had been a caretaker president, more concerned with completing the Kennedy agenda than beginning his own. Now that he had been elected to the office in his own right, he was impatient to offer his own program, to begin to make his own contribution to history, to put his own brand on the office.

That process started with his 1965 state of the union. Early in the speech he almost literally announced that the Kennedy years had ended and the excitement of the Johnson years was beginning:

No longer are we called upon to get America moving. We are moving. No longer do we doubt our strength or resolution. We are strong and we have proven our resolve.

No longer can anyone wonder whether we are in the grip of historical decay. We know that history is ours to make. And if there is great danger, there is now also the excitement of great expectations.[4]

It therefore is clear that, from Johnson's perspective, just as his months filling out the Kennedy presidency had been caretaker months, mopping-up months, so all of the Kennedy years had been caretaker years, devoted to refurbishing the strength and will of the country after years of atrophy under Eisenhower. Those years had had to take place, for we had needed to reassert ourselves, but because they were devoted to rebuilding they were not exciting. Now, however, the rebuilding was completed and we faced the prospect of moving into new realms, conquering new problems. And though these new adventures might contain some dangers, "there is now also the excitement of great expectations."[5]

Looking back through the dark prism of Vietnam, it is difficult for us today to imagine that Johnson could ever have thought that his tenure would outshine Kennedy's. Perhaps we have forgotten too much. Have we forgotten the enormity of Johnson's electoral advantage over Goldwater in 1964? Have we forgotten the self-confidence of a people living in a vibrant economy unencumbered with "stagflation?" Have we forgotten the felt security of a country clearly superior in arms to any potential foe? I will argue that we have forgotten how well Johnson operationalized the archetypes of the national community in his rhetoric to make him seem the repository of our values, the enunciator of our hopes, the initiator of our highest aspirations.

Most, if not all, of the values identified in this essay live in tension with our cultural values. The expansive view of the nation conflicts with the belief that we should not intervene in the internal affairs of other countries. The expansive view of the presidency contradicts the belief that we are a nation of laws, not men, and that we are all equal before the law. Unity and consensus conflict with individualism; economic desires conflict with non-economic values; progress conflicts with stability. Commitments to "communication" and "action" can conflict.

After 1965, Johnson felt he was forced to stress presidential action over governmental communication and problem solving. The tension became too great to maintain those commitments in balance to each other. Likewise, as divergent voices grew clamorous over Vietnam, President Johnson had to choose between presidential power and community unity. This is not to suggest that Johnson's presidential experience was unique; all presidents must steer inherently rocky roads between conflicting valuative commitments in the electorate. As Zarefsky noted in a recent piece, presidential decision-making often is "... required in just those situations in which values conflict."[6] Further, especially in times of crisis, "... perhaps one of the president's chief duties is to speak for the ordering of values to which he subscribes."[7]

Zarefsky suggests that "The hierarchy of values displayed in presidential communication during crisis is ... likely to reflect the president's intuitive value premises."[8] No denial of that thesis is suggested here, but an amendment, namely: The values displayed in presidential rhetoric early in a president's career, before crises erupt, are likely to reflect the president's intuitive value premises. And these value premises, in turn, reflect his assessment of the value commitments of the populace, for, as a practical matter, no president commits himself to values antithetical to his audience.

In most cases, including the instance under examination here, there is no need to believe that the confluence between presidential and national values results from manipulative rhetoric. The president, indeed, is of the people: His life experiences are similar enough to those of the people who elected him to incline him toward the same values they hold. In Johnson's case, his origins, his beliefs, even his physicality, mirrored the national self-image. Hailing from the expanse of west Texas, being an expansive personality, he was a natural leader for a broad and extensive country that seemed ready to view itself and the presidency expansively.

EXPANSIVE VIEW OF THE NATION

Johnson's expansive view of the country was hardly new with him. Its roots go back to the early settlers. The Puritans perceived themselves on a holy errand to Christianize the wilderness. They formed a "... community without geographical boundaries, since the *wilderness* is by definition unbounded, the *terra profana* 'out there' yet to be conquered, step by inevitable step, by the advancing armies of Christ."[9]

Soon after the formal founding of the country, the Puritan view of Americans as "God's elect" combined with their idea of the "holy errand" to produce a national egocentrism:

> One rather obvious proof of this is the tradition of July Fourth addresses. The tradition itself is said to begin with an oration delivered in 1778 at Charlestown, South Carolina, hailing "the Revolution as the beginning of a new age in human history"; and the theme continues unabated in the long procession of orations that followed through the Federalist period. "From their birth," cried Thomas Yarrow of New York, the American states were "designed to be the political redeemers of mankind!" . . . In Maine, Virginia, and South Carolina, July Fourth orators explained the correspondence between local progress and "the vast designs of providence" for the "universal redemption of the human race."[10]

Thus do we see the development of the idea that Americans have been elected to save the world, to universalize the holy errand.

Such a viewpoint impinges upon both our self-concept and our concept of others: "The significance of 'holy land' depends on other lands not being holy; the chosenness of the chosen people implies their antagonism to the *goyim,* the profane 'nations of the earth.'"[11]

There is a logical development from "sacred errand to manifest destiny, colony to republic to imperial power."[12] Thus, in the 1890s the imperialist rhetoric of the champions of Manifest Destiny ". . . was typified by an all-encompassing appeal to the political myth that it was the pre-ordained destiny of the American people, acting as agents of the Divine, to somehow go out into the world spreading American institutions and precepts."[13] While the idea of Manifest Destiny and most of the religious view of the "sacred errand" of "God's elect" became muted in the twentieth century, the major outlines of the national egocentrism continued. By the end of World War II, ". . . the tendency to equate America's way of life with the goals of civilization itself was so widespread that it had become nothing less than a national assumption."[14] Johnson's predecessor in the Oval Office, John F. Kennedy, believed the assumption:

> Other countries look to their own interests. Only the United States has obligations which stretch ten thousand miles across the Pacific, and three or four thousand miles across the Atlantic, and thousands of miles to the south. Only the United States — and we are only six percent of the world's population — bears this kind of burden.[15]

And Lyndon Johnson, product and bearer of the American culture, bought the assumption. He ". . . never questioned that this was the best of all countries."[16] And with that acceptance came a burden: "This assumption of superiority," thought Johnson, "imposed a moral obligation to share the American way with the world."[17] And this belief brought Johnson's signature into alignment with the national archetype, for "Whether rebels or reactionaries, hard hats, blue collars, middle Americans, liberals, blacks, establishment, native Americans, or power elitists, most Americans believe America can do *something* about the state of the world: America has a responsibility."[18]

As early as 1946 Johnson spoke in Congress of this burden of superiority:

> We in America are the fortunate children of fate. From almost any viewpoint, ours is the greatest nation: the greatest in material wealth, in goods and produce, in abundance of the things that make life easier and more pleasant . . . nearly every other people are prostrate and helpless. They look to us for help — for that inherent courageous leadership. . . . If we have excuse for being, that excuse is that through our efforts the world will be better when we depart than when we entered.[19]

With this confluence of national value and personal value, it is no surprise to find, in President Johnson's 1965 state of the union message, lines such as "Our concern and interest, compassion and vigilance, extend to every corner of a dwindling planet."[20] And again:

> Our own freedom and growth have never been the final goal of the American dream. We were never meant to be an oasis of liberty and abundance in a worldwide desert of disappointed dreams. Our nation was created to help strike away the chains of ignorance and misery and tyranny wherever they keep man less than God means him to be.[21]

And if Johnson's public words leave any doubt about his desire to export American values, his private reminiscence about the early days of his presidency do not:

> When I first became President, I realized that if only I could take the next step and become dictator of the whole world, then I could really make things happen. Every hungry person would be fed, every ignorant child educated, every jobless man employed. And then I knew I could accomplish my greatest wish, the wish for eternal peace.[22]

In this dream of being benevolent despot of the world we see the basis of the second element of Johnson's expansiveness — the desire to expand the office of the presidency. And, again, we see the confluence of Johnson's desire with the national desire, of signature with archetype.

EXPANSIVE VIEW OF THE PRESIDENCY

This is not to suggest that presidential expansion began with Johnson. Practically every president from Washington on expanded it beyond the bounds of his predecessor, an expansion expressive of the national orientation:

> The focus on the Presidency is part of our nationalism, our search for national unity and wholeness in a single person. All the logic and mythology of individualism — of independence, of the loner, of community service, of legitimate fame, of popularity and approval of one's equals, and of the effectiveness of *one* sturdy, adaptive jack-of-all-trades set down in the midst of a savage, chaotic wilderness — has been taken up and applied, in the mythology of modern nationalism, to the whole nation through the symbolic and representative President of the United States.[23]

And this has been especially true of the more famous presidents — Jefferson, Lincoln, Theodore Roosevelt, Wilson, Franklin Roosevelt, Truman, Kennedy — presidents holding tenure in times of war, hot and cold. What came to be called, in Arthur Schlesinger's felicitous phrase, "The Imperial Presidency,"

> was essentially the creation of foreign policy. A combination of doctrines and emotions — belief in permanent and universal crisis, fear of communism, faith in the duty and right of the United States to intervene swiftly in every part of the world — had brought about the unprecedented centralization of decisions over war and peace in the Presidency. With this there came an unprecedented exclusion of the rest of the executive branch, of Congress, of the press and of public opinion in general from these decisions.[24]

But the Imperial Presidency was not to be confined to foreign affairs. In the words of Schlesinger, "Foreign policy had given the President the command of peace and war. Now the decay of the parties left him in command of the political scene, and the Keynesian revelation placed him in command of the economy."[25]

George E. Reedy, who served Johnson both as press secretary and special assistant, believes that the public not only accepted but welcomed this growth in presidential power. As citizens, he says, "we placed our faith — our unquestioning faith — in institutions that were only brick and wood and in men who were only flesh and blood."[26] Consequently, he says, "It is virtually taken for granted that the proper objective of a study of our chief executive is to identify those inhibiting factors which frustrate his efforts to resolve national problems and to devise mechanisms which will remove those frustrations."[27]

Reedy claims that the factors which impel the public to accept an expanding presidency include our belief "that the office somehow ennobles the occupant and renders him fit to meet any crisis,"[28] that the president "works around the clock"[29] on our behalf and thus is deserving of our support, and that the president is privy to information, unknown to the rest of us, which validates his decisions.[30]

Lyndon Johnson, hardly immune to these same beliefs, also came to define the presidency in expansive terms. As early as 1941, during his first campaign for Congress, Johnson deferred to President Roosevelt's plan for "packing" the Supreme Court, telling his rural west Texas audiences, "I didn't have to hang back like a steer on the way to the dripping vat. I'm for the President. When he calls on me for help, I'll be where I can give him a quick lift, not out in the woodshed practicing a quick way to duck."[31]

Nor was this just the deference of a relatively weak candidate for Congress to the wishes of the most powerful man in his own political party as well as in the land. When he was Majority Leader of the Senate during the 1950s, when Republican Dwight Eisenhower was in the White House, Johnson still clung to the practice of deferring to the President:

> Whenever my critics in the Congress talked to me about the responsibility of creating issues, I came back to the question of where in the hell they expected the issues to come from — from our heads? If an issue is not included in the presidential agenda, it is almost impossible — short of crisis — to get the Congress to focus on it. That's the way our system works; but these fellows never understood that. They didn't understand — with all their calls for Congress to have all sorts of expertise and classified information, in order to act in foreign affairs — that the congressional role in national security is not to act but to respond to the executive.[32]

Senator Johnson, in one of those homey metaphors for which he was famous, explained to his senatorial colleagues the need for Congress to defer to the President: "If you're on an airplane, and you're flying somewhere, you don't run up to the cockpit and attack the pilot. Mr. Eisenhower is the only President we've got."[33] As Doris Kearns notes, such a view omits as a possibility what most of us, as travelers, insist upon: ". . . that the passengers might be entitled to consult with, even instruct, the pilot about where they wanted to go."[34]

But Senator Johnson never conceded that possibility. And neither did President Johnson. He had deferred to presidents when he was in Congress, and thus, notes Kearns,

> he expected the same deference from *his* Congress. After all, partisanship and public debate were enemies of a sound foreign policy. It was in the public's best interest . . . to leave the complicated questions of international affairs in the hands of the President. The public, Johnson reasoned, would only hurt itself by knowing too much. Democracy demanded good results for the people, not big debates.[35]

Again we see that the national sentiment expected and favored an expanding executive, just as did Johnson, as a congressman, a senator, and a president. So it is not surprising that we find President Johnson, in January 1965, announcing the start of "a new quest for union,"[36] asserting that U.S. military superiority "will continue to grow as long as this office is mine,"[37] and, most revealingly, explaining that although "A President's hardest task is not to do what is right, but to know what is right,"[38] and, after searching his own west Texas heritage, "I knew the answer."[39] As troubling as it may be for those of us imbued with the ideals of representative democracy to encounter a president who contends it is his job to "know what is right" for the rest of us, the trouble-someness is multiplied exponentially when that same president claims he can know that by exploring, not our wishes, but his own childhood remembrances. That is, it is now troubling as we look back through Watergate, through Vietnam, through our lessened reverence for the office. In 1965 it apparently did not trouble us at all; the national archetype and the Johnsonian signature both called for an expansion in the responsibilities and duties of the president.

Expansion of the nation and expansion of the presidency, then, are the two major points at which the valuative commitments of Johnson and the nation coalesced. And it will immediately be perceived that these also are the two points which become, over time, the major weaknesses in the Johnson presidency — the attempt to impose our values upon Vietnam and the related presidential absorption of congressional war-making powers.

But these were not the only points of convergence of national archetype and Johnsonian signature in the 1965 state of the union. Others, although less important, can be detected. Significantly, these more minor points of confluence reinforced the major ones and perhaps emboldened Johnson to travel the path that led to his eventual downfall.

REINFORCEMENTS

Unity

Paeans to national unity are commonplace in American politics, and commonplaces tend to reflect deeply held cultural beliefs. National unity grows out of an older ideal, community, and, according to James Robertson, simultaneously presupposes and idealizes homogeneity of values:

> The *real* community is a melting pot. It mixes disparate elements (different families, different classes, people from different nations and places) into a unity. It creates unity by providing individuals (regardless of race, creed, or national origin) with opportunities to move, to rise, to change, to progress, to succeed. The logic is that, by using the opportunities provided by the community, the individual will become one in basic values with all its other members. The essential democracy, classlessness, and the homogeneity of American community is thus proved by the logic of the melting pot.[40]

And the major political dichotomy of the American people, the two-party system, suggests more unity than diversity. For our two parties are not ideological; they do not disagree on ends as much as on means. According to Daniel Boorstin, "The small ideological difference between our two political parties may be accounted for by the fact that their only disagreement is over means. Both Democrats and Republicans have, on the whole, the same vision of the kind of society there ought to be in the United States."[41] For instance, in the economic arena, where the goal of both parties is a strong capitalist economy, the Democrats hold that the way to achieve the goal is through government influencing of the economic system, while the Republicans opt for the workings of private enterprise in the free marketplace. The disagreement is not over goals but means. For those outdistanced in the rough and tumble of capitalist economic battles, the Democrats favor government aid; the Republicans, private charity. Again, different means to reach the same goals. Thus it is that both Democrats and Republicans assume almost all voters are within reach and, according to Rossiter, make a gallant attempt "to mirror the entire American electorate, an attempt that is made possible in the first place by the extraordinary unity of the people in matters of ideology."[42]

President Johnson believed that the greatest resource of the American people was unity.[43] He "... stubbornly maintained a conception of America in which no one seriously disagreed with what was to be sought."[44] So Lyndon Johnson, a politician above all else, believed in

American unity of goals and came to believe that consensus was possible in all realms, goals, and methods. "Consensus," thus, came to mean not only the natural pre-existing agreement on ends but what he could convince us to do. He defined consensus as "first, deciding what needed to be done regardless of the political implications and, second, convincing a majority of the Congress and the American people of the necessity for doing those things."[45]

So he came to adopt as his favorite quotation the Biblical injunction, "Come now, and let us reason together, saith the Lord" (Isaiah 1:18). And so long as the subject was means to agreed-upon ends, that verse seemed appropriate. But eventually, especially in Vietnam, when the goals themselves were not accepted, Johnson seemed to adopt the stance of God, along with the two verses immediately following his favorite: "If ye be willing and obedient, ye shall eat the good of the land: But if ye refuse and rebel, ye shall be devoured with the sword: for the mouth of the Lord hath spoken" (Isaiah 1:19-20).

But that was to be later. In 1965, at the time of the state of the union, Johnson stressed that we were "entering the third century of the pursuit of American Union,"[46] that we had already "achieved a unity of interest among our people that is unmatched in the history of freedom,"[47] and that the remaining goal was to find a new union, "the unity of man with the world that he has built."[48]

Thus national unity, as exemplified in our non-ideological political parties, was embraced by Lyndon Johnson. Yet, argues Kearns, Johnson's idiosyncratic way of perceiving national unity on goals as identical with national consensus on policies was one source of his downfall:

> What was unique to Johnson was the confidence that he possessed powers of will and persuasion which could convince an entire nation that his policies represented the necessary and wisest course toward the kind of America that all should desire. There was much to justify this confidence, but it also made him unable to foresee the possibility of resentment based, not on objections to his social goals or to the practicality of specific measures, but on hostility to the implicit assertion of increased central authority to define the general welfare and confer benevolences which, however desirable in themselves, should not be imposed by presidential will.[49]

Johnson's idiosyncratic approach to unity, confusing unity on goals with consensus on means, interacted with his expansive conception of the presidency in such a way as eventually to erode the unity and destroy his presidency.

Desires

Zarefsky maintains that by the middle of the 1960s the American people had come to assume that prosperity was permanent: "Freed from purely material concerns, citizens could revise their aspirations upward toward a vision of quality. Buoyed by their economic success, they believed that success in social intervention also was possible."[50] President Johnson believed in this national assumption, but structured it slightly differently; he not only thought the prosperity permanent, but believed we all wanted the same things. Additionally, he believed he could specify those American desires:

> What the man in the street wants is *not* a big debate on fundamental issues; he wants a little medical care, a rug on the floor, a picture on the wall, a little music in the house, and a place to take Molly and the grandchildren when he retires.[51]

Further, Johnson believed these were not just American desires; they were universal. As early as 1947 he had declared, "the hopes and desires of a man who tills the soil are about the same whether he lives on the banks of the Colorado or on the banks of the Danube."[52] According to Kearns, "To Johnson there were foreign customs, foreign religions, foreign governments, but there were not foreign cultures, only different ways of pursuing universal desires."[53]

Sending troops to Vietnam to fight for capitalistic individualism, freedom, self-determination, and the rest of the pantheon of American values, President Johnson had no understanding that he was trying to impose upon the Vietnamese peoples a system of values alien to their culture. Nothing in Johnson's background had prepared him for a situation where a fight for the right of self-determination would be immoral because the self did not exist outside the community, and determination was God's responsibility, blasphemous for the individual to undertake.

Thus, in 1965 Johnson could say that we were in Vietnam because what was at stake was "the cause of freedom,"[54] and a major source of world unrest was "man's irrepressible ambition for liberty and a better life."[55] And our policies throughout the world were, he said, based upon "common interest and common values, common dangers and common expectations."[56] For Johnson, and presumably for the country, the universality of desires was a commonplace.

Problem Solving

If there is a unity of goals, if we all want the same things, it is reasonable to assume that all disagreements can be solved; then, lacking disagreement, we should be able to solve any problem. Indeed, as Zarefsky notes, "summoning the people through a vision of unlimited possibilities has been a recurrent appeal in the nation's rhetorical history."[57] As Americans, we tend to believe we can solve all problems. Robertson contends that our "desire to bring about change and [our] insistence that change is desirable, inevitable, and necessary are modern manifestations of the long-established American mythology of revolution, reform, and progress."[58] And Robert Heilbroner sees us embracing a philosophy of optimism which "assumes that the direction in which we seek to venture as the heroic steersmen of our destiny will be compatible with the currents and tides set in motion by history's impersonal forces."[59] If we do not quite believe in progress in the "in every day in every way we are getting better and better" mold, we do pride ourselves on being pragmatic, on getting things done, on being a nation of problem-solvers.

And Lyndon Johnson was a problem-solver *par excellence;* "None of his fellow citizen's desires were, Johnson thought, wholly beyond his ability to satisfy."[60] So, in the 1965 state of the union, Johnson proposed better education for all children, better health for all citizens, Medicare for the elderly, better aesthetics in both urban and rural settings, tax rebates for businessmen, better control of crime to calm the fearful, higher wages for workers, better protection of black voting rights, direct help for the small farmers, faster trains for the commuters, higher welfare payments for the poor, cleaner air and water for the conservationists, recognition and monetary encouragement for the artists, a more efficient government for all. Truly, something for everyone — and plenty more where that came from.

Detractors, mostly Republican, claimed that all these efforts were misguided because "you can't solve problems by throwing money at them." But President Johnson was able to mute the complaints of his conservative opposition by stressing the frugality of his programs, the possibility that the programs would pay for themselves by "making taxpayers out of taxeaters," the benefits to all rather than to narrow special interests, and the "businesslike" principles undergirding the programs.[61]

Additionally, the conservative position was undermined by the difficulty American politicians have in stating the belief (or flying in the face of public opinion by admitting) that problems cannot be solved. The national belief that solutions can be found is too strong. And an American like Lyndon Johnson, proud patriot, life-long Democrat, a living model of the Horatio Alger rags-to-riches myth, had to believe that the problems could be solved by government. The Johnson signature and the national archetype again coalesced.

Communication

If we agree on goals and believe we can solve our problems, then Americans conclude that what we need to do is sit down and talk, figure it out. Since the problem cannot be ideological, it must be perceptual. And again we hear Isaiah, and Johnson, saying, "Come, let us reason together." Johnson's "greatest gift of leadership was the ability to understand, persuade, and subdue,"[62] and he saw that power as the essence of leadership: "A true leader," he said in 1956, "is a man who can get people to work together on the points on which they agree and who can persuade others that when they disagree there are peaceful methods to settle their differences."[63]

And, because people in other countries are just like us, international disagreements also can be solved by communication. So in 1965 he proposed to let the Soviet leaders have access to United States television if they would give him access to theirs,[64] to visit "some of our friends in Europe this year,"[65] to "pay a visit to Latin America,"[66] and to "renew our commitment" to the United Nations, because "It is far better to throw these differences open to the assembly of nations than to permit them to fester in silent danger."[67]

Again, this belief in communication extended to Johnson's conduct in Vietnam. Although here the medium was bombs rather than talk, the belief in negotiating remained strong:

> I saw our bombs as my political resources for negotiating a peace. On the one hand, our planes and our bombs could be used as carrots for the South, strengthening the morale of the South Vietnamese and pushing them to clean up their corrupt house, by demonstrating the depth of our commitment to the war. On the other hand, our bombs could be used as sticks against the North, pressuring North Vietnam to stop its aggression against the South.[68]

This view of the possibility of negotiation, whether the persuasion is by words or bombs, is distinctly American, stemming from the aforementioned lack of domestic ideological battles:

Separated for two centuries from the ideological struggles of Europe, the American cultural tradition displayed little awareness that it had taken a unique, peculiarly indigenous, direction and form, that the people of other nations might be different in fundamental ways. This American tendency to project its values upon other countries was dramatized in the view held on the highest levels of decision that the Vietnamese conflict was a battle between two fixed groups of people with different but negotiable interests. By denying significance to irreconcilable moral and ideological issues in favor of calculation of bargaining and power, thus limiting the stakes to matters negotiable, Americans overlooked the reality, ultimately decisive, that the war in Vietnam was an ideological struggle, a social revolution.[69]

Lyndon Johnson and the American people both believed that problems could be solved by communication, by negotiation, by forceful persuasion. President Johnson, applying this belief in foreign affairs, led us into the conflict in Vietnam, a country suffering not a communication problem that could be talked away but an ideological civil war that one side or the other had to win.

Honorable Action

Finally, although talk and action are sometimes seen as antithetical, one strand of the American heritage holds that if something needs to be done and can be done, it would be dishonorable not to do it: "Success [has] long been, for Americans, a moral goal."[70] And, ironically, for Americans "moral exhortation" can be framed in "military terms and images"[71] as in "the war on poverty." Perhaps nowhere is this interaction of morality and conflict more evident than in the myth, and surrounding rhetoric, of the Old West: "The western rhetoric . . . is lit up by the new hope and adventure of the frontier, the spirit of conquest, a man's pride in taking a risk, in offhand daring."[72] The man who is afraid to act is a coward. Action is manly; inaction is cowardice, traitorous.

Johnson completely internalized this myth. He was fearful of even a "remote appearance of weakness or loss of face."[73] He feared that if he "lost" Vietnam people would say "That I had let a democracy fall into the hands of the Communists. That I was a coward. An unmanly man. A man without a spine."[74] He even had nightmares about it:

Every night when I fell asleep I would see myself tied to the ground in the middle of a long, open space. In the distance, I could hear the voices of thousands of people. They were all shouting at me and running toward me:

"Coward! Traitor! Weakling!" They kept coming closer. They began throwing stones.[75]

To avoid having his nightmare come true, Johnson stayed in Vietnam — and talked the tough rhetoric of the Old West. Vietnam was "'the outer frontier of disorder,'" he said, "to be tamed by the methods of the pioneers who 'had a rifle in one hand and an ax in the other.'"[76] In the White House, fulminating against those opposing the war, he cried out, "Why do they want me to put my pistol on the table and just sit here while the enemy is killing my boys?"[77] In 1967, "Addressing field commanders at Cam Ranh Bay, he asked the Lord to bless them 'until you come home with the coonskin on the wall.'"[78]

In the 1965 state of the union we see this tough-talking Western rhetoric. We see the concern for honor in Johnson's quoting of Andrew Jackson's promise that "the honor of my country shall never be stained."[79] We see the muzzle-loader over the mantle in Johnson's boast that "we have built a military power strong enough to meet any threat and destroy any adversary."[80] We see the firmly-set jaw of the cowboy in Johnson's assertion that "we have proven our resolve."[81] And we see the necessity of honoring our word in Johnson's explanation of why we were in Vietnam: "Ten years ago our President pledged our help. Three Presidents have supported that pledge. We will not break it now."[82]

What we did not see in 1965 was that Vietnam was perceived by Johnson not only as a threat to our national honor, but to his own courage:

Johnson was motivated in his critical Vietnam decisions by fear of being regarded as lacking in military will. . . . Courage, his courage, was in his mind. After he had ordered bombing raids in Vietnam, allegedly in retaliation for Viet Cong terrorist attacks, he said, "They thought they could frighten the President of the United States. They just didn't know this President."[83]

For Johnson not being a coward was not only a personal requirement, it was a foreign policy. International questions of judgment and justice were to some extent reduced to questions of personal manhood. People trying to think, "What is wise?" were pummeled with the question, "What is brave?"[84]

Lyndon Baines Johnson was president of the "home of the brave" and he meant to prove that both he and the nation deserved that musical accolade.

CONCLUSION

Throughout his 1965 state of the union message, Johnson demonstrated the meshing of his personal signature with the national archetype. There is little reason to think this was a contrived confluence, that he set out to prove that his belief system was congruent with the nation's. Rather, the conformance seems natural. Johnson's signature in this address was a microcosm of the macrocosm of his character.[85] If, as president, Johnson occasionally confused not only his office but himself with the nation, that is understandable, given the continuity between his signature and national archetypes. And if the people did not notice the confusion of those realms, that too is natural; an expansive nation and an expansive presidency, united, desiring the same things, sharing a confidence that problems can be solved, that disagreements can be resolved by communication, and that honorable action can be taken could hardly have done otherwise. President Johnson, on January 4, 1965, did not so much persuade the nation as ratify it. And 16 days later he was inaugurated not only as the elected successor to John Kennedy, but as the prototypical president of the United States.

NOTES

1.   David Zarefsky, "The Great Society as a Rhetorical Proposition," *Quarterly Journal of Speech* 65 (1979):378.
2.   Anthony Hillbruner, "Archetype and Signature: Nixon and the 1973 Inaugural," *Central States Speech Journal* 25 (1974):169–181.
3.   Ibid., p. 171.
4.   Lyndon Johnson, "The 1965 State of the Union Message," January 4, 1965 (Private recording; subsequent references titled "Johnson's speech").
5.   Ibid.
6.   David Zarefsky, "Civil Rights and Civil Conflict: Presidential Communication in Crisis," *Central States Speech Journal* 34 (1983):59.
7.   Ibid., pp. 65–66.
8.   Ibid., p. 59.
9.   Sacvan Bercovitch, *The American Jeremiad* (Madison: The University of Wisconsin Press, 1978), p. 26.
10.   Ibid., p. 141.
11.   Ibid., p. 178.
12.   Ibid., p. 92.
13.   Jeff D. Bass and Richard Cherwitz, "Imperial Mission and Manifest Destiny: A Case Study of Political Myth in Rhetorical Discourse," *Southern Speech Communication Journal* 43 (1978):228.

14. Doris Kearns, *Lyndon Johnson and the American Dream* (New York: New American Library Signet Books, 1976), p. 102.

15. John F. Kennedy, quoted in James Oliver Robertson, *American Myth, American Reality* (New York: Hill and Wang, 1980), p. 272.

16. Kearns, *Johnson and the American Dream*, p. 67.

17. Ibid.

18. Robertson, *American Myth*, p. 25.

19. Lyndon Johnson, "Remarks," *Congressional Record*, June 4, 1946, p. A3170.

20. Johnson's speech.

21. Ibid.

22. Kearns, *Johnson and the American Dream*, p. 202.

23. Robertson, *American Myth*, p. 310.

24. Arthur M. Schlesinger, Jr., *The Imperial Presidency* (Boston: Houghton Mifflin, 1973), p. 208. For a viewpoint denying that such expansion has taken place see Curtis Arthur Amlund, *New Perspectives on the Presidency* (New York: Philosophical Library, 1969).

25. Ibid.

26. George E. Reedy, *The Twilight of the Presidency* (New York: World, 1970), p. 197.

27. Ibid., p. xii.

28. Ibid., p. 18.

29. Ibid., p. 21.

30. Ibid., pp. 27–28.

31. Lyndon Johnson, quoted in Alfred Steinberg, *Sam Johnson's Boy: A Close-Up of the President from Texas* (New York: Macmillan, 1968), p. 110.

32. Johnson, quoted in Kearns, *Johnson and the American Dream*, pp. 145–146.

33. Ibid., p. 149.

34. Ibid., pp. 149–150.

35. Ibid., p. 297.

36. Johnson's speech.

37. Ibid.

38. Ibid.

39. Ibid.

40. Robertson, *American Myth*, p. 222.

41. Daniel Boorstin, *The Genius of American Politics* (Chicago: University of Chicago Press, 1953), p. 137.

42. Clinton Rossiter, *Parties and Politics in America* (New York: New American Library, 1964), pp. 20–21.

43. Kearns, *Johnson and the American Dream*, p. 103.

44. Ibid., p. 197.

45. Lyndon Baines Johnson, *The Vantage Point: Perspectives of the Presidency, 1963–1969* (New York: Holt, Rinehart and Winston, 1971), p. 28.

46. Johnson's speech.

47. Ibid.

48. Ibid.

49. Kearns, *Johnson and the American Dream*, p. 367.

50. Zarefsky, "The Great Society," p. 367.

51. Johnson, quoted in Kearns, *Johnson and the American Dream*, p. 159.

52. Lyndon Johnson, "Remarks," *Congressional Record*, May 7, 1947, quoted in Kearns, *Johnson and the American Dream*, p. 98.

53. Kearns, *Johnson and the American Dream*, p. 202.

54. Johnson's speech.

55. Ibid.

56. Ibid.

57. Zarefsky, "The Great Society," p. 378.

58. Robertson, *American Myth*, p. 348.

59. Robert L. Heilbroner, *The Future as History* (New York: Grove Press, 1959), p. 34.

60. Kearns, *Johnson and the American Dream*, p. 226.

61. Zarefsky, "The Great Society," pp. 370–372.

62. Kearns, *Johnson and the American Dream*, p. xii.

63. Johnson, quoted in ibid., p. 163.

64. Johnson's speech.

65. Ibid.

66. Ibid.

67. Ibid.

68. Johnson, quoted in Kearns, *Johnson and the American Dream*, p. 277.

69. Ibid., pp. 277–280.

70. Robertson, *American Myth*, p. 290.

71. Zarefsky, "The Great Society," p. 373.

72. Ronnie Dugger, *The Politician: The Life and Times of Lyndon Johnson. The Drive for Power, from the Frontier to Master of the Senate* (New York: W. W. Norton, 1982), p. 142.

73. Kearns, *Johnson and the American Dream*, p. 41.

74. Johnson, quoted in ibid., p. 264.

75. Ibid., pp. 264–265.

76. Johnson, quoted in Dugger, *The Politician*, pp. 131–132.

77. Johnson, quoted in ibid., p. 145.

78. Ibid., p. 144.

79. Johnson's speech.

80. Ibid.

81. Ibid.

82. Ibid.

83. Dugger, *The Politician*, p. 150.

84. Ibid., p. 151.

85. Hillbruner, "Archetype and Signature," concluded the same thing about Nixon's Second Inaugural and Nixon's character (p. 181).

Part III

THE FUTURE OF THE "RHETORICAL PRESIDENCY"

Chapter 7

"MERE RHETORIC" AND THE AMERICAN PRESIDENCY

The arts of presidential communicating should also include a sense of when to keep quiet.

Hedley Donovan

Twenty years ago, presidents enjoyed positive public support and esteem. But the 1960s and 1970s raised many questions about the fundamental nature of the U.S. presidency. During this time, the United States passed through a tremendous internal political crisis that drained the nation's energy, taxed its patience, and threatened its constitutional system. Thomas Cronin, in 1975, wrote that "under the banners of the New Frontier, the Great Society, the New American Revolution, and WIN, the presidents pledged major innovations and social change. Each also generated, however, a grievously large gap between promise and performance."[1] James Barber echoed the sentiment by writing, "if as it now appears, the public voted for activism in 1960, for peace in 1964, for tranquility in 1968, and for competence in 1972, then, somehow our calculus has been defective."[2] Even as recently as 1984, Theodore Sorensen wrote, "we have witnessed in the last several administrations a 'political ineffectiveness' cycle as relentless and as harmful to our national strength and cohesion as the ups and downs of the economic cycle."[3] The result, he argues, is the loss of confidence: "confidence in our leaders, in our government, in our political parties, even in our system."[4]

But some scholars and citizens would argue that President Reagan is reestablishing the presidency in terms of respect, grandeur, and public esteem. For us, it is not surprising that he is doing so while being called "the great communicator." We must not forget that Walter Mondale, in a press conference the day after his large defeat, noted that one of his major problems as a presidential candidate was his inability to use television. From this perspective, the better *television* communicator won.

As human beings, we continually communicate in a variety of ways and in a variety of contexts. The familiar activities of our life, however, are taken for granted. But we have attempted to recognize the variety and importance of presidential communication. How a president communicates reveals the inner motives, desires, and goals of the occupant.

Clearly, in addition to brains, good looks, and a political philosophy, we would argue that the president needs to be a communicator. Today, as never before, television specifically is as important to governing the nation as it is in getting elected. Language, according to Samuel Johnson, is the dress of thought. But politically, it has become, at the best, a costume and at its worst, a disguise. For us, rather than question the failure of human communication as a tool for solving social ills, we should question the failure of human beings to *use* communication properly.

The presidency is more than the current occupant. It has a history and a public life of its own. It is an office wherein "rhetoric, poetic, politics, dialectic, and ethics converge."[5] The presidency is essentially, according to Walter Fisher, a "rhetorical fiction." For him, "rhetorical fictions may provide pleasure and lead to contemplation, and they certainly may display ritualistic and mythic features. Rhetorical fictions also involve matters of faith, which are a part of the poetic realm . . . [they] concern the reality of the work-a-day world and their function is to advise with regard to public conduct: they are, in effect, pragmatic, public dreams."[6]

More communication in no way implies better communication. In fact, the "rhetorical presidency," narrowly defined, is problematic. It becomes too easy for leaders to rely on inspirational words rather than specific deeds, to promote empty, glorified visions than engage in social action, to identify a problem rather than to implement a solution, or to increase awareness of societal ills rather than enlarging public understanding.

Thus, our argument is twofold. First, that there is no relationship between the increase of presidential public communication and the quality of their pronouncements. We do not call for or advocate more presidential public communication. And second, that we must become citizen-critics, analyzing all types and forms of presidential communication. Therein lies the true quality of leadership and policy expectations. Hopefully we have provided examples and perhaps even a methodology for such analyses. We must ensure, as Gerald Ford recognizes, that the "ability to communicate with the public through television will not, by itself, assure a successful foreign policy. A president must first have a wise policy to communicate."[7] We must be careful in criticizing a Jimmy Carter for overexplaining and being boring when perhaps the truth is we want to hear what we want to believe about ourselves rather than what we need to know about the world. We do advocate better understanding of the nature of human communication and its application to presidential discourse.

If we are lucky, there will be life after Ronald Reagan. But, as Roderick Hart argues, we need to "get beyond" Ronald Reagan. For him, this means "the American people would have to get beyond purposeful facial expressions and nonchalant humor. To get beyond Ronald Reagan, the American people would have to distinguish more sharply between genuine economic advancement and earnest promises, between the dangers of nuclear destruction and a comforting rhetoric of military strength, between institutionalized prayers in schools and cordial civic piety, between an Equal Rights Amendment and White House receptions for women's leaders, between drastic cuts in Social Security and speeches in praise of the elderly."[8]

Presidents must penetrate both the *minds* and the *hearts* of the public. They have perfected the latter but can they do equally well with the former? As citizens, according to Cronin, "we must refine our expectations of the president and raise our expectations of ourselves."[9] Finally, all too often academics prescribe "things to do" while ignoring that doing is a product of being. In the end, the quality of our leaders are determined by what we are.

NOTES

1.   Thomas Cronin, *The State of the Presidency* (Boston: Little, Brown, 1975), p. 4.
2.   James D. Barber, *Choosing the President* (Englewood Cliffs, NJ: Prentice-Hall, 1974), p. 2.
3.   Theodore Sorensen, *A Different Kind of Presidency* (New York: Harper & Row, 1984), p. 5.
4.   Ibid., p. 2.
5.   Walter Fisher, "Rhetorical Fiction and the Presidency," *Quarterly Journal of Speech*, vol. 66, no. 2 (April 1980):122.
6.   Ibid., p. 121.

7. Gerald Ford, "With a Bow to the Medium's Power," *TV Guide,* September 19–25, 1981, p. 8.

8. Roderick Hart, *Verbal Style and the Presidency* (Orlando, FL: Academic Press, 1984), p. 229.

9. As quoted in Hedley Donavan, "Job Specs for the Oval Office," *Time,* December 13, 1982, p. 29.

INDEX

ABOUT THE AUTHORS

Robert E. Denton, Jr., has degrees in political science and communication from Wake Forest University and Purdue University. He teaches and writes in the areas of political communication, mass media, advertising, and contemporary rhetorical theory. Denton is the author of a book on the presidency and co-author of books on social movements, persuasion in contemporary U.S. life, and political communication (also with Praeger). In addition, he has published articles in the fields of political science, advertising, and communication. He is currently an associate professor in the Department of Communication Studies at Northern Illinois University.

Dan F. Hahn has degrees in political science and communication from the universities of Kansas State, Kansas, and Arizona. He teaches in the areas of political communication and rhetorical theory and criticism. Hahn has authored over 50 articles in communication and political science journals. He is currently a professor in the Department of Communication Arts and Sciences at Queens College, New York.